DISRUPTING THE CULTURE OF SILENCE

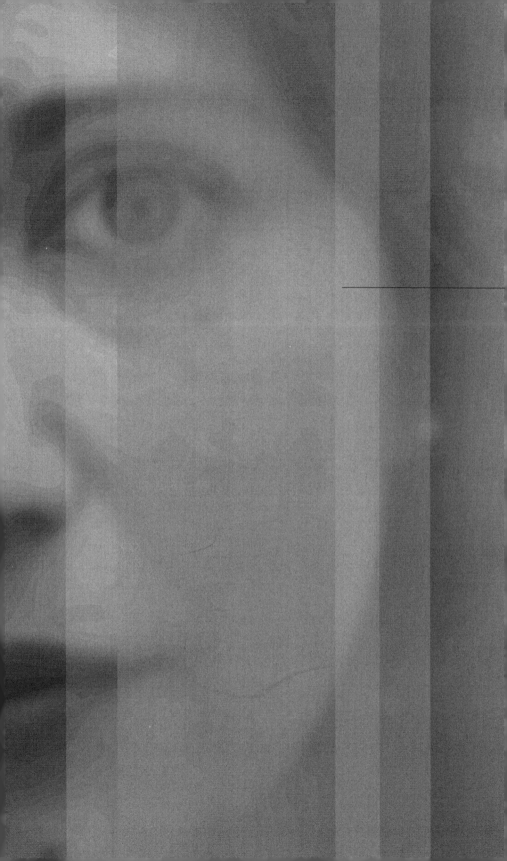

DISRUPTING THE CULTURE OF SILENCE

Confronting Gender Inequality and Making
Change in Higher Education

EDITED BY

Kristine De Welde and Andi Stepnick

Foreword by
Penny A. Pasque

STERLING, VIRGINIA

Sty/us

Published by Stylus Publishing, LLC
22883 Quicksilver Drive
Sterling, Virginia 20166-2102

Library of Congress Cataloging-in-Publication Data
Disrupting the culture of silence : confronting gender inequality
and making change in higher education / edited by Kris De Welde
and Andi Stepnick.
    pages cm
Includes bibliographical references and index.
ISBN 978-1-62036-217-4 (cloth : alk. paper)
ISBN 978-1-62036-218-1 (pbk. : alk. paper)
ISBN (invalid) 978-1-62036-219-8 (library networkable e-edition)
ISBN (invalid) 978-1-62036-220-4 (consumer e-edition)
1. Sex discrimination in higher education–United States.
2. Women college teachers–United States. 3. Women college
administrators–United States. 4. Universities and colleges–Faculty–
Employment–Sex differences–United States I. De Welde, Kris,
editor of compilation. II. Stepnick, Andi, editor of compilation.
LB2332.32.D57 2015
378.0082–dc23
                                                                2014012596
13-digit ISBN: 978-1-62036-217-4 (cloth)
13-digit ISBN: 978-1-62036-218-1 (paperback)
13-digit ISBN: 978-1-62036-205-1 (library networkable e-edition)
13-digit ISBN: 978-1-62036-206-8 (consumer e-edition)

Printed in the United States of America

All first editions printed on acid-free paper
that meets the American National Standards Institute
Z39-48 Standard.

Bulk Purchases

Quantity discounts are available for use in workshops and for
staff development.
Call 1-800-232-0223

First Edition, 2014

10   9   8   7   6   5   4   3   2

This book is dedicated to those facing and fighting injustice in academia.
We stand with you.

CONTENTS

FOREWORD

Faculty and administrators serve on myriad committees throughout institutions and within our respective international, regional, and local associations. At times, I have been extremely thankful to have finished a term on a committee—as a faculty member or as a former higher education administrator—feeling gratified by the work we accomplished. At other times, I have been disappointed to see tireless hours of effort sit on the shelf ignored by administrators. However, there is the rare occasion when service on a committee evolves into a meaningful intersection of service, scholarship, and activism. Such an intersection fosters concerted change in the academy when it questions or critiques hegemonic policies, programs, and practices and intentionally connects institutions of higher learning with equity and social justice. This book stems from such an intersection.

Kristine De Welde and Andi Stepnick served as founding members of Sociologists for Women in Society's committee on academic justice, as part of their service, and developed engaging workshops about issues facing women academics that resonated with participants. This edited volume is the culmination of their decade-long service and research efforts, and the companion website is a concrete way to share updated information and keep the dialogue about gender inequalities and progressive change in academia moving forward across disciplines and fields.

Some people have asked, "Is gender inequality still an issue? I thought it was addressed long ago." I often respond by asking the person to look up the academic hierarchy: Who makes important policy decisions about education? Who are the faculty members, department chairs, deans, provosts, presidents, board of trustee members, state education commissioners or legislators, and secretary of education? Further, what are the genders, races, ethnicities, sexual orientations, socioeconomic statuses, and dis/abilities of the people in these positions of power? The anecdotal information is compelling, the research even more so: Women still do not receive equal pay for equal work (U.S. Department of Labor 2010); few women serve as chief academic officers or provosts and far fewer identify as women of color (Allan 2011); we still need the Lilly Ledbetter Fair Pay Act of 2009 (which extends the statute of limitations on cases in which workers find they are receiving discriminatory pay); employers often hire or promote men based on signs of leadership potential alone whereas women move up the ladder or are hired only after they display a record of productivity and worth (Ropers-Huilman 2008). The chapters throughout this volume share disconcerting research that provides further evidence of these gendered patterns, and the personal narratives reflect the multitude ways gender inequity pervades the academy. The authors powerfully show how women's individual experiences are linked directly to the organizational and sociocultural milieu of their workplaces. So, for those who question the existence of gender inequality, yes, it is still an issue, even in higher education.

Also important to note, the economic, sociopolitical, and cultural context is changing rapidly in the current era of academic capitalism (Slaughter and Rhoades 2004) and neoliberalism (Cannella and Lincoln 2004). Accountability in higher education is on the rise while state appropriations are being reduced (Slaughter and Rhoades 2004; Tierney 2006). As such, it is important that feminist research, policies, and practices—including action strategies that address gender inequity in and beyond the academy—are grounded in the historical *and* ever-changing contemporary contexts.

What distinguishes this book are the engaging narratives and the compelling contemporary research that are woven throughout the text that will resonate with many readers, but the editors and authors do not stop with this important knowledge. Through real-life narratives, case studies, resources, tools, and action steps that build off of each other in an intentional manner, readers can transform this knowledge into action where they can work to make change on their own campuses and in their professional and personal lives. As such, the editors and authors walk readers through the complexities of gender inequity in higher education including the intersectionality of gender, race, ethnicity, socioeconomic status, motherhood, eldercare, academic jobs, contrapower harassment, trauma, mobbing, action strategies, and numerous other issues. In this way, *Disrupting the Culture of Silence: Confronting Gender Inequality and Making Change in Higher Education* is an important book that contains the various components a facilitator, an administrator, or a faculty member might intentionally combine to use in provost and dean training seminars, faculty workshops, courses, reading circles, and multiple venues across campuses and professional associations.

This book was not written to sit on a shelf like reports that are culminations of some service work. This book is to be opened, read, reflected upon, discussed, and acted upon. Readers will engage with the chapter authors and the anonymous faculty whose narratives reflect the experiences of many. *Disrupting the Culture of Silence: Confronting Gender Inequality and Making Change in Higher Education* interrogates inequities around gender and intersectionality, raises questions that connect individual experiences with organizational policies and practices, inspires readers to engage in the possibilities of gender equitable futures, and encourages us to make such possibilities a reality in the academy.

Penny A. Pasque
Associate Professor
Educational Leadership and Policy Studies
Women's and Gender Studies
Center for Social Justice
University of Oklahoma

References

Allan, E. J. 2011. "Women's Status in Higher Education: Equity Matters." *ASHE Higher Education Report* 37(1):iii–163. San Francisco: Jossey-Bass.

Cannella, G. S., and Y. S. Lincoln. 2004. "Dangerous Discourses II: Comprehending and Countering the Redeployment of Discourses (and Resources) in the Generation of Liberatory Inquiry." *Qualitative Inquiry* 10(2):165–174.

Ropers-Huilman, B. 2008. "Women Faculty and the Dance of Identities: Constructing Self and Privilege Within Community." In *Unfinished Agendas: New and Continuing Gender Challenges in Higher Education*, edited by J. Glazer-Raymo, 35–51. Baltimore: Johns Hopkins University Press.

Slaughter S., and G. Rhoades. 2004. *Academic Capitalism and the New Economy: Markets, State and Higher Education*. Baltimore: Johns Hopkins University Press.

Tierney, W. G. 2006. "Trust and Academic Governance: A Conceptual Framework." In *Governance and the Public Good*, edited by W. G. Tierney, 179–198. Albany: State University of New York Press.

U.S. Department of Labor, U.S. Bureau of Labor Statistics. 2010. *Highlights of Women's Earnings in 2009*. Report 1025. Washington, DC: U.S. Department of Labor, U.S. Bureau of Labor Statistics.

ACKNOWLEDGMENTS

We are indebted to the courageous women who shared their stories with us and who emerge as heroines in these pages. We are grateful for our supportive colleagues at Sociologists for Women in Society (SWS) who connected us many years ago, continue to encourage us, and show us what academic justice looks like. And, we are grateful to our contributors for their steadfast commitment to this project and to the many authors and activists whose work inspires us.

We want to express deep gratitude to our feminist colleagues who supported us throughout the long process of writing this book, particularly through the challenges we faced. While there is not enough space to name you all, Abby Ferber, Adina Nack, Ana Prokos, Dana Britton, Danielle Currier, Heather Laube, Irene Padavic, Laura Logan, Pat Martin, and Tracy Ore warrant naming.

We owe thanks to our team at Stylus Publishing, particularly John von Knorring for his enthusiastic support throughout this project and Alexandra Hartnett for her attention to detail during the final editing stages.

We are grateful to our wonderful students over the years and across several institutions, who remind us why we chose to be academics and feminists. Lastly, we owe thanks to our early workshop participants who helped inspire this book and the anonymous reviewers who helped us improve it.

Kris

I want to acknowledge, with boundless gratitude, my support team. Foremost, my husband/partner Manny Roque; he is with me through magnificent adventures, difficult times, and that which fills our lives in between. I thank him for his willingness to journey beside me all these years. My mother Armanda and my sister Adriana who are steadily enthusiastic for my career goals, patiently listen to impromptu lectures (with interest), and remind me to be joyous and grateful, and always "forward!" This trio is my anchor, and I recognize that my choices have not always been easy for them. Emma (Yeya), Yoly, and Peter, my connections to the spirit of my father, Rene, who never saw me bloom, but who manages to still bring wonder and laughter to us all. These are my biggest champions, regardless of the circumstances.

My academic path would not exist or be as rich if it were not for the following role models, colleagues, and friends: Krista Brumley, David Chiszar, John Cox, Mari DeWees, Nicola Foote, Donna Henry, Leslie Irvine, Laura Kramer, Sandra Laursen, Amy Leisenring, Kamala Kempadoo, Joan Manley, Melanie Murphy, Stephanie Nawyn, Martha Rosenthal, Joanna Salapska-Gelleri, Elaine Seymour, Elisabeth Sheff, Dave Thurmaier, Jim and Sasha Wohlpart. I am blessed to be loved and respected by these amazing people.

And, Andi Stepnick as my academic partner and confidant, I could not—would not!—have done this without her. She is wise and kind, and inspires me to share our hard fought strength with others through this book.

Andi

I am profoundly grateful to my biological sister, Shari, and my chosen sisters, Jennifer and Catherine, for their love, faith, wisdom, humor, and companionship. Their zest for life inspires me and their steadfast and unconditional support is an incredible gift.

I am fortunate to have had three parents support me over the years in ways too numerous to mention. Robert J. Stepnick's consistent enthusiasm nourished me throughout this project. He offered encouragement when things were going well and reassurance when challenges arose; that made all the difference. Arlene Stepnick and Robert Durel provided me with much needed practical and intellectual support. More importantly, they showed me what it means to stand up for what you believe in. Also, I am grateful to my brother, Bobby, whose creativity and sense of humor were a force to be reckoned with. His spirit continues to fill me and remind me of what is important.

I am thankful for the friendship and collegial support of many people, especially: Andrea, Andy, Annemarie, Ben, Beth, BJ, Bob, Bonnie, Camille, Carl, Catherine, Cynthia, Dan, Dee Dee, Denise, Destiny, D'lynn, Doug, Emily, Erin, Gene, Jamie, Jennifer, Jerry, Jimmy, Jo Dee, Joyce, Judy, Ken, Larry, Laura, Lauren, Lynn, Maria, Mark, Merrie, Michelle, Neal, Pam, Randy, Robbie, Rory, Rose, Sandy, Shelby, Suzanne, Val, Vicki, and Wendy. They show me, time and time again, what it means to be part of a community and how important it is to "walk the talk." I am honored to know them and my life is richer because of them.

Finally, I could not have done this project (or enjoyed it as much) without Kristine De Welde. I am grateful that our work over the past seven years joined us as partners and, then, as friends. She inspires me!

INTRODUCTION
From People to Policies: Enduring Inequalities and Inequities for Women Academics

Kristine De Welde and Andi Stepnick

Historically, public discourse has framed higher education as fundamental to individual advancement, intellectual development, skill building, employment potential, personal growth, character development, and social maturity. U.S. higher education has been a location for enlightened dialogue and a locus for social change including emancipation, civil rights, peace, and other justice movements. As such, the U.S. system of higher education has been and continues to be foundational to civil society and democracy. But, the academy is a changing institution: increasingly under threat from corporatization, magnified pressure for research and grants to fund faculty salaries, a reduction of faculty autonomy and academic freedom, a decrease in full-time faculty lines and reliance on contingent positions, minimization of shared governance, and legislative intrusions that primarily target social science and humanities disciplines. Fortunately, the academy is changing in positive ways, too: diversity is increasing, interdisciplinary efforts that dislocate historically entrenched intellectual divisions are being fostered, and innovations in pedagogy and research continue. These revolutionary transformations, positive and negative, can foster uncertainty, suspicion, hostility, increased workloads, and other challenges for those in academic settings. Negative outcomes trickle down to those who are either newest in the system or least powerful: women, people of color, contingent faculty, or other perceived outsiders.

Within that framework, this book explores the contemporary challenges facing women faculty in U.S. higher education. The chapters provide research and theoretical insights on workplace inequities, inequalities, and challenges. Case studies, coupled with resources and suggestions for action, are designed to help individuals navigate difficult situations. Our guiding questions include the following:

1

- What do women academics classify as challenging, inequitable, or "hostile" work environments and experiences? How do these vary by race/ethnicity, rank, sexual orientation, or other social locations?
- How do academic cultures and organizational structures work independently and in tandem to foster or challenge such work climates? How does the academy legitimize barriers faced by women faculty?
- What explains the lack of change in academia regarding the challenges academic women face?
- What actions can institutions and individuals—independently and collectively—take toward equity in the academy?

Though we focus on women faculty, these issues are not "women's issues"; they are relevant to the academy, its members and constituents, and beyond. As West and Curtis (2006) argue: "The barriers for women in higher education not only raise questions of basic fairness, but place serious limitations on the success of educational institutions themselves" (4). The academy reflects societal biases and hostilities (Chesler, Lewis, and Crowfoot 2005). Yet, it could direct social change too. Our biographies, experiences, and training in feminist scholarship compel us to disrupt complacency among those who might claim that things are "better" or "good enough." The academy is not yet equal or equitable; our work is not done. Robbins and Kahn (1985) compel us all to consider our involvement:

> Although many problems specifically affect women—such as the feminization of poverty, battering, and sexual harassment—the problem of discrimination in academe is uniquely ours, and particularly ironic in a community that prides itself on its principled stands and values. We are the perpetrators as well as the victims, the people who deny that discrimination exists as well as those who experience and document it. (8)

We concentrate on women faculty to highlight the "shared challenges women have faced and continue to face in patriarchal contexts while acknowledging how race, social class, and other identities intersect and interact with sex and gender and contribute to shaping one's professional status in profound ways" (Allan 2011, 3). But, we emphasize intersectionality (e.g., Collins 1990), despite limitations of existing research and language. As Aguirre (2000) argues, neither the term *women faculty* nor *minority faculty* refers to homogeneous populations. Yet, these categories facilitate analytic comparisons and broader patterns of experiences. When data or theory permits, we compare and contrast the experiences of women of color faculty (e.g., Latinas, Blacks, American Indians, Pacific Islanders, Asians) with those of white women faculty.[1] To deepen our understandings of the experiences of diverse women academics, we explore underexamined identities such as lesbian, feminist, and married or unmarried. We hope this approach discourages readers from conceptualizing specific issues as relevant only to women of particular statuses (e.g., white, heterosexual).

Attention to women's access to and representation in U.S. higher education has a long history, dating to 1848 and the first Women's Rights Convention in Seneca Falls, where, in drafting the Declaration of Sentiments, reformers objected to women being barred from "facilities for obtaining a thorough education—all colleges being closed against her."[2] Between the 1800s and the mid-twentieth century, women's access to higher education was uneven and fraught with struggle (see Aleman and Renn 2002). The late 1960s brought women's university commissions, and similar groups, focused on women's issues in higher education and on specific campuses or within national organizations (Allan 2011). Such commissions sought to assess the status of women on a campus and make recommendations to remedy problems, including women's representation in different areas (e.g., administration; science, technology, engineering, and mathematics [STEM] fields); sexual harassment; pay inequality; advancement; tenure; safety; family policies and resources; and representation in the curriculum (Allan and Hallen 2011; Glazer-Raymo 1999). These issues, exposed in the initial commission reports in the 1970s, remained evident into the 1990s and continue in the early twenty-first century (Allan and Hallen 2011).

By the 1970s issues of sex discrimination in higher education became major federal policy issues (Robbins and Kahn 1985) that culminated with legislation and policy efforts to remedy bias and discrimination against women. Spanning 50 years, these include the Equal Pay Act of 1963, the Education Amendments of 1972, the Vocational Education Act Amendment of 1976, and the Family and Medical Leave Act of 1993 (see Allan 2011). Some discrimination and bias required "affirmative action" to overcome limited inclusion of women and minorities (i.e., "compensation, correction, and diversification," Glazer-Raymo 1999, 201). For example, the Civil Rights Act of 1964 codified the tenets of the Supreme Court's desegregation ruling, *Brown v. Board of Education*, (1954) while Title VI and Title VII protected women and racial or ethnic minorities (and religious affiliation) from discrimination in employment, *and* reaffirmed equal opportunity employment in sectors receiving federal aid (see Glazer-Raymo 2011). Additionally, this legislation established the Equal Employment Opportunity Commission (EEOC), which now oversees Title VII, the Equal Pay Act, the Age Discrimination in Employment Act, and the Americans with Disabilities Act (Glazer-Raymo 2011). Title IX of the Education Amendments of 1972 (arguably the most impactful piece of legislation for women in higher education to date) provided legal protection to women and girls from kindergarten through postsecondary education. It included a stipulation that encouraged programs or institutions receiving federal aid to take "affirmative action" to address conditions resulting in women's differential participation in education. George H. W. Bush signed the Civil Rights Act of 1991, which "upheld affirmative action as a remedy for 'intentional employment discrimination' and 'unlawful harassment in the workplace,' extending compensatory damages to include sex and disabilities, in addition to race or national origin, and permitting punitive damages against offending organizations" (Glazer-Raymo 2011, 358).

Diversification of U.S. higher education has been controversial and continues to find its way into the Supreme Court (see Chesler et al. 2005; Glazer-Raymo 2011). Even with diversity programs, tolerance trainings, and affirmative action initiatives, progress for women and minority faculty has been uneven, benefiting white women, as a group, the most (Aguirre 2000). Part of the reason for the tempered successes of minority faculty, and minority women specifically, has been persistent stereotyping and assumptions of tokenism. Aguirre (2000) notes, "Ironically, affirmative action initiatives that were designed to increase the representation of women and minorities in the faculty ranks have resulted in an environment in academia that isolates rather than incorporates women and minorities in the academic culture" (2). He suggests that enduring social forces within the academy, such as resistance to diversification and widespread reluctance to discuss ongoing discrimination against women and minority faculty, serve the interests of white men and some white women. Despite significant legislative remedies, the attrition of well-trained, skilled, and valuable faculty often results from such enduring inequalities within the academy.

Books About Women Academics

We can trace research on U.S. women faculty to Jessie Bernard's (1964) *Academic Women*. Since then books, articles, conference sessions, and entire conferences have explored the status of academic women—sometimes specific to disciplines, other times more broadly. An exhaustive review of this literature is beyond the scope of this introduction, though a handful of texts are worth noting as we trace this literature. Some texts take an all-encompassing approach (Aleman and Renn 2002; Bank 2011). Others focus on specific issues in academe, such as work/family concerns (Bracken, Allen, and Dean 2006; Connelly and Ghodsee 2011), women's exclusion from knowledge production (May 2008), and faculty incivility (Twale and De Luca 2008). Despite the historical silence on the issues faced by academic women of color, recent scholarship attends to the structural and cultural aspects of the academy that produce inequity despite imperatives for diversification and equality (e.g., Aguirre 2000; Niles and Gordon 2011), the underrepresentation and resiliency of Black women in higher education (Gutiérrez y Muhs, Niemann, and Harris 2012; Mabokela and Green 2001), and the tensions or possibilities of allied relationships among women academics (Dace 2012).

Several texts focus on changing the academy's structures and cultures by incorporating feminist perspectives or interventions (e.g., Allan 2011; Morley and Walsh 1995, 1996). Glazer-Raymo's (e.g., 1999, 2008) influential texts on women and higher education provide evidence of women's progress in higher education and document persistent barriers to their full equality and equity. The aforementioned texts, and others (e.g., Brown-Glaude 2009), focus primarily at the organizational level of the academy, offering recommendations for and examples of institutional change, as well as ways to increase enforcement of existing laws and policies intended to ensure equity. Other texts provide advice to help individual women academics with workplace challenges (e.g., Caplan 1993; Collins, Chrisler, and Quina 1998; Toth 1997[3]). Some focus on minority populations' unique experiences (Rockquemore and Laszloffy 2008), speak to new faculty issues (e.g., Boice 2000; Lenning, Brightman, and Caringella 2010), or offer advice for administrators (e.g., Crookston 2012).

Another subgenre explores the "leaky pipeline" of women from STEM degree programs and careers in the STEM fields.[4] This scholarship centers on the limited and partial successes of legislation and affirmative action and locates women's attrition from or rejection of academic careers within an array of structural and cultural circumstances including "chilly climates," overt discrimination, lack of mentoring and role models, inadequate work-family policies, and other accumulated disadvantages. The expansion in research on women's underrepresentation in STEM fields has produced many excellent books, too numerous to list comprehensively (e.g., Bilimoria and Liang 2011; Bystydzienski and Bird 2006; Etzkowitz, Kemelgor, and Uzzi 2000; National Research Council 2007; Rosser 2004; Stewart, Malley, and LaVaque-Manty 2007; Xie and Shauman 2003).

A watershed moment in the awareness of continued bias and discrimination of women faculty (with an emphasis on STEM faculty) came with the 1999 Massachusetts Institute of Technology (MIT) report, showing that MIT's tenured women faculty in the sciences experienced marginalization and salary, space, and resource inequities. Further, their experiences worsened as they advanced. All had prominent careers: Forty percent held membership in the National Academy of Sciences and/or the American Academy of Arts and Sciences. Thus, the argument that gendered inequities resulted from poorer performance did not hold.

In contrast, the report showed that MIT's *early-career*, pre-tenure women faculty felt supported by their colleagues and were optimistic about their careers. The concern was that, over time, unconscious and subtle discrimination stalled, or made difficult, the careers of women scientists and engineers. The authors wrote: "Discrimination consists of a pattern of powerful but unrecognized assumptions and attitudes that work systematically against women faculty even in the light of obvious good will" (MIT 1999, 11). One key finding—that micro-inequities and subtle forms of bias are "what discrimination looks like"—ignited research on gender (and race) inequity in higher education, much of which was done under pressure from women faculty across the country (see Roos and Gatta 2009). National attention grew toward developing understandings of the structural (macro) and interactional (micro) practices that hampered women academics' careers. For example, in response to the MIT report,[5] in 2001, the National Science Foundation initiated the ADVANCE grant program to improve the representation and experiences of women and minority faculty by attending to the climate in academia, lack of diversity, and "pipeline" issues.

Thus, equality and equity in academia are not new research topics. What is new and significant about ADVANCE and similar initiatives is their concerted, often funded effort to give attention to complex, intersecting factors, such as the relationship between institutional structure and culture at micro and macro levels that create inequity and inequality for academic women. Recent scholarship exposes enduring aspects of discrimination against women and draws attention to shockingly low numbers of tenured women in specific disciplines (e.g., some STEM fields). Further, it documents and helps us understand patterns of stratification remaining in the U.S. system of higher education. For example:

- Women's lower salaries (compared with men counterparts), as well as their overrepresentation in lower ranks and at less prestigious institutions, confirms persistent *vertical* segregation in the academy.
- Women's overall representation in STEM disciplines is lower than in social sciences, education, or humanities, reflects *horizontal* segregation.
- Women's and men of color's representation in all levels of the academy (e.g., students, faculty, administration) are disproportionately low.

Gender Segregation in the Academy

Women continue to make notable gains in higher education according to recent U.S. Department of Education National Center for Education Statistics (NCES) Integrated Postsecondary Education (IPEDS) data (2011–2012).

However, women are outnumbered by men at *all* ranks at *all* four-year institution types (i.e., public, private for-profit, private not-for-profit), yet women outnumber men at *all* two-year institution types (public, private for-profit, private not-for-profit) (see Table I.1). That is, men faculty outnumber women except at the least prestigious institutions, with the fewest resources and lowest salaries (and at the ranks of assistant professor, instructor, and lecturer).[6] Interestingly, within those two-year private nonprofit institutions, men outnumber women at the *highest rank* one can achieve: full professor.

The American Association of University Professors (AAUP) reports that men outnumber women two to one at the rank of full professor across degree-granting institutions (Curtis 2011). Danowitz and Agans (2011, 317) suggest that the "gatekeeping process" to achieving full professor is "more unyielding for women." Additionally, men, the majority of whom are white, overwhelmingly fill the power structure of the academy, including administrators, trustees, presidents, provosts, and chancellors (Chesler et al. 2005; Curtis 2011; Danowitz and Agans 2011; Glazer-Raymo 2011). This disproportionate leadership occurs even though more white women and faculty of color are in the "pipeline" than ever before (Aguirre 2000; Allan 2011).

The "cohort effect" suggests that these disparities result from women and people of color being newcomers to academe and that we need to wait for them to rise through the ranks before seeing the effects of the previous decades' recruitment and retention efforts. (For a review of the glass ceiling and cohort

TABLE I.1.
Full-Time Instructional Faculty in Degree-Granting Institutions by Gender and Type of Institution

Type of Institution	No. of Men	No. of Women
Public 4-year	223,503	158,648
Public 2-year	51,258	61,983*
Private 4-year	147,043	106,962
Private not-for-profit 4-year	138,887	99,332
Private for-profit 4-year	8,156	7,630
Private 2-year	5,178	7,044*
Private not-for-profit 2-year	618	1,027*
Private for-profit 2-year	4,560	6,017*

Note. U.S. Department of Education, National Center for Education Statistics, Integrated Postsecondary Education Data System (IPEDS), Winter 2011–2012. Human Resources component, Fall Staff section. Based on Table 286.

* = type of institution where women outnumber men.

effects on faculty salaries see Prokos and Padavic 2005.) Marschke et al. (2007) challenge this notion by demonstrating that without any kind of intervention (in hiring, retention, or promotion) to increase the numbers of women faculty at the research-intensive university they studied, there would never be numerical equality between men and women. With a hypothetical intervention to ensure "equal hires" and "equal exits" (i.e., equal hiring, advancement, attrition, retention, and retirement), the faculty would still need *57 years* to reach simple numerical equality. Using a dramatic hypothetical intervention where only women are hired and attrition rates are equal, the faculty would reach numerical equality in 11 years. Such policy intervention would be illegal, of course. However, their analyses illustrate that colleges and universities must adopt and enforce policies to ensure equitable recruitment, hiring, and retention of faculty, among other measures, if we are to ever reach parity.

Although the vertical segregation described previously explains a significant portion of the salary gap between men and women faculty, the research attributes some of the gap to the persistent sex segregation in some academic disciplines (e.g., Bellas 1993; Roos and Gatta 2009). Women faculty are concentrated in disciplines such as education, in health fields, and in some humanities but are far less represented in the natural sciences or engineering. This horizontal segregation translates into significant salary differentials because faculty in the latter disciplines have higher salaries than those in the former. Salary data for 2011–2012 showed that newly hired assistant professors in computer science earned just over $74,500, and in engineering, $78,650. The same cohorts in education earned just over $55,600, and in liberal arts/humanities, just shy of $53,000 (unweighted averages; College and University Professional Association for Human Resources 2012). Although men *and* women in the lower-paying fields earn less than their peers in higher-paying fields, women's salaries are lower within all disciplines (Bellas 1993). That is, even if women "choose" higher-paying disciplines, they would likely earn less than similarly situated men.

The distribution of men and women at different institution types matters, too. According to AAUP's salary data (2010), the gap between men's and women's salaries was smallest at two-year colleges, where women earned 95.9% compared with their men peers (who earned less than their peers at four-year institutions). The pay gap was largest (78.3%) at doctoral-granting universities and was present at each faculty rank and at all institution types. In addition, the academic pay gap has hovered near the same level, about 80% overall, since the 1970s (Curtis 2011). Despite the range of variables that might explain existing or historical salary disparities between men and women (e.g., rank, discipline, educational attainment, institution type), "research specific to newly hired faculty confirms a wage gap for women faculty that is unexplained by other factors" (Porter et al. 2008, cited in Allan 2011, 114). Even detailed and complex analyses that account for such variables still generate an "unexplained" salary gap:

> Although it is not appropriate to attribute [the] remaining differential to discrimination on the basis of this evidence alone, the statistical analyses clearly leave a series of questions unanswered: . . . Why are women less likely to obtain full-time tenure-track positions? Why are they less likely to be employed in research universities? Why do women faculty generally spend more of their time on student advising and committee service than do men? Why do positions in the disciplines in which women faculty are concentrated generally pay less? Why are women less likely than men to earn tenure and promotion to full professor? Why do they earn less on average at every rank than their male counterparts? If we are to achieve equity for women faculty, it is necessary to confront each of these questions at the local level, and to devise more effective strategies to remove the disadvantages for women that persist even after decades of effort to remove them. (West and Curtis 2006, 12)

And while we should consider the array of factors that attempt to explain differences in men's and women's positioning in the academy, we should be leery of explanations that reduce complex issues to individual women's "choices." Curtis (2011) argues:

> Suggesting that women "choose" employment that is less remunerative implies that all career options are equally open to them. . . . The reality faced by women in academia, as in other professions, is that their "choices" are constrained by limited career options, socially gendered roles on the job and in the home, and by "simple" economics. (7)

National-level data illustrate how academic career pathways remain stratified by gender, race, and class, reflecting broader societal stratification. This is noteworthy, in part, because access to higher education is a primary means of class mobility and attainment of increased power and status. The lack of diversity in faculty ranks indicates blocked opportunity structures, antithetical to the values of the academy and U.S. society. Faculty of color constitute just 19%–20% of the faculty at public and private four-year and public two-year institutions. They comprise 32.5% of the faculty at private two-year institutions (see Table I.2), even though people of color attain PhDs at a higher rate than is reflected in faculty ranks (Aguirre 2000).

Although these snapshots of the academic "pipeline" are relevant, a "body count" (Martin 1994) cannot tell the entire story because equal numerical

TABLE I.2.
Full-Time Instructional Faculty in Degree-Granting Institutions
by Race/Ethnicity and Gender

	% of All Faculty (N = 1,523,615)	% of All Women Faculty (N = 734,418)	% of Women of Color Faculty (N = 139,178)
Black women	4.0	8.4	44
Hispanic women	2.1	4.4	23
Asian women	2.6	5.4	29
Pacific Islander women	0.1	0.2	1.2
American Indian/Alaska Native women	0.3	0.5	2.7

Note. U.S. Department of Education, National Center for Education Statistics, Integrated Postsecondary Education Data System (IPEDS), Winter 2011–2012. Human Resources component, Fall Staff section, Table 287. Figures exclude nonresident aliens (where race/ethnicity data are not collected), two or more races, and race/ethnicity unknown categories.

representation is not equity. Aggregate data cannot capture the many aspects of academic inequity (Monroe et al. 2008; Turner 2002). First, a critical mass of women in previously men-dominated fields is important; however, it is insufficient to shift inequitable academic cultures (Frehill 2006; Rosser 2004). Second, aggregate data do not expose the homogeneity of women in academia. For example, the lack of representation of women from lower socioeconomic backgrounds or first-generation students, or the overrepresentation of women from dominant categories (e.g., heterosexual, able-bodied, white). The legacy of racism in academe "pervades the curriculum, pedagogy, structure of departments and disciplines, formal and informal relationships among participants, and decision making about hiring, promotion, and retention" (Chesler et al. 2005, 19). A more nuanced picture of women's representation in higher education requires us to address intersectionality. Third, raw numbers can present the image that the problem of equality of opportunity is solved, depending on which numbers are examined. For instance, the National Education Association's (2012) *Higher Education Advocate* cites National Center for Education Statistics (U.S. Department of Education 2011–2012) data showing that between 1989 and 2011, the increase in full-time women faculty across all types of public institutions (e.g., two-year, four-year) was 98.3%. The increase across all types of private institutions (e.g., two-year, four-year; for profit/not-for-profit) was 83.4%. The largest increase in women faculty occurred in doctoral private institutions (223.1%) and doctoral public institutions (189.2%). Some could interpret this as evidence of bias against men (see Evers et al. 2006, cited in Allan 2011). However, such assertions suggest a limited understanding of the issues, because aggregate numbers do *not* reveal the ways inequality and inequity persist.

Theoretical and Conceptual Frameworks

We and many of our contributors identify as feminist scholars who recognize problems of equity as gendered. We interpret individual actions, attitudes, and experiences as well as institutionalized structures, policies, and procedures within their specific social contexts. These contexts are imbued with the dynamics of power and privilege, often difficult to recognize. Using feminist frameworks means that we aim for "social change while also emphasizing women and gender as key analytic categories" (Allan 2011, 18). As sociologists, we (and many of our contributors) seek to understand the well-documented patterns of gender inequality as outcomes of institutional and cultural arrangements existing within a particular historical time and geographical place, rather than as a collection of individual experiences that just happen to be alike. Mills (1959, 8) argues that we can only begin to understand "issues" and find their solutions by taking this approach. Individuals can take actions to alleviate their "personal troubles," but those are stopgap measures. To eradicate the "issues" for the thousands of women academics in U.S. higher education, academic structures, cultures, and climates must change.

What does it look like to apply feminist sociological frameworks to understanding gender inequality in the academy? For example, when women scientists who leave the academy are characterized as "choosing" motherhood over science (e.g., Ceci and Williams 2011), feminist sociologists would critique the shortcomings of such individualistic explanations. Instead, we focus on the structural and cultural context in which people make decisions. To highlight the need for more complex understanding of seemingly personal issues,[7] sociologists might deliberately add quotation marks to the word *choice*. When women leave their careers in academic science (or other workplaces), it is often because of inadequate family-work-life policies (Goulden, Mason, and Frasch 2011; Hochschild 1997; Mason and Goulden 2002, 2004; Perna 2005; Williams 2005), or because of (real or perceived) penalties for using existing policies (Schneider 2000). For example, university policy may allow flexible office hours, but departmental cultures that require "face time" at the lab or at late afternoon meetings might compel a new, untenured faculty member to "choose" to remain in the office. Many women, particularly in the obstinately sex-segregated fields of engineering, computer science, and physics, have struggled with an "old boys' club" (De Welde and Laursen 2011; Hewlitt et al. 2008; Rosser 2004; Still 2006), a lack of mentoring (De Welde and Laursen 2008; Fox 2003), and a lack of networking opportunities (Clark and Corcoran 1986; Sonnert and Holton 1995). Additionally, they face unequal rates of hiring and promotion, allocation of resources, and opportunities to participate in workplace decision making (Aguirre 2000; Wenzel and Hollenshead 1994). These issues can be exacerbated for women of color (e.g., Aguirre 2000; Davis 1985; Turner 2002).

When women academics decide to leave the fields in which they have invested considerable time, energy, and money, as well as significant aspects of their identities, it is with consideration of these accumulating constraints, considerations that men, particularly white men, generally, do not have to make (Valian 1998).[8] By using a feminist sociological framework, we might consider why women, but not men, have to "choose" between family and career. Or, why men scientists do not leave careers (in the same numbers as women) when they have children. Beyond the actual birth, men are equally capable of raising children and many would like to do so. Feminist sociologists would analyze the cultural pressures or structural barriers that create such gendered patterns.

To understand people's "choices," we must understand their contexts—contexts structured by unequal power relations between actors. As Bird (2011, 202) suggests, "women-centered" explanations for gender inequality and inequity in academe persist and can obscure the structural and cultural barriers that provide greater explanatory power for individual "choices" that occur as part of larger patterns (i.e., not just one woman, but many). Thus, she calls for increased dissemination of research findings about these barriers and how to transform them. We take up this call.

Theories of Gendered Organizations

Our work draws from Acker's (1990, 1998) theory of gendered organizations. She argues, "To say that an organization, or any other analytic unit, is gendered means that advantage and disadvantage, exploitation and control, action and emotion, meaning and identity, are patterned through and in terms of a distinction between male and female, masculine and feminine" (Acker 1990, 146). Thus, the structure of an organization and its culture reflect society's gender (and other cultural) ideologies. Further, gender is an essential element of the "organizational logic" (Acker 1990, 147) of work organizations: The practices, attitudes, values, and guiding principles of organizations all contribute to the "ongoing processes of creating and conceptualizing social structures." However, as Bird (2011) argues, "This is not to say that bureaucratic work structures are inherently gendered, always gendered to the same degree, or invariably masculinist" (204; see also Britton 2000). But, as Acker (1990, 147; 1998) suggests, the "gender substructure" of organizations reflects the societal gender (and race) inequalities and reproduces and institutionalizes them (see also Martin 1994; Roos and Gatta 2009). Applying these ideas, we conceptualize colleges and universities as gendered organizations (e.g., Bird 2011; Martin 1994); within them, faculty roles are gendered, and hierarchies of inequality are reproduced in part because "bureaucratic organizations and institutions themselves [like higher education] provide the legitimizing scaffolding" (Roscigno 2011, 364).

The gendered division of academic labor persists across disciplines and organizations. The labor of service and teaching is not easily quantifiable; thus, it often goes unnoticed, and women faculty "perform a disproportionate share of academic departments' care work and emotion labor" (Bird 2011, 204). Despite their necessity, academic organizations typically undervalue teaching and service, resulting in status, pay, and promotion disparities between women and men academics (Misra, Lundquist, Holmes, and Agiomavritis 2011). Another result is little diversity among those who have the authority and power to develop and implement institutional policies and practices and shape organizational cultures toward greater gender equality (Acker 1998; Bird 2011; Martin 1994; Roos and Gatta 2009).[9] Institutional policies that ensure equitable treatment of campus members must be developed with diverse experiences in mind. Otherwise, they reflect what those in power deem important or relevant, which may not reflect the experiences of those different from them (i.e., women and minority faculty). We see strong evidence of this in the current attention toward developing family-friendly policies. Throughout the academy's history, men administrators have had families, generally with wives/partners caring for them and their homes. Such administrators might not have considered the need for on-site day care, stopping the tenure clock, part-time or flexible schedules, or other family-friendly resources. As more women enter higher administration, these job-related needs enter mainstream conversation. Although research shows that many men chairs and deans support these policies (Marjukka Ollilainen, personal communication, 2012). In sum, as Bird (2011) argues:

> The segregation of academic disciplines and institutions, the construction of faculty and administrative roles in ways that are more consistent with men's lives, and the maintenance of evaluation processes that disproportionately value the disciplines and activities that men dominate are all

examples of how university structures and associated cultures and practices are gendered. (208)

Thus, we frame the academy, and colleges and universities within it, as gendered organizations imbued with gendered barriers toward advancement (Bird 2011; Valian 1998). Additionally, they reflect "incongruous gendered bureaucratic structures" (Bird 2011) because the formal and informal norms of colleges/universities and departments can conflict, partly resulting from the decentralized decision-making structures within academe. Bird (2011, 205) explains, "Incongruous, gendered bureaucratic structures produce ambiguities for individual faculty members regarding the extent to which one should follow university and departmental formal guidelines versus informal norms." For example, we see "structural incongruencies" between what departments value and what university mission statements declare as important (206)—disjunctures between structures (e.g., formal policies) and cultures (e.g., beliefs, values, norms) or climates (e.g., behaviors and informal practices). Roscigno (2011) describes this as the "decoupling between what organizations profess to do and how they actually operate" (360), which allows those in positions of power to legitimize discriminatory actions by "invok[ing] structure in a way that reifies hierarchy" (365). Furthermore, incongruity exists between the ascribed peripheral roles for women and minority faculty (i.e., service) and the stated expectations for scholarly productivity (Aguirre 2000). These inconsistencies allow for subtle discrimination or unconscious bias against women academics. They impact interactions and decision making, creating uncertainty about what constitutes valued work. These practices accrue and contribute to "accumulated disadvantages" (Clark and Corcoran 1986; Valian 1998) and "mechanisms of inequity" (Roos and Gatta 2009) that stall and slow women's careers.

Structure, Culture, and Climate

Our conceptual framework includes an emphasis on *structure* (i.e., the unique organizational arrangements of the academy) and *culture* (i.e., the norms, beliefs, and values of academic institutions). Also, we incorporate *interactions and practices*—and the dynamic and dependent relationships between transitory members of the academy (e.g., students, contingent faculty) and stable ones (e.g., administrators, full-time faculty). The relationship between academic structures and cultures is reciprocal and interactive (Hermanowicz 2005). Researchers may separate structure and culture for analytical purposes (as we do); however, in reality, these components work in tandem at micro (individual or small group) and macro (institutional) levels to shape our interactions and our understanding of social phenomena.

Although "the structure" of the academy is not monolithic, we can generalize about how academic careers and faculty life are organized (e.g., attainment of advanced degrees; ambitions for tenure; and core faculty responsibilities of teaching, research, and service). And yet, the structure of academic careers is changing dramatically across the United States because of sweeping and aggressive fiscal changes. The impact is greatest at public universities, historically funded largely by state and federal monies. Like no other time in our history, we are witnessing a growing trend in the corporatization of U.S. higher education, or "academic capitalism" (Metcalf and Slaughter 2011; Rhoades and Slaughter 2004). As state and federal investments in postsecondary institutions decline, we see increased attention on research and teaching with *commercial* potential. These forces create a "regime" that coerces academics' involvement in the global market and their dependence on private funding (Metcalf and Slaughter 2011, 15). The pressure on academics to attract external funding marginalizes and situates as less "valuable" disciplinary fields with lesser potential for partnering with industry and other profit-making ways. Further, financially driven relationships influence what subjects are taught and studied so that what is most profitable becomes equated with what is most important (e.g., national emphasis on STEM degree attainment). Pressures to serve the private, corporate good, as opposed to the public good, now extend to *all* disciplines through increasing exposure to market forces, such as through the intense marketing of distance/online education and through prepackaged curricula created primarily to generate revenue (Metcalf and Slaughter 2011).

Academic capitalism is gendered, creating "conditions within colleges and universities that allow men to recapture some of the historic privilege they have derived from higher education . . . [and] recasting the value of higher education in the process" (Metcalf and Slaughter 2008, 81). That is, the merit and value of academic work shifts from being determined within the academy, which has become increasingly diversified, to being determined by (and in) the economic marketplace, which continues to be dominated by men and masculine ideals.

Decreases in federal agency support (e.g., the National Science Foundation) intensify competition between faculty (Aguirre 2000) and increase reliance on private industry funding. These trends shift where the value of knowledge production is determined, and by whom. Rather than being evaluated by peers, outside the reach of the state or marketplace, the market determines and regulates knowledge production based on what is profitable (Metcalf and Slaughter 2008, 2011). This dynamic changes the core values of the academy and undermines it as a locus for innovation, change, progress, and ideas. Furthermore, the increased reliance on external funding for salaries, historically supported by the state as an investment in the public good, requires faculty to assume another responsibility, increasingly emphasized above teaching or research. Such changes create uncertainty for faculty and deepen historical divides between the physical and social sciences (the latter are funded less, historically), and between other fields such as business or engineering and education or the humanities.[10] These trends illustrate ways that we can speak, generally, about the structure of faculty careers.

Exploring the structure of academic careers is relevant because of assumptions that the academy is neutral and nondiscriminatory—a bureaucracy in the ideal sense (Weber 1949). Academics (and others) may operate under the assumption that it is, perhaps, the last bastion of true meritocracy where merit and peer-reviewed tenure and promotion policies and procedures guarantee reward for those who follow them. Policies presumably curtail discrimination and typically offer channels for redress for those who experience unfairness or discrimination. However, academic structures are not immune to unfair or illegal practices. How these inequalities manifest is typically less blatant than in the past, when, for example, mainstream universities and colleges barred women and people of color. Rather, "a meritocratic discourse *incorporates gender-blindness in the name of fairness*" (Acker and Armenti 2004, 19; emphasis added), which effaces important consequential differences in faculty lives. In addition, implicit bias enters into evaluation processes (e.g., Bird 2011). For example, if someone's advancement is "slow," evaluators might assume the candidate lacks dedication, has low productivity, or cannot succeed. Though this might be the case for some, these assumptions are applied to women faculty more than men, to mothers more than nonmothers, and to women of color more than white women (see Part Three of this volume). In fact, those in positions of authority and power draw on the presumably neutral policies and procedures to enact what Roscigno (2011) calls "symbolic vilification" (e.g., where women and minorities are considered as problematic or less creditable in the structure) and "symbolic amplification" (where institutional/organizational policies and practices are used to legitimize hierarchical and, thus, unequal practices) (362–364).

Finally, as Twale and De Luca (2008) suggest, the structure of the academy, with its focus on faculty governance and decisions made by committees, is especially ripe for "incubating" hostility, bullying, secrecy, marginalization, and harassment. Institutional structures unwittingly create and perpetuate silence about these problems by not having adequate policies, or by discouraging, dismissing, or minimizing incident reports. Silence can result from powerlessness, denial, embarrassment, fear of retaliation, or lack of knowledge about what actions to take (Twale and De Luca 2008). Though remaining silent is a survival strategy for some, it allows injustice to foment and become embedded in the institutional culture.

The cultures of academic careers are more diverse than the structures. Cultures vary from institution to institution, and across institution types (i.e., research universities, community colleges, liberal arts colleges) (see Hermanowicz 2005). *Academic cultures* are closely linked to the structure of the academy in that cultures are imbedded, difficult to change, and reflective of the values expressed by institutions. Academic cultures can exacerbate the negative aspects of academic structures, or they may respond in ways that benefit faculty experiencing workplace hostilities. However, even when policies change, cultures can respond slowly.

Campus climates are microlevel work environments that differ across (and within) institutions; are imbedded in cultures; and are reflective of broader social, economic, and political contexts. Climates are even more idiosyncratic and shift more quickly than structures or cultures. They are more malleable and subject to shift such as when leadership changes occur. Individuals' perceptions of their organizational culture and structure, along with their shared/collective experiences, constitute climate. In other words, a culture reflects and includes the values of an organization and its structure and is more enduring (Allan 2011). Climates have to do with current, perhaps transitory, organizational practices.

We can better understand the context of academic careers—and universities—as gendered organizations within the institution of higher education by examining structures, cultures, climates, and the relationships among them. Individuals experience discrimination or bias within a structural context permeated by an institutional culture and an immediate climate. As Roscigno (2011) argues, "Historically and culturally proscribed hierarchies become inscribed in bureaucratic structures, practices, and internal dynamics" (360). This book contributes to the extensive body of research documenting the struggles and some successes of academic women within these milieus. We explore structural and cultural aspects of the academy that continue to be biased against academic women in direct, indirect, obvious, and subtle ways. We envision our book as a toolbox to be used for creating greater equality and equity in the U.S. higher education system. By examining problematic workplace situations and how women faculty navigate them, we hope to begin shifting the enduring aspects of academic cultures that drive chilly climates, discrimination, harassment, marginalization, and other challenges facing women academics. Thus, this book fundamentally is subversive because it "repositions women from victims to change agents" (Morley and Walsh 1995, 3).

Background of the Project

For more than a decade, we have been members of Sociologists for Women in Society (SWS), an academic organization dedicated to improving women's lives, creating feminist social change by maximizing networking opportunities for women sociologists, and applying sociological insights to all aspects of society.[11] In 2007, as part of our service to SWS, we joined a newly formed committee for academic justice (CAJ). The CAJ collects and analyzes data regarding issues confronting women in higher education (i.e., inequitable university policies, race/gender/sexual orientation–based discrimination, bias in teaching evaluations). The CAJ's goal is, in part, to create a more just academy that reflects the democratic ideals of the academy.[12] In 2007, we offered a workshop on navigating inequitable and challenging work situations. To explore this terrain, we put out a "call for experiences" on the SWS Listserv.

We asked members to submit their experiences, in confidence, for use as case studies. We removed identifying information (e.g., names, geographic location) and together with workshop participants analyzed narratives and developed concrete, appropriate actions for each situation. In keeping with our committee's goal of creating academic justice, we went beyond suggesting interpersonal solutions and proposed "action" at the organizational and extraorganizational levels of colleges and universities. We realized that a broader audience might benefit from hearing about women's experiences and exploring strategies to manage them. Thus, this book project was born.

Method and Methodology of the Project

We placed a "call for experiences" similar to that on the SWS Listserv in approximately 80 electronic venues (Listservs, e-mail, organizations' newsletters, etc.) representing diverse U.S.-based academic disciplines using the CAJ's comprehensive list of academically oriented women-focused organizations, which we expanded (see Online Resources, this volume). Our goal was to shed light on topics that have remained largely invisible and give voice to women academics who have, perhaps, been silent (or been forced to be quiet) about negative work-related experiences.

We developed an online instrument that allowed for anonymous submissions. After obtaining consent, we culled lengthier narratives from our previous workshops and our online instrument as representative of areas of concern for each part of the book. Given the sensitive topics within these illustrative case studies, we took cautions to obscure any identifying details (e.g., removing university name, changing personal names, changing specifics of discipline or rank). However, most of each narrative remains unchanged.

We position ourselves as insiders of this community and claim our positionality as academic feminists who have experienced bias, discrimination, hostility, and silencing.[13] These experiences shape what we see as important to study. Feminist standpoint epistemology, or the valuing of women's situated knowledge, has guided our project from its inception. We believe that women's perspectives on their own experiences, conveyed through their interpretation of events, offer valuable empirical and theoretical insights for feminist research (Harding 1987, 31). As Narayan (1992) suggests, "[A] fundamental thesis of feminist epistemology is that our location in the world as women makes it possible for us to perceive and understand different aspects of both the world and human activities in ways that challenge the male bias of existing perspectives" (256). Standpoint epistemology should not be interpreted as an attempt to essentialize women or reify gender as a priori, suggesting that all academic women have homogeneous experiences. Instead, the communal experience of academic women, situated as such, provides a window into the conditions of their experiences. Our differences are as important as our similarities. And, we do not discount the possibility of alternative or competing explanations of accounts. We recognize that women can have positive and fulfilling careers in academe, unencumbered by negative experiences. It is precisely feminist change within (and outside) the academy that allows for women faculty to have affirming experiences. Exploring where inequality and inequity persist directs us to areas within academic structures and cultures that need our attention. We focus on providing a space for our respondents to tell their stories as they experienced them, in their words, and with their framing. We offer an analytical context to situate these narratives and suggest action steps to help women academics, and their allies, to navigate similar situations and to create change, broadly, within the academy.

Examining narratives, independently and as part of a greater set of data, allows us to appreciate the complex ways women faculty handle bias, discrimination, or other forms of workplace inequity. Further, it helps us understand how power manifests and operates, structurally and culturally, even as individuals resist, adapt, and respond to it. To date, our call for experiences has yielded 68 distinct "narratives" from women academics in 35 different disciplines, constituting our "case study database" (Yin 2009). In the introductions to Parts One through Four of the book, we feature select narratives and "Academic Women's Voices" sections as evidence of some experiences. Parts One through Four each conclude with a case study from our data that is coupled with action steps for women academics in similar situations. Part Five concludes with four real-world case studies illustrating successful, feminist institutional transformation. Because we cannot include all the experiences submitted by our participants, we analyzed the narratives systematically for themes by a process of inductive theory building (Esterberg 2002). We categorized sections of respondents' submissions with our initial categories of "hostile climates" determined, in part, from the literature on women in the academy, including:

- Sexual harassment and discrimination
- Hostility in the classroom
- Incivility, bullying, and mobbing
- Hostility to women's race/ethnicity, sexual orientation, and feminist pedagogy or research
- Work and family conflicts
- Gendered and racialized expectations for service and "emotion work"[14]
- Pay equity and other disparities in work-related resources and compensation

However, people's experiences are rarely neatly catalogued. In reviewing the narratives for themes, we discovered nuances in experiences that we had not anticipated, and we used them to develop new categories. This process required subsuming some categories within others and developing new ones in an iterative coding process that allowed us to capture the complexity of individual narratives while finding broader patterns across them. We created a matrix of categories, placing excerpts of data into those categories. Then, we further considered the relationship between the categories given the data within them (see Miles and Huberman 1994).

No one book can cover the diversity of academic women's experiences. Space limitations have prevented us from addressing ageism, postdoctoral experiences, classism, and women faculty at for-profit institutions or community colleges. Additionally, we were unable to explore in depth the positive experiences of many women faculty, which research tells us are prevalent (e.g., Harvard COACHE climate survey). Nor could we address the experiences of women staff, undergraduates, or administrators; academic institutions outside of the United States; or men's experiences in the academy. However, this volume presents an important "slice" of academic life.

The Structure of the Book

The first four parts of the book emphasize challenges facing U.S. women faculty that emerge from intersecting structures, cultures, and climates. Each of these parts opens with an introduction that intersperses narratives from our data with summaries of the part's chapters. In keeping with our book's toolbox approach to change, a case study from our data ends each part (there are four case studies for Part Five) to provide a sense of the costs that our study participants—and women academics throughout the United States—face as a result of inequitable workplaces. The case studies to Parts One through Four conclude with action steps that academics in similar situations—and their allies—can use. We intend them as starting points for action, not exhaustive lists. To avoid redundancies, and because the situations in our case studies overlap, we distribute our recommendations across the case studies.

Despite the resources and advice that we provide and that exist in other books, on websites, and via organizations, we acknowledge that some battles are not winnable. Many of the suggestions that we make are about, for example, putting policies into place to educate, protect, and prevent discriminatory and hostile situations from happening. But casualties occur. If you (or someone you know) are navigating a challenging workplace situation, we recommend reading each case study to identify the most appropriate steps and resources.

Part Five, "Tools for Changing the Academy," includes chapters that illustrate the need for broad, complementary approaches to creating change along with step-by-step ways to assess and correct the equity issues on your campus. This part ends with examples of recent, successful change initiatives from universities in the United States that we hope will inspire strategic interventions on your campus. The book ends with a list of resources that we compiled for faculty, administrators, and practitioner-researchers seeking to create a more inclusive academy. The online resources feature more than 100 organizations, groups, committees, and sources for information from a wide variety of disciplines as well as umbrella organizations.

We and the chapter contributors are hopeful not only that this book will result in institutional change but also that it will provide a sense of solidarity for women faculty who are experiencing (or have experienced) challenging, hostile, or biased academic environments. You are not alone! The narrative excerpts and case studies reflect the voices of academic women—and there are many—who stand with you. (Many academic men support you too.) We hope this book provides you with concrete ways to survive, or even thrive, in your current situation.

Notes

1. We follow Crenshaw (1991, 1244), who argues that minority categories denote cultural groups (e.g., Black, Latina, Asian) and thus constitute proper nouns requiring capitalization. Equally, "white" and "women of color" are not specific cultural groups; thus, we do not capitalize them. However, perspectives on this differ. The editors respected contributors' decisions regarding which conventions to use.

2. From The Papers of Elizabeth Cady Stanton and Susan B. Anthony Project at Rutgers University: http://ecssba.rutgers.edu/docs/seneca.html

3. Toth (2008) includes advice to men.

4. For a critique of the "pipeline" metaphor see Furhmann et al. (2011) and Xie and Shauman (2003).

5. See www.advance.cornell.edu/documents/CU_ADVANCEprop.pdf.

6. One curious exception occurs in four-year private for-profit institutions, which have more men lecturers than women.

7. Ceci and Williams (2011) state that choices may be "free or constrained," but they take for granted that it is about "motherhood"—why not a "parenting" choice? Their more sociological analysis can be found in Williams and Ceci (2012).
8. Drawing attention to men as a group does not mean that men cannot be allies. Many men are supportive allies and individual women can engage in hostile behavior. Our intention is to examine the *systems* that benefit particular categories of people; in this case, men. The flipside to men's privilege is that women, as a group, are disadvantaged.
9. Of noteworthy difference are historically Black colleges and universities (Martin 1994), tribal colleges and universities, and Hispanic-serving institutions.
10. This shift is part of a larger assault on intellectualism, a topic beyond this book's scope.
11. See www.socwomen.org
12. See www.socwomen.org/academic-justice
13. Our current workplaces are not represented in any of the case studies, narratives, or other examples of "hostility in the academy" in this book.
14. See Hochschild, Arlie Russel. 1979. "Emotion Work, Feeling Rules and Social Structure." *American Journal of Sociology* 85(3):551–575.

References

Acker, Joan. 1990. "Hierarchies, Jobs, Bodies: A Theory of Gendered Organizations." *Gender and Society* 4(2):139–158.
———. 1998. "The Future of 'Gender and Organizations': Connections and Boundaries." *Gender, Work & Organization* 5(4):195–206.
Acker, Sandra, and Carmen Armenti. 2004. "Sleepless in Academia." *Gender & Education* 16(1):3–24.
Aguirre, Adalberto. 2000. *Women and Minority Faculty in the Academic Workplace: Recruitment, Retention, and Academic Culture.* San Francisco: Jossey-Bass.
Aleman, Ana M. M., and Kristen A. Renn, eds. 2002. *Women in Higher Education: An Encyclopedia.* Santa Barbara, CA: ABC-CLIO.
Allan, Elizabeth. 2011. "Women's Status in Higher Education: Equity Matters." *ASHE Higher Education Report* 37(1). Hoboken, NJ: Wiley Periodicals.
Allan, Elizabeth, and Lisa P. Hallen. 2011. "University Women's Commissions and Policy Discourses." In *Gender & Higher Education*, edited by B. Bank, 398–405. Baltimore: Johns Hopkins University Press.
American Association of University Professors (AAUP). 2010. *Tenure and Teaching-Intensive Appointments.* Washington, DC: American Association of University Professors. http://www.aaup.org/report/tenure-and-teaching-intensive-appointments
Bank, Barbara J., ed. 2011. *Gender and Higher Education.* Baltimore: Johns Hopkins University Press.
Bellas, M. L. 1993. "Faculty Salaries: Still a Cost of Being Female?" *Social Science Quarterly* 74(1):62–75.
Bernard, Jessie. 1964. *Academic Women.* University Park, PA: The Pennsylvania State University Press.
Bilimoria, Diana, and Xiangfen Liang. 2012. *Gender Equity in Science and Engineering: Advancing Change in Higher Education.* New York: Routledge.

Bird, Sharon R. 2011. "Unsettling Universities' Incongruous, Gendered Bureaucratic Structures: A Case-Study Approach." *Gender, Work & Organization* 18(2):202–230.

Boice, Robert. 2000. *Advice for New Faculty Members.* Needham Heights, MA: Allyn & Bacon.

Bracken, Susan J., Jeanie K. Allen, and Diane R. Dean, eds. 2006. *The Balancing Act: Gendered Perspectives in Faculty Roles and Work Lives.* Sterling, VA: Stylus.

Britton, Dana M. 2000. "The Epistemology of the Gendered Organization." *Gender & Society* 14(3):418–434.

Brown v. Board of Education, 347 U.S. 483 (1954).

Brown-Glaude, Winnifred R., ed. 2009. *Doing Diversity in Higher Education: Faculty Leaders Share Challenges and Strategies.* New Brunswick, NJ: Rutgers University Press.

Bystydzienski, Jill M., and Sharon R. Bird, eds. 2006. *Removing Barriers: Women in Academic Science, Technology, Engineering, and Mathematics.* Bloomington: Indiana University Press.

Caplan, Paula J. 1993. *Lifting a Ton of Feathers: A Woman's Guide to Surviving in the Academic World.* Ontario: University of Toronto Press.

Ceci, Stephen J., and Wendy M. Williams. 2011. "Understanding Current Causes of Women's Underrepresentation in Science." *Proceedings of the National Academy of Sciences of the United States of America* 108(8):3157–3162.

Chesler, Mark, Amanda Lewis, and James Crowfoot. 2005. *Challenging Racism in Higher Education: Promoting Justice.* Lanham, MD: Rowman & Littlefield.

Clark, Shirley M., and Mary Corcoran. 1986. "Perspective on the Professional Socialization of Women Faculty: A Case of Accumulative Disadvantage." *Journal of Higher Education* 57(1):20–43.

College and University Professional Association for Human Resources (CUPA-HR). 2012. *2011–12 National Faculty Salary Survey by Discipline and Rank in Four-Year Colleges and Universities.* Knoxville, TN: CUPA-HR.

Collins, Lynn H., Joan C. Chrisler, and Kathryn Quina, eds. 1998. *Career Strategies for Women in Academe: Arming Athena.* Thousand Oaks, CA: Sage.

Collins, Patricia H. 1990. *Black Feminist Thought: Knowledge, Consciousness and the Politics of Empowerment.* New York: Routledge.

Connelly, Rachel, and Kristen Ghodsee. 2011. *Professor Mommy: Finding Work-Family Balance in Academia.* Lanham, MD: Rowman & Littlefield.

Crenshaw, Kimberlé W. 1991. "Mapping the Margins: Intersectionality, Identity Politics, and Violence Against Women of Color." *Stanford Law Review* 43(6):1241–1299.

Crookston, R. Kent. 2012. *Working With Problem Faculty: A Six-Step Guide for Department Chairs.* San Francisco: Jossey-Bass.

Curtis, John W. 2011. *Persistent Inequity: Gender and Academic Employment.* American Association of University Professors.

Dace, Karen L., ed. 2012. *Unlikely Allies in the Academy: Women of Color and White Women in Conversation.* New York: Routledge.

Danowitz, Mary A., and Lyndsay J. Agans. 2011. "Academic Career Patterns." In *Gender & Higher Education,* edited by B. Bank, 315–321. Baltimore: Johns Hopkins University Press.

Davis, Larry. 1985. "Black and White Social Work Faculty: Perceptions of Respect, Satisfaction, and Job Permanence." *Journal of Sociology and Social Welfare* 12(1):79–94.

De Welde, Kristine, and Sandra Laursen. 2008. "The 'Ideal Type' Advisor: Helping STEM Graduate Students Find Their 'Scientific Feet'." *The Open Education Journal* (1):49–61.

———. 2011. "The Glass Obstacle Course: Formal and Informal Barriers for STEM Ph.D. Students." *International Journal of Gender, Science and Technology* 3(3):547–570.

Esterberg, Kristin. 2002. *Qualitative Methods in Social Research.* Boston: McGraw-Hill.

Etzkowitz, Henry, Carol Kemelgor, and Brian Uzzi. 2000. *Athena Unbound: The Advancement of Women in Science and Technology.* Cambridge, UK: Cambridge University Press.

Fox, Mary F. 2003. "Gender, Faculty, and Doctoral Education in Science and Engineering." In *Equal Rites, Unequal Outcomes: Women in American Research Universities*, edited by L. S. Horning, 91–110. New York: Kluwer Academic/Plenum Publishers.

Frehill, Lisa. 2006. "Measuring Occupational Sex Segregation of Academic Science and Engineering." *The Journal of Technology Transfer* 31(3):345–354.

Fuhrmann, Cynthia N., D. G. Halme, P. S. O'Sullivan, and B. Lindstaedt. 2011. "Improving Graduate Education to Support a Branching Career Pipeline: Recommendations Based on a Survey of Doctoral Students in the Basic Biomedical Sciences." *CBE Life Sciences Education* 10(3):239–249.

Glazer-Raymo, Judith. 1999. *Shattering the Myths: Women in Academe.* Baltimore: Johns Hopkins University Press.

———. 2008. *Unfinished Agendas: New and Continuing Gender Challenges in Higher Education.* Baltimore: Johns Hopkins University Press.

———. 2011. "Affirmative Action." In *Gender & Higher Education*, edited by B. J. Bank, 357–366. Baltimore: Johns Hopkins University Press.

Goulden, Marc, Mary A. Mason, and Karie Frasch. 2011. "Keeping Women in the Science Pipeline." *The ANNALS of the American Academy of Political and Social Science* 638:141–162.

Gutiérrez y Muhs, Gabriella, Yolanda Flores Niemann, Carmen G. Gonzalez, and Angela P. Harris, eds. 2012. *Presumed Incompetent: The Intersections of Race and Class for Women in Academia.* Boulder, CO: University Press of Colorado.

Harding, Sandra. 1987. "Is There a Feminist Method?" *Hypatia* 2(3):19–35.

Hermanowicz, Joseph C. 2005. "Classifying Universities and Their Departments: A Social World Perspective." *Journal of Higher Education* 76(1):26–55.

Hewlitt, S. A., C. B. Luce, L. J. Servon, L. Sherbin, P. Shiller, E. Sosnovich, and K. Sumberg. 2008. *The Athena Factor: Reversing the Brain Drain in Science, Engineering, and Technology.* Boston: Harvard Business Review Research Report.

Hochschild, Arlie R. 1997. *The Time Bind: When Work Becomes Home and Home Becomes Work.* New York: Metropolitan/Holt.

————. 1979. "Emotion Work, Feeling Rules and Social Structure." *American Journal of Sociology* 85(3):551–575.

Lenning, Emily, Sara Brightman, and Susan Caringella, eds. 2010. *A Guide to Surviving a Career in Academia: Navigating the Rites of Passage* (e-book). London: Taylor & Francis.

Mabokela, Reitumetse, and Anna L. Green, eds. 2001. *Sisters of the Academy: Emergent Black Women Scholars in Higher Education*. Sterling, VA: Stylus.

Marschke, Robyn, Sandra Laursen, Joyce M. Nielsen, and Patricia Rankin. 2007. "Demographic Inertia Revisited: An Immodest Proposal to Achieve Equitable Gender Representation Among Faculty in Higher Education." *Journal of Higher Education* 78(1):1–26.

Martin, Joanne. 1994. "The Organization of Exclusion: Institutionalization of Sex Inequality, Gendered Faculty Jobs and Gendered Knowledge in Organizational Theory and Research." *Organization* 1(2):401–431.

Mason, Mary A., and Marc Goulden. 2002. "Do Babies Matter? The Effect of Family Formation on the Lifelong Careers of Academic Men and Women." *Academe* 88(6):21–27.

————. 2004. "Marriage and Baby Blues: Redefining Gender Equity in the Academy." *The ANNALS of the American Academy of Political and Social Science* 596:86–103.

Massachusetts Institute of Technology. 1999. "A Study on the Status of Women Faculty in Science at MIT." *The MIT Faculty Newsletter* XI(4).

May, Ann M., ed. 2008. *The "Woman Question" and Higher Education: Perspectives on Gender and Knowledge Production in America*. Northhampton, MA: Edward Elgar.

Metcalf, Amy S., and Sheila Slaughter. 2008. "The Differential Effects of Academic Capitalism on Women in the Academy." In *Unfinished Agendas: New and Continuing Gender Challenges in Higher Education*, edited by J. Glazer-Raymo, 80–111. Baltimore: Johns Hopkins University Press.

————. 2011. "Academic Capitalism." In *Gender & Higher Education*, edited by B. Bank, 14–19. Baltimore: Johns Hopkins University Press.

Miles, Matthew B., and A. M. Huberman. 1994. *Qualitative Data Analysis: An Expanded Sourcebook*. Thousand Oaks, CA: Sage.

Mills, C. W. 1959. *The Sociological Imagination*. New York: Oxford University Press.

Misra, Joya, Jennifer H. Lundquist, Elissa Holmes, and Stephanie Agiomavritis. 2011. "The Ivory Ceiling of Service Work." *Academe* 97(1):22–26.

Monroe, Kristen, Saba Ozyurt, Ted Wrigley, and Amy Alexander. 2008. "Gender Equality in Academia: Bad News From the Trenches, and Some Possible Solutions." *Perspectives on Politics* 6(2):215–233.

Morley, Louise, and Val Walsh, eds. 1995. *Feminist Academics: Creative Agents for Change*. London: Taylor & Francis.

————. 1996. *Breaking Boundaries: Women in Higher Education*. London: Taylor & Francis.

Narayan, Uma. 1992. "The Project of Feminist Epistemology: Perspectives From a Nonwestern Feminist." In *Gender/Body/Knowledge: Feminist Reconstructions of*

Being and Knowing, edited by Alison M. Jaggar and Susan R. Bordo, 256–269. New Brunswick, NJ: Rutgers University Press.

National Education Association. 2012. "Where's the Money?" *Higher Education Advocate* 6(2):4–9.

National Research Council. 2007. *Beyond Bias and Barriers: Fulfilling the Potential of Women in Academic Science and Engineering*. Washington, DC: The National Academies Press.

Niles, Marnel N., and Nickesia S. Gordon, eds. 2011. *Still Searching for Our Mothers' Gardens: Experience of New, Tenure-Track Women of Color at "Majority" Institutions*. Lanham, MD: University Press of America.

Perna, Laura. 2005. "The Relationship Between Family and Employment Outcomes." *New Directions for Higher Education* 2005(130):5–23.

Prokos, Anastasia, and Irene Padavic. 2005. "An Examination of Competing Explanations for the Pay Gap Among Scientists and Engineers." *Gender & Society* 19(4):523–543.

Rhoades, Gary, and Sheila Slaughter. 2004. "Academic Capitalism in the New Economy: Challenges and Choices." *American Academic* 1(1):37–60. https://69.18.221.209/pdfs/highered/academic/june04/Rhoades.qxp.pdf.

Robbins, Lillian, and Ethel D. Kahn. 1985. "Sex Discrimination and Sex Equity for Faculty Women in the 1980s." *Journal of Social Issues* 41(4):1–16.

Rockquemore, Kerry A., and Tracey Laszloffy. 2008. *The Black Academic's Guide to Winning Tenure—Without Losing Your Soul*. Boulder, CO: Lynne Rienner.

Roos, Patricia A., and Mary L. Gatta. 2009. "Gender (In)Equity in the Academy: Subtle Mechanisms and the Production of Inequality." *Research in Social Stratification and Mobility* 27(3):177–200.

Roscigno, Vincent. 2011. "Power, Revisited." *Social Forces* 90(2):349–374.

Rosser, Sue V. 2004. *The Science Glass Ceiling*. New York: Routledge.

Schneider, Alison. 2000. "U. of Oregon Settles Tenure Lawsuit Over Maternity Leave." *The Chronicle of Higher Education*, July 21, A12. http://chronicle.com/article/U-of-Oregon-Settles-Tenure/6843

Sonnert, G., and G. Holton. 1995. *Gender Differences in Science Careers: The Project Access Study*. New Brunswick, NJ: Rutgers University Press.

Stewart, Abigail J., Janet E. Malley, and Danielle LaVaque-Manty, eds. 2007. *Transforming Science and Engineering: Advancing Academic Women*. Ann Arbor: University of Michigan Press.

Still, Leonie V. 2006. "Gender, Leadership and Communication." In *Gender and Communication at Work*, edited by M. Barrett and M. Davidson, 183–194. Burlington, VT: Ashgate.

Toth, Emily. 1997. *Ms. Mentor's Impeccable Advice for Women in Academia*. Philadelphia: University of Pennsylvania Press.

———. 2008. *Ms. Mentor's New and Ever More Impeccable Advice for Women and Men in Academia*. Philadelphia: University of Pennsylvania Press.

Turner, Caroline S. V. 2002. "Women of Color in Academe: Living With Multiple Marginality." *The Journal of Higher Education* 73(1):74–93.

Twale, Darla J., and Barbara M. De Luca. 2008. *Faculty Incivility: The Rise of the Academic Bully Culture and What to Do About It.* San Francisco: Jossey-Bass.

U.S. Department of Education, National Center for Education Statistics, Integrated Postsecondary Education Data System (IPEDS), Winter 2011–2012. Human Resources component, Fall Staff section.

Valian, Virginia. 1998. *Why So Slow? The Advancement of Women.* Cambridge, MA: MIT Press.

Vetter, Betty M. 1981. "Women Scientists and Engineers: Trends in Participation." *Science* 214:1313–1321.

Weber, Max. 1949 [1917]. *On the Methodology of the Social Sciences.* Glencoe, IL: Free Press.

Wenzel, Stacy A., and Carol Hollenshead. 1994. *Tenured Women Faculty: Reasons for Leaving One Research University.* Paper presented at the Annual Meeting of the Association for the Study of Higher Education, Tucson, AZ.

West, Martha S., and John W. Curtis. 2006. *AAUP Faculty Gender Equity Indicators 2006.* Washington, DC: American Association of University Professors.

Williams, Joan C. 2005. "The Glass Ceiling and the Maternal Wall in Academia." *New Directions for Higher Education* 2005(130):91–105.

Williams, Wendy M., and Stephen J. Ceci. 2012. "When Scientists Choose Motherhood." *American Scientist* 100(2):138–145.

Xie, Yu, and Kimberlee A. Shauman. 2003. *Women in Science: Career Processes and Outcomes.* Cambridge, MA: Harvard University Press.

Yin, Robert K. 2009. *Case Study Research: Design and Methods* (4th ed.). Thousand Oaks, CA: Sage.

PART ONE

THE STRUCTURE

Blocked Advancement, Marginalization, and Resource Inequalities

P art One focuses on how institutional structures (and cultures) are gendered and contribute to continued inequity in academia. The chapters investigate how structures within higher education settings create an academic "pipeline" fraught with obstacles for women faculty. They explore how academic women's advancement can be blocked or delayed as a result of disproportionate service responsibilities or biases. Additionally, they consider how institutional policies and practices influence academic women's location in university structures (e.g., in lower or contingent ranks) and result in unequal wages, power, and resources compared to men faculty.

Sometimes individuals in positions of power—including those who create official organizational policies and practices (e.g., human resources staff, department chairs, deans)—generate, perpetuate, or exacerbate structural challenges that disadvantage women academics. However, as these chapters show, conscious, harmful intentions are not the drivers of gender inequities in academic workplaces, though they can play a role. The chapters highlight how the structure of academic careers marginalizes particular faculty, doing particular kinds of work and in specific ways. Interactions with those in positions of power may reinforce the structural inequities. Too often, women faculty experiencing negative outcomes in their careers are not able to see the structural mechanisms at play. The same problems can follow them to new workplaces. We hope to expose what are typically unseen mechanisms by highlighting how the structure of academic careers perpetuates some of these negative outcomes.

Women academics consistently earn lower wages than men colleagues even when researchers control for academic rank, institution type, human capital, productivity, and academic discipline (e.g., Curtis 2011). How can we explain persistent wage inequality? In chapter 1, "Glass Ceilings and Gated Communities in Higher Education," Hironimus-Wendt and Dedjoe offer a new approach to analyzing wage differentials between women and men academics. They examine how administrators establish wages and make hiring decisions at the organizational level. In their case study of a midsized, unionized, state university, they find that women academics earn 15% less than the men faculty. Hironimus-Wendt and Dedjoe refer to this differential as a wage *premium,* a bonus, paid to men but not to women.

Over time, differences in wages accumulate and have profound effects on finances (e.g., purchasing power, retirement savings, income-based employer retirement matches, income-based summer or overload pay, Social Security contributions). Additionally, faculty can and do interpret their salaries symbolically as a sign of their worth. When women academics earn less than their men counterparts, this wage inequality can be a source of frustration and can lead to feelings of being marginalized and silenced. This pattern was evident in the data we collected as part of this book project. Irene, an associate professor at a research-intensive university, discussed widespread pay inequalities, saying, "Women earn 20% less than men at all levels—assistant, associate, and full—in my school. I mentioned this for many years, but it fell on deaf ears so I stopped [talking about it]." Likewise, Karen, a 55-year-old full professor of biochemistry at a large state university, explained that although she held her own in research productivity, she still earned far less than men colleagues:

> I am one of the lowest paid full professors in my department and am easily the lowest paid research-active full professor (defined at my university as having a federal grant—in my case, I have a large NSF grant) in the department. My chair agrees with me—that I am grossly underpaid—but says that because we're in an era of budget cuts, that he cannot put in for me to have a salary adjustment. And we just hired three male full professors who each make more than 1.5 times what I make.

Administrators explain salary inequalities in terms of tight budgets or difficult economic times (see the case study to this part of the book). Or, they may suggest that there is a need to consider many facets when setting salaries and that averages should be dismissed (West and Curtis 2006). Even if this were plausible, an unexplained gap between men and women faculty continues even after considering an array of factors. Hironimus-Wendt and Dedjoe's analysis suggests that in addition to glass ceilings, women academics must navigate "gated communities" created by exclusionary hiring practices.

Our study yielded similar findings. One participant, Elizabeth, a 30-year-old Hispanic assistant professor in a humanities field at a liberal arts college noted with frustration her discovery of unequal pay: "I don't feel in the same position as my men colleagues. I've learned that I earn $12,000 less than an equally qualified friend. He will also be promoted to associate professor with different rules than me. This guarantees that I will earn $24,000 less than him for the next five years." Though we do not know the race/ethnicity of her "equally qualified friend," minority faculty such as Elizabeth have lower pay and tenure rates than their white counterparts (Aguirre 2000). And, "although women faculty perceive themselves to be the victims of salary inequities, minority faculty perceive themselves to be the victims of a biased reward system" that extends beyond pay scales (Aguirre 2000, 66).

In chapter 2, "Challenges of Race and Gender for Black Women in the Academy," Baldwin and Griffin explore the intersection of race and gender experienced by Black women academics and how their situated identities differentiate them from other women academics and from Black men faculty. They examine the costs borne by Black women academics including unfair expectations, microaggressions, and feelings of isolation. Baldwin and Griffin consider how persistent stereotypes in U.S. society (e.g., Sapphire, the "Angry Black Woman") trickle into academic cultures and influence how administrators, colleagues, and students view and evaluate Black women faculty and administrators. They examine the structural and cultural forces that negatively impact Black women academics including lack of mentorship, disproportionate service responsibilities, marginalized work, and challenges related to balancing work/personal responsibilities. These authors focus on how racism in academia persists at the institutional, as well as cultural, level and influences Black women's experiences.

In our study Arlene, a 37-year-old African American postdoctoral student in the social sciences, recalled similar experiences:

> During my two years in the unit, the research director has subjected me to racial slurs posing as "facts" about "browns" and my home country, insults about my research ability, professional ostracism by cutting me out of group discussions. Constant slights in front of my colleagues and also strangers, impossible target-setting, and further insults about my inability to meet them. Insulting comments about my partner and his job. None

of this stops the director from appropriating credit for the work I do and appending his own name to it.

This alarming example of racism occurs at the interactional level. However, the *structure* of this woman's current position places her, as a postdoc, at the mercy of her director and exacerbates the situation. Furthermore, it presumably decreases her advancement options because she will not have sole or primary credit for publications, presentations, or other work.

Another mechanism of academic injustice related to the structure of academic careers is the institutional reality of contingent faculty positions. In chapter 3, "Contingent Appointments and the Diminishing Voice, Agency, and Professionalism of Women," Sam and Kezar explore the increasing trend of using contingent workers. Like other authors in this part of the book, Sam and Kezar apply cultural, structural, and interactional lenses by examining how academia's structural reliance on non-tenure-track faculty (NTTF) influences policies and practices, and interactions with other faculty, creating unique challenges for NTTF. Because they are ineligible for tenure and often work on a semester-by-semester basis, contingent workers possess little job security. They earn significantly less, have fewer resources, and receive less respect from administrators, colleagues, and students compared to tenure-track or tenured faculty. Because women disproportionately fill NTTF positions in higher education, we must consider these as *gendered* institutional realities.

Contingent faculty are laudable for enduring difficult schedules, few resources (e.g., computers, office space), and often shamefully low pay, but individual strategies are not effective solutions to such working conditions (American Association of University Professors 2010). Because of their position in academic institutions, contingent workers typically have less access to governance structures. Thus, universities often exclude them from protections afforded to tenure-track faculty such as academic freedom or due process. For example, because of their structural positions, women NTTF are at greater risk for harassment, mobbing, and other hostilities compared to those on the tenure track. Yet, as Sam and Kezar explain, because of their feelings of isolation and deprofessionalization, contingent faculty may hesitate to speak up regarding issues that may be cloaked in stigma and silence. In our study, Elizabeth experienced demoralizing marginalization not just because of her NTTF status (prior to her ranked faculty position), but because of the intersections between her age and gender as well. She wrote:

> As an adjunct professor, older and higher in hierarchy male professors were always tempted to look down at me and patronize me. I always got the question of "how old are you?" that was always directed in a tone of dis-

trust of my capacities as a professor. My colleagues who were the same age, but were men, did not experience this. I always answer "I'm old enough to teach the course" and smiled, exiting the room.

Her strategy of navigating these frustrating interactions highlights her resilience. In addition, it draws our attention to how the congruence between the formal university structure—which positions her as less important—and informal practices and interactions can create situations where paternalism or "benevolent sexism" (Glick and Fiske 1996) results. Lack of access to governance structures hindered Elizabeth's ability to respond formally.

The overall structural issues shaping the realities of contingent faculty create consequences for tenured and tenure-track faculty as well. For instance, the dramatic expansion of contingent faculty in U.S. higher education often makes *tenure-track* faculty more vulnerable to increasing service demands because it shrinks the pool of faculty available for service. Again, this trend differentially impacts academic women. Research shows that the disproportionate service burdens on women and minority faculty are impediments to their success (Aguirre 2000; Misra, Lundquist, Holmes, and Agiomavritis 2011). Some suggest it "borders on incivility" to saddle women and people of color faculty with service burdens, particularly when done under the guise of "diversity" (Twale and De Luca 2008, 86).

In chapter 4, "Faculty Gender Inequity and the 'Just Say No to Service' Fairy Tale," Pyke explores how the overrecruitment of women for university service contributes to gender inequity in the academy. Although crucial for smooth organizational functioning, administrators and faculty regard service as the least important component of academic work. Decisions regarding tenure and promotion weigh heavily on research and/or teaching accomplishments—but usually not service. Because engaging in service deprives academics time to pursue the work that universities reward more highly, doing it has the potential to hurt one's chances for promotion or tenure. Thus, colleagues, mentors, and administrators may advise women faculty to "just say no" to service requests.

Pyke's chapter exposes the flaws in this individualistic approach to structural inequities and suggests looking at service as a systematic obstacle to academic women's equity and advancement. Burdening women faculty with disproportionate, unrecognized, and unrewarded service can lead to their attrition (Aguirre 2000). An example in our study is Jennifer, a white 38-year-old assistant professor of criminology at a research institution. She wrote:

Chances [for promotion] are further harmed by the chair's tactic of wasting everyone's time with unnecessary committees. The department went from

four committees when she came in to 44 last year. Only three of these produce anything. The outcome of this is that untenured faculty waste hundreds of hours on fruitless service that will not count at all toward tenure,
and also waste time they need to publish to get tenure.

While her chair's "tactic" is a problematic microinteraction that exacerbates
a structural issue and needs remedy, the problem remains: Until universities
regard service work as valuable labor for the functioning of academe, and reward
it in kind, academic women's advancement and promotion will be hampered.

Structural mechanisms of inequity—lower pay, lower status, increased
service burdens, and institutionalized racism—constitute barriers that contribute to women's slower or blocked career advancement. These realities
are not inevitable. Remedies for structural inequities exist but take time
to implement, especially if they are resisted by institutions or institutional
actors. Because the goal of this book is to promote gender equity and equality
in higher education, and provide women experiencing the negative aspects
of academic careers with tools for survival, we explore strategies for change
within the chapters and the case studies at the end of each part of the book.
We couple the case studies with suggested resources and "action steps" that
may help women facing similar situations—or for allies who wish to help.
The case at the end of Part One features the experience of a long-term contingent faculty member and illustrates the complexity of women's academic
careers encumbered by formal and informal barriers.

References

Aguirre, Adalberto. 2000. *Women and Minority Faculty in the Academic Workplace:
Recruitment, Retention, and Academic Culture.* San Francisco: Jossey-Bass.

American Association of University Professors (AAUP). 2010. *Tenure and Teaching-
Intensive Appointments.* Washington, DC: American Association of University
Professors.

Curtis, John W. 2011. *Persistent Inequity: Gender and Academic Employment.* Washington, DC: American Association of University Professors.

Glick, Peter, and Susan T. Fiske. 1996. "The Ambivalent Sexism Inventory: Differ-
entiating Hostile and Benevolent Sexism." *Journal of Personality and Social Psychology* 70(3):491–512.

Misra, Joya, Jennifer H. Lundquist, Elissa Holmes, and Stephanie Agiomavritis.
2011. "The Ivory Ceiling of Service Work." *Academe* 97(1):22–26.

Twale, Darla J., and Barbara M. De Luca. 2008. *Faculty Incivility: The Rise of the
Academic Bully Culture and What to Do About It.* San Francisco: Jossey-Bass.

West, Martha S., and John W. Curtis. 2006. *AAUP Faculty Gender Equity Indicators
2006.* Washington, DC: American Association of University Professors.

Academic Women's Voices on the Academy's Problematic Structures and Processes

The following narratives, at first glance, appear to be about the "bad behavior" of a few individuals. By focusing on the institutional aspects that structure these experiences, we are able to see the failure of institutions to adequately educate individuals about appropriate, nondiscriminatory behavior; monitor institutional processes to ensure equitable treatment of faculty; and provide remedies for harm done.

The male graduate students made working as a graduate student difficult and contributed to my decision to leave after [receiving my] MS. Discouragement by male students often seems overlooked in contributions to "the leaky pipeline" of women in STEM fields. I was never given a briefing on what constituted discrimination or workplace harassment and have never seen nor heard of a graduate school requiring them. [A] lot of male graduate students are completely unaware of the negative effects their remarks have on others—or worse, there may be a small contingent who thrive on "wiping out the competition" through active discouragement. For example, while a graduate student, I was sent to recruit a potential student. While showing him around campus, he suddenly tells me, "You are so lucky." I asked for clarification on what he meant. He tells me women have an easier time getting into graduate school because they are treated preferentially. Had he bothered to ask about my background before making that blanket statement, he maybe would have avoided the topic after learning of my multiple years of relevant undergraduate research, multiple scholarships, stellar GRE scores, multiple years of internships at a national lab as an undergrad, and a degree with a great GPA from a prestigious university. I did end up telling him about my background, and he backpedaled saying the same thing every other sexist or racist person on the planet says after saying something off-color: "I didn't mean you." Years later, he was recognized as "Graduate Student of the Year" and is now a professor at a university. . . .

The moral of the story is a large part of the problem in academia is that sensitivity training and harassment training need to begin earlier. Instead of learning the lesson early on as male graduate students that it is "OK" as long as no one says anything or you don't get caught, the lesson needs to be that the behavior in general is NOT acceptable as a graduate student OR ESPECIALLY later as faculty. Even though these young men may have changed at some point during their careers, I cannot help but wonder every now and then how they are treating their female students. Are they encouraging their female graduate students? Are they making it a point to recruit only male graduate students from some perceived unfairness due to "reverse discrimination"? Are they turning a blind eye to the poor behavior of male graduate students? Would they want to know if their female graduate students are being treated unfairly by the other male graduate students? Would they do anything about that behavior? It is for these reasons I see things not changing very rapidly for women in STEM fields.

—Joan, a 35-year-old (returning) graduate student
in a STEM field

The first challenging experience that comes to mind for me was when I was working as an adjunct at a for-profit school. I wasn't making much money, but taking my job seriously nonetheless. I once caught a student cheating—as in purchased their paper from a website. I had solid evidence and wasn't sure what the school policy was on this. I went first to the registrar, who had up to that point overseen many of the policy issues. She referred me to the dean, who basically said, "Well, that's too bad. It's up to you to deal with it however you see fit." As an adjunct, and as a woman, I felt sort of belittled by this response. First, he seemed to not be taking seriously something that I felt was very serious. Second, he seemed to be offering me no institutional or personal support in confronting the student and leveraging consequences. . . . . I felt that the institution could have risen to support me more as an instructor in this issue. There were many factors at play, not the least of which was the nature of for-profit education. Yet, it was not entirely clear to me that the dean was even sure who I was, as this was our first (and only) face-to-face meeting during my whole employment with this institution.

—Nicole, a 23-year-old white adjunct instructor of sociology

I am writing on contingent/adjunct worker issues, specifically related to resources, legitimacy, and respect. I hold a full professor faculty position at one university, and simultaneously hold an adjunct research position at another university, where I have conducted research with a federal agency's grants in various capacities, mostly as a principal investigator. When I took a leave to conduct [community-based] work, one university—rather than treating this as a leave of absence or sabbatical to enable me to continue to my duty as principal investigator—cited certain bureaucratic rules that resulted in a "downgrading" of my role to a coprincipal investigator. I do not know whether this is related to being female or not, and I do not have statistics on the difference in gender. Perhaps most disappointing is that colleagues, all male, with whom I've worked with over the years, did not stand up at all, and perhaps were even eager to take over! The outcome is that I decided to work on something else that [allows me to not have to deal with this]. Sometimes rather than trying to solve the problem, it is easier just to avoid it and to spend time on things that are productive and with people who are collaborative, and ignore the institutions.

—Melanie, a 43-year-old Asian adjunct and researcher in the sciences

I

GLASS CEILINGS AND GATED COMMUNITIES IN HIGHER EDUCATION

Robert J. Hironimus-Wendt and Doreen A. Dedjoe

Among many things, higher education is a labor market. People work in higher education settings. And although it is tempting to think of universities as representing middle-class, middle-income, highly educated employment settings, there is a great deal of variance in the competencies and compensations of workers on any campus. In brief, working for a college or university is in some ways like working for any other business—inequalities exist, and discrimination is practiced. Our study examines gender inequalities routinely found in the core, primary sector jobs in higher education: the faculty. It is here that most observers assume hiring and promotion decisions (i.e., discriminatory practices) are legitimate. After all, professors are supposedly hired first and foremost according to seemingly gender-neutral academic credentials: possession of a terminal degree, teaching experience, and publication history. Here we find explicit job descriptions and search practices. Most administrators vehemently deny the possibility that their faculty employment practices could be gender discriminatory.

Yet, any casual observer can see that gender and racial/ethnic discrimination still happens in faculty hiring. We see it in the faces of the professoriate

A previous version of this chapter, with authors in reverse order, was presented at the annual meeting of the Midwest Sociological Society, St. Louis, MO, March 25, 2011.

itself. Minorities are rare. If we look up, most of the faces we see are those of men. The proportion of women changes from college to college, department to department. A cursory glance shows women are strangely absent in some places on campus while abundant in others. Something is amiss in the queuing processes that match the queue of potential workers to the queue of available jobs in higher education (cf. Granovetter 1981).

Increasing Access, Yet Persistent Wage Gaps

Recent reports show that women earn 52.3% of all doctorate and professional degrees (Snyder and Dillow 2011; Thornton 2009). Over the past decade women's representation among all full-time faculty, across all types of institutions, has grown from 33% to 43% (Knapp, Kelly-Reid, and Ginder 2010; Toutkoushian 1999). Still, there remains a 10% gap between the number of women earning doctorate and professional degrees and the number of women among the professoriate. Moreover, women are not equally distributed across institution types. Women are overrepresented among two-year college faculty (54.2%), and underrepresented (41.6%) among full-time faculty on four-year campuses (Knapp et al. 2010). Nonetheless, women have made progress and are present in large numbers on many college campuses.

Despite the growing progress in representation on campuses, women are slower to earn tenure, and slower to be promoted to full professor (Krefting 2003; Tuckman and Tuckman 1976). As seen in Table 1.1, whereas 18.1% of men faculty are non-tenure-track, 31.1% of women faculty are non-tenure-track (Thornton 2010). Similarly, substantially less than half of all women faculty in higher education are tenured, whereas greater than 60% of men are tenured. If we only look at tenured and tenure-track faculty, the tenure ratio for men is 3 to 1, but for women it is 2 to 1.

TABLE 1.1.
Percentage of Men and Women in Tracks

	All Faculty			
	Non-tenure-track	*Tenure-track*	*Tenured*	*Total*
Men	18.1	20.5	61.4	100.0
Women	31.1	25.9	43.0	100.0
	Tenure-Track and Tenured Faculty Only			
Men	—	25.0	75.0	100.0
Women	—	37.6	62.4	100.0

Note. Data are from Thornton, Saranna. 2010. "No Refuge: The Annual Report on the Economic Status of the Profession 2009–10." *Academe* 96(2):4–32.

Full-time faculty at most colleges and universities are assumed to carry out equally the central missions of academic institutions (e.g., teaching, research, and service). Nevertheless, wage distributions among faculty often are unequal. Numerous studies have shown that women are paid less than men in higher education, after controlling for human capital attributes, productivity measures, academic ranks, type of institution, and discipline-level differences (Becker and Toutkoushian 2003; Binder et al. 2010; Travis, Gross, and Johnson 2009). Thornton (2010) shows that women are paid just under 81% of what men are paid, implying a 19% "wage penalty" for women faculty. The only exception is at the instructor level, where earnings are comparable. Additionally, Thornton shows that the wage gap persists when controlling for different types of institutions (e.g., public versus private, and across Carnegie classifications). Barbezat and Hughes (2005) and Toutkoushian and Conley (2005) report a base-level wage gap of about 20%. Umbach (2007) finds a 22% wage gap, although his analyses are limited to faculty working in Research I and II institutions.

The evidence is overwhelming that in higher education today women are underrepresented in the professoriate and consistently are paid less than men. These conclusions are hardly surprising; they mirror broader labor market patterns and the patterns of gendered institutions. Despite seemingly gender-neutral hiring processes, after statistically controlling for all conceivable predictors of worker productivity as well as tenure and rank, a gendered wage gap persists in higher education. This gap is particularly relevant given the fact that we are at the 50th anniversary of major civil rights legislation, including the 1964 Equal Pay Act, and the 42nd anniversary of the 1972 Educational Amendments (Title IX) to the 1964 Civil Rights Act. At least two generations have since enrolled in and been employed by higher education establishments. The faculty hired from the 1960s to the 1980s are either long gone or now retiring in large numbers. Thus, it is tenuous at best to suggest that women have not had sufficient time to enter "men's fields," professions, and leadership positions. Indeed, women today earn 52.3% of all doctor's degrees conferred by degree-granting institutions (Snyder and Dillow 2011) and represent a substantial majority of all college students.

Many econometric studies analyze the gendered wage gap among faculty using traditional human capital factors. Using the 1993 and 1999 *National Study of Postsecondary Faculty* (NSOPF) data, Toutkoushian and Conley (2005) found that some progress has been made in reducing wage gaps between men and women at the national level. Their study was limited to full, associate, or assistant professors employed full-time in four-year colleges. The authors utilized traditional measures of human capital as well as publication histories, receipt of grants, employment in public versus private universities, and regional variations in wages as control variables. They then analyzed effects associated with employment across Carnegie classifications. Toutkoushian and Conley (2005) demonstrated statistically significant wage gaps at research institutions and at comprehensive universities, but not among faculty at doctoral-level or liberal arts institutions. When they analyzed potential differences associated with employment across academic divisions (i.e., professional fields, arts and humanities, social sciences, physical sciences, and "all other fields"), they found that after controlling for all previous factors there were significant gender differences existed among faculty in the social sciences, physical sciences, and "all other fields." The authors concluded that although progress was made during the 1990s, the unexplained residual wage penalty of about 4% to 6% was statistically and substantively significant, especially when "these differences are compounded over a woman's career" (2005, 23).

Using the same 1999 National Center for Education Statistics NSOPF data (but alternative model specifications), Barbezat and Hughes (2005) similarly concluded that of an initial 20% wage gap, about 4% to 5% may be attributable to unexplained wage discrimination mechanisms. Umbach (2007) used these same data but introduced structural labor market variables into his analyses, using supplemental data from the National Science Foundation's *Survey of Earned Doctorates*. Umbach focused solely on faculty at Research I and II institutions. He employed HLM regression models to analyze the cumulative effects associated with including additional structural variables in the wage determination models. Although his initial model pointed to a 22% preliminary wage gap among faculty at Research I and II institutions, the inclusion of measures of human capital, individual measures of productivity, and rank reduced that gap to about 8%. After including the additional measures of labor market effects (percentage of women within each discipline, percentage of recent graduates unemployed, and percentage of faculty within each discipline with funded research), the wage gap between men and women dropped to about 7%, and remained statistically significant (Umbach 2007).

It is reasonable to conclude that women are treated differently from men in the national academic labor market. Whether we analyze overall wage gaps or residual wage gaps, earnings inequalities exist and are statistically significant. In a concluding comment, Toutkoushian and Conley (2005) note that despite rigorous attempts to explain wage-setting mechanisms, current models explain "less than half of the variation in salaries across individual faculty after controlling for a myriad of personal and institutional characteristics. While institution-specific studies generally account for more variation, they also leave as unexplained a significant portion of the salary differences across individuals" (23).

The Faculty of a Typical State University

Our project seeks to explain why women faculty in state universities are paid significantly less than men faculty. Our case study is uniquely suited for this study in several contexts. First, the university is a midsized, regional comprehensive state university, classified as a "Master's/L" (i.e., "master's large") university by the Carnegie Foundation's basic classification criteria. This institution was established as a state normal school and then became a state teachers college. About 50 years ago, the university expanded its mission to establish itself as a regional state university. It has 12,500 students and offers 66 undergraduate and 37 graduate degree programs, including one established doctoral program with two more in progress. Second, the university has a large faculty (650 full-time faculty). Third, prior research on this institution found significant, ongoing wage gaps between women and men: 18% in 1995 and 10% in 2005 (Maguire, Faulkner, and Radosh 1995; Radosh, Mathers, and Miller 1994–1995; Polly Radosh, personal communication, September 28, 2009). In light of the findings in 1995, institutional policies were enacted to address discipline-specific wage disadvantages for women faculty. These prior studies provide an institutional benchmark documenting the prior existence of a gendered wage gap at this institution and allow us to assess whether these intentional efforts to eliminate wage gaps across the institution were effective.

Because the university we examine is a public institution, all wages and salaries are available through annual budget documents. Our earnings data are from the 2008–2009 fiscal year budget. We supplemented these data with information from relevant university catalogs (e.g., year of hire, academic rank, possession of a terminal degree). The Office of Institutional Research generously provided additional information. Beyond tenured and tenure-track faculty, our sample includes a small group of "associate" faculty who are more or less permanent members of the faculty and are formally represented in the collective bargaining agreement. Most associate faculty are stable employees although they lack terminal degrees and thus are not eligible for tenure. Unlike adjunct faculty, associate faculty are eligible to apply for promotion to the (terminal) rank of assistant professor if they have records of publication and service.

We include teaching faculty with part-time administrative assignments. These few faculty typically are paid an additional month's salary (e.g., 10-month contracts) and sometimes are granted a course release. They serve as directors of graduate programs, research centers, teaching and learning centers, and so forth. We elected to include department chairs because most chairs represent internal promotions from the ranks of tenured full professors. Chairs are still obligated to teach. In this context, we view the chair position as representing a significant rung along a career ladder for internal candidates. The wages for department chairs reflect their academic rank and involve a straightforward conversion from a 9-month to a 12-month salary (i.e., the current salary is increased by 33%).

These faculty are represented by a local chapter of the American Federation of Teachers (AFT). The presence of unions tends to compress wages within given classes of workers. In theory, this practice should further diminish the potential for unjustifiable wage gaps within classes of workers. Because of the union contract, tenure status is tied to rank and appropriated salaries. A few associate professors are not tenured, and few assistant professors are. The final sample we use is thus restricted to all full-time tenured and tenure-track faculty, department chairs, and full-time associate faculty.

The dependent variable for the study is the earnings of individual faculty. The primary independent variables are gender, academic rank, and disciplinary divisions/college of employment. The university has four colleges: the College of Business and Technology (COBT), the College of Education and Human Services (CEHS), the College of Fine Arts and Communication (COFAC), and the College of Arts and Sciences (CAS). Because the CAS is substantial and represents a diverse set of disciplines, our analyses sort these faculty into three divisions associated with the arts and sciences (i.e., the humanities, the natural sciences and mathematics, and the social sciences). We include measures of the gender composition (percentage of women) of the academic units (departments/divisions/colleges), given that the gender composition of positions has been demonstrated to influence the average earnings of men and women academics (Umbach 2007). In addition, we analyze the potential effects that the gender composition of the academic ranks might have upon earnings.

Unequal Opportunities and Rewards

What makes an organizational case study like ours particularly useful is that in the context of a highly bureaucratized, unionized, public university where contracts are negotiated openly, potential salary discrepancies among otherwise comparable workers calls into question explicit departmental, divisional, and college-level policies regarding wage-setting mechanisms and hiring and promotion practices. Rather than attempting to model anew wage-setting mechanisms to determine a better fit for explaining the gendered wage gap, our project frames the wage gap issue in terms of a queuing theory of how workers are allocated to jobs. It is premised on the thesis that although national trends and patterns are informative, hiring decisions and wage-setting mechanisms ultimately play out at the establishment level (Granovetter 1974; Reskin and Roos 1990; Tomaskovic-Devey 1991). As Acker notes (2006), "Work organizations are critical locations for the investigation of the continuous creation of complex inequalities because much societal inequality originates in such organizations" (441).

Attempts to explain residual wage gaps after rational and legitimate human capital factors of variance have been controlled for must focus on the social processes by which workers are hired and promoted within organizations. They also must focus on the organizational processes by which wages are assigned to jobs. After all, wages are attached to the positions at the point of hire, not to the incumbents who fill those positions (Baron and Bielby 1980; Stolzenberg 1975, 1978), even if in some cases new hires may be able to negotiate slightly higher starting wages. At the same time, if entry-level jobs within a given organization are differentially allocated by gender, subsequent employment practices (e.g., pay raises, promotion ladders, supervisory opportunities) may be influenced by gender and thereby compound gender inequalities within establishments (Acker 1990; Reskin and Roos 1990; Tomaskovic-Devey 1993).

Table 1.2 presents information regarding the distribution of the faculty across the four colleges that comprise the university. Of the 650 full-time faculty, 526 are tenured or in tenure-track appointments (subsequently referred to as tenure track). Overall, women comprise 42% of the professoriate. Within-group analyses are revealing. Whereas relatively few of the men are instructors (12.8%), over a fourth of all women (27.7%) are employed in instructor positions. These numbers are somewhat comparable to those found at the national level, where about 31% of women in the professoriate are in non-tenure-track positions (Thornton 2010). When we combine full and associate professors, we find that men are more likely than women to be tenured (62.8% versus 44.2%), and these rates are nearly identical to the gender distribution of men and women among tenured faculty at the national level, as shown in Table 1.1.

If we look at the distribution of women and men across the ranks, it becomes apparent that the patterns differ substantively. Whereas one-third of men are full professors, only one-fifth of women are full professors. Among tenured faculty, women are outnumbered about 2 to 1. At each rung of the academic ladder, the percentage of women index shows that they are slightly less likely to be found as we progress up the rank ladder, particularly if we look across the tenure threshold (e.g., from assistant to associate professor). However, when only considering men, the percentage of men index shows that men are more likely to be found as we move up that same ladder. Women comprise 37.6% of the tenured/tenure-track faculty, but 61.3% of the non-tenure-track (instructor) rank. Excluding instructors, about 39% of men are full professors (30% of women), and 28% of men are assistant professors (39% of women). These patterns of decreasing proportions of women and increasing proportions of men as one moves up the promotion ladder are consistent with Cotter et al.'s (2001) thesis on how glass ceilings operate.

TABLE 1.2.
Distribution of Faculty Across Ranks and Divisions by Gender

		No.	% of Total	No. Men	% of Men	No. Women	% of Women	Women as % of Row
All faculty		650		376		274		42.2
Tenure track		526	80.9	328	87.2	198	72.3	37.6
Non-tenure-track		124	19.1	48	12.8	76	27.7	61.3
Rank	Full	187	28.8	128	34.0	59	21.5	31.6
	Associate	170	26.2	108	28.7	62	22.6	36.5
	Assistant	169	26.0	92	24.5	77	28.1	45.6
	Instructor	124	19.1	48	12.8	76	27.7	61.3
Division (all)	Humanities	99	15.2	39	10.4	60	21.9	60.6
	Natural sciences/math	86	13.2	61	16.2	25	9.1	29.1
	Social sciences	72	11.1	39	10.4	33	12.0	45.8
	COBT	115	17.7	83	22.1	32	11.7	27.8
	CEHS	169	26.0	91	24.2	78	28.5	46.2
	COFAC	109	16.8	63	16.8	46	16.8	42.2
		650		**376**		**274**		**42.2**
Division (tenure track)	Humanities	71	13.5	33	10.1	38	19.2	53.5
	Natural sciences/math	73	13.9	54	16.5	19	9.6	26.0
	Social sciences	67	12.7	38	11.6	29	14.6	43.3
	COBT	91	17.3	72	22.0	19	9.6	20.9
	CEHS	137	26.0	73	22.3	64	32.3	46.7
	COFAC	87	16.5	58	17.7	29	14.6	33.3
		526		**328**		**198**		**37.6**

Note. Column percentages do not sum to 100% as a result of rounding.

As one looks up the rank ladder, one sees progressively more men *and* progressively fewer women. Because of this uneven distribution effect, in some of the following analyses we analyze the full faculty; in others we exclude faculty at the instructor rank to concentrate on tenure-track faculty. When we evaluate gender effects for the entire faculty, the total number of faculty used in the analyses is 650 professors. When we exclude instructors from the analyses, the total number of faculty used is 526 professors.

The bottom half of Table 1.2 shows the distribution of women and men across the academic colleges and three arts and sciences divisions. While women constitute about 42% of the overall faculty, they are not distributed equally across these academic units. Women are underrepresented in the natural sciences and math division, and the COBT, but women are overrepresented in the humanities division. When we remove from consideration the non-tenure-track faculty, women constitute about 38% of the faculty. In this situation, the underrepresentation of women in the COBT becomes more pronounced, and the overrepresentation of women in the humanities becomes less pronounced (although still substantial). Overall, the bottom half of Table 1.2 shows that women are differentially hired into different areas of the university, and that considerations of where non-tenure-track faculty are employed is relevant to discussions of gender queuing.

Table 1.3 presents wage information for each of the academic ranks. Because the analyses use small, nonrandom samples of a single faculty, and because the manifest inequalities within these small groups are not technically generalizable toward a larger population, we present our results using two alpha levels: 0.05 and 0.10. These baseline data indicate that the overall wage gap between men and women is about $10,000, or about 15%. This gap falls between the previous findings of 18% (1995) and 10% (2005) for this university. Although this gap is somewhat smaller than gaps found at the national level, it is substantial and statistically significant. When we look within academic ranks, however, the gap diminishes substantially. Of the four ranks, only the wage gap between women and men in the associate rank approaches significance, depending on the alpha level used. Alternatively, within-rank analyses indicate that within any given rank women and men are compensated at roughly the same rate (although women still earn slightly less than men). This paradox occurs because for each rank a base pay rate is established by contractual agreement. Additionally, all faculty receive the same annual, percentage-based cost-of-living adjustment according to the agreement. Thus, when we look only within ranks, we are unlikely to detect significant wage gaps other than those associated with time in rank. At the same time, because relatively fewer women are promoted at each step along the promotion ladder, women are less likely to be found where higher wages

TABLE 1.3.
Wages Within and Across Faculty Ranks (All Faculty)

	Men's Wage	Women's Wage	Wage Difference[a]	Women's Wages as % of Men's Wages	Wage Gap (%)	Women as % of Row Category
All faculty	$66,856.85	$56,874.27	$9,982.58*	85.1	14.9	42.2
Full professor	$90,559.63	$87,852.24	$2,707.39	97.0	3.0	31.6
Associate professor	$64,860.99	$62,289.31	$2,571.68**	96.0	4.0	36.5
Assistant professor	$51,865.47	$51,384.35	$481.12	99.1	0.9	45.6
Instructor	$36,873.62	$33,970.20	$2,903.42	92.1	7.9	61.3

Note. Wage = total annual salary.
[a] *t*-tests for equality of means (equal variances not assumed): * $\alpha \leq 0.05$; ** $\alpha \leq 0.10$.

prevail. This finding is consistent with Cotter et al.'s (2001) thesis that glass ceilings represent the accumulation of serial disadvantages along the steps of a promotion ladder.

For these reasons and others, the data in Table 1.3 demonstrate that controlling for academic rank (a proxy for human capital) seemingly captures a significant proportion of wage gap differences between women and men faculty. However, it is noteworthy that women earn substantially less than men overall. This finding in conjunction with the findings reported in Table 1.2 suggests that the overall 15% wage gap is largely attributable to the unequal queuing of men and women across social locations. Whether we choose to attribute this fact (in the absence of actual proof) to human capital or worker productivity differences, the results stand. Other things being equal, women appear less likely to be promoted to the rank of full professor and are in this way overrepresented where wages are low and underrepresented where wages are high (cf. Cotter et al. 2001).

Table 1.4 examines the wage gap from a different perspective. If women are hired into different areas of the organization at different rates, then studying wage differences within these divisions makes sense. The upper part of Table 1.4 uses wage data from all faculty and the lower part excludes faculty in the instructor rank. In both parts, the wage gap between women and men is significant, although when we exclude instructors, the magnitude of that gap shrinks from 14.9% to 7.8%. In the upper part, the wage gap in the humanities division of the CAS is not only significant but also substantial (22%). Here, the wage gap exceeds $14,000. The wage gap between men and women in the COBT also is substantial ($10,222), although this gap only approaches statistical significance depending on the alpha level used. Similarly, the wage gaps in the natural sciences and in the CEHS approach significance, although not at the 0.05 alpha level. The data in the bottom part of the table indicate that excluding non-tenure-track faculty from the analysis partially explains the wage gap inequalities. Although the overall wage gap is significant among tenure-track faculty, the gap is statistically significant only among faculty in the CEHS. Still, the pattern of men earning higher incomes is present in each of the academic units with two exceptions. First, among faculty in the social sciences division the wage gap is negligible (1%). Second, when we exclude adjuncts and instructors in the COFAC, women appear to earn slightly higher wages than men. This suggests that women who are employed as full-time instructors in the COFAC are paid substantially less than full-time men instructors in that same college.

Tables 1.5 and 1.6 present simple regression models to determine whether the concentration of women in different academic divisions significantly explains any portion of the 15% overall wage gap between women and men. To the degree that women are scarce in some areas of the faculty and concentrated in others, it is reasonable to test whether the uneven distribution of women across different academic units is associated with the wage gap that exists across the faculty. To do so, we tested the effects of including a measure of the percentage of women within each academic division. Table 1.5 assesses the effects of including a measure of the percentage of women on the entire faculty, and Table 1.6 performs the same analysis excluding faculty at the instructor rank.

These tables demonstrate that for this institution the wage gap is significantly related to academic rank (as established previously in Table 1.3), and that the percentage of women within divisions is also a significant predictor of the gender wage gap. Including only the academic rank variable in Tables 1.5 and 1.6 (Models 3) reduces the gender variable to an insignificant predictor of wages. In Table 1.5, which includes all faculty, the gender variable approaches a traditional level of significance, although it falls short of the 0.05 alpha level. Introducing the percent of women in the division variable alone (Models 2) also demonstrates a significant effect in and of itself, although here the gender variable remains significant in the model that includes all faculty. A brief analysis of the R^2 values for each model confirms that a large proportion of wage variance at the individual level is captured by the inclusion of the academic rank measure (a proxy for human capital variance).

TABLE 1.4.
Wages Within and Across Academic Divisions

	Men's Wage	Women's Wage	Wage Difference [a]	Women's Wages as % of Men's Wages	Wage Gap (%)	Women as % of Row Category
All Faculty						
All faculty	$66,856.85	$56,874.27	$9,982.58 *	85.1	14.9	42.2
Humanities	$64,193.23	$50,100.00	$14,093.23 *	78.0	22.0	60.6
Natural sciences/ math	$65,123.36	$56,698.12	$8,425.24 **	87.1	12.9	29.1
Social sciences	$63,717.21	$59,575.73	$4,141.48	93.5	6.5	45.8
COBT	$77,101.67	$66,879.19	$10,222.48 **	86.7	13.3	27.8
CEHS	$63,714.24	$57,274.94	$6,439.30 **	89.9	10.1	46.2
COFAC	$63,169.98	$56,228.65	$6,941.33	89.0	11.0	42.2
Excludes Instructors						
Tenure-track faculty	$71,244.64	$65,665.73	$5,578.91*	92.2	7.8	37.6
Humanities	$67,084.00	$60,706.29	$6,377.71	90.5	9.5	53.5
Natural sciences/ math	$68,222.72	$62,548.47	$5,674.25	91.7	8.3	26.0
Social sciences	$64,386.45	$63,652.45	$734.00	98.9	1.1	43.3
COBT	$83,602.18	$80,702.95	$2,899.23	96.5	3.5	20.9
CEHS	$71,062.01	$64,209.84	$6,852.17*	90.4	9.6	46.7
COFAC	$65,808.17	$69,580.93	−$3,772.76	105.7	−5.7	33.3

Note. Wage = total annual salary.
[a] *t*-tests for equality of means (equal variances not assumed): * $\alpha \leq 0.05$; ** $\alpha \leq 0.10$.

TABLE 1.5.
Regression Models of Faculty Wage (All Faculty)

Model	1	2	3	4
Variable	β	β	β	β
Gender	−$9,982.58*	−$8,264.28*	−$1,838.21**	−$365.74
% women in division	—	−$359.60*	—	−$315.60*
Rank	—	—	$17,671.99*	$17,594.74*
Constant	$76,839.44*	$89,557.44*	$10,6859.04*	$117,889.82*
R^2	.045	.071	.695	.715
N	650	650	650	650

* $\alpha \leq 0.05$; ** $\alpha \leq 0.10$.

TABLE 1.6.
Regression Models of Faculty Wage (Instructors Excluded)

Model	1	2	3	4
Variable	β	β	β	β
Gender	−$5,578.91*	−$3,507.37**	−$1,762.82	−$225.10
% women in division	—	−$374.40*	—	−$360.99*
Rank	—	—	$19,017.23*	$18,970.25*
Constant	$76,823.55*	$88,061.78*	$108,954.65*	$119,710.99*
R^2	.018	.061	.619	.658
N	526	526	526	526

Note. In Models 2 and 4, % women in division uses the percentage of women in the division when instructors are excluded. Alternative specifications using the overall % women in division yielded the same results. * $\alpha \leq 0.05$; ** $\alpha \leq 0.10$.

Nonetheless, when rank and percent of women in the division are included simultaneously (Models 4), the evidence shows that these two factors independently account for a significant proportion of the wages faculty earn, and that the coefficient for the gender variable approaches zero (and is not significant).

These tables show that for this university the percentage of women across academic divisions matters. Although not presented here, we also found that the percentage of women within each department is significantly and inversely related to wages after controlling for academic rank. Thus, as the percentage of women across academic units of analysis (department and division) increases, professors in units with higher proportions of women among their faculty are paid lower wages, regardless of their own gender (cf. Umbach 2007). At least for this one institution, where we find fewer women we find significantly higher wages and vice versa, consistent with a queuing thesis. Whereas rank and tenure status are generally seen as measures of worker productivity, the percentage of women effect shows that organizational factors beyond human capital attributes influence wages as well. Including or excluding instructors in the gender composition of the division does not substantively change these results.

Glass Ceilings and Gated Communities

Our data indicate that the gender composition of an academic unit is a significant predictor of wages. The glass ceiling thesis suggests that wage gaps are explained partially by exclusionary, gendered, organizational practices that limit women's opportunities for promotion to positions with higher wages and greater authority. Cotter et al. (2001) argue that to demonstrate the presence of a glass ceiling, we must show that at each successive step along the promotion ladder within an organization women are increasingly absent, and in growing proportions. In academia, women are still overrepresented in the lower ranks and underrepresented among tenured faculty. This maldistribution of women across the ranks explains a substantial portion of the wage gap (Barbezat and Hughes 2005; Binder et al. 2010; Dedjoe 2010; Toutkoushian and Conley 2005; Umbach 2007). The studies just listed and our own demonstrate that if a glass ceiling exists in higher education it is found at the boundary between tenure-track and tenured positions. The tenure threshold is associated with profound differences in gender representation and explains a substantial proportion of the gendered wage gap between faculty.

Studies of gender discrimination in higher education therefore must renew their focus on the processes, practices, and criteria by which faculty become tenured and look at those criteria that systemically limit or deny women's tenure. At the same time, Barbezat and Hughes (2005), Toutkoushian and Conley (2005), and Umbach (2007) independently conclude that a significant 4%–6% gender wage gap remains after accounting for rank, human capital differences, and structural factors of variance associated with wage-setting mechanisms. Using national data, Travis, Gross, and Johnson (2009) estimate this wage penalty to be about $3,200 annually.

These studies and our own suggest that the glass ceiling argument is incomplete. We find that beyond the glass ceiling effect (which primarily is concerned with *vertical* access to opportunities within organizations) women are disproportionately absent from specific "places" across establishments (see also Binder et al. 2010; Dedjoe 2010; Umbach 2007). Although total exclusion is rare, tokenism is not. This finding demonstrates the presence of *gated communities* in institutions of higher education, where women are more or less welcomed across the academic units of a university. Employment practices regulate who is initially hired into positions with higher wages, and these practices are gendered. For example, women earned 39% of business-related PhD degrees in 2009 (Snyder and Dillow 2011). However, women comprise only 21% of the tenurable faculty in the COBT in our study. Likewise, women earned 44% of all natural science and math doctoral degrees in 2008–2009 but comprised only 26% of the faculty in the natural sciences and math division of the university under investigation. These data cast doubts on the idea that women are not available to be hired.

Reskin and Roos (1990) demonstrated long ago that as entry-level wages decline the *proportion* of women in application queues increases (as some men look to other high-paying jobs), and thus women are more likely to be hired. The converse of this finding implies that where we find higher wages we might expect to find more men being hired. Although we cannot offer direct evidence of an explicit preference for men, our case study shows that men are disproportionately found in academic divisions and departments where wages are higher, and at rates that are inconsistent with the increasing presence of women possessing PhD degrees in those fields.

In the final analysis, the employment practices used to hire new professors have resulted in fewer women being employed in departments and divisions that pay higher wages. These employment processes resemble *horizontal* exclusionary processes, in the presence of vertical exclusionary practices. The percentage of women (measured at the division and department levels) significantly predicts wage differences across horizontal locations. This implies that the gatekeeping processes used to hire men and women into the professoriate vary across locations throughout the university and are significantly associated with the wage gaps between women and men overall. As with gated residential communities, some minorities are always allowed to enter these academic domains—after all, restrictive covenants are illegal in academia, just as they are in housing markets. However, gated communities are typically less diverse relative to the broader, surrounding community. So too are some areas of the professoriate relative to the number of PhDs granted each year.

Noting that market-sensitive salaries are paid in some but not all disciplines, Maguire et al. (1995) ask, "Why should faculty in some disciplines be paid market-competitive salaries while faculty in other disciplines receive non-competitive salaries?" They conclude that "the lack of a consistent pay strategy for faculty of all disciplines . . . produce[s] general salary inequities" (45). Noting similar lower wages in disciplines dominated by women, Umbach (2007) states, "The question then becomes, why is the work done by these disciplines valued less?" (188). This question is underscored by the fact that except for those at Research I and II universities faculty generally teach, publish research, and serve. Like these studies, ours demonstrates that different wage structures across departments independently contribute to the gendered wage gap, and that this finding is unrelated to hierarchical arrangements and promotion opportunities—it is strictly about hiring decisions.

Anecdotally, we hear routinely that "some departments" must offer market-sensitive wage premiums if they are to attract competent candidates. This is at best only a theoretical proposition. It is rarely tested. Nonetheless, faculty who receive these higher wages defend the argument vigorously. Ironically, it tends to receive strong support by administrators who are co-opted into paying higher wages. This happens because, in the final analysis, this theory of external labor market pressures is framed around the need to legitimate active discrimination among otherwise equally employed faculty. All faculty are hired to teach, publish, and serve. Yet, despite this more or less equality in terms of expectations of worker productivity, some are intentionally and openly paid more, whereas others are quietly paid less.

It should not be a surprise that the beneficiaries of market-sensitive wage-setting mechanisms are disproportionately men. Given this reality, attempts to produce gender equity in wages across campuses will require either (a) the elimination of irrational market-sensitive wage-setting mechanisms that unjustly advantage some faculty over others despite expectations of equal worker productivity, or (b) intentional efforts to increase the proportion of women being hired in overcompensated, privileged faculty locations.

References

Acker, Joan. 1990. "Hierarchies, Jobs, Bodies: A Theory of Gendered Organizations." *Gender and Society* 4(2):139–158.

———. 2006. "Inequality Regimes Gender, Class, and Race in Organizations." *Gender and Society* 20(4):441–464.

Barbezat, Debra A., and James W. Hughes. 2005. "Salary Structure Effects and the Gender Pay Gap in Academia." *Research in Higher Education* 46(6):621–640.

Baron, James N., and William T. Bielby. 1980. "Bringing the Firm Back In: Stratification, Segmentation, and the Organization of Work." *American Sociological Review* 45:737–765.

Becker, William E., and Robert K. Toutkoushian. 2003. "Measuring Gender Bias in the Salaries of Tenured Faculty Members." *New Directions for Institutional Research* 117:5–20.

Binder, Melissa, Kate Krause, Janie Chermak, Jennifer Thacher, and Julia Gilroy. 2010. "Same Work, Different Pay? Evidence From a US Public University." *Feminist Economics* 16(4):105–135.

Cotter, David A., Joan M. Hermsen, Seth Ovadia, and Reeve Vanneman. 2001. "The Glass Ceiling Effect." *Social Forces* 80(2):655–682.

Dedjoe, Doreen. 2010. "An Organizational Analysis of Earnings Inequality by Gender in a Public University." MA thesis, Western Illinois University.

Granovetter, Mark. 1981. "Toward a Sociological Theory of Income Differences." In *Sociological Perspectives on Labor Markets*, edited by Ivar Berg, 11–47. New York: Academic Press.

Knapp, Laura G., Janice E. Kelly-Reid, and Scott A. Ginder. 2010. *Employees in Postsecondary Institutions, Fall 2009, and Salaries of Full-Time Instructional Staff, 2009–10*. Washington, DC: U.S. Department of Education, National Center for Education Statistics. http://nces.ed.gov/pubs2011/2011150.pdf.

Krefting, Linda A. 2003. "Intertwining Discourses of Merit and Gender: Evidence From Academic Employment in the USA." *Gender, Work and Organization* 10(2):260–278.

Maguire, Brendan, William Faulkner, and Polly Radosh. 1995. "Pay Inequity at a Midwestern University: A Case Study of Faculty Protest." *Sociological Imagination* 32(1):44–56.

Radosh, Polly, Rich Mathers, and Dave Miller. 1994–1995. "Salary Equity Revisited." Unpublished manuscript presented at Western Illinois University: Macomb, IL.

Reskin, Barbara, and Patricia Roos. 1990. *Job Queues, Gender Queues: Explaining Women's Inroads Into Male Occupations*. Philadelphia: Temple University Press.

Snyder, Thomas D., and Sally A. Dillow. 2011. *Digest of Education Statistics: 2010*. Washington, DC: U.S. Department of Education, National Center for Education Statistics. http://nces.ed.gov/programs/digest/d10/.

Stolzenberg, Ross M. 1975. "Occupations, Labor Markets and the Process of Wage Attainment." *American Sociological Review* 40(5):645–665.

———. 1978. "Bringing the Boss Back In: Employer Size, Employee Schooling, and Socioeconomic Achievement." *American Sociological Review* 43:813–828.

Thornton, Saranna. 2009. "On the Brink: The Annual Report of the Economic Status of the Profession, 2008–09." *Academe* 95(2):14–28.

———. 2010. "No Refuge: The Annual Report on the Economic Status of the Profession 2009–10." *Academe* 96(2):4–32.

Tomaskovic-Devey, Donald. 1991. "A Structural Model of Poverty Creation and Change: Political Economy, Local Opportunity, and U.S. Poverty, 1959–1979." *Research in Social Stratification and Mobility* 10:289–322.

———. 1993. *Gender and Racial Inequality at Work: The Sources and Consequences of Job Segregation*. Ithaca, NY: ILR Press.

Toutkoushian, Robert K. 1999. "The Status of Academic Women in the 1990s: No Longer Outsiders, but Not Yet Equals." *Quarterly Review of Economics and Finance* 39:679–698.

Toutkoushian, Robert K., and Valerie Conley. 2005. "Progress for Women in Academe, Yet Inequities Persist: Evidence From NSOPF:99." *Research in Higher Education* 46:1–28.

Travis, Cheryl, Louis Gross, and Bruce Johnson. 2009. "Tracking the Gender Pay Gap: A Case Study." *Psychology of Women Quarterly* 33(4):410–418.

Tuckman, Barbara H., and Howard P. Tuckman. 1976. "The Structure of Salaries at American Universities." *The Journal of Higher Education* 47(1):51–64.

Umbach, Paul D. 2007. "Gender Equity in the Academic Labor Market: An Analysis of Academic Disciplines." *Research in Higher Education* 48(2):169–192.

2

CHALLENGES OF RACE AND GENDER FOR BLACK WOMEN IN THE ACADEMY

Candice P. Baldwin and Monica D. Griffin

Structurally constrained by a combination of lower positioning, limited authority, and high levels of responsibility, Black women academics also experience marginalization as a result of perceptions of their character, abilities, and leadership. The ability of research to highlight these experiences is weakened by a general emphasis on the experiences of women overall or the experiences of Blacks without looking at the unique intersections of race and gender. Thus, the complex, informal social arrangements and subtle cultural realities for Black women academics are obscured.

Examining the intersections of race and gender in higher education can simultaneously illustrate privilege or subordination. Socially and politically charged assumptions about affirmative action hiring policies and practices position Black women as a "double minority" who may not benefit from the policies as intended. How Black women experience affirmative action, as either an advantage in their careers or an ever-present burden to navigate, is not clear or easy to document. Black women find themselves culturally at the bottom of the racial and gender hierarchy and confront distinct issues that elude Black men based on their gender status and white women based on their racial status. Making transparent the intersection of racism, sexism, and a variety of other factors that impact Black women in particular is dependent largely on Black women reporting their experiences, possibly risking their privacy, career success, and reputations. The dearth of literature on Black women academics' experiences warrants research that examines the multiple factors impacting their retention and recruitment, laying the foundation for critical considerations of their unique experiences.

Black academic women contend with differential educational attainment and employment at the start of their careers. In 2003–2004, white women earned 60% of the 23,005 doctorate degrees awarded to women, whereas Black women received only 8% of these degrees (Knapp et al. 2005). Historically, white men hold most of the faculty positions (Thompson 2008), and the growth in Black women administrators has remained virtually unchanged over the past decade (National Center for Education Statistics 2008). Although the increasing numbers of women in higher education seem promising, Black women seem to disappear at every point along the academic pipeline.

Black women graduate students and early-career faculty experience limited interaction with individuals with similar social experiences who could foster trust, mentoring relationships, or support their success (King and Chepyator-Thomson 1996; Mabokela and Green 2001), making it less likely that the practical dimensions of success are clear. The differences between the social networking and mentoring experiences of Black doctoral students and those of their white counterparts as well as the experiences of women versus those of their men counterparts can serve as a deterrence to completion. Black students report experiencing racial difficulties in their programs (e.g., unfair treatment, underestimation of their abilities, exclusions, insults, denial of opportunities) (Cooke, Sims, and Peyrefitte 1995; King and Chepyator-Thomson 1996; Mabokela and Green 2001). Women report that issues with family responsibilities, committees, internal conflicts, slow feedback, and lack of mentoring often force them to delay completion. Additionally, Black women report dealing with socially inhospitable climates; lack of financial support; and the absence of diverse mentors (in terms of race and gender), faculty, and peers (Mabokela and Green 2001; Seagram, Gould, and Pyke 1998). These experiences reflect gendered organizational practices.

Ideally, early-career socialization prepares individuals to navigate the structure of higher education and make transparent a variety of expectations for merit-based promotions. Early-career socialization for Black women also should prepare them for the social structural barriers they will have to face as Black women faculty and administrators in academia. Consider the following account from one of this chapter's authors (a first-generation college and doctoral student) regarding her early academic socialization:

> The notion of a "tenure clock" was as abstract to me as the ticking clock in *Alice in Wonderland*. Folks in graduate school talked about it in terms of

fear and loathing, while my early colleagues referred to it in terms I could only translate from my brief two years in the professional world before graduate study as something more akin to a periodical performance review by a supervisor. And even then, it was brought up as a question and not addressed as action: "Has anyone talked to you about your tenure clock or walking through the process yet?" Only when someone discovered (too late in the tenure clock) that I had taken three years to complete a dissertation (as a full-time, tenure-eligible faculty) did someone respond at the midterm evaluation. I resigned undergoing the tenure process, faced with unrealistic scholarship expectations in combination with newly emerging family responsibilities. The tenure process was neither the sort of thing that would come up in my family or friends' circles, nor was it elaborated on or structured into my orientation and early career mentoring in the academy.

"Faculty boot camps," designed to facilitate better organizational socialization and preparation of new faculty for the tenure process, for example, are a positive step toward bridging the gap between Black women and their counterparts in navigating social networks or interpersonal relationships to develop successful tenure and career profiles. These could prepare Black women for the unique issues they will face such as stereotyping, role strain, and disproportionate service expectations.

Stereotypes, unfair expectations, and campus environments affect Black academic women differently than white women and Black men, as comparable minorities with distinctive experiences. Throughout history, images, stories, and historical records presented in the dominant culture often distort accurate representations of Black women (Atwater 2009; Harley 2002). In the scholarly literature and in public and media discussion, stereotypical images often merge to symbolize the Black woman. The wounds of covert and overt racism, sexism, and xenophobia run deep for many Black women as negative images of Jezebel, Mammy, and Sapphire persist (Atwater 2009; Collins 1999; Stanley 2006; St. Jean and Feagin 1998). Sapphire is the domineering matriarch, contemporarily coined as the "Angry Black Woman," who is strong, unfeminine, and uncontrollable; Jezebel, the sexual player, links Black women's intelligence with their sexuality; and, finally, Mammy, the maternal figure, symbolizes Black women as the nurturers, caretakers, and backbone of the community or the "maids of academe" (Henderson, Hunter, and Hildreth 2010). As maids of academe, Black women faculty are often in the position of caretaking and "cleaning up" when it comes to minority student achievement, managing diversity (e.g., institutional representation, sustaining an image of inclusion), and solving problems when diversity issues emerge at institutions.

Cultural factors impact Black women academics' experiences, within colleagues' imaginations, and in the normative practices of mentoring, professional development, and collegiality as Black women academics face the challenge of managing role strain. Additionally, Black women faculty and administrators experience hostile climates, lack of community, lack of mentorship in scholarship and role models of success, and bias in performance evaluations (Thompson 2008; Turner 2002). Furthermore, they "find it difficult to speak to other colleagues regarding experiences of racism, sexism, privilege, and inequity because white or [men's] privilege becomes the lens through which these experiences are re-interpreted and dismissed" (Henderson et al. 2010, 32).

As in society, negative depictions of Black women cut across many areas of academia, which, alone or in combination, negatively impact the views of peers, superiors, and students. As suggested by Henderson et al. 2010, "No [contemporary] representation of Black women as intellectuals, persons of character, and productive colleagues" articulates Black women's experiences on college campuses (30); thus, the stereotypes persist and can be translated into the roles that Black women fill on college campuses (Atwater 2009; St. Jean and Feagin 1998; Thomas and Hollenshead 2001). One of this chapter's authors' career experiences illustrates the challenge of navigating a professional role with embedded cultural strains:

> As a young Black higher education administrator, I am constantly reminded of stereotypes and often battle these perceptions on a day-to-day basis. On a given day, in the office, I am the "Mom" that can be counted on to provide a hug, encouragement, and a smile. Once I leave the office, perceptions of being too serious, aggressive, intimidating plague my conversations and interactions. I must politely address and acknowledge how I am being perceived, and adjust accordingly. The pressure to combat perceptions and live up to sometimes contradictory expectations as a Black woman in academia is often debilitating.

Controlling images of Black women characterize their experiences as outsiders within higher education organizations, as victims of discrimination or stereotyping, and as professionals positioned within organizational hierarchies. Collins (1999) makes the case that "outsider-within identities are situational identities that are attached to specific histories of injustice—they are not a decontextualized identity category divorced from historical social inequalities that can be assumed by anyone at will" (86). Comparisons of marginalized individuals' experiences to those in dominant groups (e.g., white women compared to women of color or to Black women specifically) can potentially reduce analyses to universalization or trivialization of specific intersections of race, class, and gender that perpetuate inequality (Collins 1999).

Black women in higher education hold positions that require unique levels of responsibility (or workload) as compared to their white women and men colleagues (e.g., public relations, diversity governance, advising/ mentoring to minority students) (Stanley 2006; Thompson 2008; Turner 2002). Further, Black women administrators are concentrated in student affairs positions and other support roles where they have direct responsibility for promoting diversity initiatives (Aguirre 2000). But, Black women student affairs administrators tend to be concentrated in lower and mid-level positions and are underrepresented as *senior* student affairs administrators in most colleges and universities (Aguirre 2000; Patitu and Hinton 2003).

Service and advising are risky activities for tenure or promotion because faculty are evaluated primarily on scholarship and publication success. Yet, Black women academics are likely to be more engaged in teaching, advising, and committee-related activities than their men and (white) women counterparts (Gregory 2001). Black women find themselves disproportionately responsible for advising and mentoring students of color and for handling multiple committee assignments. Many Black women faculty must balance a sense of responsibility to students of color and to community knowing that these activities could hurt them in the tenure or promotion process (Aguirre 2000; Gregory 2001; Stanley 2006; Thompson 2008; Turner 2002).

Black women academics are differentially challenged to manage their time and responsibilities (Stanley 2006; Thompson 2008). While white women faculty experience disproportional pressures to respond to student care needs (compared to men faculty), the sociocultural role expectations for Black women to perform these duties go beyond gendered differences. For Black academic women, the expectation is largely cultural, and the practice of "racial uplift" (see Mawhinney 2011) (however beneficial to the institution) is rarely connected to merit, reward, or promotion. Instead, these practices and a broader understanding of this kind of work as "natural," not professional or skilled, work against Black women's successes. Black women administrators and faculty may practice nurturing or "mothering" responsibilities as academic mentors to students of color, whether hired to do so or not. Mawhinney (2011) describes her practice of mentoring students at historically Black colleges and universities from a Black feminist framework of "othermothering" (Collins 2000), the practice of women caring for children who are not biologically theirs. Mawhinney (2011, 11) explains that for her "othermothering came with a price," including: (a) challenges with time management because of a steady demand for attention to students (personal, academic, or financial issues), (b) health issues (e.g., depressive guilt and loss of energy related to tensions between activities rewarded for merit and those that mattered for students), and (c) the uncertainty of sustaining racial uplift programs without institutional supports. Mawhinney's role expectation to "othermother" students conceptually compares to the Mammy. Collins (1991) describes "othermothering" as an activist practice of taking on an ethic of care and personal accountability in communities with historical precedence of preserving family infrastructure for white families (e.g., as "Mammy"), and for Black children (despite mainstream assault against the Black community's advancement). In short, othermothering involves renouncing one's self in favor of group advancement.

Furthermore, Mawhinney (2011) demonstrates how othermothering is devalued by controlling cultural frames (and negative, attitudinal stereotypes) that marginalize and devalue Black academic women's personal and professional contributions. Henderson et al. (2010) argue:

> The race/gendering of . . . roles as the supportive agent whose primary reason for existing is to help others (Bova 2000) results in Black women professors being a valuable, yet overburdened professional resource for diversity initiatives and other professional service tasks (Chesney-Lind, Okamato, and Irwin 2006; Few, Piercy, and Stremmel 2007). (par. 8)

Academic and student affairs roles that engage diversity initiatives tend to place differential demands on Black women but limit their authority to implement policy or programming, the use of their time, or their ability to acquire suitable compensation for differential workload. One of this chapter's authors describes her experience:

> Despite possessing a terminal degree in policy and planning, my first higher education position at a small liberal arts college more frequently tapped me to troubleshoot and address day-to-day issues for students of color than to implement campuswide initiatives. I remember from my first all-college meeting the strategic goal was to increase diversity on campus. The bullet under the goal said "Accomplished: Hired Director of Multicultural Affairs." It was made clear very early what my main "responsibility" would be on campus. This responsibility of being the "face of diversity" on campus and "saving the diverse students" limited my effectiveness as a valued contributor and reduced my role to representative troubleshooter. Although I am proud of the retention and graduation numbers of students of color during my tenure, I am disappointed that I was not fully allowed to use my training and expertise to advance diversity and inclusion efforts on campus.

In the ideological contexts of affirmative action or diversity initiatives in academia, some may perceive Black women as underqualified, hired based on their status as Black women. This often translates into resentment, lower levels of perceived deservingness, and/or higher levels of perceived workplace inequality (Aguirre 2000; Griffin 2009). For Black women academics with roles in diversity initiatives, occupational data do not reveal the cultural tensions of navigating racial and gendered systems of marginalization.

Black academic women tend to face a variety of barriers to retention that are distinctive from those of their counterparts and are imbedded within sociocultural contexts of privilege. Henderson et al. (2010) state, "White privilege is the invisible hand of support and prestige through which White colleagues are supported, advocated for, and are given access to valuable information and opportunities, and the application of best practices with respect to mentoring, tenure, and promotion" (32). Often, Black women find a difference between the Black faculty and administrator culture and the traditionally white, men-dominated culture of academia. Professional advancement for Black women academics is further complicated by issues of collegiality, lack of understanding of cultural differences, and subtle discrimination (Aguirre 2000; Henderson et al. 2010; Stanley 2006; Thompson 2008). These challenges are coupled with other impediments to tenure and promotion including marginalization of work, feelings of isolation, and the difficulties of balancing life in dual cultures. Many Black women academics find it difficult to interpret the unwritten expectations about collegiality, often resulting in exclusion and/or alienation (Thompson 2008; Stanley 2006). One of the chapter's authors explains:

> In my role, I was responsible for the recruitment and retention of students of color; providing annual diversity training to faculty, staff, and students; and addressing issues of bias and intolerance of campus. My ability to fulfill all of these roles often came at the price of fostering positive relationships with colleagues. In many cases, once I addressed a complaint, my relationship with the individual and/or department became very contentious.

Gendered racism is one way to describe the experiences of Black women academics. They are subject to gender differences in racial discrimination experiences and racial differences in gendered experiences. Thus, Black women are subjected to unique, aggression-based and exclusion-based discriminatory behaviors by men and women counterparts in academe (Perna et al. 2007; Umbach 2006; Weems 2003). For example, despite sharing the gender inequality confronting white women, white women can create more obstacles in the advancement of Black women academics than their men counterparts. These actions vary from marginalization at social gatherings, withholding professional guidance, and limiting opportunities for professional growth (St. Jean and Feagin 1998). Often, white women's inadvertent exclusion of Black women from participating in activities that could enhance careers, including informal and formal networking, stalls the professional advancement of Black women. While organizational networks may increase chances of success for women faculty generally, Black women's exclusion from and nonparticipation in networks often precipitates their need to join or participate in race-based professional networks. However, race-based networks often focus on social events and outreach instead of socialization into the organizational cultures of higher education (Crawford and Smith 2005). Consequently, patterns of social exclusion in academic settings often lead Black women to struggle in silence, change institutions, or leave higher education (Aguirre 2000; Crawford and Smith 2005; Perna et al. 2007; Thompson 2008; Umbach 2006; Weems 2003).

Recommended Strategies

Collins (1999) suggests that "organizations should aim to eliminate outsider-within locations, not by excluding the individual Black women who raise hard questions, but by including them in new ways" (88). The academy can address Black women's differential experiences by supporting their professional development and helping them navigate the structural and cultural contexts of academia.

Monitoring Existing Institutional Norms and Values

Colleges and universities should recruit and hire Black women administrators and faculty and renew yearly commitments to evaluate and improve diversity policies and hiring practices. Increasing the critical mass of Black women will help address their isolation, discomfort, and marginalization. Creating "safe spaces" (Collins 1991; Mawhinney 2011) is as much a critical need for Black women to connect *as Black women* as it is for students of color who seek their support. Universities should find ways to formally support these relationships (e.g., faculty of color lunch to discuss issues openly with one another). Sharing knowledge would enable them to think critically about the barriers in their professional lives, educate other Black women on how to avoid the same pitfalls (Fries-Britt and Kelly 2005; Myers 2002; Stanley 2006), and change their institutions.

Creating Mentoring and Networking Opportunities

Studies suggest that building a strong foundation of support is key to the success of Black women academics (Aguirre 2000; Crawford and Smith 2005;

Jenkins 2005; Stanley 2006; Turner 2002). They possess appropriate credentials and education to achieve goals but lack workplace support for career growth. Research (Crawford and Smith 2005; Mabokela and Green 2001; Stanley 2006) shows that leadership training, diverse job skills, and mentoring are invaluable to Black women (just as they are to other professionals). Thus, institutions should create opportunities for Black women administrators and faculty to develop skills to become more competitive for tenure and leadership roles.

Mentoring is not only a way to help faculty generally but also a way to prevent the social isolation of Black women faculty and administrators in particular (Aguirre 2000; Stanley 2006; Turner 2002). Mentoring positively impacts job satisfaction; lowers attrition; and facilitates obtaining career advice, public praise of accomplishments, a confidant, and career progression (Crawford and Smith 2005; Jenkins 2005, Stanley and Lincoln 2005). Further, it improves the campus climate to one that is more inclusive and affirming. Campuses must provide opportunities for faculty to connect as a first step (Fries-Britt and Kelly 2005). Individuals should not be paired with mentors based on their racial and gender status, but on their willingness to promote inclusion and diversity within the academic community. Mentors should be trained in guiding Black women academics through the publication, tenure, and promotion process (Aguirre 2000; Stanley 2006), with attention to how race, class, and gender intersect to create unique experiences for Black women. For example, universities should offer successful tenure and promotion portfolios for all pre-tenure faculty to review and establish review boards that informally review portfolios well in advance of formal deadlines. This will diminish the structural and cultural marginalization that occur when information is shared through networks of privilege.

Additionally, universities should consider the impact of bias in student evaluations, promote workshops to assist faculty in making appropriate adjustments or responses to issues in and out of the classroom, and incorporate these factors in tenure and promotion decisions (Thompson 2008; Turner 2002), especially if bias relates to curricular structure or factors outside of the professor's control. For example, Thompson's (2008) research suggests that students often question the competence and credentials of Black women faculty, which can be exacerbated by assigning them to courses outside of their expertise (e.g., diversity-based courses; see chapter 8).

Establishing a Culture of Diversified Collegiality

Colleges and universities should support increased collegiality among all faculty and connect Black women faculty and administrators to the larger campus community (Aguirre 2000). Strategies include helping all faculty to appreciate and embrace diverse cultures; being receptive of Black women faculty and administrators; and encouraging faculty to participate in programs that will further the likelihood of Black women's retention, promotion, and tenure (Stanley 2006). Furthermore, institutions must broaden professional expectations, expand criteria for quality work, and reward diverse working styles (Thompson 2008; Yoshinaga-Itano 2006).

Similar to white women, Black women experience competition between their family demands and the workplace pressures of academic culture (Sadao 2003). Many Black women find comfort in safe spaces, such as their families, churches, and communities, and with allies who understand their experiences in academia (Stanley 2006). Opportunities to validate and fuse these cultures will help create welcoming and affirming campus environments for Black women administrators and faculty. For example, institutions might reconceptualize faculty luncheons or receptions to be openly inclusive of family, community, and other culturally supportive individuals as part of new faculty orientations (Sadao 2003; Stanley 2006; Thompson 2008). Such efforts would be supportive not only of Black women academics but also, potentially, of all faculty and staff.

Black women succeed at all levels of higher education despite these challenges. They advance to become college presidents, affiliate professionals, and scholarly leaders in a variety of academic fields. They do so often in silent vigilance against the challenges outlined in this chapter and within contexts of educational and organizational socialization and mentoring, which are often a matter of serendipitous association.

References

Aguirre, Alberto. 2000. *Women and Minority Faculty in the Academic Workplace: Recruitment, Retention, and Academic Culture.* San Francisco: Jossey-Bass.

Atwater, Deborah. 2009. *African American Women's Rhetoric: The Search for Dignity, Personhood, and Honor.* Lanham, MD: Lexington Books.

Bova, Brenda. 2000. "Mentoring Revisited: The Black Woman's Experience." *Mentoring and Tutoring* 8:5–16.

Chesney-Lind, Meda, Sakagami Okamoto, and Katherine Irwin. 2006. "Thoughts on Feminist Mentoring: Experiences of Faculty Members From Two Generations in the Academy. *Critical Criminology* 14:1–21.

Collins, Patricia Hill. 1991. *Black Feminist Thought: Knowledge, Consciousness, and the Politics of Empowerment.* New York: Routledge.

———. 1999. Reflections on the outsider within. *Journal of Career Development* 26(1):85–89.

———. 2000. "Black Women and Motherhood." *Black Feminist Thought.* New York: Routledge.

Cooke, Donna, Randy L. Sims, and Joseph Peyrefitte. 1995. "The Relationship Between Graduate Student Attitudes and Attrition." *The Journal of Psychology* 129(6):677–688.

Crawford, Kijana, and Danielle Smith. 2005. "The We and the Us: Mentoring African American Women." *The Journal of Black Studies* 36(1):52–67.

Few, April, Fred Piercy, and Andrew Stremmel. 2007. "Balancing the Passion for Activism With the Demands of Tenure: One Professional's Story From Three Perspectives." *NWSA Journal* 19(3):47–66.

Fries-Britt, Sharon, and Bridget Turner Kelly. 2005. "Retaining Each Other: Narratives of Two African American Women in the Academy." *The Urban Review* 37(2):221–242.

Gregory, Sheila. 2001. "Black Faculty Women in the Academy: History, Status, and Future." *Journal of Negro Education* 70(3):124–138.

Griffin, Tiffany Manique. 2009. "The Intersection of Race, Class, and Gender in Higher Education: Implications for Discrimination and Policy." PhD dissertation, University of Michigan.

Harley, Sharon. 2002. *Sister Circle: Black Women and Work.* New Brunswick, NJ: Rutgers University Press.

Henderson, Tammy, Andrea Hunter, and Gladys Hildreth. 2010. "Outsiders Within the Academy: Strategies for Resistance and Mentoring African American Women." *Michigan Family Review* 14(1):28–41.

Jenkins, Maureen. 2005. "Why You Need a Mentor." *Black Enterprise,* March, 80–86.

King, Susan Elizabeth, and J. R. Chepyator-Thomson. 1996. "Factors Affecting the Enrollment and Persistence of African-American Doctoral Students." *Physical Educator* 53:170–179.

Knapp, Laura G., Janiece E. Kelly-Reid, Roy W. Whitmore, Shiying Wu, Lorrie Gallego, June Cong, Marcus Berzofsky, Seungho Huh, Burton Levine, and Susan G. Broyles. 2005. "Postsecondary Institutions in the United States: Fall 2003 and Degrees and Other Awards Conferred: 2002–2003." *Educational Statistics Quarterly* 7:234–247.

Mabokela, Reitumetse, and Anna L. Green. 2001. *Sisters of the Academy: Emergent Black Scholars in Higher Education.* Sterling, VA: Stylus.

Mawhinney, Lynette. 2011. "Othermothering: A Personal Narrative Exploring Relationships Between Black Female Faculty and Students." *Negro Educational Review* 62(1):213–232.

Myers, Lena. 2002. *A Broken Silence: Voices of African American Women in the Academy.* Wesptort, CT; Greenwood Publishing Group.

National Center for Education Statistics (NCES). 2008. *Table 290. Doctoral degrees conferred by degree-granting institutions, by race/ethnicity and sex of student: Selected years, 1976–77 through 2006–07.* http://nces.ed.gov/programs/digest/d08/tables/dt08_290.asp

Patitu, Carol, and Kandace G. Hinton. 2003. "The Experiences of African American Women Faculty and Administrators in Higher Education: Has Anything Changed?" In *New Directions for Student Services, Vol. 104, Meeting the Needs of*

African American Women, edited by M. F. Howard Hamilton, 79–93. San Francisco: Jossey-Bass.

Perna, Liana, Danette Gerald, Evan Baum, and Jeffrey Miliem. 2007. "The Status of Equity for Black Faculty and Administrators in Public Higher Education in the South." *Research in Higher Education* 48(2):193–226.

Sadao, Kathleen. 2003. "Living in Two Worlds: Success and the Bicultural Faculty of Color." *The Review of Higher Education* 26(4):397–418.

Seagram, Belinda, Judy Gould, and Sandra W. Pyke. 1998. "An Investigation of Gender and Other Variables on Time to Completion of Doctoral Degrees." *Research in Higher Education* 39(3):319–335.

Stanley, Christine. 2006. "Coloring the Academic Landscape: Faculty of Color Breaking the Silence in Predominantly White Colleges and Universities." *American Educational Research Journal* 43(4):701–736.

Stanley, Christine, and Yvonna Lincoln. 2005. "Cross-Race Faculty Mentoring." *Change: The Magazine of Higher Learning* 37(2):44–50.

St. Jean, Yanick, and Joe R. Feagin. 1998. *Double Burden: Black Women and Everyday Racism.* New York: M.E. Sharpe.

Thomas, Gloria, and Carol Hollenshead. 2001. "Resisting From the Margins: The Coping Strategies of Black Women and Other Women of Color Faculty Members at a Research University." *The Journal of Negro Education* 70:166–175.

Thompson, Chasity. 2008. "Recruitment, Retention, and Mentoring Faculty of Color: The Chronicle Continues." *New Directions for Higher Education* 14: 47–54.

Turner, Caroline Sotello. 2002. "Women of Color in Academe: Living With Multiple Marginality." *The Journal of Higher Education* 73(1):74–93.

Umbach, Paul. 2006. "The Contribution of Faculty of Color to Undergraduate Education." *Research in Higher Education* 47(3):317–343.

Weems, Robert. 2003. "The Incorporation of Black Faculty at Predominantly White Institutions." *Journal of Black Studies* 34(1):101–111.

Yoshinaga-Itano, Christine. 2006. "Institutional Barriers and Myths in Recruitment and Retention of Faculty of Color: An Administrator's Perspective." In *Faculty of Color: Teaching in Predominantly White Colleges and Universities,* edited by Christine A. Stanley, 351–357. Bolton, MA: Anker.

3

CONTINGENT APPOINTMENTS AND THE DIMINISHING VOICE, AGENCY, AND PROFESSIONALISM OF WOMEN

Cecile H. Sam and Adrianna Kezar

Seventy percent of U.S. faculty are off the tenure track (Knapp, Kelly-Reid, and Ginder 2011); yet, academia has largely overlooked the effects of contingent work on women's careers. For years many non-tenure-track faculty (NTTF)—part-time and full-time faculty who are not eligible for tenure—have worked in higher education under suboptimal conditions: significantly less pay, less respect, less job security, and fewer resources (Baldwin and Chronister 2001; Gappa and Leslie 1993; Gappa, Austin, and Trice 2007; Monks 2007).[1] These inequalities create a dynamic in higher education where three distinct classes of faculty exist: tenured and tenure-track faculty, who have relative prestige; full-time NTTF, who have more limited voice; and part-time faculty, who have neither prestige nor a strong voice. Tenure-line faculty tend to be considered professionals whereas non-tenure-line faculty are considered laborers, though they increasingly have similarities in education, academic socialization, and types of work.

Despite a seemingly equitable gender split (i.e., approximately half of NTTF are women), when the total number of women in the academy is taken into account, women are overrepresented in NTTF positions and underrepresented in tenure-track positions (American Association of University Professors [AAUP] 2005). In addition, they are more likely to experience the worst of the NTTF marginalized conditions, such as isolation, lack of resources, or hostility (Hart 2011; Gappa et al. 2007). Certainly, there are some well-respected NTTF, often from business, industry, or other professions, making a change to academia—but they are usually men (Levin, Kater, and Wagoner 2006). Although women have entered academic careers in increasing numbers, they are less likely to be tenure-track professors (AAUP 2005; Schuster and Finkelstein 2006; West and Curtis 2006), and women who start as part-timers are less likely to get full-time (tenure or non-tenure-track) positions than men (Schuster and Finkelstein 2006). These are gendered institutional realities that reflect the logic of gendered organizations (Acker 1990).

We draw from two studies to highlight the issues that contingent faculty face. The first study focused on a case study of a community college with a rare reputation among its faculty for its positive working conditions[2] (Kezar and Sam 2013). From this campus, Sam (2011) conducted one-on-one interviews with 46 faculty and 9 administrators who were once faculty. The resulting sample of women included 8 current adjunct faculty, 6 full-time faculty (who were once adjuncts), and 4 administrators who were once adjuncts. Interviews focused on general information about their role and experiences at the college, their ideas about academic community, and the policies and practices that they felt contributed to a sense of community.

The second study is a multiple case study, including three different public four-year, teaching-focused institutions. Kezar (2013) examined NTTF-supportive departments compared to unsupportive departments. She conducted one-on-one interviews with 107 NTTF, 65% of whom were women from 25 departments, about their views on the following: their role, discipline, and background; their institution, department, and existing policies; departmental values, norms, and beliefs; the impact of policies on their performance and student learning; their teaching and advising related to departmental policies; and their interaction with others in the department in terms of communication, colleagueship, and information. Interviews ranged between 60 and 90 minutes.

Like most case studies, Kezar (2013) and Sam (2012) supplemented the interviews with document analysis (e.g., handbooks, departmental web pages, and faculty senate minutes) and observations. Using grounded theory techniques, they conducted several phases of data analysis, given the layers (i.e., institutional, departmental, disciplinary, contract type) of data. To ensure trustworthiness, studies relied on member checks with campus informants (approximately three to four people per campus) who were well-respected and longtime members of the community. These individuals reviewed data noting if findings resonated with their own understanding of the culture, policies, and practices.[3]

Women and Non-Tenure-Track Faculty Positions

Assuming equal abilities, why do women head into contingent employment rather than tenure-track positions? Finley (2009) offers three possible reasons, arguing that it is because of converging trends in higher education that women often cannot obtain tenure-track positions. According to Finley, the first trend is institutional, where institutions that hire the greatest number of contingent faculty have a higher ratio of women to men. In general, these institutions include community colleges and second-tier liberal arts colleges that rely heavily on contingent appointments. Second, Finley also finds that "fields that employ the highest proportion of contingent faculty or have had the largest increase in contingent hiring over time tend to be comprised of more women" (par. 8). The humanities are much more likely to use contingent faculty than the sciences. It is an intriguing trend that the institutions and fields where women have gained access have moved toward contingent employment whereas institutions where men are employed predominantly have maintained a stronger model of tenure-track faculty employment. Finally, Finley (2009) offers "choice" as the third trend that may account for women's overrepresentation among NTTF. Some women choose non-tenure-track appointments because these may facilitate flexibility to meet other life goals (e.g., family responsibilities) (Finley 2009; Ivey, Weng, and Vahajdji 2005).[4] These factors influence the trend, but the interaction between and degree to which each factor contributes is unknown.

We do not consider non-tenure-track as less valuable or unattractive compared to tenure-track positions. On the contrary, non-tenure-track appointments are a desirable option for many people. Non-tenure-track positions can provide more flexibility and work-life balance (Gappa et al. 2007). Further, NTTF positions allow professionals and freelancers to maintain connections with academia and bring their expertise into the classroom (Baldwin and Chronister 2001; Gappa and Leslie 1993). For faculty who are interested in teaching or research at specific institutions, the non-tenure-track may be a more desirable option than the tenure track (Baldwin and Chronister 2001; Gappa et al. 2007; Harper, Baldwin, Gansneder, and Chronister 2001). Many non-tenure-track positions lack service requirements, which some may prefer. Finally, NTTF positions may allow dual academic-career couples to stay in the same location because the possibility of two academics being hired on tenure lines is exceedingly rare (Wolf-Wendel, Twombly, and Rice 2003).[5] Despite possible benefits of the non-tenure-track and how it may appeal to certain individuals, numerous challenges face NTTF. These challenges create a system in which NTTF positions become "second class" to the tenure line (Cross and Goldenberg 2009; Gappa and Leslie 1993; Gappa et al. 2007; Hart 2011; Levin et al. 2006; Schell and Stock 2001).

Inequality in the Academic System

Many problems and inequalities that exist for contingent faculty stem from a lack of respect that NTTF experience within academia. Respect is the core of good working environments; however, it appears that NTTF are not well respected (Gappa et al. 2007). Because of the composition of NTTF positions, this perceived lack of respect particularly affects women.

Researchers such as Gappa and Leslie (1993) and Roueche, Roueche, and Milliron (1995) have described NTTF, especially adjuncts, as the "invisible faculty," and with good reason. Until recently, institutions paid little attention to the growing contingent faculty population. Schuster and Finkelstein (2006, 6) noted that the American professoriate has been gradually changing from tenure-track to non-tenure-track faculty. They describe this unnoticed change as a "silent faculty revolution." In the last few years, few changes in policies or practices have been instituted to meet the needs of contingents (Cross and Goldenberg 2009; Kezar and Sam 2010b). However, recent changes include orientations, and some university systems, such as the University of Maryland, have instated long-term contracts for contingent faculty.

The Silence and Isolation of Contingent Faculty

One of the marks of academic life is the opportunity for and expectation of faculty to have a voice regarding work environment, instructional content, and campus policies and practices (Gappa et al. 2007; Thompson, Constantineau, and Fallis 2005). Having a voice implies that faculty can be critical of their institution and institutional leaders, as needed. However, many contingent faculty are silenced because they lack access to governance at departmental and institutional levels and they do not have the same protections (e.g., job security, grievance options, representation) as tenure-track faculty. These conditions may make contingent faculty more hesitant to speak their concerns aloud (Baldwin and Chronister 2001; Gappa and Leslie 1993). As a once-adjunct and current dean at a community college explained (Sam 2011), "I'm sure some [adjuncts] don't want to say anything because they think their jobs would be at risk, and for some, they'd be right" (12).

Lack of Faculty Governance
In many institutions contingent faculty lack representation on campus (e.g., senate, unions, and committees) and may be unwelcome at, or not invited to participate in, departmental meetings (Kezar and Sam 2010a). Though some institutions have begun to incorporate full-time NTTF within departmental activities, the same cannot be said of part-time faculty (Hollenshead et al. 2007; Kezar and Sam 2010a). Full-time NTTF may participate at the departmental level, but they experience barriers to broader campus governance

(Kezar and Sam 2010a). Often such representation is a formality. Vanessa, a full-time NTTF member, described her exclusion from governance:

> The lecturers are not encouraged to come to faculty meetings. I used to go even though they didn't want me to. But I've stopped going in recent years because they made it so uncomfortable. And I have major issues about the curriculum that I think need to be discussed, but once you have been shut down so many times when you bring up ideas, you stop.

Without access to faculty governance, contingent faculty, most of whom are women, are unable to participate in the shared governance procedures that can improve their working conditions. The lack of representation is problematic for two reasons. First, the experiences of contingent faculty vary depending on employment status, department, type of institution, or type of faculty (e.g., aspiring academics versus recent retirees) (Baldwin and Chronister 2001; Gappa and Leslie 1993; Shaker 2008). Because their work experiences can be so different from those of tenure-line faculty, to make policies for this diverse group of faculty without any of their input can lead to policies and practices that may deter contingent faculty from their work and possibly harm student learning. Second, for many institutions, especially community colleges, contingent faculty comprise 50%–80% of the faculty (American Federation of Teachers [AFT] 2010; Knapp et al. 2011; National Education Association [NEA] Higher Education Research Center 2007). Consequently, a small group of tenure-line faculty makes decisions on policies and practices affecting a majority of the faculty without their input, thereby exacerbating the gendered patterns of inequality within these institutions.

Lack of Academic Freedom
The idea of academic freedom is synonymous with autonomy (Gappa et al. 2007). It includes, in part, the ability to voice critique of the institution, perform service that maintains the integrity of the institution, or have access to open discourse in an academic realm (Rhoades and Maitland 2008; Tierney 2004) such as the freedom of faculty to determine course content. Numerous NTTF, part-time included, have said they often did not have a voice in the institution or did not want to speak for fear it would jeopardize their employment (Baldwin and Chronister 2001; Gappa and Leslie 1993; Gappa et al. 2007; Kezar and Sam 2010a). Though many institutions' employment contracts explicitly state that they value and protect the academic freedom of contingent faculty, we need to distinguish between de jure and de facto protection. De jure protection can be found in the contract language supporting academic freedom. However, it may not translate into de facto protection because many NTTF feel their continued employment is precarious. Thus,

they cannot exercise their rights should their academic freedom be violated. Contingent contracts often do not have as many protections or rehire rights, so contingent faculty are wary of voicing dissenting opinions. Valerie, from a four-year institution, talked about this silence: "We have some significant problems in our department, and I am in the middle of conflict and know a lot about it. I could be helpful in talking to the dean, but I am hired semester to semester; I am not going to get involved. I just keep my head down and hope others will work it out."

Lack of voice regarding one's career has implications for women's advancement (e.g., the glass ceiling) and their wages. For example, if NTTF cannot offer input on policies, administration and tenure-track faculty may inadvertently keep their wages low and workload high, furthering inequalities. Because NTTF are afraid to speak up, discrimination and related workplace concerns (e.g., sexual harassment, lack of resources) can run rampant. Such a climate is ripe for incivility. Our data suggest that women NTTF commonly experience bullying and other incivilities (i.e., chilly climate). Lack of family-friendly policies or accommodations for NTTF is problematic as well. Because of their contingent status, NTTF are often not eligible for certain benefits such as maternity leave, and without access to governance, they likely never will be.

Lack of Interaction

A lack of meaningful interaction exists between many tenure-track and non-tenure-track faculty. Not only are contingent faculty often unable to participate in governance, but also many are left out of other activities such as orientation, mentorship programs, and social events that can lead to interactions (Baldwin and Chonister 2001; Gappa and Leslie 1993; Roueche et al. 1995). Some logistical issues of contingent work may prevent faculty from meeting one another informally. Contingent faculty often are assigned to teach at times less desirable for tenure-track faculty (e.g., late evenings, weekends) and when few tenure-track faculty are on campus. Jessica, a part-time faculty member at a community college, noted that she taught weekend classes and her "main contacts [were] with the custodial staff and other adjuncts." Many contingent faculty, especially part-timers, try to create a full-time schedule at different institutions, do not have workspaces on campus, or must leave quickly to go to another campus to teach another class.

This lack of interaction can make contingent faculty feel isolated from the academic community and prevent them from seeking help or advice regarding their work. Sarah, a new adjunct faculty member at a community college, talked about her concerns after her first evaluation went poorly: "I wondered about other instructors coming out of grad school, are they more prepared than I am? . . . I mean—am I the worst?" Because she rarely spoke to other faculty about anything, much less their own experiences, Sarah was unsure of what her colleagues' classes were like, or how she compared to other new instructors. Fear of garnering negative impressions prevented another community college adjunct from asking her more experienced part-time colleagues about the culture of the school and norms of teaching, so she asked the teaching assistants instead.

Not only can this isolation prevent adjuncts from seeking help; but also it can also prevent more experienced faculty from offering help. With little contact between NTTF and tenure-line faculty, the latter may not be able to dispel any preconceived notions or stereotypes they may have of contingent faculty. Instead, the NTTF stereotypes (addressed in the next section) may continue unchallenged (Kezar and Sam 2010b). Mary, a full-time contingent faculty member, described the climate of isolation in many departments in her university:

> Well, I think this really sums it up: Lecturers are people that tenure-track faculty do not interact with. When we are spoken about or thought about, it's about correcting our mistakes or keeping us in line. No assumption that we are professionals and that we should be a part of decisions or conversations. We do not deserve mentoring or socialization. Everyone else on campus, including the students or TAs, is treated with much more respect. We are as low as it gets on the totem pole.

The combination of isolation and lack of respect may perpetuate how NTTF are treated with incivility. Isolation can make bullying, harassment, and discrimination hard to prove. And, like any isolated victim, they are much less likely to escape the circumstance. Social interactions that could illuminate abusive situations as abnormal, and foster connections to get beyond the abusive circumstances, are unlikely. Without other people's input, it can be difficult to determine whether certain behaviors are normative or not. Isolation prevents collective action that can make the climate for everyone better.

Non-Tenure-Track Bias
One important element of contingent faculty's isolation and experience of marginalization is the lack of respect contingents experience from tenure-line faculty. Some tenure-line faculty may have a bias against non-tenure-line faculty regarding their assumed low quality of teaching, productivity (though many contingent faculty do not have a research component to their contracts), or degree attainment (Kezar and Sam 2010a, 2010b). Some tenure-line faculty think faculty in contingent positions are less qualified or less capable than those who obtained tenure-track positions (Langenburg 1998), ignoring evidence that three of four new faculty positions are non-tenure-track

(Schuster and Finkelstein 2006). Jan, speaking about her experience while working at a four-year institution, gave an example of a tenure-track faculty member speaking about NTTF not being "real professors":

> I briefly heard one of the new faculty say at a department meeting focused on quality, "And it's really disappointing that students do not see a real professor until their third year of school." I had to stand up and say that we lecturers are real professors even if we don't have tenure. And if he had said they do not get a professor who is on campus all the time, who can advise them, and who knows our full curriculum until the third year, I would have been okay.

The lack of respect that some tenure-line faculty have toward contingent faculty can prevent them from collegial engagement with one another. In some instances, tenure-line and non-tenure-line relationships are hostile. At a four-year institution, Elaine highlighted the intense hostility and disrespect that characterized some departments: "The climates feel authoritarian, like they are using you, you are disposable. I feel very dehumanized. I am just an interchangeable part of a machine." If contingent faculty do not receive respect for the work that they do, it makes it more difficult to gain support for policies and practices that could strengthen their working conditions. Baldwin and Chronister (2001) note how little contingent faculty can matter: "Historically, faculty off the tenure-track have been viewed from a policy perspective as an academic equivalent of migrant workers" (155). For NTTF to feel dehumanized is bad enough; for them to feel dehumanized because of someone else's perception of their professional worth is worse.

The Deprofessionalization of Contingent Faculty

There is a bifurcation of the professoriate, in which tenure-line faculty are considered professionals with the rights and obligations of the profession and NTTF are considered merely laborers. We acknowledge that contingent faculty (and tenure-line faculty) may have hybrid identities (Levin and Shaker 2011; Shaker 2008) or are managed professionals—professionals in more corporate environments and managed by others (Rhoades 1998). Yet, many institutions have policies and practices that move contingents farther from the professional end of the spectrum, which again, impacts women more.

Lack of Autonomy

Autonomy is another marker of professionalization (Rhoades 1998; Sullivan 2004). Often contingent faculty lack autonomy in their work experiences and are not able to determine their class content, their research, or their working environments (Gappa et al. 2007). For example, colleges and universities have been pushing to standardize the curriculum for lower-level college courses (particularly in general education), and that standardization dictates textbooks at times. In the case of online courses, institutions give professors completed syllabi and curricula including lecture materials and assignments. Because NTTF are often the ones teaching larger introduction or online classes, they are the ones who experience this loss of autonomy more than tenure-line faculty. Marcia, an NTTF at a four-year institution, spoke about her lack of autonomy and struggle to have input into the campus curriculum as an equal professional:

> The attitude is, come in, teach classes, and I believe that's it. . . . The climate itself makes me feel like I can't have input. I keep saying to them, "Why will you not include lecturers on issues like book selection and course outlines? Do you really think the whole world will fall apart?" I think they are coming around to the idea that I've been hammering at them for a good seven or eight years now.

Lack of Necessary Resources

Contingent faculty often lack the necessary resources that could better support their instruction (Hart 2009). For instance, many contingent faculty, especially those with part-time contracts, have neither office space nor (paid) office hours to facilitate meeting with students (Gappa and Leslie 1993; Schell and Stock 2001). In addition, faculty often rely on campus support services for various reasons ranging from materials such as paper and supplies to professional development. Campuses differ, however, as to whether they provide office space, supplies, equipment, and access to secretarial services for full-time and part-time NTTF. Full-time faculty generally have adequate support and services for their work, but several studies have demonstrated that part-time faculty have more limited access to office space, supplies and equipment, and secretarial support (Gappa and Leslie 1993; Outcalt 2002). This can be taxing to contingent faculty, who are already stretched thin. Sylvia, an NTTF member at a four-year institution, explained:

> There really is no support for faculty and I make all my own copies—I go to Kinko's and do my own support work. I bought my own computer and printer because it would've taken so many hours of work to fill out the paperwork, months to receive anything and usually what we hear after all the effort is "Sorry, no money for your request."

Lack of resources can have a negative effect on the instructional practices of contingent faculty, which may affect student learning.

Lack of Professional Development
Many NTTF are actively blocked from accessing professional development, or they are not provided with financial support to attend professional development events at other campuses. Tonya, another NTTF member at a four-year institution, spoke about the lack of opportunity for professional growth. She said: "I'm not encouraged to participate in any professional development in the department. I know there's lots going on campuswide but I've never participated because so many times the notices say that it's exclusively for the tenure-track or offered in the time that I can't go." Other times, institutions offer professional development opportunities to NTTF, but at times NTTF cannot attend because the planners do not think about NTTF schedules. This absence of professional development prevents faculty from strengthening and maintaining their knowledge and expertise.

The lack of professional treatment and support is the epitome of intellectual exclusions. This speaks to the issue of legitimacy and how campus climates work to deteriorate women's self-confidence and efficacy. For NTTF, this struggle is more pronounced as they lack autonomy *and* are excluded from professional development, mentoring, and socialization that brings the social capital necessary for legitimacy. Women of color already experience the double marginalization from being a woman and a person of color. Their NTTF position creates a third level of marginalization that they must negotiate, further affecting their self-confidence and sense of legitimacy (Stanley 2006).

The Interrelation of Challenges

As we explain how each of these contingent faculty challenges can lead to oppression within academia, it is equally important to piece these challenges together to form a holistic picture of the work environment that NTTF can face and how difficult it can be to change that environment. Experiencing one challenge is difficult enough, but this section illustrates how contingent faculty may experience multiple challenges. And, without leverage to push for change, a negative work environment will remain the status quo for many NTTF.

In Figure 3.1, we show three ways that contingent faculty experience marginalization in the workplace and illustrate how one may influence the other. When we discuss how institutions can silence contingent faculty, we have to keep in mind that governance and academic freedom are often considered marks of the professoriate (Tierney 2004). By denying contingent faculty access to governance and academic freedom, these policies can inadvertently strengthen the bias that contingent faculty are less professional and less deserving than tenure-line faculty. Likewise, without the opportunity

Figure 3.1   Ways That Contingent Faculty Experience Marginalization

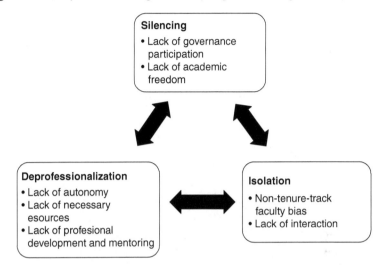

to participate in departmental or institutional meetings contingent faculty do not have a formal venue to voice concerns over existing policies or practices, such as the lack of resources that are necessary for good instruction. If contingent instruction falters, people may be more prone to attribute the poor performance to contingent faculty themselves (thus sustaining the bias against contingents), rather than to look at structural and cultural influences.

Suggestions for Culture, Policy, and Practice Changes

To alter the conditions of NTTF who experience marginalization, we need to address the systems that perpetuate the culture and structure of inequities. Faculty and administrators need to start changing academia, making it more equitable for contingent faculty and, in turn, making higher education more equitable for women.

We need to change the culture of academic departments and generate greater awareness about the problems and issues for NTTF, particularly their stereotyping and second-class citizenship. Until institutions recognize their worth to higher education, it is unlikely that policies and practices will change. NTTF are victims of a changing labor market. Their status as NTTF does not stem from lack of credentials to be tenured or on the tenure track. Mainstream academics probably lack awareness of the enormous rise in the number of NTTF or their poor working conditions. Awareness and respect will come from dialogue on campuses about the nature of the professoriate, and in other forums such as publications, professional and disciplinary associations, and online forums. These dialogues must include NTTF. In addition to raising consciousness, we need leadership from administrators and tenure-track faculty to model respect for NTTF in practice and policy. Once dialogue begins, change agents should consider some of the following recommendations.

As professionals, NTTF should be full participants in the faculty governance process (AFT 2005; Baldwin and Chronister 2001; Rhoades and Maitland 2008). They need to be invited to departmental meetings and encouraged to participate where they have the most interest or expertise. For example, business faculty may want to participate in service regarding finances. Over time, it is important to incorporate NTTF into the broader institutional governance system. Campuswide involvement in governance should include the faculty senate; campus-level committees; and departmental decisions, such as input on course selections and scheduling (Hollenshead et al. 2007; Kezar and Sam 2010a).[6] Institutions need to do more than invite faculty; they need to facilitate their involvement. This means compensating NTTF for service, if it is not included in their contracts. Because there may be times when only one NTTF member is participating on a committee, that individual may have limited voice or be perceived as a token member. Thus, contingents should have voting privileges. Leaders need to think expansively about NTTF issues and include these faculty in governance, particularly when it comes to issues concerning curriculum, teaching, and learning. This push for governance participation will give contingent faculty a voice in campus or departmental affairs as well as give them opportunities to interact. NTTF also should be included in academic freedom policies and be provided with multiyear contracts when possible. If their hiring were less contingent, they might be more willing to speak up and participate, thus changing their workplace cultures. Some campuses stand as models of NTTF equity and offer multiyear contracts and rehire rights (Chait and Trower 1997; Sam 2012).

In businesses, including academia, employers should provide the necessary supplies and support for employees to fulfill their job responsibilities. Faculty need office space that provides a place to meet with students and colleagues, prepare for teaching, and meet job responsibilities such as managing graduate assistants or field placements (Baldwin and Chronister 2001; Gappa and Leslie 1993). Additionally, they need appropriate clerical support for their teaching, service, and research demands and appropriate access to equipment (e.g., computers, photocopiers, phone, paper). Too often, NTTF, particularly part-timers, are expected to have a home office with all these materials and to buy their own supplies, putting an undue burden on faculty who are already receiving significantly less compensation than their tenure-line colleagues (Baldwin and Chronister 2001; Gappa and Leslie 1993).

NTTF need to be included in discussions about norms regarding grading policies, teaching philosophies, cocurricular activities, and other campus processes. A hallmark of professionals is that they socialize new members to the expectations and standards of the institution (Baldwin and Chronister 2001; Gappa and Leslie 1993; Sullivan 2004). Thus, institutions should create systems to professionally socialize NTTF. Tenure-track and senior non-tenure-track faculty who are familiar with the roles and responsibilities of the work should serve as mentors. Alternatively, NTTF could be included in existing orientation and mentoring systems serving tenure-track faculty. Establishing mentorship programs among faculty can help bridge the gap between tenure line and non-tenure-line faculty.[7] Providing mentoring is another way to facilitate interaction, support NTTF, and address the isolation they experience. No matter the vehicle by which professional socialization occurs, institutions can and should remove the barriers between the groups so socialization can take place more easily.

The state of women faculty's work experience is intricately connected with the state of contingent faculty's work experience. If tenure-line faculty, administration, students, and others working in higher education do not respect contingent faculty, it means that a large percentage of women faculty are not respected. However, change can happen on multiple levels. For example, in our case study of the community college, faculty realized that ensuring equitable pay for adjuncts would mean that they could hire the best instructors for their institution and ultimately benefit the students. By realizing that several leverage points can improve the work environment for contingent faculty, tenure-track women faculty and non-tenure-track women faculty may find that they have more common ground than originally expected. Together women faculty (and men allies) will have a greater impact enacting change than acting alone.

Notes

1. For this chapter we use the terms *non-tenure-track faculty* (NTTF) and *contingent faculty* interchangeably to denote full- and part-time faculty ineligible for tenure. When needed we will delineate between full- and part-time faculty and may use the term *adjunct* to denote part-time non-tenure-track.
2. For examples of positive work policies, see AFT (2002), www.aft.org/pdfs/highered/standardsptadjunct02.pdf.
3. For a more detailed description of the methods for each study, refer to Sam (2011) and Kezar (2013), respectively.
4. While research demonstrates that some women "choose" NTTF positions that offer flexibility in certain fields (e.g., health sciences), we caution that in some fields (e.g., the humanities), few options exist and they are increasingly the only choice (Finley 2009).

5. Dual positions can be an issue for women because they tend to be offered the non-tenure-track position, as opposed to men. Or perhaps women tend to be the "trailing spouse" more often (Wolf-Wendel et al. 2003).
6. See Kezar and Sam (2010a) for a discussion of how to include NTTF in governance.
7. For part-time faculty teaching in retirement and not interested in becoming part of the academic community, socialization may be less important.

References

Acker, J. 1990. "Hierarchies, Jobs, Bodies: A Theory of Gendered Organizations." *Gender & Society* 4(2):139–158.
American Association of University Professors. 2005. *Inequities Persist for Women and Non-Tenure-Track Faculty: The Annual Report on the Economic Status of the Profession 2004–05*. Washington, DC: American Association of University Professors.
American Federation of Teachers. 2002. *Standards of Good Practice in the Employment of Part-Time Adjunct Faculty: Fairness and Equity*. Washington, DC: American Federation of Teachers.
———. 2005. *Standards of Good Practice in the Employment of Full-Time Nontenure-Track Faculty: Professionals and Colleagues*. Washington, DC: American Federation of Teachers.
———. 2010. *American Academic: A National Survey of Part-Time/Adjunct Faculty*. Washington, DC: American Federation of Teachers.
Baldwin, Roger G., and Jay L. Chronister. 2001. *Teaching Without Tenure*. Baltimore: Johns Hopkins University Press.
Chait, R. and Trower, C. A. (1997). *Where tenure does not reign: campuses with contract systems. New Pathways Working Paper Series*, no. 3. Washington DC: American Association for Higher Education.
Cross, John G., and Edie N. Goldenberg. 2009. *Off-Track Profs: Non-tenured Teachers in Higher Education*. Cambridge, MA: MIT Press.
Finley, Ashley. 2009. "Women as Contingent Faculty: The Glass Wall." *Faculty Work* 37(3). http://www.aacu.org/ocww/volume37_3/feature.cfm?section=1.
Gappa, Judy M., and David W. Leslie. 1993. *The Invisible Faculty: Improving the Status of Part-timers in Higher Education*. San Francisco: Jossey-Bass.
Gappa, Judy M., Anne E. Austin, and Andrea G. Trice. 2007. *Rethinking Faculty Work: Higher Education's Strategic Imperative*. San Francisco: Jossey-Bass.
Harper, Elizabeth P., Roger G. Baldwin, Bruce G. Gansneder, and Jay L. Chronister. 2001. "Full-Time Women Faculty off the Tenure Track: Profile and Practice." *The Review of Higher Education* 24(3):237–257.
Hart, Jeni. 2011. "Non-Tenure-Track Women Faculty: Opening the Door." *Journal of the Professoriate* 4(1):96–124.
Hollenshead, Carol, Jean Waltman, Louise August, Jeane Miller, Gilia Smith, and Allison Bell. 2007. *Making the Best of Both Worlds: Findings From a National Institution-Level Survey on Non-Tenure-Track Faculty*. Ann Arbor, MI: Center for the Education of Women.

Ivey, Elizabeth, Chin-Fang Weng, and Cordelia Vahajdji. 2005. *Gender Differences Among Contingent Faculty: A Literature Review*. Sloan Foundation Report. Alexandria, VA: Association for Women in Science.

Kezar, Adrianna. 2013. "Four Cultures of the New Academy: Support for Non-Tenure-Track Faculty." *The Journal of Higher Education* 84(2):153–188.

Kezar, Adrianna, and Cecile Sam. 2010a. "Beyond Contracts: Non-Tenure-Track Faculty and Campus Governance." *NEA Almanac of Higher Education* 116:83–91.

———. 2010b. *Understanding the New Majority of Non-Tenure-Track Faculty in Higher Education: Demographics, Experiences and Plans of Action*. ASHE Higher Education Report Series. San Francisco: Jossey-Bass.

———. 2013. "Institutionalizing Equitable Policies and Practices for Contingent Faculty." *The Journal of Higher Education* 84(1):56–87.

Knapp, Laura G., Janice E. Kelly-Reid, and Scott A. Ginder. 2011. *Employees in Postsecondary Institutions, Fall 2009, and Salaries of Full-Time Instructional Staff, 2009–10 (NCES 2011-150)*. Washington, DC: U.S. Department of Education, National Center for Education Statistics.

Langenberg, Donald N. 1998. "The Subfaculty." *New Directions for Higher Education* 104:39–44.

Levin, John S., Susan Kater, and Richard L. Wagoner. 2006. *Community College Faculty: At Work in the New Economy*. New York: Palgrave Macmillan.

Levin, John S., and Genevieve G. Shaker. 2011. "The Hybrid and Dualistic Identity of Full-Time Non-Tenure-Track Faculty." *American Behavioral Scientist* 55(11):1461–1484.

Monks, James. 2007. "The Relative Earnings of Non-Tenure-Track Faculty in Higher Education." *Journal of Labor Research* 28:487–501.

NEA Higher Education Research Center. 2007. *Part-Time Faculty: A Look at Data and Issues*, 11(3). Washington, DC: National Education Association.

Outcalt, Charles. 2002. *A Profile of the Community College Professorate, 1975–2000*. New York: Routledge.

Rhoades, Gary. 1998. *Managed Professionals*. Albany: State University of New York Press.

Rhoades, Gary, and Christine Maitland. 2008. "Bargaining for Full-Time Non-Tenure-Track Faculty: Best Practices." *The NEA 2008 Almanac of Higher Education* 13:67–73.

Roueche, John E., Susan D. Roueche, and Mark D. Milliron. 1995. *Strangers in Their Own Land: Part-Time Faculty in American Community Colleges*. Washington, DC: Community College Press.

Sam, Cecile. 2011. "Conceptualizations of Academic Community." Paper presented at the Annual Meeting of the American Educational Research Association, Vancouver, BC.

———. 2012. "Institutionalization of a Positive Work Environment at a Community College." In *Embracing Non-Tenure Track Faculty*, edited by Adrianna Kezar, 100–113. New York: Routledge.

Schell, Eileen, and Patricia Stock, eds. 2001. *Moving a Mountain: Transforming the Role of Contingent Faculty in Composition Studies and Higher Education*. Urbana, IL: National Council of Teachers in English.

Schuster, Jack H., and Martin J. Finkelstein. 2006. *American Faculty: The Restructuring of Academic Work and Careers.* Baltimore: Johns Hopkins University Press.

Shaker, Genevieve. 2008. "Off the Track: Full-Time Non-Tenure-Track Faculty Experience in English." PhD dissertation, Indiana University.

Stanley, Christine. 2006. "Coloring the Academic Landscape: Faculty of Color Breaking the Silence in Predominantly White Colleges and Universities." *American Educational Research Journal* 43:701–736.

Sullivan, William M. 2004. "Can Professionalism Still Be a Viable Ethic?" *The Good Society* 13(1):15–20.

Thompson, Paul, Phillipe Constantineau, and George Fallis. 2005. "Academic Citizenship: An Academic Colleagues' Working Paper." *Journal of Academic Ethics* 3(2):127–142.

Tierney, William G. 2004. "Academic Freedom and Tenure: Between Fiction and Reality." *The Journal of Higher Education* 75(2):161–177.

West, Martha S., and John W. Curtis. 2006. *AAUP Faculty Gender Equity Indicators 2006.* Washington, DC: American Association of University Professors.

Wolf-Wendel, Lisa, Susan B. Twombly, and Suzanne Rice. 2003. *The Two-Body Problem: Dual-Career-Couple Hiring Policies in Higher Education.* Baltimore: Johns Hopkins University Press.

4

FACULTY GENDER INEQUITY AND THE "JUST SAY NO TO SERVICE" FAIRY TALE

Karen Pyke

It is common for research-intensive universities to over-recruit women faculty for service on university committees and task forces to ensure gender diversity. Ironically, this practice is an institutional barrier to women faculty's advancement because it deprives them of precious time needed to conduct research, the requisite activity for promotion. And, it is common practice in academia to advise women faculty to "Just Say No" to those who ask them to serve. Explanations of gender inequity that focus on women faculty's choices, behavior, attitudes, and biology (see Summers 2005) result in the woman as deficient model. Not only does this model fail to address the barriers to women's success, but also by blaming women, it exacerbates them. Rosser and Lane (2002) argue,

> Not surprisingly, many women [have] internalized this model and questioned whether something was wrong with them as individuals because of obstacles to success in their academic scientific careers. At best, they lost confidence in themselves and wondered where they personally had gone wrong. At worst, they dropped out of academia and science. (52)

The simplicity of the woman as deficient model makes it appealing to university administrators and faculty—it is easier to put the burden of change on individuals rather than complex bureaucratic structures. As most faculty and administrators receive no training in the study of organizational barriers to gender inequality through their disciplinary areas of research or in preparation for administrative duties, they may not recognize how university structures and bureaucratic practices produce institutional gender discrimination. Feminist sociologists, who study corporations and bureaucracies such as universities, find that these are not gender-neutral rational/technical organizations. To the contrary, they are "gendered" institutions whose organizational structures, policies, practices, and cultural presumptions reflect masculine principles, generate gendered divisions of labor, and bolster men's careers while hurting women's (Bird 2011; Cress and Hart 2009; Park 1996).

The organizational structures of today's universities, which trace their roots to the universities of medieval Europe, when higher education was the exclusive province of men, reflect men's life course trajectories and social practices, not women's (Bain and Cummings 2000; Hochschild 1975). Men continue to occupy the upper ranks of higher education, where they have failed to recognize, let alone alter, gendered institutional practices that block women faculty's advancement. Additionally, they tend to socialize in homosocial networks sometimes known as the "old boys' club" operating as "an in-built patriarchal support system," which "they do not have to make a conscious effort to be helped by" (Bagilhole and Goode 2001, 161). Women faculty typically are not part of this support system, though some might gain admission as "tokens" by not challenging the status quo (e.g., prevailing assumptions, values), not trying to bring more women into the inner circle, and not vying for top positions (Bagilhole and Goode 2001, 170). Men faculty's networks reproduce organizational practices of gender inequity and bias while simultaneously denying the existence of gendered structures (Bain and Cummings 2000; Bird 2011). Casting higher education as a gender-blind institution and failing to acknowledge structural hurdles to women faculty's advancement leads to blaming women for their failure to achieve equality and puts the onus on them to change rather than on men or the university structure. "In other words, merely allowing women faculty to meet the criteria for academic success, on terms that have been defined by men and represent their life experiences, does not necessarily guarantee equity. . . . An equitable situation should entail equal opportunities *and* equal constraints" (Bailyn 2003, 140). Bird (2011, 202) suggests that active intervention is necessary to alter these gendered practices because the current practice of "diversity" training on overtly illegal discriminatory practices and sexual and racial harassment to protect universities from lawsuits is not enough. She argues for more systematic and proactive efforts such as remedial workshops designed to identify and challenge accepted gendered assumptions and practices by training administrators and faculty to recognize systemic barriers to gender equity.

The Case Study

My campus is one of 10 research-intensive universities in the University of California (UC) system whose governance is shared among the board of regents, the system-wide president, and the representative body of tenure-track faculty, the Academic Senate.[1] Each UC campus has its own divisional Academic Senate, from whom representatives are sent to the system-wide Academic Senate. Divisional and system-wide Academic Senates have a high number of committees requiring faculty service labor to ensure the smooth functioning and maintenance of each campus, and the larger university system. The duties of Academic Senate committees and task forces include handling admissions, hiring administrators, advising chancellors and presidents on budget and administrative matters, hiring and promoting faculty, generating university rules and policies, assessing university performance, developing strategic plans, approving manuscripts for publication by the university press, overseeing undergraduate and graduate curriculum, and reporting on diversity. On my campus three dozen standing Academic Senate committees generate no fewer than 182 committee seats.

Seats must be filled from a pool of 680 nonemeriti tenure-track faculty, a number of whom are excused from Academic Senate service due to administrative duties or research leaves. Of the 680 Academic Senate faculty, only 212—fewer than 33%—are women.[2] This percentage of women faculty is typical of research-intensive universities (Marschke, Laursen, Nielsen, and Rankin 2007). In addition, the university requires faculty service on subcommittees; ad hoc committees; task forces; and the executive committees of research centers and various administrative units, such the Institutional Review Board.

Faculty must serve on departmental committees as well. For example, my department has 16 standing committees with 55 seats for a faculty of 20, some of whom are unavailable to serve at any given time due to leaves or administrative positions. My departmental colleagues also serve as members or directors of seven research centers and two academic programs; all require service duties. These figures underscore the centrality of service obligations for university faculty, and the centrality of faculty in ensuring the smooth functioning of the university. I focus only on university service, but it bears mention that faculty perform service for the profession as well. They serve as members and officers of professional associations, reviewers and editors of article and book manuscripts, members of professional award committees, reviewers of grant proposals, external reviewers of departments or faculty seeking promotion at other institutions, members of accreditation boards, invited speakers, conference organizers, textbook authors (which research-intensive universities regard as professional service rather than research productivity), and so on.

Faculty service to the university is ostensibly required to advance through the ranks. The Office of Academic Personnel on my campus posts information on its website to "underscore key aspects of the [faculty advancement] procedures in a more informal and interpretive manner" with the aim of minimizing "misunderstanding of the process and its criteria and to assist faculty in meeting its expectations." For advancement through the faculty ranks, the university expects "excellence" in the categories of "teaching, scholarship and research, professional activities and service including university and public service." However, research and teaching have priority: "Because of the need for maintenance of the intellectual and academic strength of the institution, advancement to tenure or appointment at tenure requires superior intellectual attainment with regard to research and excellence in teaching."[3] Further, it is the faculty's responsibility to "choose" carefully the amount of university service they perform as the consequences for doing too much can be a failure to receive tenure or advance through the ranks: "Maintaining a reasonable level of activity without overburdening oneself requires careful choices and sensible time management. Pre-tenure faculty, in particular, should be careful not to commit unduly to such activities."[4]

No definition in this or any other university document specifies how much service is enough, nor does the university address how faculty are to navigate the inherent structural contradiction of, on the one hand, the incessant demand for their service labor and, on the other, the need to limit their service duties so as to produce high-quality research. Although the university assigns responsibility to individual (often junior) faculty to manage their service load, it provides no mechanism for monitoring the recruitment practices of senior colleagues and administrators, or for sanctioning those who over-recruit from certain pools of faculty, such as women and men of color. In fact, it considers over-recruitment as normative:

> Women and members of a minority group may find requests for their services numerous and time-consuming, and they must be prudent in assessing their valuable input in relation to other demands on their time. Some meaningful service at this stage of the career is desirable, but not at the expense of the teaching and research responsibilities. The chair and senior faculty can provide helpful advice on selecting service involvements.[5]

University administration formally advises women and underrepresented minorities to seek advice on how to manage their service loads from senior colleagues and administrators who, as it turns out, are most likely to be men lacking experience with such pressures. Three-quarters of full professors and the vast majority of university administrators in the United States are men (Misra, Lundquist, Holmes, and Agiomavritis 2011). Because these are the same individuals who are likely to press women faculty into service, this practice is akin to asking the wolf to guard the henhouse.

The prevailing presumption at research-intensive universities that faculty "voluntarily" engage in campus service and fully control how much they do is naïve. It "demonstrates little thoughtfulness about the relations of power inside the academy" (Park 1996, 55). Department chairs and deans can and do assign faculty to department and university committees and task forces. When an administrator "asks" an assistant or associate woman professor to serve, she may not know if this is a sincere question or an assignment to which saying no could have negative repercussions. Further, university protocols instructing faculty to seek advice about service from senior colleagues and department chairs overlook how these individuals might be personally invested in redirecting service tasks from themselves to more junior faculty to preserve time to advance their own research careers. In addition, this practice ignores how senior men can regard service labor that emphasizes care work, community building, and nurturing as "feminized" tasks somehow better reserved for women faculty, thus contributing to gender inequity in divisions of labor (Park 1996).

Research-intensive universities do a better job protecting assistant than associate professors from service overloads due to their need to attain tenure (Misra et al. 2011). For example, the Academic Senate on my campus avoids asking assistant professors to serve and does so only if the committee meets seldom and the workload is light. However, this courtesy often is not extended to nonwhite faculty, especially women of color, for whom early-career service is common, especially on high-profile committees where the university seeks their presence as a symbol of its commitment to diversity (Park 1996; Turner 2002).

As is a common experience for women faculty (Porter 2007, 537; Wilson 2010), I was hit with a bevy of requests to join committees upon gaining tenure, often with the promise that the workload would be light. I soon found myself to be the most junior member on several committees with a heavier workload than I anticipated, in part because it included the remedial work I had to do to catch up with my more experienced colleagues. While serving as an elected member of the Committee on Committees (COC) charged with filling the seats of the Academic Senate Committees, I observed and participated in the committee practice of targeting women faculty for service to ensure gender diversity.[6] Because women faculty make up less than one-third of the Academic Senate faculty, and a high proportion of women faculty are at the assistant rank, where they are largely (though not entirely) off limits, women faculty available for service are in short supply, thus necessitating extra efforts to successfully recruit from the small pool. Thus, it was customary practice for COC members to pressure women faculty who initially rejected a service request to reconsider, underscoring the committee's need for a woman. I do not recall a time when the committee issued a repeated request to a man faculty member who said no, because men were not in short supply. Hence, men faculty and administrators are better able to control their service labor by saying no than can women faculty, who must say no more often, and repeatedly, while also ignoring any obligation they feel to represent women on campus.

At the same time I was issuing repeated pleas to women faculty to serve on Academic Senate Committees, I participated in faculty reviews of personnel files where colleagues commonly denigrated faculty service labor. I saw how the service labor I was pushing on women faculty as a member of the COC could slow their advancement through the ranks and rob them of much-needed wage increases. These contradictions prompted my interest in "unsettling" the accepted practices of institutional gender discrimination, aptly referred to as the "ivory ceiling of service work" (Misra et al. 2011).

The "Ivory Ceiling of Service Work"

The relationship between women's slower advancement through the faculty ranks and greater share of service duties is fairly clear (Misra et al. 2011; see also Bagilhole 1993; Mason et al. 2005; West and Curtis 2006). While women take more time to attain the rank of full professor than men (Lisberger 2011; Modern Language Association 2009), they are recruited more for university service and spend more time on service duties and less on research than men faculty (Bird 2011; Bird, Litt, and Wang 2004). One study found that women faculty at doctoral universities serve on 50% more committees than men faculty (Porter 2007).

When I began to challenge the "Just Say No" approach to the problem of women faculty's service load, I found little sympathy from senior colleagues and administrators. One highly rewarded professor, a white man, wrote the following to me on the topic:

> It has been clear to me for some time that women at the junior level are asked more than men to serve on all sorts of committees, with the expectation that they should do so. . . . In the end, the expectations will only

change if individual faculty say "no." I know this places the burden on the individual, not the system, but the system is always looking for people who will not say "no." (personal correspondence, March 20, 2009)

Colleagues were aware of the problem but unwilling to grapple with its structural roots, preferring instead to put the onus for change on individual women. I grew particularly disheartened upon hearing my disciplinary colleagues reiterate the "Just Say No" mantra because doing so requires turning down the volume knob on sociological insights and analytic methods. Why did they not find it odd, as I did, to structure an occupation on the premise that employees will be asked (or told) by their superiors to do more service labor than they ought to perform, and for which they may be punished with a career stall and lost wage increases should they do so?

In failing to address the structural root of the problem, the "Just Say No" approach exacerbates gender-blind sexism in academia. Like the rhetoric of Nancy Reagan's "Just Say No to Drugs" campaign, this discourse transfers responsibility for the problem from the larger social and political context to the individual. As I describe elsewhere (Pyke 2011):

> While drug pushers are criminalized as evil wrongdoers, academic "service pushers" are neither demonized nor blamed. Indeed, they are among the highest status members of the academy. Like drug pushers, however, "service pushers" often misrepresent the negative effects of that which they push by overestimating the rewards and underestimating the costs. (86)

And like the "Just Say No to Drugs" campaign, this approach has failed miserably to achieve its goals (Rosenbaum and Hanson 1998; West and O'Neal 2004). Given the unequal gendered division of university service labor, blame for doing too much is gendered—it falls disproportionately on the shoulders of women. When women faculty internalize the myth that they have the power and responsibility to limit their service loads, they can likewise blame themselves rather than structural inequities, and regard their lower wages and stalled careers as their own fault. This can lead to downward spirals in their self-esteem and morale (Rosser and Lane 2002; Valian 1998).

Although the intent of the "Just Say No to Drugs" public relations campaign is a "drug-free" society, faculty and university leaders who advocate a "Just Say No to Service" approach cannot hope to secure a "service-free" university. Faculty service labor is essential for the maintenance of institutions of higher learning; thus, a "service-free" university is an oxymoron. Those who espouse the "Just Say No" discourse suggest that faculty shirk their fair share of the service load and transfer the service burden to other faculty. They are effectively saying, "Let their research and careers suffer rather than yours." This suggestion overlooks how, for women faculty, saying no can mean saying yes to the structures, policies, and practices in academia that discriminate, oppress, and ignore the needs of women on campus. Also, it overlooks the greater ease with which men faculty can say no without facing additional pressure to serve, and do not feel an obligation to serve in order to address gender inequity and diversity, as is often the case with women faculty.

Structural Hurdles to Gender Equity in Faculty Service

Although academia is often cast in popular discourse as a bastion of left-leaning liberalism and many scholars and campus administrators pay lip service to diversity and gender equality, the reality can be quite different (Shea 2003). As an American Association of University Professors report notes, "Women face more obstacles as faculty in higher education than they do as managers and directors in corporate America" (West and Curtis 2006, 4). Research finds gender bias in faculty peer reviews of personnel records of scholarly accomplishments. Faculty are more likely to recommend promoting and rewarding men faculty on the basis of their perceived potential, while evaluating women faculty on the basis of what they have already accomplished (Bailyn 2003; Valian 1998). In experimental comparisons of identical curriculum vitae, one with a woman's name and the other with a man's name, faculty rate the one with the man's name higher (Valian 1998).

Not only do women take longer to advance through the academic ranks than men faculty, they are also less likely to get hired in the first place. The number of women in faculty positions has not kept pace with the numbers receiving doctorates (Marschke et al. 2007; Monroe and Chiu 2010). Women are also less likely to be recruited and hired into academic posts and less inclined than men to see academia as a good environment for pursuing a career. In addition, women graduate students are less likely than their men counterparts to desire an academic career, and their interest in academic careers declines the longer they are in graduate school and learn how their gender will count against them (Rice 2012). Furthermore, those women who enter into faculty positions are more likely to leave academia than men faculty (Rosser and Lane 2002; West and Curtis 2006). For those who do stay, they earn less than men with comparable experience and research records (Valian 1998). Sadly, projections of current trends suggest that without serious interventions women faculty will not achieve gender equity in the foreseeable future (Marschke et al. 2007; Monroe and Chiu 2010).

Fewer Tenure-Track Faculty to Fill Service Roles

Recent academic employment trends that favor the hiring of part-time lecturers have increased the service burden for tenure-track faculty. Nearly 70% of faculty in 2007 had non-tenure-track appointments whereas only 31% had full-time tenure-track jobs (American Association of University Professors 2007, see chapter 3 of this volume). As non-tenure-track teaching-only appointments that do not carry service obligations have grown, the core of tenure-track faculty who perform university service has shrunk. That means a smaller number of faculty are responsible for a university service load that has not decreased with time and, if anything, has increased. Ongoing state budget cuts at public institutions of higher learning have contributed to mushrooming class sizes, further expanding the time faculty need to devote to teaching and mentoring—with women faculty already devoting more time to teaching and mentoring than men faculty (Bagilhole 1993; Park 1996). This means that faculty have less time to devote to research and writing for publication than in the past. In this context of rising service loads and teaching burdens, women faculty are asked more than men faculty to perform service for reasons I explain next.

Underrepresentation of Women Faculty and Need for Diversity

At every tenure-track rank men far outnumber women, with the gender disparity increasing as the rank rises (Monroe and Chiu 2010; see chapter 1 of this volume). The proportion of women faculty deteriorates as faculty rank increases and as institutional status rises. Among tenured faculty at master's and baccalaureate colleges, women comprise slightly more than one-third of tenured faculty; at doctoral universities, where research is central to one's career advancement, they account for one-quarter of tenured faculty (West and Curtis 2006, 10).

Due to this gender disparity, requests for service are not equitably distributed in academia (Hult, Callister, and Sullivan 2005). As they comprise a smaller core, women faculty endure more requests to serve. Women of color are particularly hard hit because of their smaller faculty numbers and their ability to contribute to gender *and* racial diversity in their service (Turner 2002). Hence, women serve more as a mere function of being asked more.

Women faculty serving on committees to guarantee diversity can be asked to serve on subcommittee assignments, if the need arises, to ensure gender diversity. Another factor contributing to women's larger service load are the committees and task forces charged with addressing gender inequity issues, often requiring the collection and analysis of data, and the preparation of reports. Women typically comprise committees tasked with improving women's status within the institution, an often invisible form of "institutional housekeeping" (Bird et al. 2004, 194). Not surprisingly, a major source of women faculty's dissatisfaction with their academic careers is the pressure they feel from being overloaded with committee assignments (Hult et al. 2005).

Women Faculty Serving Earlier and Above Their Skill Level

Because women faculty are disproportionately represented at the assistant and associate ranks, the need for their presence on committees means they are asked to serve much earlier in their careers than men, and at a rank when service can have more deleterious and long-lasting effects on their careers. Serving earlier in their careers means women often serve as the most junior and least experienced members of committees. Further, they often serve on committees with high, specialized workloads, including prestigious task forces and executive search committees where their performance is highly visible to university leaders. It is easy to regard an "invitation" to serve on a high-status committee with senior colleagues as an "honor," making it nearly impossible to say no. Saying yes, however, can require immense remedial learning to "catch up." When women faculty find they are the lone woman on committees, they can feel additional pressure to appear competent as representatives of all women; thus, they may be more afraid to ask questions that appear naïve. Meanwhile, they do not enjoy easy access to the networks of senior colleagues and administrators—the "old boys' club"—in which men share information about the unwritten rules, policies, and politics of the institution and trade favors and resources (Bagilhole and Goode 2001). Women faculty's inability to receive remedial training through traditional networks puts greater mentoring pressure on the small core of senior women, already overtaxed with service, when junior women seek their advice about how to perform service duties that exceed their skill set and pay grade.

When women faculty are charged on committees with, in part, representing the interests of women on campus, they have more at stake than men colleagues who might be freer to be less diligent in their committee work and skip meetings without enduring notice or negative sanctions. These different, gendered experiences can have other effects that are beneficial for men faculty but negative for women: Service assignments accrue to those judged diligent and competent whereas those whose service work is substandard or who appear disinterested can be "rewarded" with fewer service requests (i.e., more time to engage research and move up through the ranks).

Although structural gender inequities create a situation that foists service labor on women faculty to serve earlier in their careers than men faculty, their lower rank disqualifies them for elite administrative positions that require high rank and advanced skills. These positions tend to come with course releases, staff support, research money, and decision-making power.

So, although women at the assistant and associate levels can easily engage more service than men faculty at their rank and above, they are less likely to receive resources to mitigate the time they lose from their research. Moreover, women faculty who advance to full professor more slowly, or not at all, can hit an administrative glass ceiling despite having more service experience than the senior men who occupy elite posts (Park 1996). This happens because their slower movement through the professorial ranks counts against them, and appointments to elite positions depend on strong sponsorship from "old boys' club" networks more difficult for women to attain (Bagilhole and Goode 2001). Women who break through the glass ceiling into the pipeline of power are frequently "tokens" who as "one of the boys" are eager to fit in and avoid disappointing their sponsors (Bagilhole and Goode 2001, 170). The "Just Say No" framework overlooks the fact that faculty service assignments are neither equitable nor truly optional. Moreover, it obscures the structural forces of institutional gender discrimination in academia. We can replace the "Just Say No" mantra toward service with the far more apt slogan "Just Don't Ask." "But, if you do ask me for service, be prepared to acknowledge and reward my service labor. Otherwise, 'Just Don't Ask!' "

Notes

1. See the University of California website at www.universityofcalifornia.edu/aboutuc/governance.html.
2. Data are from the Academic Senate's website (http://senate.ucr.edu/; downloaded May 4, 2012) and the executive director of the Academic Senate (May 4, 2012).
3. See "Advancement and Promotion at UCR," p. 3 (http://academicpersonnel.ucr.edu/resources/CNASAdvandPromoUCRiverside.pdf) (downloaded May 4, 2012).
4. Ibid., p. 9.
5. Ibid.
6. A distinguished professor asked me to run, and another senior professor, soon to be dean of my college, nominated me. I was flattered by their confidence in me, making it more difficult to "Just Say No."

References

American Association of University Professors. 2007. "Trends in Faculty Status, 1975–2007." http://www.aaup2.org/research/TrendsinFacultyStatus2007.pdf.

Bagilhole, Barbara. 1993. "How to Keep a Good Woman Down: An Investigation of the Role of Institutional Factors in the Process of Discrimination Against Women." *British Journal of Sociology of Education*, 14(3):261–274.

Bagilhole, Barbara, and Jackie Goode. 2001. "The Contradiction of the Myth of Individual Merit, and the Reality of a Patriarchal Support System in Academic Careers: A Feminist Investigation." *European Journal of Women's Studies* 8:161–180.

Bailyn, Lotte. 2003. "Academic Careers and Gender Equity: Lessons Learned From MIT." *Gender, Work & Organization* 10:137–153.

Bain, Olga, and William Cummings. 2000. "Academe's Glass Ceiling: Societal, Professional-Organizational, and Institutional Barriers to the Career Advancement of Academic Women." *Comparative Education Review* 44(4):493–514.

Bird, Sharon. 2011. "Unsettling Universities' Incongruous, Gendered Bureaucratic Structures: A Case-Study Approach." *Gender, Work and Organization* 18(2): 202–230.

Bird, Sharon R., Jacqueline Litt, and Yong Wang. 2004. "Creating a Status of Women Report: Institutional Housekeeping as Women's Work." *National Women's Studies Association Journal* 16:194–206.

Cress, Christine M., and Jeni Hart. 2009. "Playing Soccer on the Football Field: The Persistence of Gender Inequities for Women Faculty." *Equity and Excellence in Education* 42(4):473–488.

Hochschild, Arlie. 1975. "Inside the Clockwork of Male Careers." In *Women and the Power to Change,* edited by F. Howe, 47–80. New York: McGraw-Hill.

Hult, Christine, Ronda Callister, and Kim Sullivan. 2005. "Is There a Global Warming Toward Women in Academia?" *Liberal Education* 91(3):50–57.

Lisberger, Jody. 2011. "The Politics of Data: Gender Bias and Border Mentality in the EEOC Job Category Compliance Chart and How Transnational Gender Mainstreaming Can Offer Best Practices for Change." *Wagadu* 9:89–111.

Marschke, Robyn, Sandra Laursen, Joyce McCarl Nielsen, and Patricia Rankin. 2007. "Demographic Inertia Revisited: An Immodest Proposal to Achieve Equitable Gender Representation Among Faculty in Higher Education." *The Journal of Higher Education* 78(1):1–27.

Mason, Mary Ann, Angelica Stacy, Marc Goulden, Carol Hoffman, and Karie Frasch. 2005. "Faculty Family Friendly Edge: An Initiative for Tenure-Track Faculty at the University of California." http://ucfamilyedge.berkeley.edu/ucfamilyedge.pdf.

Misra, Joya, Jennifer Hickes Lundquist, Elissa Holmes, and Stephanie Agiomavritis. 2011. "The Ivory Ceiling of Service Work." *Academe* 97(1). http://www.aaup.org/AAUP/pubsres/academe/2011/JF/Feat/misr.htm.

Modern Language Association. 2009. "Standing Still: The Associate Professor Survey." http://www.mla.org/assocprof_survey.

Monroe, Kristen, and William Chiu. 2010. "Gender Equality in the Academy: The Pipeline Problem." *PS: Political Science and Politics* 43(2):303–308.

Park, Shelly M. 1996. "Research, Teaching, and Service: Why Shouldn't Women's Work Count?" *The Journal of Higher Education* 67(1):46–84.

Porter, Stephen. 2007. "A Closer Look at Faculty Service: What Affects Participation on Committees?" *The Journal of Higher Education* 78(5):523–541.

Pyke, Karen. 2011. "Service and Gender Inequity Among Faculty." *PS: Political Science and Politics* 44:85–87.

Rice, Curt. 2012. "Why Women Leave Academia and Why Universities Should Be Worried." *The Guardian,* May 24. http://www.guardian.co.uk/higher-education-network/blog/2012/may/24/why-women-leave-academia.

Rosenbaum, Dennis P., and Gordon S. Hanson. 1998. "Assessing the Effects of School-Based Drug Education: A Six-Year Multilevel Analysis of Project D.A.R.E." *Journal of Research in Crime and Delinquency* 35(4):381–412.

Rosser, Sue V., and Eliesh O'Neil Lane. 2002. "Key Barriers for Academic Institutions Seeking to Retain Female Scientists and Engineers: Family-Unfriendly Policies, Low Numbers, Stereotypes, and Harassment." *Journal of Women and Minorities in Science* 8:161–189.

Shea, Christopher. 2003. "What Liberal Academia?" *Boston Globe*, October 12. http://www.boston.com/news/globe/ideas/articles/2003/10/12/what_liberal_academia/.

Summers, Lawrence H. 2005. Remarks at NBER Conference on Diversifying the Science and Engineering Workforce. Cambridge, MA, January 14.

Turner, Caroline Sotello Viernes. 2002. "Women of Color in Academe: Living With Multiple Marginality." *The Journal of Higher Education* 73:74–93.

Valian, Virginia. 1998. *Why So Slow? The Advancement of Women*. Boston: Massachusetts Institute of Technology.

West, Martha S., and John W. Curtis. 2006. *AAUP Faculty Gender Equity Indicators 2006*. Washington, DC: American Association of University Professors.

West, Steven L., and Keri K. O'Neal. 2004. "Project D.A.R.E. Outcome Effectiveness Revisited." *American Journal of Public Health* 94(6):1027–1029.

Wilson, Robin. 2010. "The Ivory Sweatshop: Academe Is No Longer a Convivial Refuge." *The Chronicle of Higher Education,* July 25. http://chronicle.com/article/The-Ivory-Sweatshop-Academe/123641/.

CASE STUDY

LECTURER BARNES: LONG-TERM CONTINGENT FACULTY

I came to East Coast University (ECU) through my spouse, who took a tenure-track position there. My living abroad at the time prevented prearrival negotiation for a tenure-track spousal hire position. But, this was more or less promised. After two years, ECU decided that I would not make tenure. Initially, I was given a full-time "senior lecturer" position on a five-year contract that would, eventually, get renewed annually. On the quarter system, full-time lecturers taught five courses per year. I had auxiliary research projects that supplemented my income. I taught half time (2.5 courses per year, teaching three one year, two the next), and did research half time. So, I had full-time and summer pay.

My applied research was not considered as appropriate for tenure-seeking faculty in spite of my consistent publishing record, albeit mostly book chapters and pieces outside of peer-reviewed journals. In short, tenure expectations effectively pigeonholed my research as unimportant and unworthy of tenure consideration. Still, I was able to continue the work I enjoyed without having a long-distance relationship. After all, my partner had followed twice before to other jobs; it was my turn.

I worked at ECU in this position for 10 years, with few raises beyond the cost of living, averaging 2% to 3% a year, barely keeping up with inflation. In my 10th year, ECU decided to mandate a lecturer workload of six courses.

This essentially meant a 17% pay cut. I appealed to ECU via all the appropriate channels, and was told the university did not have to honor spousal hire or any other previous agreements.

Recently, due to serious budget shortfalls and declining grant funding, senior faculty moved back into the classroom, meaning less money for salaries, overall. Thus, ECU decided to adjust my appointment (and other lecturers') to 50% of pay and workload. ECU kept appointments at 50% so lecturers would continue receiving full benefits. Unlike before, I could not increase my teaching beyond 50% when grants decreased. Additionally, lecturers lost their vote in faculty meetings, effectively silencing them. I stopped attending. Even though I could comment, it felt awkward and "out of place" to speak on proposals I could not vote on. This increased my feelings of isolation.

Also, I was impacted negatively by budget cuts in my externally funded projects. Due to budget shortfalls, ECU resolved the crisis by not returning indirect costs on grants to principal investigators. In short, they decided to balance the budget on the backs of the non-tenure-track faculty. The senior faculty are buying second homes; the lecturers are facing foreclosures. Like many spousal hires, my options for work at other universities nearby are few and poorly compensated.

My status as non-tenure-track faculty was revealed to me in a powerful juxtaposition. Faced with continuing budget cuts, numerous proposals were put forth. One suggested senior faculty teach an extra course, of their choosing, per year. This idea was presented at a faculty meeting on April 1 and was quickly revealed as an April Fool's Day joke. However, at the following faculty meeting, a serious proposal was put forth to increase the lecturers' workload from six to seven courses a year! Fortunately, the proposal did not pass, but senior faculty seemed surprised at objections, as some units in the university had such a workload (but under different conditions, e.g., with TAs).

I am concerned about my increasing workload, diminishing status, and substandard salary. Over the last decade, according to public data, the average professor at ECU has gone from earning 1.8 times that of lecturers to 2.6 times as much. From another perspective, professors have gone from making $42,000 *more* than lecturers to $96,000 *more*. The average annual *percent* increase over this decade for full professors was 7.4%, while for lecturers it was 2.7%. No promotion or advancement system exists for lecturers. And, despite the grants lecturers or other non-tenure-track faculty might secure, one's salary is determined by one's teaching, not one's grants.

I am considering leaving ECU, but my partner has significant ties to ECU and to the area. Plus, I have family obligations that make relocation difficult, if not impossible. I feel as though ECU knows that they "have" me. I also feel my early years, participating in creating curriculum, sitting on admissions committees, and so on—work that was expected of "regular" faculty—was never rewarded or appreciated. Now, I do my teaching and research, and get my reward from the latter—which practically funds itself. But, this is not a long-term viable solution. One can go a decade without promotion or reward, but decades?

If I could do it over, I would have tried to arrange the spousal hire previous to my arrival at ECU. Once my spouse was here, we no longer had any leverage. And, it felt as if I was seen as less valuable, not seen in my own right. Indeed, it was probably only because of personal relationships that I got an appointment at all. When the department head stepped down, the next ones did not value me at all. I've learned that spousal hires are really difficult to make work, especially for women, even now. So, organize, organize! When the TAs and RAs organized at ECU, there was some movement to organize non-tenure-track faculty. But in my department, only the faculty of color and gay faculty wanted to work together. There was a divide-and-conquer strategy by the department head, and none of the negative decisions above were reversed, whatever one's status regarding ethnicity or sexual orientation.

What Can We Learn From This Case Study?

This situation is challenging on emotional, interpersonal, and financial levels. Unfortunately, most colleges and universities do not give contingent faculty status, rights, or resources equivalent to those of tenure-track faculty. Administrators who value contingent faculty and want to "do right" by them may intend to keep verbal promises like those given to Lecturer Barnes. Yet, institutional constraints and/or workplace changes may prevent them from doing so. One lesson here: Get all agreements in writing.

When considering potential actions, women academics in similar situations will need to take the specific culture and structure of their institution(s) into account. Institutions tend to change slowly. Before pursuing a course of action, anyone seeking change and redress should prioritize goals. Then, boundaries to protect precious time and energy should be created. Help from others should be enlisted whenever possible.

Actions Involving Individual Resources

- Connect with other contingent faculty on one's campus and meet regularly. One goal of such gatherings is to listen to others' ideas for organizing as a group and voicing concerns collectively. Another goal is to work together to identify and address challenges for differently situated contingent faculty. Collective actions can be more effective than individual ones. As a side benefit, working with others can provide a sense of solidarity and support to counterbalance the stress and negative emotions that emerge in difficult work environments.

- Counterbalance stress from dealing with hostile workplaces through counseling, spiritual practice, meditation, social supports, recreation, and other mechanisms that support mental and physical health. Although we consider it a last resort, some women academics who work in hostile workplaces may wish to leave them.

Actions Involving Institutional Resources

- Seek opportunities for involvement in departmental or university life. Doing so can be difficult for contingent faculty; however, it is important for faculty to demonstrate value to the institution. The following are ways to navigate barriers to inclusion:

  o Ask to be included on e-mail lists about departmental and university-wide events (e.g., teaching or grant-writing workshops, meetings). Attending can provide opportunities to gather useful information and to remind colleagues of your consistent contributions to the department and university.

  o Explore opportunities to broadcast your accomplishments in electronic newsletters or other institutional publications that document faculty activities and accomplishments.

- Develop departmental and university-wide contacts who may know about campus opportunities to supplement your income (e.g., policy centers that could benefit from your expertise). Be sure that others, campuswide and beyond, know who you are and your areas of professional expertise. Do not be shy in letting others know that you are seeking extra work.

- Seek and develop allies for non-tenure-track faculty. These could be administrators or tenured/tenure-line faculty who could use their status to make visible the needs of contingent faculty (e.g., in department meetings, in the faculty senate, in other relevant committees or task forces). Some organizations listed in the following list and in the online resources at the end of the book identify effective strategies for doing so.

- Reignite conversations about organizing with contingent faculty across the campus. Document *everything* related to the process of institutional change. For example, who does what on your campus? What responses do you receive and from whom? Online resources such as Google Docs or Dropbox allow multiple users to work collectively and conveniently.

Actions Involving Extrainstitutional Resources

- Use your knowledge to formulate a case for addressing the needs of contingent faculty on your campus and beyond.[1] When educating others, the following resources are good starting points:

  o AAUP statements on contingent/non-tenure-track faculty at www .aaup.org/aaup/comm/rep/nontenuretrack.htm.

  o The New Faculty Majority (NFM), an organization "dedicated to improving the quality of higher education by advancing professional equity and securing academic freedom for all adjunct and contingent faculty" in a variety of ways (www.newfacultymajority.info/equity/ learn-about-the-issues/mission-a-identity/nfm-mission-statement). The NFM website features numerous resources for contingent faculty.

  o The Delphi Project on Changing Faculty and Student Success, cofounded by Adrianna Kezar (see chapter 3), offers a variety of resources to assess and improve contingent faculty working conditions within specific institutional contexts. In particular, see Tool Kits for creating institutional change at www.thechangingfaculty.org.

  o The On Hiring blog of *The Chronicle of Higher Education*, particularly Adjunct Life (http://chronicle.com/blogs/onhiring/category /adjuncts) and The Two-Year Track (http://chronicle.com/blogs/ onhiring/category/the-two-year-track). Authors offer erudite, timely posts on broad topics of importance to contingent faculty. Posts often end with a question for readers (e.g., Do you bring anything unique to the table that your students might not get from tenure-track professors?) that encourage feedback from readers, thus providing another source of ideas and a way to connect with similarly situated faculty.

  o The Adjunct Project website includes informational archives and job listings in higher education and those in "new fields categorized as the 'alternate academy' " (www.adjunctproject.com/about-the-project/).

The website includes a member-driven spreadsheet regarding adjunct pay, benefits, and other working conditions created by more than 1,500 contingent faculty workers across the United States. Use this information to illustrate to your school's administrators just how well your campus compares with others—or does not.

o AdjunctNation.com acts as a clearinghouse of useful information for non-tenured faculty, including articles, blogs, book reviews, job search information and tips, interviews, and discussion forums (e.g., teaching online, job hunting, using technology in the classroom). Significantly, AdjunctNation.com includes information regarding international news of relevance. It offers a free trial. After that, 6- and 12-month subscriptions can be purchased from $20–$30.

• Consult online communities (e.g., Listservs, blogs) for personal and professional advice including useful resources and recommendations for action. For example, gather information about similar schools that have successfully addressed the needs of contingent faculty (e.g., converting yearly contracts into multiple-year contracts, or schools that include contingent faculty in professional development opportunities and governance). The following are examples of useful online communities:

o The H-Adjunct Listserv is "an open, inter-disciplinary forum for issues involving adjunct, part-time and temporary faculty at universities, colleges and community colleges" (www.h-net. org/~adjunct/). The Contingent Academics Mailing List (http:// adj-l.org/mailman/listinfo/adj-l_adj-l.org) is ideal for connecting with list members.

o The University of Venus, "a collaborative venture bringing together the voices of GenX women in higher education from around the globe" (http://uvenus.org/about/), provides biweekly Twitter-based conversations (#Femlead) on topics of interest such as "Alternative Academic Careers." To ground these discussions, #Femlead recommends relevant readings. Archived discussions and reading links are located at http://uvenus.org/femlead-chat/.

o *The Chronicle of Higher Education's* Non-Tenure-Track forum[2] (http://chronicle.com/forums/index.php/board,52.0.html).

o Facebook. At the time of this writing, AdjunctNation.com and AdjunctWorld.com had active Facebook pages (www.facebook.com /AdjunctNation and www.facebook.com/AdjunctWorld). A Google search for "facebook.com and adjunct" identifies other groups as well.

- Develop networks in other areas of professional competence to amend your income. If opportunities for teaching, research, grant writing, or other university-related work are limited, consider using this time to develop additional "real-world" experience that can contribute to your institutional value. Think outside the box regarding opportunities to develop and demonstrate your skills. Consider writing editorials for the local paper or offering a night or weekend class to interested groups.
- Consider communicating with legislators regarding the negative impact of working conditions for contingent faculty on learning outcomes.

Consult the online resources at the end of the book and the case studies to the other parts of the book for additional information that might be helpful.

Notes

1. See www.aaup.org/AAUP/pubsres/policydocs/contents/conting-stmt.htm and www.aaup .org/AAUP/comm/rep/teachertenure.htm.
2. Accessing the forum requires a subscription log-in and password. Many universities should be able to provide access to this resource via departmental, college, or library subscriptions.

PART TWO

STRUCTURE MEETS CULTURE

Work-Family Conflicts

Recently, academics have paid significant attention to the conflicts between the competing responsibilities of work and personal/family life. These conflicts are deeply gendered in that women, more than men, continue to shoulder domestic and family responsibilities in heterosexual couples. Women routinely cite work-family conflicts as a reason for "opting out" of the paid labor force (e.g., Stone 2007; Williams 2005, 2010). These challenges may be exacerbated for women faculty. Full-time faculty work more hours than people in other professions (Winslow-Bowe and Jacobs 2011): full-time men faculty work an average of 54.8 hours per week, while their women counterparts report an average of 52.8 hours. Among academics, 38.1% of men and 32.5% of women report 60-hour workweeks, compared to men and women in other fields, who work an average of 46 and 39.5 hours, respectively. The chapters in this part of the book explore women's academic work-family challenges and how they navigate the related structures and cultures that work against them (or at least do not work in their favor).

The academy as a gendered organization (Acker 1990; Bird 2011; Martin 1994) reflects structures and cultures (i.e., policies and procedures; interactions and identities) that appear to be gender neutral but are not. In reality, most organizations reflect historical, unarticulated assumptions of employees as men "whose life centers on his full-time, life-long job, while his wife or another woman takes care of his personal needs and his children" (Acker 1990, 190). Many of those assumptions remain unaddressed. Thus, comprehensive work-family policies are not yet universal or commonplace. Such policies include access to paid and unpaid leave, ability to stop the tenure clock, flexibility in teaching (e.g., modified teaching loads, part-time teaching), on-site or university-sponsored childcare, *and* a culture that does not stigmatize people who use them (see Ward and Wolf-Wendel 2004).

Research suggests that academic men benefit from having children; however, women's careers are impacted negatively (Mason and Goulden 2002, 2004). Williams (2005) refers to this as the "maternal wall." Furthermore, family responsibilities can be a barrier to women's entering the professoriate (van Anders 2004). The conflict between simultaneous "biological" and tenure clocks is one primary obstacle related to the structure of academic careers (De Welde and Laursen 2011; Martin 1994; Williams and Ceci 2012). Beyond biological (sex) conflicts are gendered conflicts. Because women academics are more likely than men to be responsible for home and childcare responsibilities, institutional expectations during pre-tenure years place them under even greater strain. Our study respondents identified difficult decisions about when, or whether, to have children. Susan, a 25-year-old white PhD business student at a research university, noted perceived differences:

> There were very few tenure-track women in the department, and all the full professors are men. Many times they refer to experiences that they had in graduate school or going up for tenure and make it seem as though their way could work for everyone, and thus we should all manage graduate school and tenure track in the same way that they did. But whenever they offer this unsolicited advice, all I can think about is how different it is for them than it is for me because I am a woman with a young child and they are men—many [of whom] have stay-at-home wives. I don't feel like they really understand that I have a different experience because of my different situation and that the commonly held beliefs about what is appropriate for my stage along my career path just doesn't work the same for me.

Then, she described the conflicting, unsolicited advice given "half jokingly" by one of the women faculty:

> She'll say things like "Have children during graduate school because that's the best time to do it, it only gets worse after that." Other times she'll say, "Don't have kids, because it makes it too hard" (referencing her struggles in the tenure process), but then she'll make a comment . . . [like] "If you do have them, have them during graduate school."

Susan's narrative highlights how gendered ideologies manifest in the supposedly neutral policies and practices of the academic career pathway. As Acker (1998) argues, the ideological "gender substructure" of organizations "helps to recreate [*sic*] the gendered divide between paid work and unpaid family reproductive work, consigning the latter, and women, to a subordinated and devalued position as practice and belief put the demands of the work organization first over the demands of the rest of life" (107). Though well-meaning, Susan's professors reinforced the inequitable realities many academic women face.

The "advice" Susan received could, in a different context, close options for women who want to delay having children because they think a faculty career is off limits because they did not have children "early enough." Such discourse influences women's career pathways and, ultimately, the potential pool of applicants for faculty jobs. Even women who *follow* the "early babies" formula (Mason and Goulden 2002) can experience negative results. Heather, a white 31-year-old social sciences PhD student, had this to say:

> Generally speaking, I did not feel disadvantaged by being a woman in an academic environment until I decided, during the second year of a PhD program, to have a baby. Since then, I have had the distinct sense that I am considered a different "type" of student than my peers. Faculty and other graduate students almost always begin conversations with me by asking about my child instead of my research. And I feel I am taken far less seriously than other students around me, perhaps because I am necessarily less a part of the life of the department than I was before becoming a mother.

In some cases, well-meaning faculty advisors steer women out of academia because they subscribe to the outdated notion that the roles of faculty member and mother do not mix.

Stereotypes about mothers as less committed to and less effective at their jobs as a result of the demands of family responsibilities persist (Wallace 2008). Yet, does the job performance of women faculty suffer because of their family responsibilities? Are they less committed? In chapter 5, "The Influence of Departmental Culture on Academic Parents' Pro-Work Behaviors," Kmec, Foo, and Wharton investigate mothers' and fathers' pro-work behaviors (PWB) such as their engagement at work and their perceived level of work intensity. By investigating how departmental culture impacts the relationship of parenthood and pro-work behaviors, they bring an important new analytical component to this discussion. Drawing on survey research with faculty in STEM (science, technology, engineering, and mathematics) and non-STEM fields at a large research university, they discover surprising patterns. For example, mothers performed higher levels of PWB regardless of departmental culture, perhaps, as the authors suggest, because of women's internalized expectations that they are held to a higher standard. Further, their research suggests that academic mothers effectively use multitasking strategies at home and at work to meet responsibilities. Although women faculty reported spending more time on caregiving and housework than academic fathers, they reported greater pro-work behaviors too.

Kmec et al.'s findings challenge faulty assumptions about the mis-match of mothering and faculty work. Thus, their findings have important consequences for the "pipeline" of women faculty and for their institutions.

In our research we encountered Emily, a white 39-year-old PhD student in education who had been fortunate to work with a major professor supportive of her family circumstances. However, when her mentor took a position abroad, Emily had to navigate a tricky situation when the new members on her dissertation committee offered her uninvited career advice. She explained:

> I told them that I was expecting my second child in about seven months and wondered how this might affect my progress. The female junior faculty member took the lead of the conversation and began talking about her role as a mother. As [she] continued talking, she began pointing out my writing challenges and emphasized my intentions to seek a career outside of academia. The pivotal point of this meeting was when she advised that a PhD was not necessary for my career aspirations and an EdS may suffice and better suit my family circumstances. Her words still echo in my head as she then advised me to consider dropping out of the program to be a mom.

Another example of an academic mother being treated unjustly because of her "mother" status is Tiffany, a white 37-year-old senior lecturer at a university. She reported, "I worked hard in education to achieve my present position and even delayed my pregnancy." But, by singling her out, her manager created a negative work atmosphere:

> When I found out I was pregnant I was worried to tell my male manager. After I told him, I was often subject to comments he made about me in staff meetings about me "being an older mother," or "she's off on maternity leave so don't bother asking her," etc. I consider myself to be an assertive and intelligent woman but could only summon the courage to laugh it off

partly due to shock and partly because I didn't want any stress affecting my unborn child. After going on maternity leave I was informed by a colleague that my male manager had been making negative comments about me being away such as I'm too busy playing "mommies and daddies." I am dreading returning to work because I feel this is a precursor to further comments and being penalized by this manager for having the gall to go on maternity leave. I also feel my colleagues, men and women, enjoyed seeing me squirm, feeling that I'd got my "just desserts" because I'd left them in the lurch so to speak, because no financial cover was brought in when I went on maternity leave so they resentfully covered my work.

Tiffany's narrative highlights the need for understanding the impact of women's multiple social locations on their workplace experiences. Further, it suggests the importance of effectively trained managers, supportive organizational cultures, and policies that facilitate maternity (and paternity) leave—including attention to how leaves may impact colleagues. Without such support, Tiffany and her colleagues faced unnecessary, stressful challenges. The hostilities generated in such a context may remain after she returns to work, potentially damaging workplace relations and reducing departmental effectiveness. (This underscores our point in Part Five, "Tools for Changing the Academy": Responsive and progressive policies are insufficient without cultural shifts that enable people to use them without penalties.) Otherwise, people may see them as ways to accommodate *women,* not *parents.* Judy, a 40-year-old associate professor of sociology at a comprehensive university, illustrates the importance of the congruence between the cultural and structural level of gendered organizations. Her department is "family focused," but not in a modern way. She reported:

I work for a university that is steeped deeply in 1950s expectations of traditional family. By that I mean faculty members are assumed to be traditional creatures: straight White men with wives at home taking care of children. This might seem too harsh a statement, but the university (and the faculty) consider people not as professional individuals, but as narrowly defined family members. In addition to not being valued as intellectual capital, or as professional individuals working for an educational institution, it is also assumed/desired that we are all (happily) coupled. I am a straight single child-free woman. . . . My campus and the community surrounding it values couplehood and family over and above everything and anything else, and although the campus claims to practice "family friendly" policies, only a traditionally defined nuclear family can really benefit from such policies, and even then not very much.

Judy's narrative reminds us to think broadly about "family" (e.g., child-free, single, partnered) and to be wary of cultural assumptions about separate spheres that pervade U.S. society. That is, the notion that women's "natural" expressive tendencies should be expressed at home (the private sphere) and men's "natural" instrumental traits should be applied at work (the public sphere). Such ideas create significant tensions for women academics whose careers are based, presumably, on a gender-neutral structure with gender-neutral processes for evaluation and advancement.

Beyond the subjective experiences of marginalization and stereotyping that many women experience as a result of their choices to mother or not mother (and when), work-family balance concerns weigh heavily on women academics. Some scholars (Young and Wright 2001) suggest that work-family conflicts negatively impact women's rates of promotion and tenure. However, in chapter 6, "Assimilating to the Norm: Academic Women's Experiences With Work-Family Policies," Solomon shows the profound impact organizational policies and cultures can have on academic women's success and stress levels by analyzing the experiences of women faculty at two universities—each with different work-family policies. Solomon illustrates that policies help some academic mothers in the short term, workplace cultures that expect faculty to prioritize work over everything else require academic mothers to strategize vigilantly to meet their responsibilities, particularly in settings with inadequate policies. Thus, to reverse the historical tendency to construct faculty roles in ways that favor men and men's lives, we need to identify how policies and cultural norms may work against women (Bird 2011).

Most of the literature on work-family balance addresses childcare challenges for parents. Yet, as the U.S. population ages, eldercare-related concerns will become a significant family-work issue. In chapter 7, "The Eldercare Crisis and Implications for Women Faculty," Leibnitz and Morrison focus on elder caregiving needs within academia. They find that women faculty express greater stress about eldercare issues than men faculty or other women employees. Yet, many feel unable to discuss their concerns. Additionally, their research confirms the negative impact of caregiving on social networks: As women academics provide eldercare, their support networks diminish, and when needed most.

Part Two highlights the stressors that carework exerts on women academics and how inadequate workplace supports exacerbate work-family tensions. Work and family are no longer separate, and cultural stereotypes about "uncommitted" women faculty on the "mommy track" are outdated and problematic. To attract and retain the best employees, and to support faculty lives and productivity, academic workplaces require policies and practices for twenty-first-century families.

The case study for Part Two features a graduate student who attempts to navigate gendered interpersonal dynamics and cultural contexts regarding issues of pregnancy, childcare, and competing professional obligations. Her narrative illustrates persistent notions of the "ideal worker" (Acker 1990) and the need for supportive academic workplaces.

References

Acker, Joan. 1990. "Hierarchies, Jobs, Bodies: A Theory of Gendered Organizations." *Gender and Society* 4(2):139–158.

———. 1998. "The Future of 'Gender and Organizations': Connections and Boundaries." *Gender, Work and Organization* 5(4):195–206.

Bird, Sharon R. 2011. "Unsettling Universities' Incongruous, Gendered Bureaucratic Structures: A Case-Study Approach." *Gender, Work and Organization* 18(2):202–230.

De Welde, Kristine, and Sandra Laursen. 2011. "The Glass Obstacle Course: Formal and Informal Barriers for STEM Ph.D. Students." *International Journal of Gender, Science and Technology* 3(3):547–570.

Martin, Joanne. 1994. "The Organization of Exclusion: Institutionalization of Sex Inequality, Gendered Faculty Jobs and Gendered Knowledge in Organizational Theory and Research." *Organization* 1(2):401–431.

Mason, Mary A., and Marc Goulden. 2002. "Do Babies Matter? The Effect of Family Formation on the Lifelong Careers of Academic Men and Women." *Academe* 88(6):21–27.

———. 2004. "Marriage and Baby Blues: Redefining Gender Equity in the Academy." *The ANNALS of the American Academy of Political and Social Science* 596:86–103.

Stone, Pamela. 2007. *Opting Out? Why Women Really Quit Careers and Head Home.* Berkeley: University of California Press.

van Anders, Sari M. 2004. "Why the Academic Pipeline Leaks: Fewer Men Than Women Perceive Barriers to Becoming Professors." *Sex Roles* 51:511–521.

Wallace, Jean E. 2008. "Parenthood and Commitment to the Legal Profession: Are Mothers Less Committed Than Fathers?" *Journal of Family Economic Issues* 29(3):478–495.

Ward, Kelly, and Lisa Wolf-Wendel. 2004. "Fear Factor: How Safe Is It to Make Time for Family?" *Academe* 90(6):16–19.

Williams, Joan C. 2005. "The Glass Ceiling and the Maternal Wall in Academia." *New Directions for Higher Education* 2005(130):91–105.

———. 2010. *Reshaping the Work-Family Debate: Why Men and Class Matter.* Cambridge, MA: Harvard University Press.

Williams, Wendy M., and Stephen J. Ceci. 2012. "When Scientists Choose Mother-hood." *American Scientist* 100(2):138–145.

Winslow-Bowe, Sarah E., and Jerry A. Jacobs. 2011. "Faculty Workloads." In *Gender and Higher Education*, edited by B. Bank, 335–343. Baltimore: Johns Hopkins University Press.

Young, Diane S., and Ednita M. Wright. 2001. "Mothers Making Tenure." *Journal of Social Work Education* 37(3):555–568.

Academic Women's Voices on Family Resources and Policy Issues

The following narratives illustrate the concerns and challenges facing women as they strive to meet the intense demands of their family lives and academic careers. The women in these narratives are diverse: single and partnered, straight and gay, women of color and white women. Yet, their narratives echo the common need for effectively trained administrators, supportive work-place cultures, and institutional policies and practices that facilitate family life in all of its manifestations.

I'm now 14 weeks pregnant and too scared to tell my department chair and the dean. By becoming a mom, I fear to be sentenced to academic death.

—Elizabeth, a 30-year-old Hispanic assistant professor of
cultural studies

Probably the most difficult was transitioning from corporate to academia. I moved across country with a small child for my new position at the university, and within a month or two, it was clear that it would be a challenge from the standpoint of pay, not having family or friends around, and having such a steep learning curve at the same time I'm juggling elder care issues for my mom (back East) and child care issues for my young son in my new city. It was a challenge to find child care in the evenings or early mornings when my deans needed me to moderate an evening panel or come in for an early morning breakfast or represent the school at conferences. I was able to piece together care for him. I had to move my mom across country to her home state so relatives could help me because I could no longer afford to fly back and forth to check on her myself.

—Rory, a 48-year-old African American professor of media

I have a same-sex partner and we had a child a few years ago. Because we do not have hard benefits for domestic partners (DPs) at my institution, we are not able to be on the same insurance plan as a family. We are finally able to join the Rec Center as a family. I am working individually and with others to have DP benefits institutionalized at the university. The administration and HR are supportive but must fight a state-mandated insurance plan. I feel that things could be moving along faster, though.

—Rosanna, a 43-year-old white associate professor of social work

I have had a nearly lifelong situation dealing with profound health issues that my father has suffered: a "benign" brain tumor that did not kill him, but left him

impaired in many ways. He was more than one person could handle. He was more than my mother could handle. Because of these things, "eldercare" was longer term for me than for many others, which also delayed my start into academia. Eldercare has some significant differences from that of child care. [First, the] duration is unknown. Children age at predictable rates. They grow up. Elderly parents can stay in need for unknown periods of time. [Second, it] tends to be harder for others to care for parents. [Third, geography] is crucial. Children follow their parents. But, when parents grow old and/or become disabled, moving them can be, in effect, ruining their lives. They need to stay around what they know—locations, friends, doctors. This means that the children of parents in need are geographically limited—and this is, of course, the evil of academia. When someone is single and needs to live in a certain location the message is simple—you don't belong in this job. Your priorities are wrong. Still, I believed the party line given by virtually all universities and the U.S. government that we need talent and creativity in engineering, and specifically a U.S.-born female presence.

When I was hired, I made it plain that I needed to stay close to my parents, and that the situation was something of a wild card. I sacrificed being married to care for them and have a career, and so that should have been enough to say that I was committed to both. The department head that hired me told me that there was precedent for faculty to travel each weekend, but that he had a "good" reason—he was separated from his wife and wanted to see his kids. Presumably my reason was not good. . . . It was certainly true that my career path was affected—and I'm sure I told a few people that it was, even as just a means to ask for them to consider that despite my not taking a traditional path, I might just have tremendous potential. But, academia is such that talent is not valued. Rather, being in the club of top schools is valued. While up for tenure, I had to drop everything and get my father placed in a vet's home. He, all of a sudden, could no longer live at home. After three years there, he died. But, my mother is now in need of care. And so, I still live an almost completely underground form of existence, telling virtually no one how I live. Because, I do what I must do now in order to fulfill what I believe to be dual commitments to my mother and my career. There is not one soul in this department who understands, and most are openly hostile—and, really worse, doing all sorts of things behind the scenes. Most of this is on record. This is not only not the life I expected, it is simply not remotely what it should be. Years from now people will look back on this kind of situation and it will be viewed the way we view the way women and children were treated in the industrial revolution—as indecent.

—Michelle, a white 51-year-old associate professor of engineering at a
research institution

5

THE INFLUENCE OF DEPARTMENTAL CULTURE ON ACADEMIC PARENTS' PRO-WORK BEHAVIORS

Julie A. Kmec, Shanyuan Foo, and Amy S. Wharton

As in other professions, the demands for success in academia are high; productivity is the norm, especially in the early-career stages when faculty may be considering parenthood. Thus, many academics find themselves balancing the most demanding times of their career with parenthood. Moreover, expectations of the "ideal" academic and the "ideal" mother are at odds. The "ideal" academic, like the "ideal" worker, works long hours, is dedicated to her or his job, and has limited family interruptions (see Acker 1990; Williams 2001). The "ideal" mother spends most of her time and energy caring for children, even if she is a professional (Hays 1996; Ridgeway and Correll 2004). By contrast, "ideal" academics and "ideal" fathers are a better fit. An "ideal" father monetarily supports his family and fatherhood signals traits the academy rewards, including stability and dedication (Hodges and Budig 2010; Jacobs and Gerson 2001; Williams 2002). These different, gendered views of parenthood and job compatibility impact the experiences of academic parents—particularly mothers (see Gatta and Roos 2004; Mason and Goulden 2002, 2004a, 2004b; Rosser 2004; Ward and Wolf-Wendel 2004; Wolf-Wendel and Ward 2006). In fact, parenthood is a greater barrier to the professoriate for women than men (van Anders 2004). Academic institutions can be arduous places for parents, especially academic mothers, who report greater responsibility for family care than academic fathers (Halpern 2008; Jacobs and Gerson 2004; Jacobs and Winslow 2004; Suitor, Mercom, and Feld 2001).

Despite challenges for academic parents, few have investigated whether mothers and fathers engage in different levels of pro-work behaviors (PWB) that are consistent with those of "ideal" academic workers, including work intensity, engagement, and avoidance of negative home-to-job spillover. Few have studied how departmental culture—particularly the extent to which departments foster research productivity—shapes the parenthood-PWB relationship. Faculty members' departments exert a strong influence on their experiences (Callister 2006) and departmental culture affects faculty PWB.

This chapter offers empirical evidence on the effect of academic cultures of productivity on PWB and how they shape the parenthood-PWB relationship. We explore these questions: Do reports of PWB differ for academic mothers and fathers? To what extent does perceived departmental culture of productivity affect mothers' and fathers' PWB?

Cultural beliefs about mothers, especially the notion that mothering should take priority over everything else, shape the perception of employed mothers as less competent, less committed, and less work oriented than employed fathers and childless workers (Blair-Loy 2003; Correll, Benard, and Paik 2007; Hays 1996; Wallace 2008). Little research explores differences in PWB among academic mothers and fathers. That which does focuses on research productivity (i.e., publications), with some studies finding a negative relationship between children and women's research productivity (Hargens, McCann, and Reskin 1978; Sonnert and Holton 1995), others no relationship (Cole and Zuckerman 1987; Fox 1991), and some a positive relationship between parental status and research productivity (Bellas and Toutkoushian 1999).

King (2008) examined the levels of work involvement, commitment, flexibility, and interest in advancement of faculty who are parents and compared these self-reports to senior faculty members' perceptions. Academics who are mothers had lower expectations for advancement than fathers, but mothers' and fathers' work attitudes were similar. However, mothers expressed higher levels of work involvement than fathers and a greater intent to stay with their university. By contrast, senior faculty colleagues perceived mothers as having less work involvement and flexibility for advancement than fathers; they even rated the women's levels of work involvement lower than the mothers themselves did. This study reveals a disjuncture between the actual and perceived work attitudes of mothers and fathers in academe. Like King (2008), we are interested in the attitudes of faculty who are parents toward their work, but extend her study by considering how departmental culture conditions these views.

Additionally, family and household responsibilities demand time and effort and can deplete one's energy. Workers with high family demands may use their energy reserves at home, leaving less for PWB (Kmec and Gorman 2010). For these reasons, workers with children—especially young children—and those who are married or partnered may limit their PWB.

Workplace social context shapes faculty members' perceptions and behaviors. For most faculty, the proximal work group is the department; departmental leaders play key roles in evaluating and mentoring faculty, and departmental processes shape resource allocation, work assignments, and advancement. Along with formal policies and procedures, departments develop informal practices and schemas for interpreting their own and others' experiences. Research on academic and nonacademic workplaces shows that workplace cultures influence and mediate a range of work outcomes (Bilimoria et al. 2006; Callister 2006; Castilla and Benard 2010; Turco 2010).

At research universities, institutional missions and policies reinforce research productivity as a core value, although these expectations may be unevenly implemented and embraced by departments. We focus on departments' "productivity culture," which creates the conditions for faculty research productivity; this is a culture where opportunities, expectations, and rewards for research are high and, in theory, meritocratically distributed.

Many studies show how organizational context can blunt or magnify ascriptive biases in workplaces (Baron, Hannan, Hsu, and Kocak 2007; Castilla and Benard 2010; Ridgeway 2009). Contexts associated with a reduction in ascriptive biases include those in which organizationally based identities, such as researcher, are foregrounded to a greater degree than nonwork identities, such as parent. This suggests that parents in departments with a strong productivity culture should be more likely to engage in PWB. In addition, we suspect that the emphasis on research in a department with a strong productivity culture may override prescriptive stereotypical notions of intense motherhood (Hays 1996), making it "acceptable" for mothers to engage in levels of PWB as high as or higher than those of fathers.

We draw on data from the Faculty Caregiving and Workplace Culture survey administered in 2011 at a large, multicampus research-intensive (R1) public university in the Pacific Northwest. We drew respondents from a complete list of tenure-line faculty derived from yearly performance reviews. To recruit faculty, we e-mailed them a letter and confidential URL linked to the study. Of the 840 eligible tenure-line faculty, 308 participated (36% response rate). Forty-three percent of respondents were women; of these 27% were assistant professors, 34% were associate professors, and 39% were full professors. The typical respondent was employed by the university for roughly 13 years. Because our focus was on parents, we dropped the 130 nonparents from our analyses. Table 5.1 includes a description of variables in the model. The outcomes we measured replicated those of national studies (see Kmec 2011).

Our scale measuring department culture of productivity captures faculty perceptions of department support, expectations for research productivity, and whether a department equitably rewards faculty for doing research. Scale items measure the extent to which respondents agreed with the following statements about their department:

- My department leadership (e.g., department chair/head, senior faculty) actively nominate faculty for awards, honors, and growth opportunities.
- I feel appreciated and valued by departmental colleagues for my research work.
- I get constructive feedback, guidance, and suggestions from my departmental colleagues.
- Faculty voluntarily expend energy to achieve departmental goals and objectives.
- I have a high degree of say in how much time I spend fulfilling each of my faculty roles.
- The department provides me with resources to conduct my research.
- I am encouraged to establish a schedule that allows me to protect periods of uninterrupted time to conduct research.
- The climate in my department contributes to high faculty research productivity.
- It is a goal of my department to reward all faculty members equitably.
- When money is available, my department has systematic and fair mechanisms for monetarily rewarding faculty research achievements.
- I have enough time to conduct research projects.
- Has systematic and fair mechanisms for non-monetary recognition of faculty research achievements.
- Faculty raises are determined by performance.

Table 5.2 shows that mothers worked at higher levels of intensity, had less irritability at work resulting from stress at home, and did not reduce needed sleep because of their home commitments compared with fathers. Mothers and fathers were similar in terms of their work engagement, the amount of effort family responsibilities took from work, and the extent to which they worked hard as a result of family needs. These comparisons reveal that mothers and fathers were quite similar in work and home activities. The only difference in individual-level attributes between mothers and fathers was in experience (fathers had more) and

TABLE 5.1.

Description and Coding of Pro-Work Behaviors and Their Predictors

	Description	Coding/Range
Pro-work behaviors		
Work intensity	Work very intensively/ are very busy trying to get things done.	1 = never; 2 = rarely; 3 = some of the time; 4 = most of the time; 5 = all of the time
Engagement	So involved in work that forget about everything else, even the time.	
Home *does not* reduce job effort	Personal/family responsibilities reduced effort could devote to job in past year (reverse coded).	1 = daily; 2 = few times per week; 3 = few times per month; 4 = few times per semester; 5 = never
Home stress *does not* lead to work irritability	Home stress led to irritability at work in past year (reverse coded).	1 = never; 2 = few times per semester; 3 = few times per month; 4 = few times per week; 5 = daily
Home *does not* reduce sleep needed for job	Home activities prevented sleep needed to do job well (reverse coded).	
Independent variables		
Departmental culture of productivity scale	13-item scale (α = 0.92) (see text for items)	1 = strongly agree; 2 = disagree; 3 = agree; 4 = strongly agree
Work experience	Years in current academic institute.	1.56–41.53
Tenured	Current academic rank. We combined full and associate because statistical tests suggested they had a similar impact on PWB.	1 = full or associate professor; 0 = assistant professor

(Continues)

TABLE 5.1.
Description and Coding of Pro-Work Behaviors and Their Predictors
(Continued)

	Description	Coding/Range
Weekly research hours	During the typical semester, weekly hours spent doing research.	0 = none; 1 = 1–3 hours; 2 = 4–6 hours; 3 = 7–9 hours; 4 = 10–12 hours; 5 = 13–15 hours; 6 = 16–18 hours; 7 = 19–21 hours; 8 = 22–24 hours; 9 = 25–27 hours; 10 = 28–30 hours; 11 = 30+ hours
Weekly teaching hours	During the typical semester, weekly hours spent on teaching.	
Weekly mentoring/ advising hours	During the typical semester, weekly hours spent on mentoring/advising.	
Weekly service hours	During the typical semester, weekly hours spent on service.	
Weekly hours on chores	During the typical semester, weekly hours spent doing household chores.	0 = none; 1 = 1–3 hours; 2 = 4–6 hours; 3 = 7–9 hours; 4 = 10–12 hours; 5 = 13–15 hours; 6 = 16–18 hours; 7 = 19–21 hours; 8 = 22–24 hours; 9 = 25–27 hours; 10 = 28–30 hours; 11 = 30+ hours
Weekly hours on child and eldercare	During the typical semester, weekly hours spent doing child and eldercare.	
Number of children	Number of children in household for at least half of year.	1–4
Preschool-aged child	Denotes a preschool-aged child in home.	1 = preschool-aged child(ren) in home; 0 = not
Marital status	Current marital status.	1 = married or cohabiting; 0 = not

self-reported weekly service (fathers reported more).[1] Mothers reported more hours dedicated to caregiving than fathers and were more likely to be married or cohabiting. In short, mothers and fathers spent equivalent time on research, teaching, mentoring, and chores and were employed in similar ranks.

TABLE 5.2.
Mean Scores on Variables for Mothers and Fathers

	Mothers	Fathers
Work intensity	4.36* (0.07)	4.19 (0.06)
Work engagement	3.28 (0.09)	3.13 (0.09)
Home *does not* reduce work effort[a]	2.96 (0.15)	2.76 (0.14)
Home *does not* reduce needed sleep[a]	3.61* (0.15)	3.31 (0.13)
Home stress *does not* lead to work irritability[a]	4.30** (0.09)	3.95 (0.11)
Department culture of productivity scale	2.41 (0.12)	2.55 (0.11)
Work experience	10.86* (0.71)	12.64 (1.01)
Tenured	0.76 (0.05)	0.77 (0.04)
Weekly research hours	6.04 (0.34)	6.76 (0.35)
Weekly teaching hours	5.39 (0.29)	4.99 (0.26)
Weekly mentoring hours	2.90 (0.21)	3.01 (0.20)
Weekly service hours	2.87* (0.24)	3.37 (0.28)
Weekly chore hours	3.58 (0.26)	3.31 (0.22)
Weekly caregiving hours	5.97*** (0.55)	4.37 (0.40)
Number of children	1.82 (0.12)	1.80 (0.09)
Preschool-aged children	0.30 (0.05)	0.26 (0.04)
Married/cohabiting	0.92*** (0.03)	0.78 (0.04)
n	71	106

Note. Mean difference was significant at *$p < .10$, **$p < .05$, and ***$p < .01$.
[a] Outcomes were coded so higher values indicate more positive PWB.

TABLE 5.3.

Results From Ordered Logistic Regression Predicting Pro-Work Behaviors

	Work Intensity	Engagement	Home does not reduce job effort	Home does not reduce needed sleep	Home does not lead to work irritability
Mother (reference category: father)	0.86** (0.36)	0.56* (0.33)	0.66** (0.32)	0.76** (0.32)	0.88*** (0.34)
Department culture of productivity scale	0.09 (0.41)	−0.35 (0.38)	0.05 (0.36)	−0.02 (0.38)	−0.31 (0.37)
Work experience	0.01 (0.02)	−0.03 (0.02)	0.02 (0.02)	0.006 (0.02)	0.02 (0.02)
Tenured (reference category: untenured)	−0.20 (0.47)	−0.40 (0.45)	−0.34 (0.42)	−0.13 (0.41)	−0.22 (0.47)
Weekly research hours	0.09 (0.05)	0.06 (0.05)	0.04 (0.05)	0.09** (0.05)	0.04 (0.05)
Weekly teaching hours	0.07 (0.07)	0.13ᵗ (0.07)	−0.02 (0.06)	−0.05 (0.06)	−0.03 (0.07)
Weekly mentoring hours	0.20** (0.10)	0.27*** (0.09)	0.17* (0.09)	−0.14* (0.09)	−0.23** (0.09)
Weekly service hours	0.002 (0.08)	0.18** (0.08)	−0.03 (0.07)	−0.01 (0.07)	0.05 (0.07)
Weekly chore hours	−0.04 (0.09)	0.0003 (0.08)	−0.14* (0.08)	−0.18** (0.09)	−0.13** (0.08)
Weekly caregiving hours	−0.09 (0.06)	−0.07 (0.05)	−0.14*** (0.07)	−0.07 (0.05)	−0.07 (0.05)
Number of children	0.40* (0.22)	−0.13 (0.22)	0.25 (0.21)	0.26 (0.19)	0.06 (0.21)
Preschool-aged child	0.23 (0.46)	−0.56 (0.45)	−0.56 (0.41)	−0.74* (0.40)	0.20 (0.44)
Married/partnered (reference category: all other)	−0.20 (0.60)	0.14 (0.55)	−0.60 (0.52)	−0.43 (0.51)	0.26 (0.56)
Intercept 1	−0.79	−3.27	−2.09	−3.62	−4.99
Intercept 2	2.97	−1.62	−0.69	−2.29	−4.40

(Continues)

TABLE 5.3.
Results From Ordered Logistic Regression Predicting Pro-Work Behaviors
(Continued)

	Work Intensity	Engagement	Home does not reduce job effort	Home does not reduce needed sleep	Home does not lead to work irritability
Intercept 3	—	1.44	−0.06	−1.07	−2.66
Intercept 4	—	4.05	2.00	0.32	−0.56
Log likelihood	−126.45	−172.20	−226.96	−226.81	−170.55
n	163	164	157	156	152

*$p < .10$; **$p < .05$; ***$p < .01$.

As Table 5.3 shows, 297 answer to our first question—Do mothers and fathers report different PWB?—is straightforward. Compared with fathers, mothers worked more intensely and were more engaged in their jobs, reported that personal/family life reduced their job effort significantly *less* than fathers, reported being deprived of sleep *less* frequently, and were significantly *less* likely to report being irritable at work because of stress at home. The mother-father differences in job engagement and reduced job effort are only marginally significant ($p < .10$), but a clear pattern emerges. Consistent with King's (2008), findings, academic mothers in our sample did *not* avoid PWB.

Regarding our second question, we saw little influence of a culture of productivity on PWB; the influence of perceived culture of productivity did not affect mothers' and father's PWB differently. Nor was the relationship between motherhood and PWB different across departmental cultures. In short, our findings are consistent with those of reports of PWB in a national sample (see Kmec 2011). Although mothers reported less time doing research than childless men and less time doing service than men and women without children, mothers spent similar amounts of time teaching and mentoring as nonparents. However, multivariate analyses (not shown) found mothers' PWB to be similar to that of nonparents of both genders.

The effects of some family-level control variables are noteworthy. For both mothers and fathers the number of children in the home increased work intensity, possibly because having children limits the time available to work outside of "normal" business hours, forcing faculty parents to engage in intense work when they are in the office, but did not impact other PWB outcomes. Having preschool-aged children reduced mothers' and fathers' ability to get the sleep they needed to complete their jobs but had no influence on other PWB.

Despite concerns over motherhood penalties at work (see Correll et al. 2007) and cultural understandings that motherhood and academic work are incompatible (King 2008), mothers in our sample reported higher levels of PWB than fathers, *although* mothers reported more hours toward caregiving and similar hours toward most academic and household tasks than fathers (see Table 5.2). This suggests that the mothers may transfer the skills used at home (i.e., task prioritizing, multitasking, efficiency, and creativity) to benefit their jobs. Successful academics must juggle service, research, teaching, and mentoring; mothers may gain this "experience" from their role as primary caretakers in the home more than fathers.

Another explanation for mothers' higher levels of PWB than fathers' is that women perceive that their employers hold them to a higher work standard than men (see Gorman and Kmec 2007). If mothers overestimate performance expectations, they may overcompensate by exerting greater PWB to avoid sanction (see Kmec 2011). Selection processes may be at work as well. Analyzing data on doctoral recipients, Mason and Goulden (2002) found that women in all disciplines who achieved tenure were more likely to be single and less likely to have children compared to men. This suggests that successful academic mothers may be different from men counterparts. That is, our sample, like any sample of academic mothers, reflects women who have "figured out" how to navigate work and family.

Our findings reveal that mothers' and fathers' perceptions of departmental culture of productivity neither directly nor indirectly influence PWB. Mothers are no more or less likely to report engaging in PWB in departments they perceive as having a strong culture of productivity. We caution that our culture measure may be too broad to clearly differentiate departments with high versus low productivity expectations. Alternatively, other aspects of department culture, such as a culture that protects faculty from bullying, may be important moderators and mediators of PWB.

Research Implications for Disrupting the Culture of Silence

Societal assumptions about mothers' supposedly low PWB negatively impact women who intend to advance in academia (see Mason and Goulden 2002). Our study debunks the notion that academic mothers are disengaged from work and are too overwhelmed with interruptions from home to be fully engaged and productive at work. Academic administrators should pay close attention to our findings. One way they can begin disrupting the culture of silence is to recognize that academic workplaces are gendered organizations. To dismantle outdated ideas of the "ideal worker," we must recognize (and reward) the PWB of mothers and affirm that having children is not the end of women's academic productive careers.

We encourage researchers to study academic mothers' higher levels of PWB and to investigate the levels and consequences of bias against mothers in light of the data. Furthermore, scholars should consider what shapes faculty perceptions of academic culture. Do different departmental attributes, such as demographics, shape mothers' and fathers' perceptions? Scholars working with multi-institutional samples should consider the role institutional factors (e.g., family leave policies) play in the perceptions of departmental culture and PWB, as well as explore parent versus nonparent differences in perceived culture and PWB to better understand how having children affects work behaviors.

Our findings have important implications. At every level on the tenure track, men's earnings are higher than women's (*The Chronicle of Higher Education* 2010). The institute we analyzed is no different; in analyses not shown, we found that at every rank, men outearned women. The academy stands to gain from understanding why mothers' PWB do not translate into better pay or recognition. As women earn more degrees than men and the combination of work and family becomes increasingly more socially acceptable, it is possible that more women academics will be mothers. The academy will lose this important resource if the gulf between what mothers do and the rewards for their work does not close.

Note

1. Women professors perform more service work than men, especially at the associate level (see Misra, Lundquist, Holmes, and Agiomavritis 2011; chapter 4 of this volume). We have identified two possible reasons why our findings are inconsistent with those of others. First, there may be survey response bias. Men who chose to respond to a voluntary Internet survey sponsored by a university NSF-ADVANCE grant may be a select group that engages in more service than men who did not respond. Second, these men may feel compelled to inflate their service to give the impression of "pulling their weight" on a survey supported by an NSF-ADVANCE grant and fielded by a woman faculty member.

References

Acker, Joan. 1990. "Hierarchies, Jobs, and Bodies: A Theory of Gendered Organizations." *Gender and Society* 4:139–158.

Baron, James N., Michael T. Hannan, Greta Hsu, and Özgecan Kocak. 2007. "In the Company of Women: Gender Inequality and the Logic of Bureaucracy in Start-up Firms." *Work and Occupations* 34:35–66.

Bellas, Marcia L., and Robert K. Toutkoushian. 1999. "Faculty Time Allocations and Research Productivity: Gender, Race, and Family Effects." *The Review of Higher Education* 22:367–390.

Bilimoria, Diana, Susan R. Perry, Xianfeng Liang, Eleanor Palo Stoller, Patricia Higgins, and Cyrus Taylor. 2006. "How Do Female and Male Faculty Members Construct Job Satisfaction? The Role of Perceived Institutional Leadership and Mentoring and Their Mediating Processes." *Journal of Technology Transfer* 31:355–365.

Blair-Loy, Mary. 2003. *Competing Devotions: Career and Family Among Women Executives.* Cambridge, MA: Harvard University Press.

Callister, Ronda R. 2006. "The Impact of Gender and Department Climate on Job Satisfaction and Intentions to Quit for Faculty in Science and Engineering Fields." *Journal of Technology Transfer* 31:367–375.

Castilla, Emilio J., and Stephen Benard. 2010. "The Culture of Meritocracy in Organizations." *Administrative Science Quarterly* 55:543–576.

The Chronicle of Higher Education. 2010. "Average Faculty Salaries for Men and Women by Rank, 2009–10." http://chronicle.com/article/Chart-Average-Faculty/64999/.

Cole, Jonathan R., and Harriet Zuckerman. 1987. "Marriage, Motherhood, and Research Performance in Science." *Scientific American* 256:119–125.

Correll, Shelly, Stephen Benard, and In Paik. 2007. "Getting a Job: Is There a Motherhood Penalty?" *American Journal of Sociology* 112:1297–1338.

Fox, Mary F. 1991. "Gender, Environmental Milieu, and Productivity in Science." In *The Outer Circle: Women in the Scientific Community,* edited by Harriet Zuckerman, Jonathan R. Cole, and John T. Bruer, 188–204. New Haven, CT: Yale University Press.

Gatta, Mary L., and Patricia L. Roos. 2004. "Balancing Without a Net in Academia: Integrating Family and Work Lives." *Equality, Diversity and Inclusion: An International Journal* 23:124–142.

Gorman, Elizabeth, and Julie A. Kmec. 2007. "We (Have to) Try Harder: Gender and Workers' Assessment of Required Work Effort in Britain and the United States." *Gender and Society* 21:828–856.

Halpern, Diane F. 2008. "Nurturing Careers in Psychology: Combining Work and Family." *Educational Psychology Review* 20:57–64.

Hargens, Lowell L., James C. McCann, and Barbara F. Reskin. 1978. "Productivity and Reproductivity: Fertility and Professional Achievement Among Research Scientists." *Social Forces* 57:154–163.

Hays, Sharon. 1996. *Cultural Contradictions of Motherhood.* New Haven, CT: Yale University Press.

Hodges, Melissa J., and Michelle J. Budig. 2010. "Who Gets the Daddy Bonus? Organizational Hegemonic Masculinity and the Impact of Fatherhood on Earnings." *Gender and Society* 24:717–745.

Jacobs, Jerry A., and Kathleen Gerson. 2001. "Overworked Individuals or Overworked Families?" *Work and Occupations* 28:40–63.

———. 2004. *The Time Divide: Work, Family and Gender Inequality.* Cambridge, MA: Harvard University Press.

Jacobs, Jerry A., and Sarah E. Winslow. 2004. "The Academic Life Course, Time Pressures and Gender Inequality." *Community, Work, and Family* 7:143–161.

King, Eden B. 2008. "The Effect of Bias on the Advancement of Working Mothers: Disentangling Legitimate Concerns From Inaccurate Stereotypes as Predictors of Advancement in Academe." *Human Relations* 61:1677–1711.

Kmec, Julie A. 2011. "Are Motherhood Penalties and Fatherhood Bonuses Warranted? Comparing Pro-Work Behaviors and Dimensions of Mothers, Fathers, and Non-Parents." *Social Science Research* 40:444–459.

Kmec, Julie A., and Elizabeth Gorman. 2010. "Gender and Discretionary Work Effort: Evidence From the United States and Britain." *Work and Occupations* 37:3–36.

Mason, Mary Ann, and Marc Goulden. 2002. "Do Babies Matter? The Effect of Family Formation on the Lifelong Careers of Academic Men and Women." *Academe*. http://www.jstor.org/stable/40252436.

———. 2004a. "Do Babies Matter (Part II)? Closing the Baby Gap." *Academe*. http://www.jstor.org/stable/40252699.

———. 2004b. "Marriage and Baby Blues: Redefining Gender Equity in the Academy." *The Annals of the American Academy of Political and Social Science* 596: 86–103.

Misra, Joya, Jennifer Hickes Lundquist, Elissa Holmes, and Stephanie Agiomavritis. 2011. "The Ivory Ceiling of Service Work." *Academe*. http://www.aaup.org/article/ivory-ceiling-service-work.

Ridgeway, Cecelia L. 2009. "Before We Know It: How Gender Shapes Social Relations." *Gender and Society* 23:145–160.

Ridgeway, Cecelia L., and Shelly J. Correll. 2004. "Motherhood as a Status Characteristic." *Journal of Social Issues* 60:683–700.

Rosser, Sue V. 2004. *The Science Glass Ceiling: Academic Women Scientists and the Struggle to Succeed*. New York: Routledge.

Sonnert, Gerhard, and Gerald J. Holton. 1995. *Gender Differences in Science Careers: The Project Access Study*. New Brunswick, NJ: Rutgers University Press.

Suitor, Jill A., D. Mercom, and I. S. Feld. 2001. "Gender, Household Labor, and Scholarly Productivity Among University Professors." *Gender Issues* 19:50–67.

Turco, Catherine J. 2010. "Cultural Foundations of Tokenism: Evidence From the Leveraged Buyout Industry." *American Sociological Review* 75:894–913.

van Anders, Sari M. 2004. "Why the Academic Pipeline Leaks: Fewer Men Than Women Perceive Barriers to Becoming Professors." *Sex Roles* 51:511–521.

Wallace, Joan E. 2008. "Parenthood and Commitment to the Legal Profession: Are Mothers Less Committed Than Fathers?" *Journal of Family Economic Issues* 29:478–495.

Ward, Kelly, and Lisa E. Wolf-Wendel. 2004. "Academic Motherhood: Managing Complex Roles in Research Universities." *The Review of Higher Education* 27:233–257.

Williams, Joan. 2001. *Unbending Gender: Why Work and Family Conflict and What to Do About It*. Oxford: Oxford University Press.

———. 2002. " 'It's Snowing Down South': How to Help Mothers and Avoid Recycling the Sameness/Difference Debate." *Columbia Law Review* 102:812–833.

Wolf-Wendel, Lisa E., and Kelly Ward. 2006. "Academic Life and Motherhood: Variations by Institutional Type." *Higher Education* 2006:487–521.

6

ASSIMILATING TO THE NORM

Academic Women's Experiences With Work-Family Policies

Catherine Richards Solomon

Scholars increasingly pay attention to how women professors manage work and personal responsibilities. Although research documents the difficulty that women academics have in juggling their various duties (Mason and Goulden 2004; Solomon 2011; Ward and Wolf-Wendel 2004; Young and Wright 2001) as well as their underrepresentation among full-time faculty (August 2006), there is little research on how these women use university work-family policies in their work-life management. The reason for this lack of research could be related to the fact that few universities have such policies (American Association of University Professors 2001; Sullivan, Hollenshead, and Smith 2004) and for those that do the policies vary widely. Most universities offer six weeks of paid maternity leave for mothers following the birth of a child (Center for the Education of Women [CEW] 2007; Sullivan et al. 2004). Some allow women to take a full semester of paid leave and extend their tenure clock for a year following the birth or adoption of a baby (CEW 2007; Sullivan et al. 2004; UC Faculty Family Friendly Edge 2003). Few schools offer more than these measures.

Scholars know little about how professors experience these policies or whether they help with work-and-family obligations. We know that faculty benefit from formal policies immediately following the birth or adoption of a child in that they feel less stressed about getting tenure and meeting work demands (Drago and Colbeck 2003). However, few faculty use the policies (Drago, Crouter, Wardell, and Willits 2001; Sullivan et al. 2004) and some fear negative repercussions if they do (Drago et al. 2001). Effective work-family policies may help academe move toward gender equity by increasing the number of women among tenured faculty (Mason, Goulden, and Frasch 2009). Mason et al. (2009) showed that women graduate students opt out of working at research universities, like those in the present study, because they perceive such schools as hostile to having a family and an academic career.

As part of a larger project, I interviewed 19 untenured tenure-track assistant professors and one associate professor—all women—to explore how they experienced work-family policies and what strategies they used to manage work-family responsibilities. I used website faculty lists from two large research universities in a Northeastern state (pseudonyms are used herein), each with different work-family policies, to randomly select participants, whom I then recruited through e-mail. Hilltop University (HU) offers a one-year tenure extension policy and a semester off from teaching with full pay for the birth or adoption of a child. HU has on-site childcare, but at the time of the interviews, it had a yearlong waiting list. Valley University (VU) does not have a tenure extension policy but allows six weeks of paid maternity leave, three days of paid paternity leave, and up to seven months of unpaid leave to faculty for childcare purposes. VU does not offer childcare but allows employees to deduct pre-tax money from their salaries toward dependent care, under a state plan. I focus on parental leave policies most salient to respondents because they considered this policy most helpful in managing professional and family responsibilities.

Of the participants, 12 had children, one was pregnant with her first child, and seven did not have children. Two were African American (both had children) and two were Asian American (neither had children); the remaining participants were white. Women's ages ranged from 28 to 49 years, and they worked in diverse disciplines including physical sciences, humanities, social sciences, fine arts, education, and business. Five were single and 15 had partners and/or were married. Of the 12 participants with children, who ranged from infants to teenagers, the number of children was one to four. I asked women about their career trajectories, work responsibilities, tenure expectations, family and living situations, daily schedules, university leave policies, and childcare arrangements. Following Bogdan and Biklen's (1998) analytical approach, I looked for patterns in the data, grouping those into codes representing key categories, and then grouped codes into larger themes that illustrated dimensions of experiences. I gave participants pseudonyms.

Participants expressed preference for progressive policies for work-life management (e.g., policies to provide sufficient paid time off to have or adopt a child). For example, Amy (at VU) said, "[I] definitely [would like] paid maternity and paternity leave. Twelve weeks, I think, would be wonderful." However, women's experiences differed depending on their workplace. This is not surprising given the fact that universities offered different leaves. Women at VU found its policy inadequate because it did not mesh with their teaching schedules. Jamie said:

> But the maternity leave [policy] doesn't really work for faculty because they give you six weeks so it's just the normal regular policy, right? It's six weeks off and [because] I'm due in August, I'm not going to be able to take six weeks off [because] then it would be eight weeks into the semester [when I'd come back] and then resume professional responsibilities. Like [I'm going to tell my students], "Hi, students, how ya doing? Having fun for eight weeks while I wasn't here?" [Laughs]

HU participants commented positively about its policies. Kendra said, "I think they're really generous policies. I think that they are ways to encourage women to really balance professional obligations and family, to be able to have a professional career but have a family too." Mothers felt that HU's parental leave policy created desirable situations for their children and lessened this stressful life transition because they had a semester to spend time with their babies. For example, Sydney described how important it was to take a semester off after adopting her daughter:

> [Parental leave for that semester was] absolutely crucial. Because then that semester I was the full-time caregiver and [my daughter] was not in daycare at all. So that meant the first year after we got her from the orphanage, she didn't have to be in group daycare at all. She was with either myself, my partner, or for a while my partner's mother was living in an addition on the back of the house. She was with an adult all the time, one of the family. So it was crucial for me.

Most mothers wanted to see their universities' childcare situation improve. Jill (HU) said:

> Our contracts always start the week before classes start officially. [Hilltop] daycare doesn't start until the week classes start. So how about [changing] that? My chair can legitimately schedule an all-day retreat for me the week before classes start and what do I do with my kids? [Chuckles] [My husband] will take a day off [from] work. We can manage it but it's those sorts of [things], it would be nice if the daycare were open.

Though HU had a childcare center, it had limited spaces and hours of operation that might not work with professors' schedules. This restricted women's flexibility with work arrangements and their ability to take advantage of the center.

As with women's experiences taking parental leave, many felt standards of professionalism and motherhood constrained their ability to press for change. Calista (VU) said:

Even when I have a family conflict, I won't voice [it] if I can try to figure a way around it. We have faculty retreats sometimes and they're all day on Friday. Sometimes if [my son] is off from school, I won't volunteer that information and say that I can't make it. I'll try to find some daycare.

[CRS: Why is that?]

I don't know. I guess I'm feeling that as a professional and as a mother that's my responsibility and I need to work it out.

Overall, when work-family policies fit faculty schedules and allow for a semester off, they help parents manage work-life responsibilities in the short term. Participants felt universities providing childcare on-site benefited them, but needed improvement.

Given that parental leave policies provide for short-term leave, department culture was important for day-to-day management of family-work responsibilities. Many participants felt their colleagues accepted their non-work responsibilities. Sydney (HU) shared:

I have a very supportive department. It's very supportive of its junior faculty especially.

[CRS: So, can you give me some examples of how they're supportive?]

Oh, they let me show off the pictures, they let me complain about being jet-lagged. They just don't make any snide comments about "Well if you'd been around." I never have heard any comments like that. If I have to miss a meeting, I don't [get] rebuked for it. People ask about how my partner or my daughter are doing.

Colleagues with children and working spouses provided vital support for participants. They experienced a great deal of acceptance, more than participants whose colleagues did not have children or had stay-at-home spouses. This acceptance made work-life management easier. Roxanne (HU) said:

People were very sweet and very supportive and a number of my colleagues brought us food once the baby was born and brought presents for [my son] and came to see him. I think it makes a difference having two women faculty who have just had children. Also the majority of the senior male faculty members have wives that are professionals. . . . Most of them are double PhD kinds of families and I think that makes an incredible difference because there is an awareness of how hard it is and that both sides have to compromise.

However, some departmental cultures hampered women's work-life balance by having high expectations for "face time" (i.e., having to be in their offices daily for a certain number of hours), which eroded their ability to use the flexibility inherent in academic careers. Participants explained this expectation as necessary for departmental collegiality but said it seemed unfair. Annemarie (HU) shared:

There's a kind of culture of people hanging around and doing [discipline] and it's noted [who is around]. Not in a hostile way, there's no big repercussions to not [being around] but it's noted if you're not around, if you're never going out or you're never coming to anybody else's seminars, if you're never having conversations with people outside of your own classes about [your discipline], if you're never in your office, that kind of thing. It's noted [that] you're just a bad departmental citizen. It's hard to figure [out] what the repercussions of that exactly would be except if you're like the person who most of us are, it's not nice to be judged that way. [Laughs]

Though Annemarie said no "repercussions" exist for minimal involvement in department life, faculty believed they would be viewed negatively—a repercussion. Participants cared about how colleagues perceived them because they valued collegial relationships and because collegiality could influence tenure decisions.

Participants with young children at HU mentioned that scheduling of work-related activities (e.g., meetings) and classes was an issue; however, participants at VU did not report any issues with such scheduling. Basically, HU's participants felt unable to participate fully in university life when activities occurred in the evenings. Additionally, they expressed irritation when departments only scheduled meetings or activities for late afternoon hours, when they needed to be with their children after school. Angela said:

It's hard especially in the [department] because of the demands on your time outside of the set hours that classes are going on. There are things like lectures that you're kind of expected to go to once a week. Every Wednesday night there's a lecture. They usually start at 7:00, I think. I've made it to two maybe.

In addition, when classes were scheduled sometimes resulted in conflicts for mothers at HU. Jill shared:

> This is always a battle [over when people teach] because there's always a hierarchy in departments. I understand why Tuesday and Thursday at 10:00 is prime time and senior faculty should get it because they're senior faculty. On the other hand, I'm the only person in the department with young kids who doesn't have a spouse at home. There are two others but they have spouses at home taking care of the kids. So I'm the only one trying to juggle. . . . I do get frustrated that it has to simply be a matter of seniority.

Some mothers said they had colleagues who acted hostile toward them because of their personal responsibilities, leaving participants feeling silenced when it came to discussing their families. In general, participants said that their profession supported a culture that expected "disembodied workers" (Acker 1990) because it did not accommodate personal responsibilities. Disembodied workers exhibit a sole commitment to their professional lives and either have no responsibilities outside of work or have someone else (i.e., spouse/partner) to tend to them (Acker 1990). Participants felt an expectation to have someone at home caring for their families and found this assumption offensive because (a) it negated their own sense of priorities, which they thought they should determine, and (b) living up to professional standards proved almost impossible because all women's spouses worked full-time. They felt frustrated by a standard that they could never meet or meet only with great difficulty (e.g., a live-in nanny). For example, Jill talked about needing a shift in attitudes to make academe more accommodating of professors' personal responsibilities:

> [I like the] semester off, which is nice for new mothers and new fathers. . . . But then once they come back, [the university should] not think of us as just minds who are capable of sitting on various committees but that we're people with certain constraints in our personal lives and those with children are just gonna be different than those without children and to try to accommodate that. . . . I guess [I'd like] more acceptance. Being a parent with young kids with no one at home taking care of them feels like . . . what it must have felt like to just be a woman at all in the academy [during the] 60s or 70s. Where you're not seen or you're seen as different but the difference . . . [the university] doesn't want to accommodate [it] so it's only how much you can

assimilate to the norm. That's what it feels like. . . . When I said to [my colleague], "I think I'm saying too much about the kids and I need to be quiet," she said, "Yes, you should, [because] people are saying things." And this is a very supportive department, this is a department that really is supportive compared to [others]. I have friends in other departments who are not supportive. [Laughs] The fact that my just vocalizing concerns and frustrations about the imbalance is read as being negative, [as] that kind of feminist bitchiness [is frustrating].

Jill's comment about how faculty felt they had to "assimilate to the norm" shows how policies and colleagues' perceived support remain insufficient to change work-family challenges. This underscores how structural and cultural factors shape professors' work-life management.

To compensate for insufficient policies and to navigate the chilly climate of academe (Hall and Sandler 1984) and its maternal wall (Williams 2004), participants employed individual strategies to meet professional responsibilities and personal priorities. Many wanted to make efficient decisions about work activities so they could spend time with their families. Jenny (HU) said:

I am just very attentive to what I'm doing. I make lists of what I need to accomplish that day and I do that in both settings. At home I've got a list and at work I have a list. Like tonight I will know exactly what I am doing tomorrow, barring anything unusual happening, of course, any emergencies. But I know at what point in the day I'm doing different things. I'm extremely organized and structured, both for the work setting and for the home setting, and I try not to mix the two very much.

But being efficient (and thus productive) proved difficult for others. Jill had to negotiate with her husband for weekend work time:

The time that I have [to do] my work is incredibly circumscribed and I have to be immensely disciplined. I have colleagues who say, "Well I've got this conference paper to write but I'll spend all weekend writing it." That's nice, how nice. [Laughs] I'm really lucky if I get [time on the weekend]. . . . Like tomorrow (Saturday) I worked out with my husband to let me go into the office for a few hours. I might get three hours tomorrow afternoon in the office and I'll get tomorrow morning. . . . I generally get up around 4:00 a.m. . . . But everything is a trade-off, Cathy, I think that's the [thing], whereas people without children or people [who] have somebody else taking care of the children, they can really focus on their work whereas for me it's always: If I do this, then I'm not getting that done. If I talk to you, then I'm not doing my class prep. If I play with the kids, then I'm not doing as much on class prep. But if I do class prep, then I'm not playing with my kids. That algorithm is constant and it takes a lot of mental energy to parse that constantly.

Part of working efficiently meant limiting workplace socializing. Participants mentioned doing little socializing with colleagues or students to take maximum advantage of the hours in the office. Women with children, especially those working toward tenure, noticed a change. Meg (HU) reported:

> I actually had a social life at work, and post-kid, all of that . . . is cut back to almost nothing. . . . When I first came back after having the baby that seemed like a big deal to me, that I was really worried, like just not enough interaction with them outside of seeing them in a department meeting or scheduled kind of event. But I got over that kind of quickly [laughs] because I figured that all the time that I'm in my office doing stuff and not going out to lunch is time I can go home and read *Clifford* or play with blocks. And now, I don't go through that [so] what should I be doing? It's more I wish I had more time to do both things.

Being organized and efficient were key components of success that helped them focus intensely on getting necessary work done. Having family responsibilities made it hard for participants because they had to manage their lives efficiently, without room for error, to meet workplace productivity standards. This was stressful and exhausting. For example, Jill described her afternoon routine with her children: "We [arrive] here [at home]—it's on the dot—my life is run like a German train. [We laugh] Five minutes to five we're home and all I want to do is collapse. [Laughs]." Jamie felt similarly:

> The only time my life functions well is when I work every single day . . . when I can't be sick, I can't take a break. I can't go, "Oh, this weekend we're going away for the weekend." When I do those things it really throws my schedule off and screws things up.

[CRS: What do you mean by "functions well?"]

> The only time I'm not stressed out. [It's] the only time I eat good healthy meals, the only time I have time to exercise, the only time I'm not scrambling for something for my class, whether it's to get something handed back that I've said I would get graded, or whether it's getting a lecture together, which I don't want to be doing an hour before class. So, the only time I'm not rushing or giving up something like healthy eating or exercising is when I am very disciplined and I work every single day . . . like, no downtime. I have to be like this [snaps fingers] all the time. It never used to bother me . . . [but now] I'm kind of burned out.

Several participants mentioned wanting to time children's births for summer months and/or after tenure. Summer births help participants avoid arranging for midsemester leave and were especially important for VU faculty, with only six weeks' paid leave. However, even HU professors used this strategy. Amy reported, "Ideally I'll plan it so that I have a baby in May or June and I'm home June, July, August and then come back in the fall. So, hopefully I'm not going to have to deal with any of it [negotiating for leave]." Participants viewed summer as a "legitimate" time to stop work because summers were unpaid and they might not teach or have service responsibilities. Having babies during the summer allowed participants to fulfill demands for personal and work responsibilities (in the short term).

Having children after tenure may be a preferable time among professors (Mason and Goulden 2004; Ward and Wolf-Wendel 2004; Young and Wright 2001). However, many participants realized that this timing might not be possible because of biological constraints. Still, participants viewed having children pre-tenure with trepidation. Elizabeth (HU) said:

> If I wait till 2006, I'll be 34, say I get tenure and then we start trying, I'll be 34. I might be able to get pregnant right away and have one child but we want two. [Laughs] So then, you can really hear the biological clock ticking and it's like, "Gosh should I just do it now?" . . . I feel very conflicted because I don't want to wait too long and blow my chances either. Because a lot of women think, "Oh, well, after 35, I'll still be able to get pregnant." And indeed that could be true, but your fertility is decreasing and so then it's just like, "Oh, should I just go ahead and do it?" . . . I'm just going to have to see. If I can get the book manuscript done and have it sent off to someone . . . and start the process [of trying to get pregnant], then I'll be on schedule, but until I know I'm on schedule, then I'll just be worried about adding something else to my plate.

Like creating individual leave plans and working in incredibly disciplined and efficient ways, planning children for the summer and/or after tenure is an individual solution to universities' insufficient leave policies and to occupational pressures. Participants fill in the gaps of occupational structures. Reliance on these strategies reflects the internalization of occupational and societal expectations that professionals will solve their own conflicts between work and family life without relying on employers (Blair-Loy 2003; Cooper 2002; Hertz 1986; Hochschild 1997).

Universities' work-family policies provide short-term help to women academics; but the structure of academia is not conducive to work-life balance. Participants expressed a desire for leave policies that fit the academic calendar. Commonly offered six-week maternity leave, like VU's, did not work for participants because if they had a baby during or near the start of the semester they would have to miss part of the semester or take unpaid leave, financially untenable for many (Sullivan et al. 2004). My participants are untenured, so they may be hesitant to push for policy change that some may view as uncollegial or "bitchy." Besides policies, intense career demands, explicitly or implicitly hostile department climates, and unsupportive colleagues hampered participants' work-life management. Because policies only partially aided their efforts to negotiate home and work, my participants employed the follow-ing strategies to "assimilate to the norm": (a) being as efficient as possible at home and work, (b) minimizing workplace socializing (possibly affecting professional networks, opportunities, and tenure decisions), and (c) timing children's births for post-tenure years or the summer. These strategies repre-sent practical choices but serve to maintain an image of the productive scholar whose personal responsibilities do not (and should not) interfere with work.

Academe remains a gendered institution where women academics face occupational expectations to be "disembodied workers" (Acker 1990) married to spouses who are responsible for home and family. Thus, it's no surprise that women academics continue to leave academe or that women graduate students choose teaching-oriented colleges or careers outside of aca-deme where they think managing work and personal responsibilities will be easier (De Welde and Laursen 2011; Mason et al. 2009). To stem the flow of talented women out of academe, the academy needs to address these cultural and structural factors.

References

Acker, Joan. 1990. "Hierarchies, Jobs, and Bodies: A Theory of Gendered Organiza-tions." *Gender and Society* 4:139–158.

American Association of University Professors (AAUP). 2001. "Statement of Princi-ples on Family Responsibilities and Academic Work." *Academe* 87:55–61.

August, Louise. 2006. "It Isn't Over: The Continuing Under-representation of Women Faculty." Center for the Education of Women. http://www.cew.umich.edu/sites/default/files/femrep06_0.pdf.

Blair-Loy, Mary. 2003. *Competing Devotions: Career and Family Among Women Exec-utives.* Cambridge, MA: Harvard University Press.

Bogdan, Robert, and Sari Knopp Biklen. 1998. *Qualitative Research for Education: An Introduction to Theory and Method.* 3rd ed. Boston: Allyn & Bacon.

Cooper, Marianne. 2002. "Being the 'Go-To Guy': Fatherhood, Masculinity, and the Organization of Work in Silicon Valley." In *Families at Work,* edited by N. Gerstel, D. Clawson, and R. Zussman, 5–31. Nashville, TN: Vanderbilt University Press.

De Welde, Kristine, and Sandra Laursen. 2011. "The Glass Obstacle Course: Formal and Informal Barriers for STEM Ph.D. Students." *International Journal of Gender, Science and Technology* 3:547–570.

Drago, Robert, and Carol Colbeck. 2003. "Final Report From The Mapping Project: Exploring the Terrain of U.S. Colleges and Universities for Faculty and Families for the Alfred P. Sloan Foundation." The Pennsylvania State University, University Park, December 31.

Drago, Robert, Ann C. Crouter, Mark Wardell, and Billie S. Willits. 2001. "Final Report to the Alfred P. Sloan Foundation for the Faculty and Families Project." The Pennsylvania State University, University Park, March 14.

Hall, Roberta M., and Bernice Resnick Sandler. 1984. *Out of the Classroom: A Chilly Campus Climate for Women?* Washington, DC: American Association of Colleges.

Hertz, Rosanna. 1986. *More Equal Than Others: Women and Men in Dual-Career Marriages.* Berkeley: University of California Press.

Hochschild, Arlie Russell. 1997. *The Time Bind: When Work Becomes Home and Home Becomes Work.* New York: Metropolitan Books.

Mason, Mary Ann, and Marc Goulden. 2004. "Do Babies Matter (Part II)? Closing the Baby Gap." *Academe* 90(6):10–15.

Mason, Mary Ann, Marc Goulden, and Karie Frasch. 2009. "Why Graduate Students Reject the Fast Track." *Academe* 95(1):11–16.

Solomon, Catherine R. 2011. "'Sacrificing at the Altar of Tenure': Assistant Professors' Work/Life Management." *The Social Science Journal* 48(2):335–344.

Sullivan, Beth, Carol Hollenshead, and Gilia Smith. 2004. "Developing and Implementing Work-Family Policies for Faculty." *Academe* 90(6):24–27.

UC Faculty Family Friendly Edge. 2003. "The UC Faculty Family Friendly Edge: Turning a Problem Into UC's Competitive Advantage." http://ucfamilyedge. berkeley.edu/index.html.

Ward, Kelly, and Lisa Wolf-Wendel. 2004. "Academic Motherhood: Managing Complex Roles in Research Universities." *The Review of Higher Education* 27:233–257.

Williams, Joan. 2004. "Hitting the Maternal Wall." *Academe* 90(6):16–20.

Young, Diane S., and Ednita M. Wright. 2001. "Mothers Making Tenure." *Journal of Social Work Education* 37:555–568.

7

THE ELDERCARE CRISIS
AND IMPLICATIONS FOR
WOMEN FACULTY

Gretal Leibnitz and Briana Keafer Morrison

Elder caregiving will equal, if not surpass, childcare as the primary work-family issue of the twenty-first century (Smith 2004). Given the "greedy" nature of academic work and caregiving (Ward and Wolf-Wendel 2004), women faculty have significant work-life challenges. Challenges may be more acute for isolated, underrepresented women academics in historically men-dominated STEM (science, technology, engineering, and mathematics) disciplines (e.g., Hill, Corbett, and St. Rose 2010; Hopkins and Potter 1999; Sandler 1986). Unable to balance care and work reasonably, women academics with care responsibilities may leave academia (e.g., Mason and Goulden 2004). Even as work-life balance for women faculty in STEM fields has received significant attention, the impact of eldercare has not been explored (Canizares and Shaywitz 2010).

Eldercare in the United States

The composite profile of the average eldercare provider is a 46-year-old married woman employed full-time and providing care for her widowed mother who does not live with her (American Federation of State, County and Municipal Employees [AFSCME] 2005). Given that biology (e.g., gestation, delivery, lactation) does not dictate who cares for elders, one would think greater gender equity would exist regarding such care (Smith 2004). Similar to childcare, although men are involved, women provide the majority of care, regardless of their employment status (MetLife Mature Market Institute 2011; Smith 2004).

Although one in four households currently provides eldercare, most people believe the number of families impacted is far less (Burke 2003). Such ignorance compounds the challenges for eldercare providers. Consequently, people most able to assist employees (i.e., supervisors) are unaware of eldercare resources. The effects of eldercare for employers include increased employee absenteeism, "presenteeism" (i.e., the employee is present but distracted by eldercare concerns), productivity losses, and replacement costs for the increasing number of caregivers who quit to care for their elders (Burke 2003; MetLife 2011).

Eldercare and the Academy

Despite decades of research on work-life concerns, role theory and role-strain development, and sophisticated understandings of time- and strain-based work-family conflict, "it appears that providing care for elders has been overlooked by most work/family conflict studies as a major family responsibility" (Lee, Foos, and Clow 2010, 19). We identified only one published article that wed "eldercare" and "higher education" (and its variants) in the title (Joslin 1994). A few articles explored eldercare as one aspect of family caregiving responsibilities in the context of academic work life (e.g., Civian, Costikyan, and Nuter 2009; Elliot 2008).

Eldercare is of particular concern in academe because, unlike marriage/partnership and, arguably, children, women do not choose to become daughters. Given that elderly people are living longer, it is likely that an academic daughter will have living parents. Further, given that baby boomers may have just one child, academic daughters may have sole responsibility for eldercare (Rogerson and Kim 2005). The isolation academic women face, particularly those in STEM fields, will be reflected in eldercare support structures. This exacerbates the negative impact of providing eldercare: undermining institutional progress and efforts to recruit, retain, and advance academic women.

Eldercare Impact Study

In 2009, we investigated how eldercare responsibilities affected faculty and staff at a research-intensive university in the northwest United States. We used a comprehensive 49-question survey and seven in-depth interviews based on the "Model Eldercare Survey" referenced in AFSCME (n.d.).

The survey included a combination of dichotomous, multiple-choice, and open-ended survey questions covering issues such as care responsibilities, the nature and extent of caregiving responsibilities, characteristics of the elder for whom care was provided, the impact of caregiving responsibilities, and awareness of resources. The survey was available online to all university employees (approximately 4,000) for five weeks and advertised through electronic media. We sent targeted advertising to women and faculty in STEM fields delineated as historically men dominated.

Additionally, we conducted seven semistructured in-depth interviews from a convenience sample of respondents. Of 313 respondents, 25% were faculty (non-tenure-track and tenure-track), 39% were administrative professionals, and 36% were classified staff. Two hundred seventy respondents had either provided eldercare or expected to provide eldercare in the next five years. Consistent with previous research profiling eldercare providers, most were women (84%), between the ages of 46 and 65 (73%), with full-time positions (89%). More than two-thirds (72%) had been at the university longer than five years. More than one-fourth (28%) provided concurrent care for dependent children. Unless indicated otherwise, our analysis here focuses on faculty responses.

Gendered Nature of Caregiving

Although the survey was open to all faculty, 71% of respondents were women. This disproportionate response suggests that academic women are more likely to care for elderly family members than their men counterparts (Joslin 1994). Some faculty expressed that eldercare continues to be the responsibility of women. For example, one woman commented, "Eldercare falls disproportionately on the shoulders of middle-aged women and affects our health and professional well-being a great deal." Likewise, an interviewee stated, "And when you're female, in a family, you are the emotional tender in the family."

Counter to research suggesting that women academics are more likely to be "sandwiched" in providing care for children and elders (Wolfinger, Mason, and Goulden 2008), more faculty men than women reported concurrent care of elders and children (33% and 19%, respectively). This most likely results from women academics forgoing having children compared to men (p = .012).

Increased Stress

Stressors of eldercare impact faculty in a variety of ways. Because many elders were unable to afford care and necessary supplies, the financial burden fell to caregivers. Eighty-six percent of women faculty reported struggling financially because of eldercare responsibilities. After exhausting paid leave, some needed to take leave without pay, creating additional financial difficulties. Judy, a faculty administrator, said, "It's kind of hard to have to go into leave without pay and it affects how much money you have." Likewise, Nancy, a full professor, reported, "Financially, I think it can be very difficult. Health care is incredibly expensive. This kind of care that we're doing—dressing somebody, showering them, cooking for them, shopping for them—that's not covered by Medicare." The frequency of these comments confirms that financial concerns add to caregiver stress.

The stress of eldercare took a toll on the physical and emotional health of faculty. One woman academic (whose husband was an academic) related, "It's affected our health. My husband's on medical leave because of the stress of doing this and doing his job." Among women academics, 79% indicated that eldercare responsibilities negatively impacted their relationships with friends and families, and 97% said eldercare led to emotional strain.

Need for Emotional and Informational Resources

Necessary support for caregivers is difficult to find in the academy. Many women indicated that a university support system would allow them to focus on their work. Judy, a single faculty member, spoke of how childcare and eldercare affect faculty productivity:

> I think there is some kind of university responsibility for sharing information about childcare because, of course, lots of people have children, and how well that childcare works impacts their ability to work productively or not. Maybe something like a parallel of that for people who are connected with eldercare might be nice.

Other faculty echoed the need for open conversation about eldercare issues. For example, a new assistant professor remarked that providing emotional and informational support is essential to faculty health:

> You know, I'd like a lot more proactive support available out there in the open about people dealing with these issues. It should be available as a support service for people as a wellness activity that's encouraged because people do need that support. . . . I'm in an area where I don't have colleagues doing the same thing I am, so it'd be nice to talk with other people who are going through the same things.

In addition to support groups and informational sessions, women indicated the potential usefulness of institutional resources such as flextime (46%), the ability to use sick leave for family care (43%), and a compressed work-week (31%).

Overall, 91% of faculty respondents, men and women, revealed being unaware of university policies and procedures for eldercare. Women were more likely to be aware of these, but of those, most described the policies and resources as unsupportive (67%). Because information about benefits or leave options was not readily available, faculty were forced to engage in the time-consuming task of locating information about eldercare resources while coping with emotionally challenging situations. For example, one respondent commented: "I don't know what [an] employee assistance program is. Information about state and social services is difficult to negotiate and find when circumstances suddenly land in your lap with [an] elder/developmentally disabled person [who] needs help and you are the only decision maker." In short, women academics are in situations with few available eldercare resources, available resources may not provide needed support, and identifying information about existing resources is time-consuming and difficult.

A Culture of Silence Around Eldercare Issues

Much of the difficulty in finding information about eldercare resources stems from the culture of silence about eldercare issues. More than half (54%) of faculty, men and women, indicated reticence in discussing eldercare concerns with their department chairs. Women faculty (15%), in particular, found their chairs to be unsupportive of their need to manage eldercare and faculty responsibilities. One said her chair was "not understanding of others' personal difficulties." In explaining why they had not spoken with their department chairs about eldercare responsibilities, women academics gave responses such as "I think it is inappropriate and would be viewed as inappropriate" and "Personal business has no place in the workplace." In short, faculty feared that, in gendered workplaces modeled on outdated frameworks that attempt to separate work and family (Acker 1990), their eldercare responsibilities might be misunderstood or counted against them during evaluations. Nancy, a full professor and longtime university employee, noted:

> Many, many people in this community are taking care of elderly parents. When you are in that situation, you hear other people say, "Oh yeah, I'm doing that too," but before you didn't really hear about it. It's not talked about as a public problem, so that's one struggle—just kind of getting that recognition that you're under this kind of stress.

Similarly, Diana, a middle-aged academic, explained the lack of response from her colleagues when she learned that she needed to care for her terminally ill father:

I think the academic workplace, that you just don't . . . you're not supposed to have emotions in the workplace and you're not supposed to have lives in the workplace. . . . Anything for faculty, if you make it a stress management issue they're not going to go to it because it's a sign of weakness. You don't want to be seen as weak because you get dumped in the faculty world. It's not very safe on college campuses for faculty to attend to those sorts of things—it's really sad. It should be available as a support service for people as a wellness activity that's encouraged because people do need that support.

Our results indicate that faculty are concerned that merely *talking* about eldercare with colleagues might give the appearance of "weakness," impacting their careers negatively.

Preliminary evidence indicates that the "culture of silence" is particularly strong in men-dominated STEM fields, increasing caregiver stress and the need for university-based support. Faculty in STEM fields were significantly less likely to know university policies about eldercare ($p = .044$). In addition, STEM faculty reported significantly less frequently that their department was supportive of their eldercare responsibilities ($p = .067$). Women academics were three times less likely to report departmental support than faculty men.

Faced with increased financial, emotional, physical, and other eldercare-related stresses, women academics, especially in STEM fields, are overwhelmed. To alleviate such stress, 21% of these women indicated that they were seriously considering leaving their universities. Additionally, 9% reported that they were considering another position at the university, with intent to reduce impact associated with eldercare and presumably provide greater flexibility. Women in STEM fields were five times more likely than men in these fields to consider leaving their jobs or finding another position because of the lack of support for their eldercare responsibilities. These numbers do not capture individuals who may have already left the institution as a result of eldercare stress. Thus, the individual costs (i.e., loss of employment and income) as well as the institutional costs (i.e., losing and needing to replace employees) may well be greater than reported here. Replacement costs for even one faculty member are significant. Further, given the emphasis in academia to be inclusive of the best and brightest diverse workforce, action must be taken to ensure support for those engaged in or anticipating caring for elders. Even for the most educated workers, gender-related biases and attitudes change slowly (Greenhaus and Parasuraman 1999).

Action Steps

Corporate practices provide promising models for academia. Klein and Shum (2004) conclude that companies are responding to eldercare needs by conducting needs assessments; bolstering policies; providing programs for employees and supervisors; and offering support, information, and enhanced benefits. Academic institutions can and should respond similarly. Benchmarking faculty work-life satisfaction, inclusive of eldercare issues, will provide information on the extent and nature of needs, as well as help determine budget allocation for support programs. Engagement in consistent faculty work-life needs assessment will help institutions be proactive and responsive in addressing dependent care needs.

Work-family policies that include support for the broad range of caregiving activities relevant to faculty lives are critical to faculty productivity, job satisfaction, and retention. Workplace policies that support eldercare also will foster women's advancement in academia (see Anderson, Morgan, and Wilson 2002). Further, results from our study support having adequate work-family–friendly policies and actively promoting and disseminating information about them. Benefits for eldercare providers will be critical for sustaining women faculty's involvement in academia. Consistent education for faculty and administration about eldercare resources would be beneficial, and low-cost support groups or seminars by local experts could effectively and inexpensively help caregivers meet their needs.

With nationwide implementation of the Family Medical Leave Act, academia has some benefits similar to those of corporate institutions. However, they vary across institution types and by location. National legislation, coupled with public awareness about eldercare issues, could positively impact the consistency and availability of supportive benefits for eldercare providers. Further, using institution-specific work-life satisfaction assessments to determine benefits will ensure that the benefits provided are needed to maximize workforce involvement. Just as it has been found that proactive academic work settings are more likely to have on-site childcare centers than large corporations (Raabe 1997), so might the academy lead the corporate sector in modeling the positive impact of providing eldercare services for employees.

Conclusion

The changing workforce demographics illustrate the critical emerging need for eldercare-provider support in U.S. academic workplaces (Bond, Thompson, Galinsky, and Prottas 2002; Klein and Shum 2004). Arguably, just as childcare benefits have served academe in broadening and deepening the quality of the workforce, so will eldercare benefits strengthen the academy by maximizing the engagement and contributions of faculty. By learning from corporate models and applying information gained from institution-specific assessments, higher education will maximize the involvement of diverse faculty in a future where eldercare will have significant implications for all, especially women faculty.

References

Acker, Joan. 1990. "Hierarchies, Jobs, and Bodies: A Theory of Gendered Organizations." *Gender and Society* 4:139–158.

American Federation of State, County and Municipal Employees. (n.d.). *Eldercare: An AFSCME Guide for Families and Unions.* http://www.afscme.org/news/publications/life-management-and-health/eldercare-an-afscme-guide-for-families-and-unions.

———. 2005. *Fact Sheets.* http://www.afscme.org/members/education-and-trainings/education-resources/fact-sheets/eldercare.

Anderson, Donna M., Betsy L. Morgan, and Jennifer B. Wilson. 2002. "Perceptions of Family-Friendly Policies: University Versus Corporate Employees." *Journal of Family and Economic Issues* 23(1):73–90.

Bond, James T., Cindy Thompson, Ellen Galinsky, and David Prottas. 2002. *Highlights of the National Study of the Changing Workforce Executive Summary.* New York: Families and Work Institute.

Burke, Mary E. 2003. *SHRM 2003 Eldercare Survey.* http://www.shrm.org/Research/Articles/Articles/Documents/SHRM%20Eldercare%20Survey.pdf.

Canizares, Claude R., and Sally E. Shaywitz. 2010. *Gender Differences at Critical Transitions in the Careers of Science, Engineering, and Mathematics Faculty.* Washington, DC: National Academies Press.

Civian, Jan, Nancy Costikyan, and Julie Nuter. 2009. "Work-Life Best Practices: Prioritizing in Demanding Fiscal Times." Paper presented at the College and University Work/Family Association (CUWFA) Conference, Providence, RI, April. http://dev.cupahr.org/eastern2009/program.asp#top.

Elliot, Marta. 2008. "Gender Difference in Causes of Work and Family Strain Among Academic Faculty." *Journal of Human Behavior in Social Environment* 17(1):157–173.

Greenhaus, Jeffery H., and Saroj Parasuraman. 1999. "Research on Work, Family, and Gender: Current Status and Future Directions." In *Gender and Work*, edited by G. N. Powel, 391–412. Thousand Oaks, CA: Sage.

Hill, Catherine, Christianne Corbett, and Andresse St. Rose. 2010. *Why So Few? Women in Science, Technology, Engineering, and Mathematics.* Washington, DC: AAUW.

Hopkins, Nancy, and Mary C. Potter. 1999. "Special Edition: A Study on the Status of Women Faculty in Science at MIT." *MIT Faculty Newsletter* 11(4):1–15.

Joslin, Daphne. 1994. "Eldercare in Higher Education: One Campus Experience." *Gerontology and Geriatrics Education* 15(2):19–29.

Klein, Donna, and Mike Shum. 2004. *Elder Care Practice Survey of Corporate Voices Partners.* Washington, DC: Corporate Voices for Working Families.

Lee, Jo Ann, Paul W. Foos, and Chase L. Clow. 2010. "Caring for One's Elders and Family-to-Work Conflict." *The Psychologist-Manager Journal* 12:15–39.

Mason, Mary Ann, and Marc Goulden. 2004. "Marriage and Baby Blues: Redefining Gender Equity in the Academy." *ANNALS, AAPSS,* 596:86–103.

MetLife Mature Market Institute. 2011. *The MetLife Study of Caregiving Costs to Working Caregivers: Double Jeopardy for Baby Boomers Caring for Their Parents.* https://www.metlife.com/mmi/research/caregiving-cost-working-caregivers. html#key%20findings.

Raabe, Phyllis. 1997. "Work-Family Policies for Faculty: How 'Career- and Family-Friendly' Is Academe?" In *Academic Couples: Problems and Promises,* edited by M. A. Ferber and J. W. Loeb, 208–225. Urbana: University of Illinois Press.

Rogerson, Peter, and Daejong Kim. 2005. "Population Distribution and Redistribution of the Baby-Boom Cohort in the United States: Recent Trends and Implications." *Proceedings of the National Academy of Sciences* 121:15319–15324.

Sandler, Bernice. 1986. *The Chilly Climate Revisited: Chilly for Women Faculty, Administrators and Graduate Students.* Washington, DC: Association of American Colleges.

Smith, Peggie R. 2004. "Elder Care, Gender, and Work: The Work-Family Issue of the 21st Century." *Berkeley Journal of Employment and Labor Law* 25(2):351–399.

Ward, Kelly, and Lisa Wolf-Wendel. 2004. "Academic Motherhood: Managing Complex Roles and Research Universities." *The Review of Higher Education* 27(2):233–257.

Wolfinger, Nicholas H., Mary Ann Mason, and Marc Goulden. 2008. "Alone in the Ivory Tower: How Birth Events Vary Among Fast-Track Professionals." Paper presented at the 2008 annual meeting of the Population Association of America, New Orleans, LA, April. http://paa2008.princeton.edu/abstracts/81253.

CASE STUDY

GRADUATE STUDENT CHASTAIN: NAVIGATING GENDERED FAMILY-WORK EXPECTATIONS

I am Hispanic, and 35 years old. Being a woman in academia can often feel like we are nothing more than uteruses waiting for a rental opportunity. I have been asked about my "plans for children" more times since coming to graduate school than I did when working at a children's clinic. We are talked to about planning children around major exams, tenure-track time, and dissertation-writing time. Everyone has opinions about when we need or should do it. My partner is in law school. He has been working for two semesters with a professor emeritus of law and urban planning from another major university. We finally met at a reception. The professor waxed on and on about how he loves geography (my field) and taught geography classes at University X. He then asked, "So when are you having kids? You're in your late 20s, aren't you?" "No, I'm actually in my mid-30s." A look of horror passed over his face. He nearly shouted, "You better hurry up! You're running out of time! Don't you plan to have kids?!" When I calmly explained that we planned to adopt older children once we settled in our careers, he shuffled uncomfortably—giving me that look—the one that says, "Yeah, right."

When we left the reception, I asked my partner if that question had ever come up. "Never!" He looked shocked. Not once was I asked about my work, my career goals, or my research plans—even when offered by my partner to get conversation going. The only interest the professor had was in my plans for my uterus. If that'd been the only incident, I would have let it pass—an old man's peculiarity—but this is constant. I've had this conversation so many times that I blurted to one faculty member, "My partner is snipped! Don't worry. We're not having kids!" I've gone to meetings with faculty to ask for project help and ended up getting the "Helpful Advice About When to Have Children" lecture.

Three things bother me: First, my faculty ask this question repeatedly so they can report to potential future universities about my child-bearing plans. They're looking out for me. Second, without their input, I could be in serious trouble when looking for a job! No one, especially now with tight budgets, wants to lose a faculty member, soon after hiring her, to maternity leave. Third, if I did decide to have a child, *my* own year of sabbatical would get pushed out further because of my "year off" for maternity needs. I have watched men in this program . . . their wives have children. Suddenly, they're in the department all the time. The wives and babies are invisible—appearing once or twice in the course of their program, names barely muttered. Conversely, I've seen women nearly lose their funding because they're "taking too long" to complete their dissertations—even though they're taking so long because they've had a baby—in the time frame they've been told to! Women can't leave ourselves at home while we go to work. We can't bring a baby in with us. The school doesn't provide adequate childcare support. Some women have been forced to bring children to class because they have no familial support nearby. They stop coming to functions and being a part of the department because there's no room for children here. Even tenured faculty don't bring their children to events. They set the tone. We look to them for guidance. The message is clear: Family and relationships have no place in academia. In the past few years, I've found the "baby" issue hostile to women, generally. I was even advised that I may need to decide between a research institute and no children, or a small liberal arts college and children: my career or my life.

I don't hear about men being spoken to this way. I've asked several men in the department if they go through baby-vetting. They don't. Women graduate students already face issues with children and career. We struggle deciding how we need to shape our lives and futures. To be faced with outside pressures constantly is stressful. I don't think we thought we'd face this when we came to the academy.

Recently, I met a young professor from another university. We talked about the academy and gender biases came up. He proclaimed: "It doesn't still exist!" I glared. Somewhat bitterly and amused, he asked: "You think it still does?" It's difficult to explain to men the pressures women face—from family, friends, colleagues, partners, faculty, ourselves. Men have their own issues to deal with (e.g., parents who can't understand why their sons are still in school or not doing "real men's work"). It's not to take away from that. But, what is particularly frustrating is that people essentialize us to our "biological function as women." I understand the implications. I just don't see men being essentialized in the same ways—as if my work and worth is secondary to my baby-making-ness and my ovaries' youthfulness. I haven't addressed it—except to ask men in the program about their experiences. I don't know how to address it.

I realize these questions come up so often because people want us to be able to "do it all" and want to help us make the "right" decisions. But, this is a bigger issue than pointing out the anti-woman-esque nature of the battery of questions women academics face. It's an institutional issue of the academy. Women faculty who gave up having children for their careers 20 years ago now urge young women to never choose between them. Women who had children *and* their careers feel that they need to help others choose "correctly"—learn from their successes or failures.

The issue of daycare came up last year because our union contract was up for bargaining. Those involved in bargaining have fought for more childcare support for grad students. Several men were *angry* about it. [When] I noted the second biggest reason for leaving graduate school was inadequate childcare support, more than one blurted out, "Well So-and-So [a single mother in our department] is doing just fine!" But, it is not just about women. Men quit school because of lack of childcare support, too. But, the assumption is that it's women whining about lack of support. Additionally, I would fail a student who pointed to *a single person* as evidence for an argument. I was struck by the vehement hostility held against women, generally, and women graduate students with children, specifically. The request for childcare support was for *all* graduate students, not just women. But the assumption's still there. What do we do about it?

What Can We Learn From This Case Study?

Situations like these are frustrating, especially because they occur frequently. University cultures and structures create the context in which gendered assumptions and differential treatment can occur. What can student Chastain and women academics[1] in similar situations do to manage unwanted advice or personal inquiries and begin crafting twenty-first-century workplaces that respond to work-family realities? We provide different conversational approaches for use in managing microlevel interactions, as Chastain's narrative asks for. Additionally, we identify resources and tools that can be used to change workplace structures and cultures. As always, it is important to keep personal and professional goals, university culture, and interactional contexts in mind before taking action.

Actions Involving Individual Resources

- Organize a family-friendly gathering on campus, at a public park, or at someone's home to remind people that life exists outside the office and that they share commonalities besides work. Consider the goals for this event and set the tone accordingly (e.g., casual but professional, informal and fun). Consider the most effective ways to encourage networking (e.g., formal introductions, activities).
- Use your knowledge to help others understand the complexity of issues and to dismantle faulty assumptions (e.g., family issues are "women's issues"; only women quit school because of lack of childcare support). Also, share information about recent research such as this new study on flexibility stigma: www.insidehighered.com/news/2014/04/01/work-place-flexibility-stigma-affects-non-parents-too-study-suggests.
- Remember that you do not have to explain personal choices. It may help to assume people's good intentions while guiding them toward more appropriate topics. Consider different approaches. If these approaches are not right for you, perhaps they can inspire other styles.
  - In the *honest approach,* keep personal comments honest and brief. Then, shift the discussion toward a more appropriate direction by opening a line of conversation you would like to explore. Asking people about themselves may be useful, too. People may try to engage you back into conversations about personal matters, but do not let them—even if that means excusing yourself to "use the restroom." Here is an example of how you can redirect the conversation: "I appreciate your concern. But, we're not interested in having kids yet. Have I told you about _____ [e.g., research, current events]?" If you prefer to be more direct, try: "That feels a little too personal. Why don't you tell me about your _____ [e.g., research, current events]?" Or, point out the double standard by asking something like: "My women friends and I get questions like this all the time but none of the men ever do. What do you make of that?"
  - The *humorous approach* aims to defuse awkward situations with a wink and a nod. It can be useful in situations when being direct seems problematic. For example, jokingly say something like: "Did my mother hire you? She is so darn eager to become a grand-mother!" Then, change the subject. If the person persists, consider a follow-up such as, "Wow! You're good! Have you ever thought of becoming an investigative journalist? Such questions!" Such a

follow-up usually does the trick, but if it doesn't, try one of the other suggested approaches.

○ The *sociological approach* shifts the focus away from you and toward the related "public issue." Depending on the situation, you could incorporate a call to action. For example: "I appreciate your concern. Your question, in fact, speaks to wider challenges facing women in academia. Would you be interested in joining a committee on [family-work issues] or signing a petition for [on-site childcare]? We could really use your talents."

Actions Involving Institutional Resources

- Locate allies on your campus who can bring awareness, resources, and legitimacy to important workplace issues (e.g., tenured faculty, administrators). Use their knowledge of informal rules and institutional players and practices to develop action strategies. Whenever possible, try to create win-win solutions for everyone. For example, although women currently provide a disproportionate amount of care work when compared to men, consider framing this as a "workplace issue," not a "women's issue."

- Conduct a climate study or culture audit and gather feedback. Assess needs, concerns, and potential areas of agreement across university constituents (e.g., graduate students, faculty, staff). For example: What family-work issues need prioritizing? What factors inhibit widespread support of campus childcare? If your institution will not allocate resources to gather this information, consider online survey managers such as SurveyMonkey.com, Zoomerang.com, and googleforms.com.

- Encourage campuswide discussions about work-family issues (e.g., childcare, eldercare, flexible work arrangements and policies). Consider ways that different campus groups (e.g., graduate students, faculty, and staff parents) might work together. Ask to put relevant topics on formal meeting agendas.

- If you do not have a formal graduate student organization to address concerns on a broader level, contemplate organizing one (Chastain does, but these are not always present). If you move forward, use traditional and social media to your advantage and be creative in your publicity. For example, try using eye-catching materials that blend facts with humor such as "Inadequate childcare support is the second biggest reason bright, hardworking people leave graduate school. That stinks like a dirty diaper!"

- Write a letter or proposal that outlines the issues, have all your supporters sign it, and send it to your university provost and president as well as campus newspapers. Define the issues, ask for specific outcomes, and use evidence to support the argument. Articulate how the proposed actions align with the institutional mission and culture. Keep potential repercussions in mind before taking action.

Actions Involving Extrainstitutional Resources

- Consider ways to bring others on board regarding how "family-friendly" policies and practices can serve employees and the institution. For example:
  - The 2012 National Study of Employers examines data from more than 1,000 U.S. employers about workplace benefits including those related to caregiving (e.g., flextime, eldercare). The data suggest that work and family are no longer separated as they were in the past. To attract and retain the best employees, reduce absenteeism, improve workplace morale, and increase productivity, workplaces must adapt. Read the report at the Families and Work Institute at http://familiesandwork.org/site/research/reports/NSE_2012_.pdf.
  - The Workflex: Employee Toolkit summarizes various "flexible" employment arrangements, suggests tools for assessment, and provides ideas to maximize successes. See www.whenworkworks.org/be-effective/guides-tools/workflex-employee-toolkit.
- Network and see what other institutions are doing. Investigate effective models that your institution could adapt. Read and consider posting questions in *The Chronicle of Higher Education*'s Chronicle Forums (http://chronicle.com/forums/). See, for example, "Grad-School Life" and "Balancing Work and Life." Consider posting to "Department Chairs and Deans" to see what administrators think might work or what's preventing change.
- Connect with the relevant section of a disciplinary organization to which you belong. What are they doing about these issues? Adding your talents to efforts already underway could help with cultural and structural shifts to make change beyond your own university.
- Investigate universities that lead the way on work-family issues. The American Council on Education–Alfred P. Sloan Foundation Projects on Faculty Career Flexibility provides a "snapshot" including "winning institutions" and best practices (e.g., inclusive policies, "respectful,

humane treatment") at www.portal.advance.vt.edu/Advance_2009_
PI_Mtg/PIMtg2009_ACE%20Poster.pdf.

- Write editorials for the local or state media regarding the need for
  workplaces to adapt to twenty-first-century needs and why this will
  benefit students, faculty, staff, organizations, and communities to
  do so.

Consult the online resources at the end of this book and the case studies to
the other parts of this book for additional information that might be helpful.

Note

1. Our book focuses on the workplace experiences of women academics. Some issues, such as
   the one in this case study, are relevant to men faculty and to staff.

PART THREE

EXCLUSIONARY CULTURES
Intellectual and Identity Inequalities

A
s noted in the introduction, *structure* refers to institutional arrangements, systems, procedures, and other mechanisms that help organizations or institutions meet their goals. *Culture* includes—but is not
limited to—beliefs, values, norms, language, symbols, stories, rituals, and
other practices that influence its members' thoughts and actions. Aspects of
culture may be unstated, unacknowledged, or known by only some members.
Further, it is not unusual to see a disjuncture between what an organization
professes to value and what it manifests in routine practice, as the chapters
in this part of the book suggest (see also Bird 2011). As structure and culture interact, they shape people's behaviors at the microlevel (e.g., individual,
small group) of "*climate.*" Part Three emphasizes the role that departmental
and organizational cultures play in marginalizing women academics for who
they are (i.e., lesbians, women of color) or the subjects they study and teach
(i.e., interdisciplinary or queer studies).

Despite high numbers of women in the academic pipeline, and increasing numbers of tenured women professors throughout the United States,
exclusionary beliefs and practices continue to marginalize many women academics. As this part shows, these range from implicit or overt discrimination
to standards for promotion and tenure that exclude certain women and the

work they do. In addition, women's identity categories can be sources of their marginality within academia. Women of color, lesbians, transwomen, mothers, and nonmothers, for example, may be unwelcome. When marginalized, women academics can become disconnected from informal and formal networking, advancement opportunities, and other institutional participation.

Exclusionary ideologies contribute to academic women's attrition from academia and lower career satisfaction for some who remain. In chapter 8, "Perpetuating Inequality Through the Canons of Disciplinary Knowledge," Katuna explores how rigidity within social science disciplines perpetuates racism, gender inequality, and heteronormativity within academia. Through case studies, Katuna explores four women academics' intellectual and institutional exclusion; they pushed boundaries of traditional canons and suffered as a result. She notes that women in marginalized social categories often teach and do research in undervalued areas, or use interdisciplinary frameworks to address issues such as race, class, gender, or sexual orientation. Doing so in joint appointments can create career obstacles when faculty have differing sets of expectations to fulfill. Additionally, these marginalized women may be responsible for developing interdisciplinary curricula or teaching "diversity" courses (e.g., focusing on women and minorities) that tenure and promotion committees may evaluate as less important. These appointments disproportionately fall to women and minority faculty (see Aguirre 2000; chapter 2 of this volume). As such, interdisciplinary scholars can encounter barriers when being evaluated by colleagues and administrators who uphold traditional forms of scholarship and teaching.

In our research, we found similar patterns of women struggling to have their work validated. Joyce, who did not disclose her demographics, wrote, "I currently work with Latino populations in an academic environment. . . . The people who make the policies and rules are blind or misinformed about the lives and context of people of color. I am used to that struggle, but academically, the kind of work others like me do is not valued." Another participant, Shelby, a white 43-year-old assistant professor of ethnic studies at a research university, learned that colleagues questioned the legitimacy of her work when she applied for tenure. She explained:

> Faculty were required to have at least 10 well-placed journal articles, of which more than half had to be first- or sole-authored. I went up for tenure with 20 peer-reviewed journal articles, a sole-authored book, a teaching award, and a *lot* of service. My journal articles were in higher-ranked sociology journals than most of the faculty had. . . . Nonetheless, I had tenure problems. Throughout my career, I have been dedicated to engaging in the kind of work that makes a real difference in people's lives. I was being invited . . . to Washington, DC to meet with lawmakers. The fight

over tenure revolved around whether or not my work was "important." Those who opposed my tenure said (a) since my work was policy oriented it wasn't theoretical, and (b) I should have spent more time publishing and less time in Washington. Ultimately, the grounds for opposing my tenure were that only eight of my peer-reviewed articles were first- or sole-authored; thus, I had not met the "half" standard. (Of course, if I had *only* published the required 10 articles, I would have more than met the "half" standard. There was no consideration of the book published by a scholarly press.) I cannot assert that my issues involved gender. . . . In my department, it was the men who made comments such as "that's not sociology," and "that's just social work." In the end, the department had a split decision on my tenure. Both the College Committee and the University Committee unanimously voted to approve me for tenure and promotion, and I was tenured.

Clearly, Shelby is productive. She publishes prolifically, attends to service obligations, and has been recognized formally for teaching excellence. The resistance to her tenure suggests intellectual exclusion and a failure of process linked to departmental culture. Because of their key locations in the institutional structure, small numbers of decision makers have the power to make tenure decisions, establish hierarchies of intellectual canons, and make other work-related choices for faculty. When they are unfamiliar with or do not appreciate the totality of subjects involved in knowledge production, women academics like Shelby and Joyce will face professional hazards for the work they do.

In chapter 9, "Characteristics and Perceptions of Women of Color Faculty Nationally," Castro addresses similar exclusions. She considers why so few women of color faculty work in higher education, despite their increases in PhDs in the 1990s. Drawing on a nationally representative faculty survey from the Higher Education Research Institute (HERI), Castro deconstructs the unique professional experiences of academic women of color whose workplace experiences result from their marginalized statuses as women and as people of color, respectively. She finds they encounter cultural and structural barriers to their advancement; the isolation they experience exposes them to discrimination because they are on the margins. Echoing Katuna, Castro suggests that many academic women of color defy workplace norms by teaching and doing scholarship on nontraditional subjects. In challenging institutional hegemony, they face challenges to their legitimacy, attempts to block their advancement, and pressures to conform to organizational values and practices at odds with their values and goals. Within this context, many suffer isolation, compounded by challenges to their authority from students and colleagues.

In our study, Erin, a 38-year-old Hispanic early-career faculty member at a comprehensive university described how men colleagues undervalue her work and ignore her as an expert. She sees the contentious interactions with her colleagues as gendered—although her early-career status, ethnic identity, and subject matter may have contributed to those dynamics. She wrote:

> It's the silent things that happen sometimes. Male colleagues not talking to you or wanting to suggest you as a media expert. And, making this point of telling you to your face. "Oh, I forgot that I could suggest you." Please. Recently, [I] was told by a senior colleague that my upcoming position as the president of the major women faculty advocacy group is not deserving of a two-course release. And, the way in which it was stated was as if everyone on campus agrees.

In this narrative we see the disjuncture between structural and cultural dimensions of faculty life: The university structural policies support her service with release time, but her immediate colleagues do not see this work as legitimate. How can she negotiate these competing expectations? Academic workplaces often value women faculty of color, particularly for their role in meeting organizational diversity goals. On one hand, Erin is valued for this work, but, on the other, she runs the risk of censure from her colleagues during future evaluations. Similarly, Castro argues that institutions encumber academic women of color with disproportionate service obligations because of their location within the university's structure and articulated organizational values of diversity. She calls this phenomenon "diversity double duty" and, like our other contributors (see chapter 4), notes that it takes time from more respected and compensated institutional responsibilities (e.g., research), potentially derailing women on the path to tenure.

Chapter 10, "Women Sociologists and the Question of Inclusion in the Academy," provides a glimpse into the work experiences of successful women sociologists with academic careers. Marsh's inquiry for participants "Tell me about your experiences in your career" yields mixed results. Most respondents like their current job but describe workplace climates ranging from "warm" to "chilly." She finds that departmental cultures, and the interpersonal dynamics within them, can exacerbate or mitigate the institutional climate that is, in part, established by formal policies and practices. Marsh argues that sociology, as a discipline, constitutes a proxy for a "neutral" academic discipline because it is neither overtly hospitable nor hostile to academic women. Thus, it is not surprising that her participants report parallels to the individual and institutional factors that "chill" or "warm" workplace environments documented throughout this book. Like Baldwin and Griffin explain in chapter 2, Marsh's respondents indicate that mentoring helps their professional development and supports them when facing institutional and cultural challenges at work.

One of our respondents, Sherry, a white 41-year-old assistant professor at a teaching institution, wrote about how "warm" gestures from colleagues helped her endure the distressing "chilly" experience she had going up for tenure, being denied tenure, and appealing the decision. She wrote:

> A third colleague, and coauthor on a paper, has written a letter setting straight the record about my contribution to our joint paper. He stated that my contribution had been essential to the paper's publication, and not, as was claimed, insignificant. A fourth person and chair of a different department wrote a long letter carefully laying out all the different ways in which injustices had been done in my review. Importantly, she reviewed my case carefully and stated it would without a trace of a doubt have gotten full support in her department. None of these letters were requested by me. These people spoke out because they felt compelled to do so in the face of gross injustices. My dean conducted a so-called "investigation" into the allegations made in [other] letters. He determined that none of the allegations of my [other] colleagues' misconduct were true. The support of the four letter-writers, and of other colleagues, has been *very* affirming. I can live on because of the whistle-blowing letters. After a long period of hostility and feeling alone, without a voice, as my carefully built career was being trashed by a clearly subjective colleague, while everyone looked the other way, I feel vindicated by the support and am applying for work again, feeling able to move beyond this.

In chapter 11, "Not the Ideal Professor: Gender in the Academy," Hirshfield considers how beliefs and norms about gender impact how students, colleagues, and administrators view women faculty in light of expectations about the "ideal professor." When *professor* is defined narrowly or stereotypically, women of color, feminists, and scholar-activists, among others, may be excluded from certain aspects of academic life or held to different standards than men faculty. Hirshfield's interview respondents reported that students challenge the professorial authority of women faculty in overt and subtle ways such as calling them by their first name instead of their title; the use of first names is a courtesy usually granted to men faculty. This is an aspect of how the academy is a gendered organization (e.g., Acker 1990; Bird 2011; Martin 1994) with faculty roles gendered in invisible ways. Not only are women not seen as "the ideal professor," they are also held to stereotypical expectations of femininity. Our respondent Vicki, a 51-year-old white assistant professor of architecture at a research university, told us about difficulties navigating others' expectations: "As a feminist in academic architecture I was seen as a problem: Either I talked too much or not enough. My classes were labeled 'not rigorous' because I taught humanely. When I was more authoritarian, I was a 'bitch.'" Pat, a 58-year-old white associate professor at a research-intensive university was reprimanded by her dean for "not [being] nurturing and motherly to [my] students"—an expectation that seems hard to imagine being applied to men (i.e., you are not "fatherly" enough). Karen, a 55-year-old biochemistry professor at a large state university, wrote:

> The president said that he had gathered us together because we were all active researchers. When it came my turn for my introduction, I gave my unsolicited opinion that there were too few women at the gathering (there were about 35 of us, with three of us female). The president agreed. A male engineering faculty member was seated to my left. He proceeded to tell me that the reason there were few women was that women were unsuitable to be engineers. When I pointed out that 30 years ago women were thought to be unsuitable as medical doctors, but now about 50% of graduating MDs are women, he told me that medicine is primarily a service profession and women are suitable for being service providers, but that engineering is a field that is hard science and math and women just aren't up to the task. I have written to our university's provost outlining the situation and asking that he do something, but besides two e-mails from him, nothing further has come of it.

In this scenario, Karen's workplace culture is entrenched in masculine norms and gendered ideologies that perpetuate stereotypes about women situating them as tokens in men-dominant careers. Her actions might be a reasonable short-term strategy, similar to those adopted by Hirshfield's respondents who try to look older, or change their classroom strategies. However, they do not address the larger cultural or structural forces that reify the notions of the "ideal professor." By e-mailing her provost, Karen attempts to disrupt the silence around such matters and suggests her desire for a more equitable organizational approach. In doing nothing, the provost enables such troubles to continue and suggests Karen's concerns are not legitimate.

Chapter 12, "Intersectional Invisibility and the Academic Work Experiences of Lesbian Faculty," reveals how lesbian faculty experience and cope with pervasive invisibility in academic workplaces. Like academic women of color (e.g., see chapters 2 and 9), lesbian faculty embody intersecting and subordinate identities: gender and sexual orientation. Bilimoria and Stewart's intersectional framework helps us understand the difficulties lesbian faculty experience at work based on how their situated statuses align with workplace cultures and climates. Because academic workplaces mirror the dominant U.S. culture, people assume that others are heterosexual, leaving lesbian (and gay men) faculty feeling invisible and unsure about how to navigate others' assumptions. In the academy, such heteronormativity grants privileges—often unacknowledged ones—to heterosexual and cisgender people (whose gender matches their ascribed sex category). Through in-depth interviews, Bilimoria and Stewart explore the consequences of heteronormativity for lesbian faculty. Their participants question how others will react to their sexual identities, and whether they should disclose them. Additionally, participants reported having to tolerate homophobic discourse or pressures to follow appearance norms (i.e., to "look straight"). These challenges constitute "microinequities" (Rowe 1974), differential treatment for "outsiders" that, when repeated over time, contributes to a "chilly" workplace atmosphere that inflicts harm. Such microinequities contribute to "silence" on sexuality issues.

Cultures within gendered organizations have the potential to marginalize members who challenge the idealized, normative worker. Despite the strategies employed by women academics to manage challenging interactions with students, colleagues, and administrators, accumulated disadvantages (Clark and Corcoran 1986) and microinequities (Rowe 1974) can take their toll. Undervaluing the diversity of who scholars are, and the scholarship and pedagogy in which they engage, marginalizes many women academics, as the chapters and case study to Part Three show. The case study of Professor Liu illustrates multiple marginality (Turner 2002) resulting from her ethnicity, identity as a feminist, status as an immigrant, and gender-focused courses. Despite being well received by most students, some colleagues and students make her workplace climate hostile.

References

Acker, Joan. 1990. "Hierarchies, Jobs, Bodies: A Theory of Gendered Organizations." *Gender and Society* 4(2):139–158.

Aguirre, Adalberto. 2000. *Women and Minority Faculty in the Academic Workplace: Recruitment, Retention, and Academic Culture.* San Francisco: Jossey-Bass.

Bird, Sharon R. 2011. "Unsettling Universities' Incongruous, Gendered Bureaucratic Structures: A Case-Study Approach." *Gender, Work & Organization* 18(2): 202–230.

Clark, Shirley M., and Mary Corcoran. 1986. "Perspectives on the Professional Socialization of Women Faculty: A Case of Accumulative Disadvantage?" *The Journal of Higher Education* 57(1):20–43.

Martin, Joanne. 1994. "The Organization of Exclusion: Institutionalization of Sex Inequality, Gendered Faculty Jobs and Gendered Knowledge in Organizational Theory and Research." *Organization* 1(2):401–431.

Rowe, Mary. 1974. "'Saturn's Rings': A Study of the Minutiae of Sexism Which Maintain Discrimination and Inhibit Affirmative Action Results in Corporations and Non-profit Institutions." In *Graduate and Professional Education of Women,* 1–9. Washington, DC: American Association of University Women.

Turner, Caroline S. V. 2002. "Women of Color in Academe: Living With Multiple Marginality." *The Journal of Higher Education* 73(1):74–93.

Academic Women's Voices on Marginalization and Exclusion

The following narratives demonstrate the marginalization and exclusion of women academics based on some aspect of who they are (e.g., woman with a disability, woman of color). Some exclusions seem blatant and intentional. Others are subtle, perhaps unconscious. Though the sources and forms of marginalization vary, the subsequent personal and professional consequences vary less. Our respondents reported continually having to assess and navigate workplace waters, leaving them feeling stressed, fatigued, isolated, depressed, and frustrated. When unchecked, the potential for further victimization seems likely.

As a woman of color, one of the problems that plagues me is knowing when to assert which identity in which situation. This is likely true for anyone, but the "intersectionality" literature becomes palpable to me when I am the only or one of the few people of color in the room, along with being the only or one of the few women. So I find myself "code-switching" constantly—even in the same conversation with one person. I am always internally gauging how much my audience wants to hear my view on something as a woman, my view on something as a person of color, or as a social scientist versus a natural scientist or humanist, or as an administrator versus a faculty member. Many times I stop short of making my full point because of worry that my colleagues will think, "Oh, there she goes playing the race card" or whatever card they think I might play, even though the issue of gender or race might be very germane to the conversation or decision and no one else is mentioning it! So I guess what I am saying is that I am sort of paranoid about being seen as a militant woman of color (which would not go over well at my institution). I think that is part of what makes me create an appearance that is nonthreatening (i.e., very feminine and professional), a voice that is nonthreatening (i.e., quiet, apologetic). So I sort of feel like I am acting all the time. It can be tiring.

—Lisa, 46-year-old Hispanic associate professor of geography

I am an untenured, tenure-track faculty member with an autoimmune disorder. I was diagnosed early career, and faced the decision of quitting or of persevering and rethinking how I could execute my career on my terms. I had to make several life-changing decisions. The most disruptive was to move closer to family members that could help watch our children in times of need. During interviews, I was faced with the awkward interview question of why I was moving midcareer pre-tenure. My stock answer was that I wanted to be closer to family. Besides the occasional ergonomic item, I don't require special treatment. There are fantastic new drugs for [my condition] that allow me to live the life I want. But, different incidents remind me that the people I work with see me not only as a woman, but as someone disabled. I don't look disabled and on most days I don't feel disabled, but that doesn't seem to change perceptions of me. I asked a senior administrator whether I should disclose my condition to my students or colleagues. The administrator emphatically said, "No, because anyone who doesn't already know will then see you differently, and not necessarily in a good way." I left the administrator's office feeling conflicted. I want those around me to understand why I can't do certain things or why I am sick all the time. But I don't want people to discount me on account of these limitations.

—Denise, 32-year-old white assistant professor of engineering

I am often the only person of color with a PhD in the room. If I miss a meeting, it is immediately noted. Peers don't seem to recognize the role of race in reality. Although not overtly racist, some actions are influenced based on the nondiverse environment. It is common for committees to be formed without any consideration for diversity. Most people are savvy enough to avoid blatant acts of ugliness yet unconscious acts can be far more detrimental. I am often the butt of jokes because "you can take it." The reasons may be personal, professional, factual, or racial. Who knows? It's sometimes difficult to discern when you're dealing with racist behavior, low self-esteem, or both. Managing the academic culture becomes easier over time. Sadly, it's part complacency, complicity, and complete exhaustion. Pointing out the obvious is exhausting especially when denial is a viable excuse.

—Linda (no demographics given)

I am not only a woman, but am disabled. I am in a department that is male dominated. Upon joining the university, there was only one other female faculty member in our school, and she was only in her second year. I've received numerous comments over the time I've been here: "Who are you kidding? You won't be here long. You're a young woman, you'll get married and move back to _____" "You don't bake? That's because you don't have a family. Someday you'll have to put down those books and bake for your family." "You were only hired because you are disabled. You know that." "We hire women here because we need someone with compassion and sensitivity." I love what I do, but hate my job and am depressed.

—Jacqueline, 31-year-old white adjunct faculty

8

PERPETUATING INEQUALITY THROUGH THE CANONS OF DISCIPLINARY KNOWLEDGE

Barret Katuna

A trend for colleges and universities in the United States is to promote scholarship that bridges disciplines. For example, professors with appointments in sociology departments and who explore race-, gender-, or sexuality-based questions may partner with historians, political scientists, anthropologists, and others to investigate social problems that require broad-based inquiry. This interdisciplinary phenomenon is changing how academic departments respond to knowledge production and can pose challenges for professors who seek support from colleagues whose work is not interdisciplinary. Who is most likely to challenge core disciplinary foundations through research and teaching? What kinds of problems do interdisciplinary scholars encounter? Why is it important for scholars, students, and administrators to be aware of the risks that these interdisciplinary scholars take?

Social scientists often study issues that are personally and intellectually meaningful to them (Glenn 1997). Women of color, whose research may focus on gender and race, and lesbian and transgender women, who may specialize in queer studies, often confront institutional barriers in their professional trajectories. Additionally, they may face opposition when applying for tenure and promotion (Menges and Exum 1983). What is the relationship between an institution's fixed commitment to disciplinary standards and the experiences of women in marginalized social locations who work in interdisciplinary or underappreciated academic areas?

Why Disciplines Matter

Disciplines, especially at elite universities, mark the intellectual foundations of scholarship (Abbott 2002) and serve organizational and practical functions. Department names (e.g., Political Science department) identify the discipline. Each discipline has qualifying principles and standards for scholarship. Disciplines organize traditions of thought that enable students to develop awareness of their theoretical and methodological guiding principles. Furthermore, disciplines facilitate a unified scholarly community. Academic departments expect tenure-track faculty to publish in peer-reviewed journals that reflect the core values of their discipline. Given these traditions, scholars working across disciplinary boundaries risk consequences.

Rigid regard for disciplinary authority poses obstacles to social science scholars who pursue problem-based knowledge inquiries rather than problem-portable research inquiries. Problem-based research includes studies that incorporate core disciplinary frameworks to address social inequalities for historically marginalized groups (e.g., people of color, women, or lesbians and gays). Problem-portable research generates knowledge that can be applied broadly (Abbott 2002). Problem-based knowledge relies on problem-portable knowledge given that problem-based scholars borrow theoretical insights from problem-portable knowledge to address particular social problems. Interdisciplinary arrangements support a relationship between problem-based and problem-portable knowledge that enables problem-based scholars to make arguments that reflect disciplinary tenets (e.g., an interdisciplinary women's studies scholar with a joint appointment in sociology may adopt a sociological framework). Although problem-based and problem-portable knowledge are associated with the social sciences, scholars from other disciplines such as law (Williams 1991) or philosophy (Aptheker 1999; Davis 2005) may introduce nontraditional areas of inquiry into their research.

"Interdisciplinarity presupposes disciplines" (Abbott 2001, 135). Thus, problem-based scholars rely on core disciplines such as political science, sociology, anthropology, and psychology to establish esteem for their arguments. We are presently seeing movement toward interdisciplinary projects at colleges and universities: Institutions are establishing interdisciplinary majors and minors, hiring full-time area studies and problem-based studies professors, and creating dual appointments in area studies and core disciplinary departments.

The relationship between problem-based and problem-portable research may appear to be straightforward. Interdisciplinarity provides an alternative academic space and acknowledges the diversity of intellectual and vocational interests among student populations in a globalized, market-driven economy (Abbott 2002; Shumway 1999). However, scholars with problem-based research agendas report hostility from core disciplinary departments that may not deem their research to be "true" biology or political science. Scholars committed to problem-based knowledge inquiries that divert from the core discipline face obstacles in assimilating into traditional departments.

Similarly, professors whose research is situated outside of traditional modes of inquiry present challenges to market-oriented rankings, given that interdisciplinary interests may lead to publications not as widely valued within the core disciplines. Many colleges and universities are committed to rising in the *U.S. News & World Report* (*USNWR*) rankings. Faculty publishing in lesser-known area studies journals pose a threat to a university's reputation because of the *USNWR* ranking formula (Espeland and Sauder 2007, 2009; Espeland and Stevens 1998; Shumway 1999).

Beyond the external implications of a strong adherence to disciplinary standards, tenured white men professors are likely accustomed to a homogeneous academic environment. In this context, these scholars are producing work that is in dialogue with other knowledge in the discipline and they resemble one another through similarities in race, gender, and sexuality. That is, the phenomenon of the academic "clone" is probably more acceptable to higher-ranking scholars more comfortable with sustaining the field with like-minded scholars whose work expands on their contributions (Essed 2004). However, for some scholars, establishing an interdisciplinary academic home is more suitable.

Marginalization Through a Disciplinary Authority Framework

Scholars with problem-based research agendas that challenge academic canons, particularly scholars from marginalized populations, may experience a kind of knowledge-based violence analogous to state, or institutional, violence that scholars address in critiques of racism, gender inequality, homophobia, and other oppressions (Alexander 2005; Davis 1998, 2005; Frankenberg 2001; Hong 2006). Foucault's (1977) contribution to understanding state power suggests that the state maintains latent authority over the bodies and actions of its citizens. This "judicial reticence" takes away rights without physical pain. This is similar to the regulation that marginalized populations, including those of non-Western individuals, people of color, homosexuals, and women, confront in the U.S. academy. Scholars of marginalized populations face standards of their academic departments' regulatory frameworks that endorse strict disciplinary canons. If scholars must seek out joint or full appointments in area studies to find a friendly academic space, they constitute victims of "judicial reticence." Agathangelou and Ling (2009) acknowledge the need for academics to redress the production of limiting, homogeneous studies. They identify an "overarching hegemonic project" of knowledge production that perpetuates power structures and reinforces disciplinary canons that white men initially established. Alternatively, women of color feminists (e.g., Agathangelou and Ling 2002; Alexander 2005; Anzaldúa 1999; Davis 2005; Moraga and Anzaldúa 1983) attend to the intersections of racism, sexism, and homophobia that present underlying challenges for women of color faculty. In this context, women of color may face more challenges than white women, and lesbians may face more impediments to becoming part of the scholarly community than heterosexuals (see also chapter 12).

I make this argument based on three claims. First, Menges and Exum (1983) note the difficulty women and minorities have attaining elevated positions in departments historically dominated by men (e.g., engineering). Second, women and individuals of historically marginalized backgrounds may be inclined to study problem-based social phenomena that are personally meaningful to them and that cross disciplines. Third, Hurtado and Sharkness (2008) confirm the exceptional difficulties associated with interdisciplinary work and the tenure review process. Case studies of women scholars who address marginalization and hostile work environments exemplify the problems associated with adherence to disciplinary authority and provide insight on the problems that can arise when disciplinary departments undermine and devalue interdisciplinary work.

Four Case Studies of Inequality in the U.S. Academy

Women professors of historically marginalized backgrounds have published autobiographical accounts that document challenges in producing problem-based research. These narratives reveal the systemic inequality that plays out in departmental cultures and characterizes disciplinary power structures. The structures that privilege disciplinary canons relate to broader discussions about the gendered, racialized, and other discriminatory practices within academia occurring formally and informally throughout higher education.

For example, problem-based scholars are likely to publish in nontraditional venues. Discipline-specific peers may not understand or value interdisciplinary, problem-based research, resulting in discrimination when tenure reviews happen because tenure decisions are based on evaluations of publications that may not coincide with the promotion, tenure, and reappointment committee's views on acceptable scholarship. Further, teaching evaluations largely disadvantage women of color (Agathangelou and Ling 2002; Anderson and Smith 2005; Centra and Gaubatz 2000; Hendrix 1998; Houston 2005a, 2005b). Unfortunately, tenure and promotion committees generally do not acknowledge these biases. This highlights how policies and procedures at the structural level of academia interact with norms and values at the cultural level to produce inequitable outcomes for already marginalized scholars.

M. Jacqui Alexander, a woman professor of color with research and teaching interests in queer and feminist studies, documented her struggles at the New School for Social Research in New York. This case is noteworthy because the president at the New School did not grant Alexander permission to develop a student-supported gender studies program. Gender studies, a problem-based concentration, did not meet the administration's disciplinary guidelines. Students at the New School, disappointed with course selection and hiring and salary discrepancies for women of color, formed a coalition and went on a hunger strike, known as the Mobilization (Alexander 2005). Today, the Mobilization's legacy endures at the New School through the student publication, *canon*, which supports interdisciplinary work.

Alexander confronted disciplinary standards that impeded her from carrying out research of interest to her, other faculty, and students. She called attention to the "de facto revolving-door policies with regard to faculty of color, which guaranteed that 'whites only' would be the permanent guardians of knowledge and that men and women of color would be assigned the permanent work of service" (Alexander 2005, 143). Alexander related her marginalization with the curriculum and her tenure-related struggles to her social location as a woman of color scholar with gender and queer studies interests. Alexander's work was too radical to find a disciplinary home at the New School in 1997. She left the New School and is now professor of women's studies and gender studies at the University of Toronto. Looking back, Alexander acknowledged her role at the New School as a representative of diversity, but with minimal power to carry out work that was personally and politically meaningful to her.

Other key women of color scholars, Angela Davis and Patricia Williams, have documented their experiences with racism in academia. For example, Davis, known (in part) for her 1970 arrest after being named to the FBI's "Ten Most Wanted" list as a result of her association with a violent court uprising, faced obstacles within the Philosophy department at UCLA prior to her arrest.[1]

Similarly, Williams (1991), a law professor, notes the unequal power structure dynamic that she faced with students and colleagues. Williams writes also of the racism that she encountered with academic journal submissions and recounts how journal editors doubted reports of racism in her article submissions and the adversity that she faced when speaking of her grievances in academic lecture settings. Such responses provide examples of how a "culture of silence" around concerns of marginalization can be perpetuated.

In spite of their educational and class statuses, Alexander, Davis, and Williams confronted barriers within academia largely based on their race, gender, and scholarly interests. Today, as Zweigenhaft and Domhoff (2006) argue, people of color and people in other marginalized social locations have leadership roles in political, corporate, and academic spheres through election, nomination, and appointment. The power elite, once reserved for white men of privilege (Mills 1956), is more diverse today than when Mills wrote about it; however, elevations in academic status do not necessarily level the playing field. Scholars of color whose studies may challenge problem-portable social science disciplinary canons may be especially prone to similar challenges. Privileged scholars who challenge "canons" also face censure.

For example, Pierce (2003b), a sociologist of queer studies, writes about challenges with achieving tenure in a sociology department that did not value her research. Pierce, more accustomed to an environment that embraced diversity during her graduate school days at Berkeley, took a tenure-track position within the Department of American Studies at the University of Minnesota. She recounts the harassment and distress that she endured while trying to achieve validation for her scholarly contributions from a department of sociologists who, largely, could not see the merit of her work based on its feminist and queer underpinnings.

These cases demonstrate how academia can structurally and culturally endorse the vestiges of racism, gender discrimination, and homophobia. Disciplinary implications exist for individuals who are not of the historically patriarchal paradigm of the power elite. Though the presence of women and faculty of color threatens the historical power structure (Agathangelou and Ling 2002; Davis 2005), the homogeneous legacy of departments comprising men is not deconstructed easily by adding women and faculty of color (Essed 2004). However, if women and faculty of color with problem-based research agendas reach critical mass in academic departments, it is possible to change disciplinary standards and tenure review processes that would legitimate problem-based scholars.

Members of academe should be aware of the link between disciplinarity and marginalization resulting from canonical departmental structures.

Privileging traditional, problem-portable studies that do not call attention to social inequalities resulting from gender, race, and sexuality-based discrimination can lead to a hostile work environment for problem-based scholars. The experiences of Alexander, Davis, Williams, and Pierce, as well as others in this book, demonstrate the need for those who are not targets of such oppression to form solid bonds with those who are victimized. In doing so, we can counter this institutional form of oppression that has costs for individual scholars, their students, and the academy.

Moraga's "theory in the flesh" rationale offers insight for those of us who wish to address disciplinary hostility rooted in sexism, racism, and homophobia. She writes:

> Oppression is systematic and structural. A politics of discourse that does not provide for some sort of bodily or concrete action outside the realm of the academic text will forever be inadequate to change the difficult "reality" of our lives. Only by acknowledging the specificity and "simultaneity of oppression," and the fact that some people are more oppressed than others, can we begin to understand the systems and structures that perpetuate oppression in order to place ourselves in a position to contest and change them (Moraga, Loving 128). (Moya 1997, 135)

Conclusion

Throughout this chapter, I have illustrated ways that universities perpetuate racism, gender inequality, and homophobia through structural and cultural processes that protect core disciplinary canons. Women scholars' testimonials of marginalization that they associate with their social locations and research agendas suggest that discrimination within academia is insidious. The accounts in this chapter are not exhaustive. Rather, Alexander, Davis, Williams, and Pierce were fortunate to express their views in publications linked to their research. Their experiences indicate that we must attend to how universities structurally exercise power over research by reifying disciplinary standards. Furthermore, administrators must collect data on the social locations of scholars who hold joint and area studies appointments at universities and be aware of the differential tenure/promotion review processes that nontraditional appointees may confront.

Because U.S. institutions of higher education often veil internal diversity problems with grandiose images of a multicultural student body in admissions brochures and through creative misreporting of diversity-related data, it is not easy to identify how disciplinary authority is exercised. An institution's reputable track record with respect to diversity meets the academic capitalist goals of the institution (Kirp 2003; Newfield 2008; Slaughter and Rhoades 2004) and detracts from the racialized, gendered, and homophobic nature of academia with respect to disciplinary authority. This chapter, however, warrants us to "identify and dismantle those structures in which racism [and gender inequality] continue[s] to be embedded" (Davis 2005, 29).

We need to grapple with these challenges. For example, Pierce (2003a) recognizes that members of the white, power elite can unknowingly contribute to a racist environment through defensiveness and inability to see their own racist underpinnings. Her message echoes the messages of earlier women of color scholars (Moraga and Anzaldúa 1983) who expressed fervent disappointment with the lack of solidarity from white feminist colleagues. In addition, the timing of scholarly publications hampers the ability of scholars who want to write about their inequitable treatment to reach intended audiences promptly. For instance, Alexander published the struggles that she experienced in 1997 eight years later, in 2005. Today, the prevalence and wide readership of web-based forums through professional organizations' Listservs and media such as *The Chronicle of Higher Education* remedies this formerly onerous and time-consuming process of reaching the masses. Furthermore, efforts must be made across disciplines to enable professors to quickly counteract the inequalities they face. As members of academia, we bear witness to such instances of inequality. Yet, competition, apathy, professional obligations, structural and cultural barriers, and our inability to see the injustices that our colleagues face may prevent us from taking action.

Note

1. During the controversy, the philosophy department resolved its disagreement over Davis's Marxist views and supported Davis, who faced scrutiny from the university's board of regents. The regents ultimately fired Davis even after the UCLA administration had ruled in favor of keeping her on as a lecturer (Aptheker 1999). Davis's (2005) account of these events evidences the challenges that she faced when her views and scholarship were outside of the disciplinarily acceptable canons.

References

Abbott, Andrew. 2001. *Chaos of Disciplines*. Chicago, IL: University of Chicago Press.
———. 2002. "The Disciplines and the Future." In *The Future of the City of Intellect: The Changing American University*, edited by Steven Brint, 205–230. Stanford, CA: Stanford University Press.
Agathangelou, Anna M., and L. H. M. Ling. 2002. "An Unten(ur)able Position: The Politics of Teaching for Women of Color in the U.S." *International Feminist Journal of Politics* 4:368–398.

———. 2009. *Transforming World Politics: From Empire to Multiple Worlds.* London: Routledge.

Alexander, M. Jacqui. 2005. *Pedagogies of Crossing: Meditations on Feminism, Sexual Politics, Memory, and the Sacred.* Durham, NC: Duke University Press.

Anderson, Kristin J., and Gabriel Smith. 2005. "Students' Preconceptions of Professors: Benefits and Barriers According to Ethnicity and Gender." *Hispanic Journal of Behavioral Sciences* 27(2):184–201.

Anzaldúa, Gloria. 1999. *Borderlands/La Frontera: The New Mestiza.* San Francisco: Aunt Lute Books.

Aptheker, Bettina. 1999. *The Morning Breaks: The Trial of Angela Davis.* Ithaca, NY: Cornell University Press.

Centra, John A., and Noreen B. Gaubatz. 2000. "Is There Gender Bias in Student Evaluations of Teaching?" *The Journal of Higher Education* 71(1):17–33.

Davis, Angela Y. 1998. "Rape, Racism and the Capitalist Setting." In *The Angela Davis Reader*, edited by Joy James, 129–137. Malden, MA: Blackwell.

———. 2005. *Abolition Democracy: Beyond Empire, Prisons, and Torture.* New York: Seven Stories Press.

Espeland, Wendy Nelson, and Michael Sauder. 2007. "Rankings and Reactivity: How Public Measures Recreate Social Worlds." *American Journal of Sociology* 113(1):1–40.

Espeland, Wendy, and Michael Sauder. 2009. "Rating the Rankings." *Contexts* 8(2):16–21.

Espeland, Wendy Nelson, and Mitchell L. Stevens. 1998. "Commensuration as a Social Process." *Annual Review of Sociology* 24:313–343.

Essed, Philomena. 2004. "Cloning Amongst Professors: Normativities and Imagined Homogeneities." *Nordic Journal of Feminist and Gender Research* 12(2):113–122.

Foucault, Michel. 1977. *Discipline and Punish: The Birth of the Prison.* Translated by Alan Sheridan. New York: Vintage.

Frankenberg, Ruth. 2001. "The Mirage of an Unmarked Whiteness." In *The Making and Unmaking of Whiteness,* edited by Birgit Brander Rasumussen, Eric Klinenberg, Irene J. Nexica, and Matt Wray, 72–96. Durham, NC: Duke University Press.

Glenn, Evelyn Nakano. 1997. "Looking Back in Anger? Re-remembering My Sociological Career." In *Feminist Sociology: Life Histories of a Movement*, edited by Barbara Laslett and Barrie Thorne, 73–102. New Brunswick, NJ: Rutgers University Press.

Hendrix, Katherine G. 1991. "Student Perceptions of the Influence of Race on Professor Credibility." *Journal of Black Studies* 28:738–764.

Hong, Grace Kyungwon. 2006. *The Ruptures of American Capital: Women of Color Feminism and the Culture of Immigrant Labor.* Minneapolis: University of Minnesota Press.

Houston, Therese. 2005a. *Empirical Research on the Impact of Race & Gender in the Evaluation of Teaching.* Center for Excellence in Teaching & Learning, Seattle University, October.

———. 2005b. *Research Report: Race and Gender Bias in Student Evaluations of Teaching.* Center for Excellence in Teaching & Learning, Seattle University, October.

Hurtado, Sylvia, and Jessica Sharkness. 2008. "Scholarship Is Changing, and So Must Tenure Review." *Academe* 94:37–39.

Kirp, David L. 2003. *Shakespeare, Einstein, and the Bottom Line: The Marketing of Higher Education.* Cambridge, MA: Harvard University Press.

Menges, Robert J., and William H. Exum. 1983. "Barriers to the Progress of Women and Minority Faculty." *The Journal of Higher Education* 54:123–144.

Mills, C. Wright. 1956. *The Power Elite.* Oxford: Oxford University Press.

Moraga, Cherríe. 1983. *Loving in the War Years: lo que nunca pasó por sus labios.* Boston: South End Press.

Moraga, Cherríe L., and Gloria E. Anzaldúa, eds. 1983. *This Bridge Called My Back: Writings by Radical Women of Color.* New York: Kitchen Table: Women of Color Press.

Moya, Paula M. L. 1997. "Postmodernism, 'Realism,' and the Politics of Identity: Cherríe Moraga and Chicana Feminism." In *Feminist Genealogies, Colonial Legacies, Democratic Futures,* edited by M. Jacqui Alexander and Chandra T. Mohanty, 125–150. New York: Routledge.

Newfield, Christopher. 2008. *Unmaking the Public University: The Forty-Year Assault on the Middle Class.* Cambridge, MA: Harvard University Press.

Pierce, Jennifer L. 2003a. "'Racing for Innocence': Whiteness, Corporate Culture, and the Backlash Against Affirmative Action." *Qualitative Sociology* 26:53–70.

———. 2003b. "Traveling From Feminism to Mainstream Sociology and Back: One Woman's Tale of Tenure and the Politics of Backlash." *Qualitative Sociology* 26:369–396.

Shumway, David. 1999. "Disciplinarity, Corporatization, and the Crisis: A Dystopian Narrative." *The Journal of the Midwest Modern Language Association* 32:2–18.

Slaughter, Sheila, and Gary Rhoades. 2004. *Academic Capitalism and the New Economy: Markets, State, and Higher Education.* Baltimore: Johns Hopkins University Press.

Williams, Patricia. 1991. *The Alchemy of Race and Rights: Diary of a Law Professor.* Cambridge, MA: Harvard University Press.

Zweigenhaft, Richard L., and G. William Domhoff. 2006. *Diversity in the Power Elite: How It Happened, Why It Matters.* Lanham, MD: Rowman & Littlefield.

9

CHARACTERISTICS AND PERCEPTIONS OF WOMEN OF COLOR FACULTY NATIONALLY

Corinne Castro

This chapter focuses on the experiences of women of color faculty, and particularly how intersections of race and gender illuminate some of the gendered and racialized processes—specifically regarding university service, mentoring, teaching, and research—that create fundamentally different professional experiences for faculty in academia.

Generally, the existing literature relevant to the experiences of women of color faculty is embedded in the research on either people of color generally *or* women faculty (Aguirre 2000; Moore, Alexander, and Lemelle 2010; Stanley 2006; Turner and Myers 2000). However, a small emergent pool of scholarship has opened discussion about the work lives of minority women faculty (Berry and Mizelle 2006; Holmes, Land, and Hinton-Hudson 2007; Margolis and Romero 1998; Thomas and Hollenshead 2001; Turner 2002; Vakalahi and Starks 2011; Vargas 2002). When examining this literature, three themes emerge as relevant to this chapter's goals: (a) the underrepresentation and isolation that women of color faculty often encounter at their institutions; (b) the disproportionate service burden academic women of color face, or what I call the *diversity double duty*; and (c) the systemic repeal and delegitimization of affirmative action,[1] which brings into question the authority and validity of women of color's scholarship, pedagogies, and professional accolades. These professional challenges for women of color faculty can seriously affect their career advancement, health, and well-being (Vakalahi and Starks 2011).

First, women and people of color continue to be underrepresented as tenure-track faculty, especially at the highest levels (full professors and administrators) and at the most prestigious institutions (Turner and Myers 2000). One theory to explain this underrepresentation is the notion of *multiple marginality*, explained as "the more ways in which one differs from the 'norm,' the more social interactions will be affected within multiple contexts. Situations in which a woman of color might experience marginality are multiplied depending on her marginal status within various contexts" (Turner 2002, 77). Another possible explanation is the concept of *interlocking matrices of oppression/domination,* which describes the

> overall social organization within which intersecting oppressions originate, develop, and are contained. In the U.S., such domination has occurred through schools, housing, employment, government, and other social institutions that regulate the actual patterns of intersecting oppressions that Black women encounter. (Collins 2000, 227–228)

Within academia, women of color experience both phenomena; their marginal status influences their interactions, which are reinforced by structural realities. This population often encounters extreme isolation and underrepresentation at their home institutions and in their disciplines (Turner 2002). The consequences of this isolation contribute to the dearth of mentors and collaborators, which can have detrimental effects on career progress, especially promotion (Holmes et al. 2007). Because tenure and promotion processes lack transparency in most institutions (Quimby, Ross, and Sanford 2006; Tierney and Bensimon 1996), faculty often cannot be successful without mentors and colleagues to provide them with valuable information. Significantly, because tenure and promotion relies heavily on publications, especially at research universities, colleagues and mentors are vital for potential coauthorship opportunities or for providing feedback on drafts before submission for publication.

Second, similar to their white women counterparts, faculty of color experience service and mentoring burdens (Acker and Feuerverger 1996; Gibson 2006; Misra, Lundquist, Holmes, and Agiomavritis 2011; Park 1996; see chapter 4 of this volume) deemed university "carework" (Acker 1995; Murray 2006). With the implementation of diversity curriculum requirements at many universities,[2] administrators turn often to faculty of color to teach these courses and develop curricula, regardless of whether race is one of their research or teaching areas (Moore, Acosta, Perry, and Edwards 2010; Perry et al. 2009; see chapter 2 of this volume). The concept of *cultural taxation*[3] describes the burden that faculty of color experience as a result of such additional responsibilities (Joseph and Hirshfield 2011). Women of color faculty are more vulnerable to this racial, cultural, *and* gendered taxation, what I call the *diversity double duty*.

Finally, some research examines issues of legitimacy and authority experienced by faculty of color in the classroom and with colleagues regarding nonmainstream scholarship and/or methodologies (Aguirre 2000; Perry et al. 2009; Stanley 2007; Turner and Myers 2000). Nonmainstream research includes topics or methods that would unlikely be published in top-tier journals or receive federal or prestigious foundation grants (i.e., most research on people of color; women; and lesbian, gay, bisexual, transgender, and queer communities). Moore, Acosta, Perry, and Edwards (2010) argue that most faculty of color find themselves trapped within a *devalued secondary labor market* structured by the gendered and racialized emotional labor that comes with teaching diversity courses and serving as diversity representatives throughout their institutions. The emotional labor often includes daily attacks on authority and credibility in classrooms despite culturally embedded assumptions that instructors of color and women are better suited to teach courses on race and gender. Moreover, the documented experiences of minority faculty who teach diversity course requirements continually attest that students perceive them negatively as "biased" and/or having political agendas, whereas majority faculty who teach similar content often receive praise as "objective" sources of knowledge (Perry et al. 2009; Vargas 2002). Moore et al. (2010) also argue that demands to contribute to diversity education continue post-tenure. Yet the emotional labor and differential burden that instructors of color at all ranks experience goes unacknowledged.

The research reviewed here creates a foundation for scholars, policy makers, and administrators to understand resilient structures of inequality in academia today, particularly those based on gender and racial hierarchies that are reflective of society. However, most of the empirical research fails to address fully the *intersectional* experiences of academic women of color. The few studies that focus on the professional lives of women of color base their analysis on case studies of faculty at a single institution or use the *autoethnographic*[4] technique (Berry and Mizelle 2006; Holmes et al. 2007; Thomas and Hollenshead 2001; Turner 2002; Vakalahi and Starks 2011; Vargas 2002). Using nationally representative data allows for a much-needed macrolevel analysis that reveals larger patterns of inequality among faculty, providing a necessary backdrop for past, present, and future qualitative studies.

Methods

For my study, I draw from the 2004–2005 Higher Education Research Institute (HERI) Faculty Survey, designed to provide institutions with information about their faculty workload, teaching practices, job satisfaction, and academic climate. Since 1989 more than 350,000 faculty and administrators from 1,200 two- and four-year institutions have participated in this survey, which is administered every three years.[5] My analysis primarily is descriptive, consisting of mostly bivariate and three-way analyses regarding the professional lives of women of color faculty nationally to assess indicators that may impair their recruitment and retention.

The HERI data I use are limited to faculty with a PhD or equivalent who hold appointments in the liberal arts or education departments at Carnegie-designated research universities.[6] My analysis includes non-white women: African American/Black, American Indian, Asian American/Asian, Native Hawaiian/Pacific Islander, Mexican American/Chicano, Puerto Rican, Other Latino, or Other. I excluded respondents who identified as both white and another category. In this sample of women of color, foreign-born respondents account for about 46%, but the clear majority are U.S. citizens (78%).[7] Including foreign-born people in groups labeled "people of color" is a common practice at many state and federal institutions, and in past research on non-white populations.

Within academia, women of color generally belong to a younger cohort.[8] Reflective of the larger population, the sample in this analysis is overrepresented by assistant professors, 40% versus 22% for all other faculty (see Table 9.1).[9] Further, only 50% of women of color are either associate or full

TABLE 9.1.
Academic Rank

	Women of Color Faculty (%)	*All Other Faculty (%)*
Professor	16.0	45.6
Associate professor	33.9	26.3
Assistant professor	39.7	21.7
Lecturer	4.3	3.0
Instructor	7.7	1.2
Other	4.3	2.3
Total	100 (531)	100 (11,508)
Chi-square value	197.759****	

****$p < .001$; ***$p < .01$; **$p < .05$; *$p < .0.1$.

professors, while 72% of all other faculty fall into these ranks (see Table 9.1). In this sample, 63% of women of color faculty received PhDs and 77% started their current position after 1992; therefore, we can infer that the women of color in this sample are generally a newer population of faculty in academia. However, the literature shows that the cohort effect is not the sole underlying factor contributing to the underrepresentation of women of color as tenured and full professors. Thus, I reexamined some key indicators of professional identity to determine the degree to which a cohort effect exists. To make this assessment, I ran a series of three-way analyses using academic rank as a control variable.

Although the women of color faculty sample I draw from for my analyses varies in their racial, ethnic, and citizenship identities, as well as in their tenure status and rank, this chapter narrowly focuses on the ways that academia continues to be structured by gender and race in particular. To construct a clear and concise analysis, I chose not to examine all possible significant intersections. Moreover, a clear limitation of using national-level quantitative data is the lack of a more fine-tuned intersectional lens characteristic of using qualitative data, with its ability to uncover more nuanced processes from multiple intersections of identities—beyond race and gender.

Beliefs About Legitimacy

One of the most significant findings connected to past studies is a concern about feelings of legitimacy. My analysis of the HERI data indicated that 45% of the women of color sample indicated that they "to a great extent" have to work harder to be perceived as legitimate scholars, compared to only 19% of all other faculty feeling this way (see Table 9.2). This result implies that despite increased representation and inclusion of women of color faculty, particularly in the assistant professor ranks since the 1990s, there exists a strong perception among the sample of continually having to assert oneself as a legitimate professional to colleagues, students, and sometimes entire academic institutions.

Table 9.3 presents the percentage of respondents, by rank, who believed they had to work harder "to a great extent" to be perceived as legitimate scholars. In the previous analysis, women of color faculty were more than twice as likely as all other faculty to agree with the statement "I have to work harder to be legitimate" (see Table 9.2). Remarkably, controlling for academic rank seemed to have little effect on these perceptions (see Table 9.3). Controlling for rank resulted in just a 1%–3% change for women of color faculty who believed they had to work harder "to a great extent" at the full, associate, and assistant professor levels, with the differences remaining statistically

TABLE 9.2.
Beliefs About Legitimacy

	Women of Color Faculty (%)	All Other Faculty (%)	Chi-Square Value
Have to work harder to be legitimate			
To a great extent	45.3	18.8	
To some extent	33.5	31.2	
Not at all	21.2	50.0	
Total	100 (519)	100 (11,253)	258.709***

****p < .001; ***p < .01; **p < .05; *p < .01.

TABLE 9.3.
Three-Way Analysis of Legitimacy by Rank

	Women of Color Faculty (%)	All Other Faculty (%)	Chi-Square Value
Have to work harder to a great extent to be legitimate			
Full	42.7 (82)	14.3 (5,102)	57.047****
Associate	46.6 (176)	20.4 (2,954)	80.711****
Assistant	47.6 (208)	22.8 (2,452)	69.920****
Lecturer	23.8 (21)	38.9 (337)	3.242
Instructor	33.3 (9)	28.1 (128)	2.772
Other	52.4 (21)	23.0 (252)	10.066***

****p < .001; ***p < .01; **p < .05; *p < .01.

significant at $p < .001$. Senior (full professor) women of color were almost three times more likely than all other faculty in the same rank to believe that they had to work harder "to a great extent" to be perceived as legitimate scholars: 43% compared to 14%, respectively. These results indicate that inclusion and promotion of minority faculty are not the only solution to solving persistent inequality. Rather, we need to investigate the more subtle mechanisms such as the *diversity double duty* (discussed in the following section).

Desire to Leave Academia

Another significant finding was the effect of academic rank on the desire to leave academia (see Table 9.4). In the original bivariate analysis (table not shown), women of color faculty as a whole were 13% more likely than all

TABLE 9.4.
Three-Way Analysis of Leaving Academia by Rank

	Women of Color Faculty (%)	All Other Faculty (%)	Chi-Square Value
Yes, considered leaving			
Full	26.8 (82)	14.5 (5,137)	9.700***
Associate	37.8 (180)	27.7 (2,980)	8.592***
Assistant	35.3 (207)	34.7 (2,464)	0.031
Lecturer	30.4 (23)	34.9 (338)	0.191
Instructor	55.6 (9)	44.7 (132)	0.401
Other	68.2 (22)	40.6 (252)	6.316**

****$p < .001$; ***$p < .01$; **$p < .05$; *$p < .01$.

other faculty to consider leaving academia (37% versus 24%, respectively). However, when controlling for academic rank, this difference remained predominantly for women of color at the full professor or associate professor level compared to all other faculty, with a 12% and 10% difference, respectively. The chi-square values were significantly lower and the p value slightly increased: 9.700 ($p = .002$) and 8.592 ($p = .003$), respectively, for full professor and associate professor. However, a <1% difference between women of color and all other faculty existed at the assistant professor level on this measure. Consistent with other studies, the data imply that for women of color tenure and promotion do not grant a solid sense of security, belonging, and satisfaction compared to their colleagues who do not strongly consider leaving academia (Castro 2010; Turner 2002).

What is most significant about the previous analysis is that women of color who were associate professors were more likely than full professors to consider leaving academia (38% versus 28%, respectively) (see Table 9.4). We can assume that because the former presumably have had less time since they came up for tenure they have particularly vivid sentiments, perhaps even unpleasant ones, about academia and its processes. Also, it is possible that many more advanced associate professors feel that their potential for being promoted to full professor is stifled as a result of increasing standards for publications and greater service expectations post-tenure. Associate women of color in particular likely have lost most departmental protections against administrative invitations for diversifying university committees (Misra et al. 2011; Pyke 2011). Despite some of the observable effects academic rank has on whether faculty considered leaving academia, women of color comparatively, and particularly the tenured faculty, continue to express more feelings of dissatisfaction and doubt about academia. What these results signal is the importance of invisible systems of inequality that function in academia, particularly those related to the pressures that women of color faculty experience with the push toward diversifying their institutions.

Perspectives on Institutions

In this analysis, I found that women of color faculty were twice as likely to think their institutions have no respect for diverse values and beliefs. Twenty percent of women of color faculty compared to 10% of all other faculty believed there is no respect for the expression of diverse values and beliefs (see Table 9.5). Additionally, 25% of women of color faculty compared to only 9% of all other faculty would describe their institutions as having a lot of racial conflict (see Table 9.5). These results suggest that women of color are significantly more likely to perceive that institutional

TABLE 9.5.
Beliefs and Opinions About the Institution

	Women of Color Faculty (%)	All Other Faculty (%)	Chi-Square Value
Faculty are not rewarded for good teaching.	34.2	28.1	9.052***
Total	100 (524)	100 (11,292)	
There is no respect for diverse values and beliefs.	20.0	10.0	53.116****
Total	100 (520)	100 (11,267)	
There is a lot of racial conflict.[a]	24.5	8.7	145.001****
Total	100 (521)	100 (11,698)	
My department does not mentor new faculty well.[b]	49.1	39.1	24.51****
Total	100 (521)	100 (11,721)	
The criteria for advancement/promotion are not clear.[b]	41.7	25.2	69.500****
Total	100 (513)	100 (11,148)	

[a] The percentage includes respondents who "agree somewhat" and "agree strongly" with the original statement.
[b] The percentage includes respondents who "disagree somewhat" and "disagree strongly" with the original statement.
****$p < .001$; ***$p < .01$; **$p < .05$; *$p < .01$.

climates are unfriendly or even hostile throughout their academic careers. Consequently, their feelings of isolation and alienation may be further exacerbated, which can negatively impact their professional relations and development.

These drastic differences between women of color and all other faculty about perceptions of *racial conflict* may also be a result of divergent definitions of the term. In a post–civil rights era, commonly held and lawfully enforced definitions about racial or sexual discrimination involve overt acts of misconduct from one party against another. Popular discourse mistakenly ignores the less visible and covert "microaggressions" experienced by people in most marginalized communities (Solorzano, Ceja, and Yosso 2000). Additionally, widespread notions about diversity and multiculturalism are often limited to ideas of numerical representation and cultural sensitivity. Therefore, societal understandings and practices regarding discrimination and diversity together can create pervasive and unchecked color blindness that often contributes to people's inability to perceive racial conflict, even among liberal, well-educated, and well-intentioned academics (Bonilla-Silva 2006; Brown 2003; Lewis, Chesler, and Forman 2000).

My analysis also illustrates important patterns regarding faculty perspectives on mentoring and promotion. Specifically, women of color faculty were significantly less likely to believe that departments mentor new faculty well, and they were less likely to perceive promotion criteria as clear (see Table 9.5). Given the critical importance of mentorship and transparency of promotion criteria and processes (Aguirre 2000; Boyle and Boice 1998; Gibson 2006), women of color seem to be at considerable risk for tenure denial given the multiple challenges they already face with systemic undervaluing of their scholarship, teaching, and service (Acker and Feuerverger 1996; Murray 2006; Park 1996; Stanley 2006; Thomas and Hollenshead 2001; Turner 2002; Turner and Myers 2000). These findings suggest differential institutional experiences for academic women of color, some of which have detrimental effects for advancement. These results shed light on the institutionalized racial and gendered inequalities inherent in academic promotion. Ultimately, I argue that these findings indicate the need to reexamine and revise tenure policies and practices.

Research and Teaching Commitments

The literature suggests that women of color are more likely to teach, write, and research in areas less valued[10] in terms of the most prestigious funding and publishing sources. According to my analysis of the HERI data, women of color are nearly three times more likely than other faculty to research and write on issues faced by racial and ethnic minorities and more than twice as likely as other faculty to research and write about women and gender issues (see Table 9.6). The irony is that although many academics consider research examining race, gender, and international issues to be cutting-edge scholarship, the academic rewards systems at most institutions do not acknowledge the additional work and/or challenges encountered by most of these scholars, which ultimately can harm their hiring and promotion possibilities (see chapter 8 of this volume).

Women of color continue to carry disproportionately the burden of diversifying academia, what I call the *diversity double duty*. They were four times more likely to have taught an ethnic studies course and almost three times more likely to have taught a women's studies course than other faculty (see Table 9.7). That is, although academia has recognized the need to diversify the faculty (and student populations), and have acknowledged the importance of implementing multicultural/heterogeneous curricula, the responsibility rests on people of color, especially women, to carry out these mandates and do the heavy lifting of institutional change. Furthermore, as research indicates, classes dealing with sensitive or controversial discussions about race, ethnicity, and gender are generally more challenging to teach as a result of student resistance, misperceptions of instructor bias, and prominent discourses of color-blind racism (Bonilla-Silva 2006; Joseph and Hirshfield 2011; Moore et al. 2010; Perry et al. 2009; Vargas 2002). Ultimately, the *diversity double duty* poses serious costs for women of color faculty (i.e.,

TABLE 9.6.
Research Activities

	Women of Color Faculty (%)	All Other Faculty (%)	Chi-Square Value
Research/write on racial/ethnic minorities			
Yes	61.2	23.7	316.093****
Total	100 (446)	100 (9,786)	
Research/write on women/gender issues			
Yes	48.4	22.4	155.532****
Total	100 (434)	100 (9,728)	
Research/write on international/global issues			
Yes	46.7	32.4	38.884****
Total	100 (437)	100 (10,010)	

****$p < .001$; ***$p < .01$; **$p < .05$; *$p < .01$.

TABLE 9.7.
Teaching Activities

	Women of Color Faculty (%)	All Other Faculty (%)	Chi-Square Value
Taught an ethnic studies course			
Yes	34.9	8.7	336.009****
Total	100 (453)	100 (9,874)	
Taught a women's studies course			
Yes	23.2	8.3	116.776****
Total	100 (448)	100 (9,858)	
Taught a service-learning course			
Yes	28.8	19.4	23.549****
Total	100 (445)	100 (9,844)	

****$p < .001$; ***$p < .01$; **$p < .05$; *$p < .01$.

negatively impacting scholarship production or emotional/physical well-being). Though many women faculty report heavy service burdens, women of color experience the "double duty" because they are targeted for service as women and as people of color.

Since the 1990s the number of women of color earning doctoral degrees and acquiring tenure-track positions has grown significantly—about 63% and 77% of my sample, respectively. Yet, national statistics indicate that this population remains marginal in academia.[11] Strong evidence suggests that academia is far from a transformed institution. Its standards and definitions of the profession remain stable despite newcomers' attempts to rearticulate and redefine academic cultures and despite national engagement with diversity challenges.

The data suggest that women of color faculty as newcomers to academia do not experience smooth socialization into the hegemonic culture, values, and discourses of academia. Rather, these women continually redefine what it means to be a professional through their scholarship, teaching, and service. That is, women of color faculty often shape their professional priorities to align with their personal values and beliefs, despite going against the grain of their disciplines. However, academic cultures have not yet been effectively transformed by the growing number of minority faculty who challenge established norms about what it means to be an academic (Tierney 1997). Women of color faculty face significant institutional challenges including their shared perceptions about their lack of legitimacy; the contentious racial climate that can go unacknowledged by most members of the academy; and the inequitable academic rewards system that advantages particular research, teaching, and service over others.

Attention to the affective realities of academic women of color expands our understanding of the importance of embodied experiences. Being an academic involves considerably more than excelling in research, teaching, and service. Dominant groups in academia are likely to take the academic culture for granted. The often unquestioned legitimacy of majority faculty makes their path through academia more like a moving walkway and less like the obstacle course experienced by many academic women of color.

Although women of color are increasingly incorporated into the academy and sometimes favored by university administration as potential agents of change and diversity, pressures to conform to established values and practices of "hegemonic academic professionalism" exist. The taken-for-granted and seemingly neutral norms that guide workers in various institutions and organizations such as universities are gendered (e.g., Acker 1990) and racialized. Professionalization is a gendered and raced process in which "doing" the professional requires performing masculinity and whiteness (Cheney and Ashcraft 2007; Trethewey 1999). Hegemonic professionalism relies on traditional, Western-centered, or neoliberal sources of knowledge, research methods, pedagogies, and ethics. As women of color academics develop professional identities that better align with their values and priorities, they encounter institutional resistance and are systematically delegitimized. Diversifying the academy will require an expansive definition of professionalism that recognizes a multiplicity of contributions and commitments. Ultimately, unfair practices and systems of delegitimization are antithetical to the goals of inclusion and public good often purported in academia. More important, merely increasing representation of minorities will not alleviate systemic inequalities. Rather, we must critically examine and change academic cultures that covertly reproduce white patriarchal power structures and silence the marginalized.

One practical method to begin uncovering subtle forms of academic inequality is to seriously reevaluate the academic rewards system for tenure and promotion. Overhauling this system, particularly establishing equitable weight for research, teaching, and service, would significantly improve the professional lives of many minority faculty, especially at research universities. Attention to whether or not certain professional priorities are unjustly valued or devalued through the established tenure and promotion processes would alleviate considerable problems. The additional emotional tax and burdens of diversity work, especially teaching diversity curriculum, must be formally recognized and valued, as suggested by Moore et al. (2010). For example, the actual time and weight of teaching courses on sensitive, controversial, and politicized topics, especially as a minority faculty, is qualitatively different from that of most courses taught by majority faculty. This reality should be taken into account when examining student evaluations or when assigning course loads. All faculty and administrators share the responsibility and burden of diversifying universities, such as by ensuring that all faculty actively engage in mentoring students of color and first-generation students and teaching diversity courses. For social institutions to advance and achieve racial and gender equity, diversity work must be prioritized and expected for every member of academic communities, not relegated to the unpaid labor of minorities.

Notes

1. Important cases include California's Proposition 209 in 1995, a successful mandate to the University of California regents to eliminate the consideration of race and ethnicity in admissions policies. See also Supreme Court cases *Gratz v. Bollinger* and *Grutter v. Bollinger* in 2003, which challenged and limited race-conscious policies at the University of Michigan. For an empirical analysis detailing the negative consequences of eliminating affirmative action in American law schools, see Chambers, Clydesdale, Kidder, and Lempert (2005).
2. The American Association of Colleges and Universities has documented that 63% of colleges and universities have a diversity education component in their undergraduate curriculum (Moore et al. 2010), including courses about the historical significance of race, or immigrant experiences in the United States.
3. Drawn from Padilla (1994).
4. "A turning of the ethnographic gaze inward on the self (auto), while maintaining the outward gaze of the ethnography, looking at the larger context wherein self-experiences occur" (Ellis and Bochner 1996, cited in Denzin 1997, 227).
5. See www.heri.ucla.edu/facoverview.php for more information.
6. Currently, this classification includes research universities with very high research activity (RU/VH) and with high research activity (RU/H).
7. Many of the foreign-born respondents have become naturalized U.S. citizens.
8. Cohort can be indicated by the year members received highest degree and by the year of appointment.
9. All statistical results presented in the text are rounded to the nearest whole number for simplicity. See individual tables for precise results.
10. The process of valuation and devaluation in the academy is complex. One important source is the ranking system of journals, or the *impact factor*, which has been critiqued for potential bias. Stanley (2007) has written on biases within the editorial process and likens journal editors to "disciplinary gatekeepers."
11. Data from the National Center for Education Statistics' *2013 Digest of Education Statistics* (http://nces.ed.gov/programs/digest/d13/tables/dt13_315.20.asp) showed that in 2011 40% of women of color filled non-tenured ranks compared to the national average of 32.9% for all faculty, white women (37.6%), men of color (27.8%), and white men (26.2%).

References

Acker, Joan. 1990. "Hierarchies, Jobs, Bodies: A Theory of Gendered Organizations." *Gender and Society* 4(2):139–158.

Acker, Sandra. 1995. "Carry on Caring: The Work of Women Teachers." *British Journal of Sociology of Education* 16(1):21–36.

Acker, Sandra, and Grace Feuerverger. 1996. "Doing Good and Feeling Bad: The Work of Women University Teachers." *Cambridge Journal of Education* 26(3):401–422.

Aguirre, Adalberto. 2000. *Women and Minority Faculty in the Academic Workplace: Recruitment, Retention, and Academic Culture.* San Francisco: Jossey-Bass.

Berry, Theodorea Regina, and Nathalie D. Mizelle. 2006. *From Oppression to Grace.* Sterling, VA: Stylus.

Bonilla-Silva, Eduardo. 2006. *Racism Without Racists.* Lanham, MD: Rowman & Littlefield.

Boyle, Peg, and Bob Boice. 1998. "Systematic Mentoring for New Faculty Teachers and Graduate Teaching Assistants." *Innovative Higher Education* 22(3):157–179.

Brown, Michael K. 2003. *Whitewashing Race: The Myth of a Color-Blind Society.* Oakland: University of California Press.

Castro, Corinne. 2010. "In the Margins of the Academy: Women of Color and Job Satisfaction." In *Dilemmas of Black Faculty at Predominantly White Institutions in the United States: Issues in the Post-Multicultural Era,* edited by Sharon E. Moore, Rudolph Alexander, Jr., and Anthony J. Lemelle, Jr., 135–157. Lewiston, NY: Edwin Mellen Press.

Chambers, David L., Timothy T. Clydesdale, William C. Kidder, and Richard O. Lempert. 2005. "The Real Impact of Eliminating Affirmative Action in American Law Schools: An Empirical Critique of Richard Sander's Study." *University of Michigan Legal Working Paper Series* 50. University of Michigan Law School Scholarship Repository. http://repository.law.umich.edu/cgi/viewcontent.cgi?article=1050&context=law_econ_archive

Cheney, George, and Karen Lee Ashcraft. 2007. "Considering 'the Professional' in Communication Studies: Implications for Theory and Research Within and Beyond the Boundaries of Organizational Communication." *Communication Theory* 17(2):146–175.

Collins, Patricia Hill. 2000. *Black Feminist Thought.* New York: Routledge.

Denzin, Norman K. 1997. *Interpretive Ethnography: Ethnographic Practices for the 21st Century.* Thousand Oaks, CA: SAGE.

Ellis, Carolyn, and Arthur P. Bochner. 1996. *Composing Ethnography.* Walnut Creek, CA: Rowman Altamira.

Gibson, Sharon K. 2006. "Mentoring of Women Faculty: The Role of Organizational Politics and Culture." *Innovative Higher Education* 31(1):63–79.

Holmes, Sharon L., Lynette D. Land, and Veronica D. Hinton-Hudson. 2007. "Race Still Matters: Considerations for Mentoring Black Women in Academe." *The Negro Educational Review* 58(1–2):105–129.

Joseph, Tiffany D., and Laura E. Hirshfield. 2011. "'Why Don't You Get Somebody New to Do It?' Race and Cultural Taxation in the Academy." *Ethnic and Racial Studies* 34(1):121–141.

Lewis, A. E., M. Chesler, and T. A. Forman. 2000. "The Impact of 'Colorblind' Ideologies on Students of Color: Intergroup Relations at a Predominantly White University." *Journal of Negro Education* 69(1–2):74–91.

Margolis, Eric, and Mary Romero. 1998. "'The Department Is Very Male, Very White, Very Old, and Very Conservative': The Functioning of the Hidden Curriculum in Graduate Sociology Departments." *Harvard Educational Review* 68:1–32.

Misra, Joya, Jennifer Lundquist, Elissa Holmes, and Stephanie Agiomavritis. 2011. "The Ivory Ceiling of Service Work." *Academe* 97(1): 22–26. http://www.aaup.org/article/ivory-ceiling-service-work.

Moore, Helen A., Katherine Acosta, Gary Perry, and Crystal Edwards. 2010. "Splitting the Academy: The Emotions of Intersectionality at Work." *Sociological Quarterly* 51(2):179–204.

Moore, Sharon E., Rudolph Alexander, Jr., and Anthony J. Lemelle, Jr. eds. 2010. *Dilemmas of Black Faculty at Predominantly White Institutions in the United States: Issues of the Post-Multicultural Era*. Lewiston, NY: Edwin Mellen Press.

Murray, Jean. 2006. "Constructions of Caring Professionalism: A Case Study of Teacher Educators." *Gender & Education* 18(4):381–397.

Padilla, A. M. 1994. "Ethnic Minority Scholars, Research, and Mentoring: Current and Future Issues." *Educational Researcher* 23(4):24–27.

Park, Shelley M. 1996. "Research, Teaching, and Service: Why Shouldn't Women's Work Count?" *The Journal of Higher Education* 67(1):46–84.

Perry, Gary, Helen A. Moore, Crystal Edwards, Katherine Acosta, and Connie Frey. 2009. "Maintaining Credibility and Authority as an Instructor of Color in Diversity-Education Classrooms: A Qualitative Inquiry." *The Journal of Higher Education* 80(1):80–105.

Pyke, Karen. 2011. "Service and Gender Inequity Among Faculty." *PS-Political Science & Politics* 44(1):85–87.

Quimby, J., D. Ross, and D. Sanford. 2006. "Faculty Perceptions of Clarity in Promotion and Tenure Evaluations." *The Teachers College Record*. http://www.tcrecord.org/Content.asp?ContentID=12668.

Solorzano, Daniel, Miguel Ceja, and Tara Yosso. 2000. "Critical Race Theory, Racial Microaggressions, and Campus Racial Climate: The Experiences of African American College Students." *The Journal of Negro Education* 69(1/2):60–73.

Stanley, Christine A. 2006. *Faculty of Color: Teaching in Predominantly White Colleges and Universities*. Bolton, MA: Anker.

———. 2007. "When Counter Narratives Meet Master Narratives in the Journal Editorial-Review Process." *Educational Researcher* 36(1):14–24.

Thomas, Gloria D., and Carol Hollenshead. 2001. "Resisting From the Margins: The Coping Strategies of Black Women and Other Women of Color Faculty Members at a Research University." *The Journal of Negro Education* 70(3): 166–175.

Tierney, William G. 1997. "Organizational Socialization in Higher Education." *The Journal of Higher Education* 68(1):1–16.

Tierney, William G., and Estela Mara Bensimon. 1996. *Promotion and Tenure: Community and Socialization in Academe*. Albany, NY: SUNY Press.

Trethewey, A. 1999. "Disciplined Bodies: Women's Embodied Identities at Work." *Organization Studies* 20(3):423–450.

Turner, Caroline Sotello Viernes. 2002. "Women of Color in Academe: Living With Multiple Marginality." *The Journal of Higher Education* 73(1):74–93.

Turner, Caroline Sotello Viernes, and Samuel L. Myers, Jr. 2000. *Faculty of Color in Academe: Bittersweet Success*. Boston: Allyn & Bacon.

Vakalahi, Halaevalu F. Ofahengau, and Saundra Hardin Starks. 2011. "Health, Well-Being and Women of Color Academics." *International Journal of Humanities and Social Science* 1(2):185–190.

Vargas, Lucila. 2002. *Women Faculty of Color in the White Classroom*. New York: Peter Lang.

IO

WOMEN SOCIOLOGISTS AND THE QUESTION OF INCLUSION IN THE ACADEMY

Kristin Marsh

While women[1] are increasingly represented among college and university faculty, this representation is uneven among organization types, faculty ranks, and disciplines (Fox 2001; Frehill 2006; West and Curtis 2006). Further, women faculty do not seek or receive promotion to full professor at the same rates as men (Thornton 2009). But why? Existing scholarship recognizes differences in family obligations—extending beyond childcare to the care of elderly relatives or partners with health or ability challenges (Bracken, Allen, and Dean 2006; Philipsen 2008). In addition, research points to inequitable distribution of service and teaching obligations at work (Bird, Litt, and Wang 2004; Misra, Lundquist, Holmes, and Agiomavritis 2011; Winslow 2010; see also chapters 4 and 9 of this volume).

Contrasting with research that emphasizes the continuing importance of addressing gender inequity because of the negative effect it has on faculty careers, general, casual conversations educators have about women's inclusion in academia imply that the problem has been solved. For example, the online newsletter *Inside Higher Ed* reported on research by the Collaborative

The author would like to thank the participants in her study; they selflessly gave their time from too-busy professional lives to share with me their career experiences with frankness and honesty. This ongoing project has been made possible through time off from teaching afforded through faculty development support at the University of Mary Washington.

on Academic Careers in Higher Education (COACHE) that found differences in job satisfaction by gender and discipline, but readers' comments
questioned the importance of the issue (Jaschick 2010). Select posts characterized the women as "complainers":

> Maybe men are just more easy-going and willing to suck it up and do the
> job despite the conditions, so perhaps women will *never* be as satisfied as
> men overall. If this is the case then maybe we should simply give everyone
> equal opportunity and quit listening to the professional complainers. We'd
> probably get a lot more real work done. (posted by "mb")

The poster suggests that women academics have choices and an equal opportunity to succeed at work. This individual does not consider the gendered
structures and cultures of academia. The trend toward greater representation is cited to prove inclusion, without critical discussion of terms. And any
limits to a woman's career success reflect the choices she continues to make
as an individual (including whether she is willing to "suck it up" at work),
rather than the gendered structures and cultures of paid work.

These differing interpretations—one of persistent inequalities versus one
of opportunity and equal treatment—reflect a complex, fluid reality. Certainly,
positive changes have occurred in the profession, even as other still-gendered
aspects of women academics' lives and careers resist transformation. In this
chapter, I explore the issue of inclusion from the perspectives of 20 women
sociologists holding associate or full professor rank. Some are (or have been)
in administrative posts. According to professional standards, they are accomplished; some are well known in their subfields. I am interested in how they
experience their career trajectories, whether they consider themselves successful, and whether they have felt fully included, valued, and rewarded. Women's
stories—in their terms—provide an understanding of how gendered academia
remains, and the extent to which hierarchies persist, even as academia strives to
be equitable, meritocratic, and inclusive (Harding 1991; Smith 1987, 1990).

Further, I explore reported support and inclusion versus chill in women's
current and prior positions (e.g., as graduate students, in first jobs). The concept of a chilly climate has long informed studies about educational inclusion.
Reports focused our attention on classroom, then campus climate (Hall 1982,
1984) and illustrated the importance of mentoring in shaping successful academic experiences for women students, faculty, and administrators (Hall 1983;
also Sandler 1991, 1992 and Sandler, Silverberg, and Hall 1996). I use the
concept of climate to include immediate aspects of workplace culture and structure that women experience as unwelcoming or undermining of their contributions (chilly) versus environments that signal recognition of value and inclusion
(warm).

A Focus on Sociology

The study discussed in this chapter is part of an ongoing project exploring professional socialization/aspirations and perceptions of accomplishment among sociologists in academic careers. As a social science, sociology historically has been neither idiosyncratically closed nor particularly inclusive of women. Women sociologists in the United States, for example, were active in the young academic discipline. As influential men defined *sociology* as a scientific endeavor in the positivist tradition, they excluded women's contributions from textbooks and marginalized their work (Deegan 1990, 1991; Lengermann and Neibrugge 2007). Currently, the makeup of sociology departments depends on the type and rank of the institution, with women disproportionately at teaching colleges and at lower ranks whereas men dominate PhD-granting departments and higher ranks (American Sociological Association 2008). Longitudinal data indicate a narrowing gap, even though in 2006–2007 women made up only 32% of full professors in sociology (American Sociological Association 2008). In essence, sociology has been neither a bastion of gender neutrality and women friendliness nor the predominantly men's domain that traditionally characterizes engineering, law, and the natural sciences (Epstein 1983; Fox 2001; Hagan and Kay 1995). Sociology represents somewhat of a middle ground, where we can presume neither gender neutrality nor preference.

Moore (2007) suggests that women may be included as "one of us" only to the extent that they go along with the premise of equality within patriarchal structures and only to the extent that they conform to normative expectations of "unbiased" (i.e., nonfeminist) research. To what degree and in what contexts are women sociologists with critical perspectives in feminism and/or race theory allowed to participate and thrive as sociologists? Departmental and institutional contexts shape women's careers, but women's achievements in academic sociology occur within a context valuing sociology at the bottom among social sciences (at least in terms of pay) (Spalter-Roth and Scelza 2009). Examining women sociologists' experiences contributes to an understanding of the stakes when a profession seems to have reached a threshold of gender inclusiveness (Bottero 1992) while struggling with its status among peer disciplines (Jaschick 2009).

I draw on unstructured, in-depth interviews with 20 women sociologists in midlevel and advanced academic careers. Because subjective experience is not observable, qualitative methodology allows for exploration of emergent themes, attention to detail, and nuanced understanding of experience (Patton 2001; Silverman 2010). In my multitiered sampling strategy, I identified women associate and full professors as listed on sociology department websites. I sent an introduction and invitation to participate by e-mail, then added a second snowball strategy when participants offered names of potential contacts. Additionally, I contacted faculty at local, regional, and national conferences. These secondary strategies expanded the pool of respondents in general, and women of color in particular.[1] There were 15 white women from the United States, 1 white woman from the United Kingdom, 3 African American women from the United States, and 1 Indian woman from India in the sample. All have tenure; four are full professors and 17 are associate professors. The interview location varied by respondent preference. I conducted two interviews by phone and 18 interviews in person. Interviews ranged from 45 to 120 minutes, with most lasting approximately 90 minutes.

In this chapter I aim to illustrate themes related to work environment that emerged in my interviews.[2] Space limitations preclude inclusion of direct quotes from all respondents, though I have been careful to reflect issues salient to women at different ranks and in different institutional settings (research university versus teaching college). Issues of confidentiality and anonymity present a serious concern and commitment in qualitative research, and researchers vary their approaches to protecting respondents' identities. These issues are heightened because of the overlap between the community from which respondents are drawn and my intended audience. I use pseudonyms throughout, and I exclude nonessential references to institution type, location, or research specialty. This is not an easy decision because work environments are framed by institution type (i.e., university size and rank). But, it is pivotal to protecting respondents.

The Question of Climate

Historically, especially in professions dominated by men, hostility and discrimination have been an institutionalized part of work for women (Jacobs 1989; Kanter 1977). This state continues in many fields and work settings, especially to the extent that sex segregation persists. I would posit that the question of a chilly climate remains pertinent in sociology, a profession that has been increasingly inclusive of white women; has farther to go toward inclusion—or even representation—of women of color; and currently struggles with labor market segmentation and men's continued dominance in rank, recognition, and pay. Because my central interview question was not "How chilly was the climate?" but "Tell me about your career experiences," I uncovered nuanced understandings of work environments and women's understandings of merit in their careers.

When asked about their experiences at work and in graduate school, most respondents said they like their current jobs. However, respondents identified specific factors that complicated neat conclusions about whether a workplace is experienced as supportive and inclusive of women; some aspects of the work environment can "warm" or "chill" the climate.

Table 10.1 lists the "warming" and "chilling" factors organized by whether they operate on an interpersonal or institutional level. However,

TABLE 10.1.
**Signifiers of Support Versus Chill as Operating at Interpersonal
and Institutional Levels**

	Support	*Chill*
Interpersonal	• Mentoring (informal) • Colleague help negotiating (in meetings or one-on-one) • Coauthoring • Welcoming gestures/comments (of person or work)	• Hostile comments • Sexual harassment • Bias against research • Silence on institutional expectations or strategies ("playing the game")
Institutional	• Mentoring (formal) • Family care provisions (daycare; courses off; stopped clock) • Professional development support (space; travel; time off) • Merit for diverse kinds of service/teaching priorities	• Undue or undervalued service or teaching expectations • Left out of advancement opportunities and lower pay • Static values and assumptions about legitimate work

the table simplifies complex social processes. In reality, interactions occur within an institutional context, and university policies are enacted through (or resisted by) individuals. Institutional arrangements can provide rationale for bias against an individual or they can provide resources and legitimacy for more inclusive processes. Respondents in this study frequently distinguished department from university context—a supportive department can help buffer the effects of a static or uncompromising college administration and vice versa. Finally, both support and chill can emanate from the presence of specific policies or interactions, or by their absence.

The Importance of Personal Interactions

A few respondents reported nothing but support throughout their careers. A few carry a burden of not fitting in, feeling accepted, or feeling valued by their colleagues. But, most participants told a more complicated story. Gail and Hannah shared stories about blatant sexism or racism. Gail, an African American associate professor, recalled a graduate school experience:

> I remember the comment of this individual and I'm not going to name him because he's very, very famous, but I remember him saying something to the effect that, he said something about "if you are still here next semester. . . ."

I took that to imply that somehow I didn't merit my acceptance into the program. I was very offended and I didn't say anything aloud because of his power over me, but at the same time I was sitting there thinking, "That's what you think." He didn't know who he was talking to.

Later, Gail mentioned that other African American students experienced similar treatment from this professor, supporting her interpretation that this was bias.

Hannah, who is white and a full professor at mid-career, remembered specific chilling experiences such as an interview that foreshadowed a potentially hostile work environment, enough so that she turned down the job offer:

> [T]he chair of that department was so inappropriate in a gendered way. It wasn't sexual harassment, but it was clear that he, it seemed like he . . . I don't know how to describe what happened . . . but he picks me up in a car that has a lipstick kiss on the window, like . . . a woman had walked up to the car and kissed the car. . . . He never said anything inappropriate to me . . . but it was clear that he enjoyed spending time with students and having drinks with students and, again, I'm like, "Whoa, okay." . . . It was an atmosphere that seemed weird.

While clear in their memories, these moments do not characterize the overall narrative for Gail or Hannah. The predominant theme for Gail is one of support and encouragement. In particular, peers and women mentors in her undergraduate and MA programs helped her chart her course. Without them, she said, she would not have thought about earning a PhD.[3] Gail faced difficult environments in graduate school and in her first professional appointment, but since then her professional life has been fulfilling, and her current position is one that she said works well with her personality. She feels responsible for mentoring students and returned to this theme as we closed our interview:

> I know one thing I would like to say . . . that I'm mentoring my students. And that's very important to me. You know, it's important to me because people did it for me and I'm encouraging a lot of my undergraduate women to go to grad school who maybe hadn't even considered it. . . . That's just something I wanted to add. Mentoring is very important. It made the difference in my life.

Like Gail, Hannah deemphasized the relevance of what she relayed as isolated chilling moments. When speaking of her current position, she conveyed happiness and the feeling of being supported and valued:

Hannah: I do really feel like [the university] has been an incredibly supportive space for me.

Interviewer: That's great. Both in the department . . . and . . . ?

Hannah: Primarily in the department, but also from the administration. They haven't worked against me. [T]he general environment of the university is supportive, yes, particular individuals more or less so, but yeah . . . that's true.

While several participants emphasized early mentoring relationships and lasting friendships from graduate school carrying them throughout their careers, others reported a change in work climate over their tenure. Magda, a white woman, reported, "[I] can't believe I have such a great job. It's fantastic." She mentioned difficulties her first year, including alarming and unexpected hostility:

At the beginning, you know, there was a dose of homophobia, there was a dose of disciplinary narrowness. I had the chair call me in one day and [he] said, "You know, we don't like anything with a post in front of it" (because I do poststructural analyses). So I said, "Why did you hire me? That's what I do." And he said, "Well, yeah, that is our problem."[4]

This direct challenge to her expertise was compounded by an expectation to teach courses outside her training, and her chair's dismissive attitude toward "junior" (versus pre-tenure) faculty. As an older new faculty member, her initial job experiences presented a contradiction: She expected to be treated with respect as an adult and a professional, but she was treated with condescension. This hostility was further punctuated by anonymous, cryptic phone calls and a second encounter with the chair, who asked her why she thought nobody liked her. Magda said she often visualized leaving academia, which is striking given how much she loves her job now. What changed? For Magda, it was not just time passing or getting tenure that made the difference: Her university had to change for the departmental environment to change, specifically for her work to be supported. When administrators decided things needed to change, they implemented necessary policies and supports, illustrating the crucial role institutional arrangements play in shaping work environments.

Institutional Arrangements and the Ideal Worker

As poignant as stories of interactional hostility or support can be, institutional arrangements (i.e., workplace culture) figure more prominently in women's narratives about what makes for a supportive work environment. Perhaps their emphasis on institutional context relates to sociology.[5] Participants agreed that the organization of work in academia suffers from persistent, unrealistic distinctions between work and nonwork life and from still-gendered and racialized expectations for the "ideal worker" (Cha 2011; Williams 2000; see also chapter 11 this volume).

Support for Family Responsibilities

When asked whether universities are doing enough to support family/life responsibilities, many respondents—particularly mothers or those who have been in other intensive caretaker roles—said absolutely not; universities could do more. On-site daycare, effective family leave policies, and reimbursement for daycare at conferences were concrete suggestions for universities. Amie, a white associate professor, recalled:

> When I went to ASA[6] one year, I ended up bringing my baby because I was still breast feeding. I wasn't quite ready to be away, you know, which was just me, and it was great to bring him along. But if I could have just had three hours of childcare when I had to go do my presentation paid for by the university because the university [should understand] that I am a faculty member with a family and that they're not always completely separate. So, of course, I did have to pay for three hours of childcare.

Amie defined *family needs* as part of worker needs, challenging the social organization of family as being separate from work:

> But, you know, the university understands that I need to eat, and they understand I need to sleep. So they understand that I am a living human being. And yet they don't care that my baby is a living human being who might need my actual physical body. You know? He is nourished by my body that you're feeding and housing. And so we might need to take that into account. . . . They understand you need pens and paper to do your job. They don't care that you need childcare to do your job.

Respondents reported that family support is improving at their universities but that the department culture and supportive chair represent an important interface between institutionalized policies and actual practice (see chapter 6 this volume). Several participants reported having to negotiate for family leave. Amie, for example, said that new parents are allowed to take a one-semester leave, but she had to negotiate hard for a one-course teaching reduction the semester she had her son. Yet Magda reported having her chair's full support in scheduling classes to avoid conflicts with caretaking needs. Hannah mentioned that her university's family policies, including a one-semester paid maternity leave, are unusually supportive. Kara, a white associate professor, explained that in the last few years her university has implemented supportive leave policies:

> They passed a parental leave so you get a semester off, a full-paid leave. Yeah, so I was on leave when I had my baby. I had [him] at the end of April and then I had the summer off as I usually do. (I don't teach in the summer.) Then in the fall when I would have gone back, I was able to have an entire semester of paid leave.

She said that parental leave at her university applies to everyone, "men or women or lesbian couples or people who adopt or whatever, and I have several colleagues at top institutions that don't have anything remotely like that." Further, she contrasted this with the policies at her husband's university:

> He went and spoke to his chair about, you know, what options [there] are and they basically laughed. I mean [my husband's field] is so fundamentally male oriented in every way, shape, and form. And so, you know there's no leave. So my husband went back to work full-time and I pretty much stayed home with our son.

Some universities are farther along in adopting family-friendly leave policies than others. At some institutions, the gendered organizational structure of the academy remains unchanged, and family leave is seen as a "woman's" issue. Kara had university support but lost time from her work and productivity; her husband's work trajectory was uninterrupted.

Formal Mentoring Relationships

Mentoring is an important support mechanism that often emerges informally (as Gail emphasized earlier). But, a few respondents pointed to formal mentoring arrangements, especially in their current appointments, as playing a pivotal role in their transition to the new environment. Kara noted the importance of both types of mentors. When she joined her current university, she was assigned a formal mentor:

> I learned so much from him and I just shut up and let him teach me. . . . My writing was not that great when I first came out, and I mean we would work on drafts and he would just mark it up and I would do my best to not let it get me and then I learned to be a better writer from him. I learned to ask important questions a lot from him. I mean, I got that from a lot of people, but I'm saying I really got a lot of one-on-one experience from my mentor.

Mentoring also seems to matter in its absence. Janice, a white associate professor, found out that a man colleague, three years her junior, had a higher starting salary than she was making as an associate professor. Upon asking her chair about it, she was told it was because he negotiated his salary when joining the university. Janice saw the lesson here as twofold: Women need to learn to negotiate, and we need to be mentoring women so that they know these things. Janice said, "No one mentioned to me to negotiate my salary." However, once Janice learned the importance of negotiation and assertively asked for what she needed, she met with resistance. Janice had difficulty making the most of her successes after receiving external funding for research. She said her department and university "didn't know how" to support her. It became clear as she relayed her story that they didn't really step up to the task of trying to figure it out—or of letting her ask them for the things she needed. Her department rejected requests for things such as office space for her research team:

> People told me that I had to break down all the barriers to getting grants and that's what I did, and when I got the biggest grant that we had in our college—and even then it was almost like some people were jealous—it wasn't really mentioned that much. I tried to get a room and had to fight for it even though I was hiring three people, you know; no one understood. They really didn't understand so I became sort of known as always like the person who's trying to get this and trying to get that, so I just sort of backed off and quit asking, you know. . . . Someone even said, "Oh, you're always complaining, what are you complaining about now?"

Like Janice, Aminah, an African American associate professor, did not have the benefit of either formal or informal mentoring in her current position. She reported feeling marginalized in a context in which a lot of faculty do collaborative, coauthoring work. She told me she thinks this marginalization is more about race than gender. Her colleagues never ask her to collaborate or to read or comment on their work. Nor are they willing to spend minimal time to give input on her own work. One colleague refused to read a five-page proposal. In this context, Aminah is struggling to finish a book-length project in the face of a heavier teaching load than most in her department. She expressed a sense of "always running uphill": "There's this feeling of assessment like somehow I'm being assessed as deficient, you know, as not meeting the real standards of research that are part of the profession, you know, and not really knowing how that decision is made or what I can do to change that." And, it results in a contradiction: "They raise your teaching load because you're not doing enough research, but then by definition they're consuming my time with teaching. And then I'm supposed to do what? I'm supposed to run uphill." Aminah's narrative reflects both the importance of workload and the importance of transparency in expectations. In her position at a research university, she is evaluated primarily in terms of her scholarly productivity, though it is less clear exactly how productivity is measured and how the decision was made to raise her teaching load instead of someone else's.

Limiting Service and Teaching Obligations

Aminah suggested that a more supportive approach might be to encourage productivity in research by temporarily reducing or limiting teaching and service obligations. Like Aminah, Nancy understood that a discrepant workload can limit one's scholarly productivity. But her experience is one of a long career of administrative and service obligations. Nancy spoke of her loyalty and commitment to her university. She has a successful career, one in which she has felt valued, but she expressed that she has stayed at the associate professor level for too many years. She described her productivity as inadequate for application to full professor. Yet she also identified as someone who is central to the life and health of the university: "The kinds of work I've done in the institution [are things that] keep the place going day to day but which one also recognizes are ultimately not the things that the university thinks build the reputation of the institution." Her service has included work on several department and university search committees as well as on governance- and planning-related committees, and administrative roles both in the department and in interdisciplinary programs. As she described her ongoing service and administrative obligations, I was overwhelmed by the weight and breadth of her commitments. In almost the same breath, she took responsibility for these choices in her professional life and recognized the structural problem of service for midcareer sociologists: "Very honestly I am quite unhappy with my professional life right now because I feel so burdened by it and I allow it, but I really would like to be able to do more scholarship."

This problem of heavy service for midcareer sociologists is one that is increasingly recognized in scholarship on higher education (Bird et al. 2004; Misra et al. 2011; Winslow 2010; chapters 4 and 9 of this volume). And Nancy, a white associate professor, reported that her university's administration understands this: "They say we've got this bulge of women who have, you know, been tenured in some cases for 15 years and they're not in a position . . . to go up for promotion. . . . There's a recognition that it's women and that . . . they are carrying a very heavy service load. They really are." At the same time, Nancy does not experience her service burden as an indication of a lack of support or being undervalued by her university. Promotion is still a personal goal and a goal that the university has for her. She continues to experience the climate as welcoming and supportive.

Questioning Gender

Study participants responded cautiously to questions about the influence of gender on their experiences of departmental and university climate. In much the way that Feagin and Sikes (1994) describe racism in a society that no longer allows or accepts overt expressions of racism, gender discrimination remains ubiquitous but much more subtle, almost hidden. Participants reported not being sure whether there was discrimination or not: Was that a sexist, racist, or homophobic throwaway comment or "am I imagining it"? In their day-to-day lives, they may opt to ignore or reinterpret ill treatment. Or they may err on the side of assuming the best. As they relayed their stories, participants were generous in their interpretations, referring to the ignorance of the offender, or perhaps of a different generation and the "old" way of doing things. Additionally, respondents reported carrying the burden of handling these situations—they were aware of what they were about to say and took responsibility for reeling themselves in before situations got out of hand. Further, of my respondents who shared stories of interactional chill relayed them as remembrances from graduate school, first professional appointments, or—rarely—a probationary period in their current positions. It is possible that explicit expressions of sexism are less prevalent than in the past, but also that the security and status of tenure serve as a protection from these interactions.

Situating Our Experiences in the Larger Profession

Participants in this study have achieved mid- and late-career success in a discipline and profession that has seen dramatic changes on several fronts. In terms of the gender makeup of the profession, women are now well represented among PhD sociology students and graduates; they are increasingly represented among tenure-line sociology faculty at research universities. But they continue to predominate the ranks of contingent (adjunct and nontenured full-time) faculty at a time when universities are relying more and more on these positions (Thornton 2009; West and Curtis 2006; chapter 3 of this volume). As long as women continue to shoulder the burden of family care, and to the extent that workplaces are organized around hard-set conceptions of separate spheres (domestic versus public), the challenges of work-family balance will disproportionately affect women's faculty careers. Further, to the extent that research remains the singular determinant of university prestige and faculty achievement, women who value intensive teaching methods or are drawn to the intrinsic rewards of teaching or service will find themselves resigned to associate-level rank at mid- and into late-career.

It is tempting to make sense of these patterns in terms of women's choices. After all, if the profession has long been one that values and rewards research over teaching and service, then women who knew these institutional priorities from the start could have reordered their individual priorities accordingly. Indeed, the advice is often to "just say no" to additional committee work and to burdensome student requests for advice or mentorship (see chapter 4). The success of some women sociologists in achieving top ranks suggests that many academic women value their research and have a productive publication agenda. My interviews indicate, however, that these women are juggling burdensome obligations and working long hours, and that their personal lives suffer. They are getting the research done *on top of* time-intensive service and teaching.

It is possible to reshape a profession in which teaching is valued as much as research and service obligations at midcareer are shared equally (Park 1996). An insidious trend toward a two-tiered system means a heavier teaching load shouldered by the growing contingent faculty (who are predominantly women). At the same time, considerable attention is given to measuring assessment of student outcomes throughout higher education (Katz 2010). If outcomes assessment truly represented a commitment to quality teaching, faculty would be given increased autonomy in shaping assessment practices and setting learning goals. More to the point for faculty careers, universities and colleges would champion teaching accomplishments and scholarship on pedagogy equally with research success.

For the respondents in my study, the interactional climate is much improved even since their own time in graduate school and in their early careers. But, many of the institutional challenges remain for these sociologists, reflecting persistent contradictions between how workplaces are set up—as gendered organizations (e.g., Acker 1990; Martin 1994)—and workers' needs. Workplaces cannot really be distinct spheres of our lives, separate from our home selves, our parent selves, and our partner selves (Bracken et al. 2006). And the rewards of high-profile, high-quantity scholarship reflect only a piece of what these sociologists are asked to accomplish throughout the workweek (and into the weekend). While their particular experiences varied, the respondents seemed to agree that our colleagues and administrative faculty help shape a welcoming environment when they are cognizant of the many pressures on our workday, and when they help us balance, instead of juggle, work and family. The most welcoming work environment is the one that values our work selves as part of our whole selves.

Notes

1. My focus in this chapter is on gender, but never can gender be separated from other aspects of self, such as race, class, age, and sexuality. The imperative to incorporate intersectionality of experience is furthered by the interview-based design of this study. However, privileging respondents' stories in the context of a relatively small population of U.S. academic sociologists heightens the risk of identifying respondents located in certain organization types (e.g., historically Black colleges and universities, women's colleges) and individual women of color in predominantly white colleges and universities. My respondents' stories convince me that although sociology may be at a crossroads in terms of women's representation we have not effectively recruited or supported Black and Latina women.
2. See Nippert-Eng (1996) for a discussion of reporting practices in qualitative research.
3. Several respondents reported that graduate school never occurred to them until an undergraduate advisor suggested it.
4. As this quote suggests, poststructuralism has not been fully accepted as legitimate sociology. But, the interpretation of the situation depends on one's standpoint. Madga's narrative incorporates the multidimensionality of the interaction (and the matrix of domination; see Collins 1990). Her chair, though, had directly challenged only her methodology, rendering invisible other biases shaping his critique.
5. Two respondents identified Dorothy Smith's (1987) theoretical work as influencing their interest in sociology and as being instructive in their thinking about inclusion in professional organizational contexts.
6. The American Sociological Association (ASA), the primary national professional organization in sociology, holds meetings each August.

References

Acker, Joan. 1990. "Hierarchies, Jobs, Bodies: A Theory of Gendered Organizations." *Gender and Society* 4(2):139–158.

American Sociological Association. 2008. "Annual Sociology Faculty Salaries by Rank, Gender and Type of Institution, AY 2006/07." http://www.asanet.org/research/stat_sociology_programs/facsal01072.cfm.

Bird, Sharon, Jacqueline Litt, and Yong Wang. 2004. "Creating Status of Women Reports: Institutional Housekeeping as 'Women's Work.'" *NWSA Journal* 16(1): 194–206.

Bottero, Wendy. 1992. "The Changing Face of the Professions? Gender and Explanations of Women's Entry to Pharmacy." *Work, Employment and Society* 6(3): 329–346.

Bracken, S. J., J. K. Allen, & D. R. Dean, eds. 2006. *The Balancing Act: Gendered Perspectives in Faculty Roles and Work Lives.* Sterling, VA: Stylus.

Cha, Youngjoo. 2011. "Reinforcing Separate Spheres: The Effect of Spousal Overwork on Men's and Women's Employment in Dual-Earner Households." *American Sociological Review* 75(2):303–328.

Collins, Patricia Hill. 1990. *Black Feminist Thought: Knowledge, Consciousness, and the Politics of Empowerment.* Boston: Unwin Hyman.

Deegan, Mary Jo. 1990. *Jane Addams and the Men of the Chicago School: 1892–1918.* Piscataway, NJ: Transaction Publishers.

———. 1991. *Women in Sociology.* Westport, CT: Greenwood Press.

Epstein, Cynthia Fuchs. 1983. *Women in Law.* Garden City, NY: Anchor Books.

Feagin, J. R., and M. P. Sikes. 1994. *Living With Racism: The Black Middle-Class Experience.* Boston: Beacon Press.

Fox, Mary Frank. 2001. "Women, Science, and Academia: Graduate Education and Careers." *Gender & Society* 15(5):654–666.

Frehill, Lisa M. 2006. "Measuring Occupational Sex Segregation of Academic Science and Engineering." *Journal of Technology Transfer* 31:345–354.

Hagan, John R., and Fiona Kay. 1995. *Gender in Practice: A Study of Lawyers' Lives.* New York: Oxford University Press.

Hall, Roberta M. 1982. *The Classroom Climate: A Chilly One for Women.* Washington, DC: Association of American Colleges.

———. 1983. *Academic Mentoring for Women Students and Faculty: A New Look at an Old Way to Get Ahead.* Washington, DC: Association of American Colleges.

———. 1984. *Out of the Classroom: A Chilly Campus Climate for Women?* Washington, DC: Association of American Colleges.

Harding, Sandra. 1991. *Whose Science? Whose Knowledge? Thinking From Women's Lives.* Ithaca, NY: Cornell University Press.

Jacobs, Jerry. 1989. *Revolving Doors: Sex Segregation and Women's Careers.* Stanford, CA: Stanford University Press.

Jaschick, Scott. 2009. "Waiting for the Call." *Inside Higher Ed.* http://www.insidehighered.com/news/2009/08/13/sociology

———. 2010. "Job Satisfaction and Gender." *Inside Higher Ed.* http://www.insidehighered.com/news/2010/07/12/coache

Kanter, Rosabeth Moss. 1977. *Men and Women of the Corporation.* New York: Basic Books.

Katz, Stanley N. 2010. "Beyond Crude Measurement and Consumerism." *Academe* 96(5):16–20.

Lengermann, Patricia Madoo, and Gillian Niebrugge. 2007. "Present at the Creation: Women in the History of Sociology and Social Theory." In *The Women Founders: Sociology and Social Theory, 1830–1930: A Text/Reader*, edited by Patricia Madoo Lengermann and Gillian Neibrugge, 1–21. Long Grove, IL: Waveland Press.

Martin, Joanne. 1994. "The Organization of Exclusion: Institutionalization of Sex Inequality, Gendered Faculty Jobs and Gendered Knowledge in Organizational Theory and Research." *Organization* 1(2):401–431.

Misra, Joya, Jennifer Hickes Lundquist, Elissa Holmes, and Stephanie Agiomavritis. 2011. "The Ivory Ceiling of Service Work." *Academe* 97(1):22–26.

Moore, Wendy Leo. 2007. "'I Thought She Was One of Us!': A Narrative Examination of Power and Exclusion in the Academy." In *Feminist Waves, Feminist Generations: Life Stories From the Academy*, edited by Hokulani K. Aikau, Karla A. Erickson, and Jennifer L. Pierce, 250–269. Minneapolis: University of Minnesota Press.

Nippert-Eng, Christena. 1996. *Home and Work: Negotiating Boundaries Through Everyday Life.* Chicago: University of Chicago Press.

Park, Shelley N. 1996. "Research, Teaching and Service: Why Shouldn't Women's Work Count?" *The Journal of Higher Education* 67(1):46–84.

Patton, Michael Quinn. 2001. *Qualitative Research and Evaluation Methods.* 3rd ed. Thousand Oaks, CA: Sage.

Philipsen, Maike Ingrid, with Timothy Bostic. 2008. *Challenges of the Faculty Career for Women: Success and Sacrifice.* San Francisco: Jossey-Bass.

Sandler, Bernice R. 1991. *The Campus Climate Revisited: Chilly for Women Faculty, Administrators, and Graduate Students.* Washington, DC: Association of American Colleges.

———. 1992. *Success and Survival Strategies for Women Faculty Members.* Washington, DC: Association of American Colleges.

Sandler, Bernice R., Lisa A. Silverberg, and Robert M. Hall. 1996. *The Chilly Classroom Climate: A Guide to Improve the Education of Women.* Washington, DC: National Association for Women in Education.

Silverman, David. 2010. *Doing Qualitative Research: A Practical Handbook.* 3rd ed. Thousand Oaks, CA: Sage.

Smith, Dorothy E. 1987. *The Everyday World as Problematic: A Feminist Sociology.* Boston: Northeastern University Press.

———. 1990. *The Conceptual Practices of Power: A Feminist Sociology of Knowledge.* Boston: Northeastern University Press.

Spalter-Roth, Roberta, and Janene Scelza. 2009. *Sociology Faculty Salaries AY 2008–09.* Washington, DC: American Sociological Association.

Thornton, Saranna. 2009. "On the Brink: The Annual Report on the Economic Status of the Profession, 2008–09." *Academe* 95(2):14–44.

West, Martha S., and John W. Curtis. 2006. *AAUP Faculty Gender Equity Indicators 2006.* Washington, DC: American Association of University Professors.

Williams, Joan C. 2000. *Unbending Gender: Why Family and Work Conflict and What to Do About It.* New York: Oxford University Press.

Winslow, Sarah. 2010. "Gender Inequality and Time Allocations Among Academic Faculty." *Gender and Society* 24(6):769–793.

11

NOT THE IDEAL PROFESSOR

Gender in the Academy

Laura Hirshfield

ender socialization and rules of gender performance influence men's and women's choices about their education, careers, and behavior in the workplace. By interacting with others, we display, "do," or perform our gender so often that we begin to see these performances as who we ("naturally") are (Butler 1990; Goffman 1976; West and Zimmerman 1987). Additionally, expectations about which choices are gender appropriate and which are not cause men and women to be understood and evaluated differently by their colleagues, superiors, and students (Valian 1998). I argue that the role of professor, inside and outside of the classroom, is gendered and that its gender is masculine. This gendering of key positions in academia may lead to inequities for women such as unequal compensation or promotion compared to men peers.

Two major consequences of gender in the classroom most frequently examined are gender bias in students' evaluation of their instructors (Basow and Silberg 1987; Crombie et al. 2003; Feldman 1993; Sprague and Massoni 2005) and sexual harassment of instructors by students (Berdahl 2007; Champion 2006; DeSouza and Fansler 2003). The data in these empirical analyses have been mainly students' ratings and reports about professors' behavior. Faculty voices are less commonly analyzed. Researchers have discussed the *effects* of gender norms (Berdahl 2007; Sprague and Massoni 2005), but few, if any, have explored how gender norms and gender performance *produce* and *constrain* faculty choices. In my study, I address this gap by exploring the gendered nature of the profession.

Gendered Organizations

Acker (1990) describes how organizational structures are gendered, directly contributing to marginalizing women within them. She stresses the gendered nature of organizations as seen through a "hypothetical or universal worker," which she argues is that of a man/boy "whose life centers on his full-time, life-long job, while his wife or another woman takes care of his personal needs and his children" (190).

This hypothetical or universal worker is similar to Salzinger's (2003)[1] concept of interpellation, used to express how individuals are turned into subjects in the process of a person recognizing himself or herself as something or someone as a result of the way another person describes that person, such as as an employee, a prisoner, or a friend. In her research on manufacturing plants along the U.S.-Mexico border, Salzinger (2003) explains how managers came to imagine specific, embodied workers in the positions they were hiring for, and how the workers came to embrace the stereotypes that matched managers' expectations. Employers particularly valued submissiveness, agility, and lack of family. Similarly, in her research on toy stores, Williams (2006) uses the concept of interpellation to analyze how jobs were gender typed. She identified some roles gender typed as masculine, and discussed the difficulties that men faced when asked to perform jobs gender typed as feminine.

In academia, the concept of the hypothetical/universal worker surfaces in several ways. First, research demonstrates that identical research portfolios and curricula vitae identified with a man's name are evaluated more positively than those with a woman's (Steinpreis, Anders, and Ritzke 1999; Wenneras and Wold 1997). Seemingly, evaluators imagine a hypothetical academic man that women academics cannot live up to. Such studies suggest that people may have lower expectations for men than for women, which may be related to gendered ideas regarding what it means to be a professor. Second, women professors receive harsher assessments from students than men professors (Anderson and Smith 1995; Basow 1995). Third, students judge professors more harshly when they deviate from gender-specific expectations (Andersen and Miller 1997; Sprague and Massoni 2005). When students describe their best and worst professors, often they praise funny, entertaining men professors and caring, warm women professors, while criticizing men professors who are "boring" (i.e., not entertaining) and women professors who are "mean" or "bitchy" (i.e., not warm) (Sprague and Massoni 2005).

Thus, we can see how the concept of the "ideal worker" in academia affects how others (especially students) evaluate professors. However, a knowledge gap exists regarding how professors experience this construct in their lives and how race and other intersectional identities (e.g., age, sexual identity) impact ideas about the hypothetical/universal professor. To address this gap, I asked: How do faculty members make sense of what it means to be an "ideal professor"? How is this concept of the ideal professor gendered? and How does the gendering of the ideal professor impact their experiences?

Data for this analysis come from the Faculty Members and Diversity Classrooms project, a long-term study at a large, predominantly white Midwestern public university, which sought to explore how faculty members' social identities impact their university experiences.[2] The research team (two faculty members and several advanced graduate students) identified and recruited faculty in two ways. First, respondents were asked to participate if they had been awarded distinguished teaching or service honors from the university. Second, others were recruited via snowball sampling, using colleagues' recommendations of highly talented faculty committed to diversity. Our goal was not to gather a representative, generalizable sample; rather, it was to find an articulate and sophisticated set of respondents to speak about diversity, pedagogy, and the academic experience. Recruitment techniques resulted in 66 faculty interviews that were diverse by gender (34 men, 32 women), race (18 white, 20 African American, 13 Asian American, 9 Latino/a, 4 Native American, and 2 Arab American), and discipline (26 social science, 22 natural science, and 18 humanities). The response rate was 90.4%.

Researchers interviewed participants for approximately one to one and a half hours using a semistructured format. The primary goal of the faculty diversity project was to examine how race and ethnicity influenced teaching experiences and relationships with colleagues in the university. As the project developed, the team's focus shifted to how race and ethnicity and other social identities affected faculty experiences. The final interview protocol centered on these themes: (a) racial/ethnic biography, (b) teaching/academic career path, (c) pedagogy, (d) thoughts about the effects of social identities on teaching, (e) racialized/gendered experiences with the academy, and (f) diversity in higher education.

The semistructured interview format allowed interviewers to touch on the same themes while also giving them flexibility to follow the interviewee in a conversational format.[3] Interviews were audio-recorded and transcribed except for those of participants who requested that they not be.[4] My analytic strategy involved open and focused coding (Emerson, Fretz, and Shaw 1995). Specifically, I began noting recurring themes in close readings of each transcript. Next, I coded the transcripts inductively and deductively, with the help of a qualitative software program (NVivo). Themes I noted involved gender in the classroom and those related to peers, emotions, authority, and conflict.

The Ideal Professor Construct

Though most of the participants did not use the terminology of ideal *academic* or *hypothetical/universal professor,* they invoked this construct throughout their interviews to describe their experiences in class and with their peers. Several respondents, especially the natural scientists, described the role of "professor" as something shaped by history. As Howard[5] said, "I do have to recognize and say, way up front, we're talking about a discipline that has been white, male" (white, natural sciences). Howard explained that his department and discipline are largely made up of (white) men; he believed that this affected the tenor of conversations in faculty meetings and in social interactions with peers. Ellen described the stereotype of science as largely performed by men, and how this impacted the way her colleagues evaluated her and her students. When asked if her research group was looked at differently because it was all women, Ellen replied,

> Well, sure. It's never going to be as good as if it was all men. . . . This is science, you know. I mean, science . . . males do science and they're the ones that do it right. But my students . . . it's also recognized that I do train my students very well. And my colleagues know that. And the other students know that. (white, natural sciences)

Ellen was resigned to the knowledge that people may think less of her lab because of the stereotype that men are better at science. She did not address why her lab was made up entirely of women students, but there is evidence suggesting that women students seek out women mentors, especially when they are in the minority. Thus, this was more likely to be a common experience for Ellen given her men-dominant field (Hirshfield and Joseph 2012).

Phyllis recounted what she believed an "ideal" professor looked like, and how she did not feel that she, as a woman of color, could ever attain those qualities:

My ideal of a teacher is somebody, something, that I don't think I could physically ever approach. . . . I always admired professors who were kind of older, senior men. . . . They had a lot of authority in the classroom, precisely because they were big people. They were big in many senses, right? . . . They . . . have a lot more authority, but also they're able to be kinder in the classroom. . . . Because students in some way kind of fear them a little bit. . . . There's something like a power issue that they're aware of, that the professor can then kind of use to make himself seem a little bit less intimidating. . . . Whereas I'm kind of a small person, right? And, a woman, and Asian, right? . . . But oftentimes, I feel like . . . the only way that I can do that is if I appear very old. So I . . . [think] trying to appear old is a way to kind of offset those things.

Interviewer: Interesting. As age is . . .

Phyllis: You know, that's the only way I think I can change my appearance, because I feel like no matter what I do, I'm still perceived as not this other ideal teacher. But I also think the students also have expectations of what they think is an ideal professor. . . . So I'm still working with that, I'm really hoping that I'll look old at some point, really old, you know. So that . . . those things will just kind of be offset. (Asian American, humanities)

Phyllis described the additional flexibility that older men professors have in the classroom because they induce fear in the students because of who they are; thus, they are able to use less psychological intimidation or be more sympathetic without losing their authority like she might as a small, Asian woman. In her view, because Phyllis did not look like the prototypical, "ideal" professor, she felt that she was not automatically granted the same authority in the classroom as her men colleagues. Phyllis endeavored to attain an image closer to the ideal professor; yet this ideal directly contradicted the usual youthful and attractive ideal for women in our society. Although Phyllis was the only participant to explicitly discuss student conceptions of the ideal professor, others described experiences in which they felt aware of their peers' views of what professors should be like: older, white, and male.

Challenged by Students

Phyllis's belief that her size, race, age, and gender might affect how students grant her authority was echoed by many of her women colleagues. For example, Rebecca thought the issue of having less authority and being challenged by students might be common to most women faculty. She explained:

Oh, yeah . . . I think women as a whole, women faculty, and women of color faculty, it seems to me are [an] easier target. And I think a lot of times it's very . . . unconscious on the part of the students. It's a socialization process. And in a situation where there are male faculty and female faculty, a student may call male faculty Dr. So-and-So . . . [but] we try to not be called by, uh, first name. Well, I get a lot of e-mail . . . [with] "Hi, [Rebecca], Dr. So-and-So suggested that I talk to you." . . . That's sort of their socialization. They don't say, "Okay, let's call [Rebecca Rebecca], let's call [him] Dr. So-and-So." But it's a very natural part of how they perceive things and people. So it's pretty stressful. (Asian American, social sciences)

Rebecca described one of the ways that students undermine women faculty members' authority in ways that she did not see men colleagues experiencing. When students use titles to address faculty, they acknowledge their authority and expertise. When students highlight men's credentials but not women's, women may feel disrespected compared with men peers (Messner 2000).

Women faculty described not being taken seriously by students when they started as professors. Brenda counterbalanced this by acting tough:

I have had students, particularly where I had larger classes, I had them say that I was really tough, and I kind of like that. I took pride in that because I see myself as a softie, and getting students to sort of take me seriously when I started out when I was younger, now I'm feeling older, but looking young and being a woman, and being a woman of color, there are always these issues of "How are you qualified to teach me?" (African American, humanities)

Being "tough," a characteristic often associated with men, gave Brenda a sense that she had more control and power. As Phyllis described earlier, getting older has boosted her authority but her gender still affects her ability to fully garner the respect and authority she feels that she deserves.

Jessica has avoided dealing with authority issues by changing her classroom authority structure to a more egalitarian approach. She sees this as her best strategy, given her identity as a woman professor of color:

Well, the big thing is kind of reconstituting authority in the class. You know, because like I said, if you're a white guy, you can get this kind of unearned authority, essentially by virtue of who you are. And you can't get that if you're not. So the response seemed to be to insist on even more authority, like, to be more of a hard-ass. And I just felt like, well, I've asked why are we giving the profession that much authority to begin with? . . . [But] if you don't put yourself on a pedestal, you can't get knocked down. . . . So I'm not going to play those authority games with you. This is your class. Then you become less of a target and then it becomes more of their focus on their own learning. (American Indian, humanities)

Jessica challenges the structure and concept of what it means to be a professor. However, her comment identifies an important tension for women faculty. They can continue as they are within the system as it is, maintaining that women faculty can be just as successful as men. Or, they can argue that the system is flawed, that women do not have to be like men, and that women's styles of teaching may be better.

The "Ideal Professor"

Respondents do not see the role of professor as gender neutral, race neutral, or age neutral. Instead, as the logic of gendered organizations (e.g., Acker 1990) suggests, respondents understand that men, generally older white men, have held those positions. That legacy means that those who are not older white men must work harder and differently to achieve authority and respect in the classroom. Women faculty do not feel that they can ever achieve the same degree of authority and respect as older white men and, thus, the flexibility to be lenient with their students. Further, women differ regarding whether achieving traditional "authority" in the classroom is a useful goal. Several have chosen other routes, such as democratic, nonhierarchical classroom structures that create dynamics where their authority is questioned less. The research about the consequences of this type of classroom for students' evaluations is limited; it is difficult to predict how this type of professor strategy might affect women's promotion and tenure. However, alternative teaching styles are more likely to be accepted in teaching-oriented colleges and universities, which tend to have lower salaries, less prestige, and higher teaching loads than research-oriented universities, as well as an overrepresentation of women.

Respondents embraced gender, race, and age expectations of the "ideal professor" and provided examples of interpellation, as described by Salzinger (2003) and Williams (2006). Because student evaluations play an important role in faculty members' promotion and tenure, their expectations about the "ideal professor" must be taken into account when committees make decisions about faculty members' teaching effectiveness (Hirshfield and Joseph 2012). Research demonstrates that students have limited knowledge about the effects of student evaluations; however, for faculty, evaluations may influence significantly their chances for promotion and tenure, and are a major concern (Sojka, Gupta, and Deeter-schmelz 2002).

This intersectional analysis of gender, race, age, and the academy contributes to literature on women faculty, as well as to the general literature on identity in the academic workplace. These findings highlight the importance of using a qualitative approach, given that most previous studies on gender in the classroom have been quantitative. These studies have focused largely on students' thoughts about the classroom and have overlooked the experiences of professors. The Faculty Members and Diversity Classrooms project, which did not originally emphasize gender, demonstrates the need for additional research focusing specifically on identity to understand how identity impacts classroom and peer dynamics for faculty. My analysis highlights the need for more work on intersectional identities, particularly on intersections of age, race, and gender, to explore how these influence students' and faculty members' judgments and evaluations of professors who may not fit perfectly within the construct of the "ideal professor." In addition, it suggests the need for further research into alternative methods of evaluation of faculty, such as through peer observations or more comprehensive, qualitative evaluations by students. Using these (and other) metrics, promotion and tenure committees may be better able to avoid the pitfalls of gender and racial bias and begin to combat stereotypes and consequences of the "ideal professor."

Notes

1. Salzinger was not the first to develop the concept of interpellation; however, her application of Althusser's concept fits closely with the interpellation I describe.
2. For more details about the methods used for the overall study, see Chesler and Young (2013).
3. Thus, respondents were not asked consistently about the effects of social identities other than race.
4. In those cases, extensive field notes were taken during and after the interviews.
5. All names have been changed.

References

Acker, Joan. 1990. "Hierarchies, Jobs, and Bodies: A Theory of Gendered Organizations." *Gender and Society* 4(2):139–158.

Andersen, Kristi, and Elizabeth D. Miller. 1997. "Gender and Student Evaluations of Teaching." *PS: Political Science and Politics* 30:216–219.

Anderson, Kristin J., and Gabriel Smith. 2005. "Students' Preconceptions of Professors: Benefits and Barriers According to Ethnicity and Gender." *Hispanic Journal of Behavioral Sciences* 27(2):184–201.

Basow, Susan A. 1995. "Student Evaluations of College Professors: When Gender Matters." *Journal of Educational Psychology* 87(4):656–665.

Basow, Susan A., and Nancy T. Silberg. 1987. "Student Evaluations of College Professors: Are Female and Male Professors Rated Differently?" *Journal of Educational Psychology* 79(3):308–314.

Berdahl, Jennifer L. 2007. "Harassment Based on Sex: Protecting Social Status in the Context of Gender Hierarchy." *The Academy of Management Review* 32(2): 641–658.

Butler, Judith. 1990. *Gender Trouble: Feminism and the Subversion of Identity.* New York: Routledge.

Champion, David R. 2006. "Sexual Harassment: Criminal Justice and Academia." *Criminal Justice Studies* 19(2):101–109.

Chesler, Mark, and Alford A. Young, Jr. 2013. *Faculty Social Identity and the Challenges of Diversity: Reflections on Teaching in Higher Education.* Boulder, CO: Paradigm.

Crombie, Gail, Sandra W. Pyke, Naida Silverthorn, Alison Jones, and Sergio Piccinin. 2003. "Students' Perceptions of Their Classroom Participation and Instructor as a Function of Gender and Context." *The Journal of Higher Education* 74(1):51–76.

DeSouza, Eros, and A. Gigi Fansler. 2003. "Contrapower Sexual Harassment: A Survey of Students and Faculty Members." *Sex Roles* 48(11/12):529–542.

Emerson, Robert, Rachel Fretz, and Linda Shaw. 1995. *Writing Ethnographic Fieldnotes.* Chicago: University of Chicago Press.

Feldman, Kenneth A. 1993. "College Students' Views of Male and Female College Teachers: Part 11—Evidence From Students' Evaluations of Their Classroom Teachers." *Research in Higher Education* 34(15):1–19.

Goffman, Erving. 1976. "Gender Display." *Studies in the Anthropology of Visual Communication* 3(2):69–77.

Hirshfield, Laura E., and Tiffany D. Joseph. 2012. "'We Need a Woman, We Need a Black Woman': Gender, Race & Identity Taxation in the Academy." *Gender and Education* 24(2):213–227.

Messner, Michael. 2000. "White Guy Habitus in the Classroom: Challenging the Reproduction of Privilege." *Men and Masculinities* 2(4):457–469.

Salzinger, Leslie. 2003. *Genders in Production: Making Workers in Mexico's Global Factories.* Berkeley: University of California Press.

Sojka, Jane, Ashok K. Gupta, and Dawn R. Deeter-schmelz. 2002. "Student and Faculty Perceptions of Student Evaluations of Teaching: A Study of Similarities and Differences." *College Teaching* 50(2):44–49.

Sprague, Joey, and Kelley Massoni. 2005. "Student Evaluations and Gendered Expectations: What We Can't Count Can Hurt Us." *Sex Roles* 53(11–12):779–793.

Steinpreis, Rhea E., Katie A. Anders, and Dawn Ritzke. 1999. "The Impact of Gender on the Review of the Curricula Vitae of Job Applicants and Tenure Candidates: A National Empirical Study." *Sex Roles* 41:509–528.

Valian, Virginia. 1998. *Why So Slow? The Advancement of Women.* Cambridge, MA: MIT Press.

Wenneras, Christine, and Agnes Wold. 1997. "Nepotism and Sexism in Peer Review." *Nature* 387:341–343.

West, Candace, and Don H. Zimmerman. 1987. "Doing Gender." *Gender & Society* 1(2):125–151.

Williams, Christine. 2006. *Inside Toyland: Working, Shopping, and Social Inequality.* Berkeley: University of California Press.

12

INTERSECTIONAL INVISIBILITY AND THE ACADEMIC WORK EXPERIENCES OF LESBIAN FACULTY

Diana Bilimoria and Abigail J. Stewart

The everyday experiences and career consequences of the climate for sexual minority faculty remain relatively understudied, and those of lesbian faculty are particularly understudied. In an important theoretical intervention, Purdie-Vaughns and Eibach (2008) provide an explanation for the lack of attention to lesbian faculty members' experiences. They argue that individuals who have multiple subordinate-group identities such as lesbians (who are both women and sexual minorities) are defined as non-prototypical members of their respective identity groups (women and sexual minorities). Straight women and gay men are viewed as prototypical, and therefore more visible group members, rendering lesbians invisible as women and as sexual minorities on account of their non-prototypicality. As "marginal members within marginalized groups," people with intersecting subordinate identities (such as lesbians) are in positions of acute social invisibility (Purdie-Vaughns and Eibach 2008, 381).

In this chapter, we draw on and extend our recent study of the climate experienced by science and engineering lesbian and gay faculty at two research universities (Bilimoria and Stewart 2009). In that study, faculty who identified as lesbian or gay described their perceptions of the workplace climate for lesbian, gay, bisexual, and transgender (LGBT) faculty; the role pressures and choices they faced; and the effects of the climate on their work performance and careers. One of the main findings of the study was that LGBT faculty face a climate in which their gayness or homosexuality is invisible and that heterosexuality is routinely assumed.

Intersectional invisibility refers to a "general failure to fully recognize people with intersecting identities as members of their constituent groups. Intersectional invisibility also refers to the distortion of the intersectional persons' characteristics to fit them into frameworks defined by prototypes of constituent identity groups" (Purdie-Vaughns and Eibach 2008, 381). Advantages and disadvantages exist because of intersecting subordinate identities, which lesbians have as sexual minority women; these are all related to intersectional invisibility. The advantage of intersectional invisibility is that being a non-prototypical member of a subordinate group can protect individuals from being the target of direct aggression. That is, lesbians "may escape the more active forms of discrimination . . . gay men face" (382). Purdie-Vaughns and Eibach point out that "their relative invisibility shields people with intersectional identities from the brunt of oppression directed at their groups" (383). At the same time, people with intersectional subordinate group identities also live with particular disadvantages; they "face a continuous struggle to have their voices heard and, when heard, understood" (383).

Thus, we anticipated that lesbian faculty experience the academic workplace as an environment in which they feel invisible, excluded, and with little influence—an environment that attempts to systematically distort, disempower, misrepresent, and marginalize their intersectional experience. We employed qualitative analysis of open-ended interviews to explore these facets of intersectional invisibility affecting the academic work experiences of lesbian faculty. We drew on in-depth interviews with 11 women faculty who identified as lesbian at two research universities. Participants for the study were obtained by being listed publicly as willing to mentor LGBT students, by being individually known and out to the researchers, by being recommended by an interviewee, or by responding to an e-mail sent to an LGBT Listserv requesting participation in the study. Participants were faculty in liberal arts, engineering, social work, and medical schools within the two universities. Six of the participants were on the tenure track and three were tenured; they were drawn from the following academic ranks: lecturer (4), assistant professor (3), associate professor (3), and administrator (1).

As described in Bilimoria and Stewart (2009), we employed an open-ended interview protocol, which began by asking each participant to describe the climate for herself and other LGBT faculty at her university and in her department. In the original study we analyzed only interviews with faculty in science and engineering fields but included both women and men. In the present analysis, we focused only on interviews with lesbian faculty but include those in other fields. We asked all participants about the recruitment process they underwent when they came to the university, the positive and negative experiences they have had as a lesbian faculty member, their feelings about the importance of LGBT "community" and any efforts they had made to belong to it at the university, and their perceptions of the experiences of LGBT graduate students and postdoctorates. The focus of the interviews was on the nature of the job experiences and career outcomes faced by the participants as sexual minority faculty. The interviews analyzed here were about an hour long; we took detailed notes (including some verbatim quotations) during the interviews because of potential concerns about tape-recording sensitive data. We wrote up summaries of the interviews immediately afterward. We collected data according to procedures approved by the Institutional Review Boards at both institutions, including participants' informed consent.

We used conventional content analysis procedures (see Boyatzis 1998; Smith 1992) to review our notes and identify interview themes, share observations, and add examples or themes. By mutual consent, we consolidated themes after reviewing our notes. Primary themes focusing on intersectional invisibility emerged: (a) the various facets of intersectional invisibility reported by lesbian faculty participants, (b) the ways by which lesbian faculty navigate intersectional invisibility, and (c) the consequences of intersectional invisibility for lesbian faculty. Some of the themes reported in the following sections were also identified in our earlier study of LGBT faculty in academic science and engineering (Bilimoria and Stewart 2009) because the samples used in the two studies overlap to some extent.

Facets of Intersectional Invisibility in the Academic Workplace

One of the most common aspects of the work environment reported by the lesbian faculty in our study was their sense that their *being lesbian is unseen.* For example, one participant commented, "[Being a lesbian] is not part of the discourse; it's therefore hard to figure out where people are coming from. Mainly it is just completely invisible." Another participant reported that when she asked why her department did no programming for lesbian students, she was told, "There aren't any." Yet another noted that it is easier for LGBT faculty to be out if partnered, and that they are invisible if not partnered. Even when being lesbian is acknowledged, it is marginalized. One participant described a conversation about a potential speaker with a male colleague's stay-at-home wife, who wanted to know if the speaker could come but "not mention that she's lesbian."

Discussing *heterosexual privilege*, a participant stated that for a second trip during her recruitment process at which she brought her partner, the department did not reimburse her partner's travel expenses, although for married heterosexual couples the department routinely pays the expenses for both the interviewee and the spouse. Another participant shared that straight women faculty colleagues at her university with whom she was having an argument did not even know what Proposition 2 (a state-level antigay proposition) was.

Closely tied to this invisibility are unconscious attempts to make non-prototypical identity group members (lesbians) adhere to prototypical identity (straight women) characteristics. One participant noted that it is easy to assume everyone fits a straight norm because "personal lives are not on the table much" in the academic workplace. Another said,

> In the past, when I was not so out, I would occasionally talk about things (like going on a vacation), but do this without gender-based pronouns. Immediately the person I was talking to would apply male pronouns (oblivious to the fact that I had not used any, and continued not to do so). This would always force the issue as to whether or not to be "out," or to simply give the appearance of not having a life. With the appearance of no life, a couple times folks have tried to "fix me up" with a male.

A facet of intersectional invisibility and exclusion brought up by some of the study participants was the *conflation of "woman" and "lesbian"* bias. Some participants experienced the double bind of being both a woman and a lesbian in their academic workplaces. For other participants, gender-based discrimination was far more critical than LGBT bias. One participant specifically noted her lack of prototypicality as a woman when she said that she was tired of women's issues being brought up as if "'women' doesn't include me."

Some participants reported on the *pervasive sense of silence and awkwardness* surrounding their lesbian status, another contributor to invisibility. One participant noted that "gays are a foreign country" for many in the academy. This faculty member had two residents in her lab, both from small-town, very religious Christian backgrounds, and all three of them (she and they) remained perpetually silent about her sexual orientation. In the academic workplace, discomfort about minority sexualities among academic colleagues often manifests in subtle cues and signals. As one study participant noted, "I find in academics that if people are uncomfortable with this, they are quiet about it. . . . They don't want to create friction."

A unique aspect of invisibility experienced by some lesbian faculty participants was attempts to make their looks better fit heterosexual norms. In direct and subtle ways, these women were told to look more prototypical as heterosexual women. For example, during a job interview one participant was told by an interviewer to "tone down her gay look" because "people will think you're gay," revealing the heterosexist assumption that a lesbian look would be detrimental to her chances of being hired. Another participant spoke about the issue of weight discrimination that she experienced in the academic workplace. For some lesbians, weight discrimination is an issue of conforming to heterosexual norms about female thinness.

We note that all of the forms of invisibility, silence, and pressure to conform to prototypical characteristics outlined here fit the intersectional invisibility framework. Moreover, they represent a different kind of experience than direct discrimination, expressions of hostility or derogation.

Navigating Intersectional Invisibility

As Purdie-Vaughns and Eibach (2008) suggest, "The struggle to be recognized or represented is the most distinctive form of oppression for people with intersectional subordinate-group identities," such as lesbian faculty (383). Moreover, Beatty and Kirby (2006) argue that invisibility poses particular challenges in workplace social interactions because it creates burdens on the employee to disclose (become visible) or not (remain invisible). Our study's participants described engaging in constant computation about whether and when to disclose their sexuality to their colleagues, staff, and students. They described how they were sensitive to the effects of coming out in professional relationships and continually evaluated and reevaluated the implications of doing so. As members of an invisible minority (Ragins, Singh, and Cornwell 2007), lesbian faculty are burdened by not knowing how their disclosure will affect the way others view and/or treat them (cf. Crocker, Major, and Steele 1998). Further, several participants commented that they expended considerable labor trying to interpret cues. One said she "has the constant experience of wondering if things are occurring because of gayness or because of other factors."

Some participants described how other lesbian faculty contribute to their pervasive invisibility by *acting straight*. One woman described another professor "who made up an entire story about having a husband who was a merchant marine. She even wore a ring. The lie got dangerously elaborate." Law professor Kenji Yoshino (2006) describes these kinds of identity pressures as demands for "covering," and linked them to Goffman's (1963) understanding of a social response to stigma. Yoshino argues that all subordinate groups are pressured to fit into the norms of the dominant group, and that keeping their stigmatized identity out of view makes social situations more comfortable for most. He points out that the majority's implicit demand to "cover" one's identity (or "to tone down a disfavored identity to fit into the mainstream," (ix) constrains the full personhood of minority group members' self-expression, and for that reason it is experienced as deeply painful over time.

Some participants assimilated into the dominant male heterosexual culture by remaining silent and not addressing overt discrimination. For example, a participant who heard derogatory gay jokes, mostly about gay men, in faculty meetings said that she kept silent because she felt that she had enough problems as a woman and did not want to stir up trouble for herself. Another participant said that it is okay to be "known" as a lesbian "but not to say anything." As this woman faculty member said, "Being gay is never useful in science."

Other participants responded to their pervasive invisibility by choosing to be out in specific circumstances or as a general way of expressing one's self. Various participants gave examples of strategic identity disclosure acts such as having a rainbow flag in their offices, supporting and encouraging LGBT students by creating a safe space in their labs or offices, mentoring LGBT students and postdoctoral students, wearing LGBT-supportive jewelry, and belonging to an LGBT Listserv. Even with this openness, one participant observed that she worried about whether her current strategy of being out was really safe, and thought that being out to students might be a battle that she could not win.

Consequences of Intersectional Invisibility

Our participants described how invisibility leads to a number of deleterious consequences including both internal (individual) consequences and career consequences. Participants described their own internal discomfort about and fear of being their whole selves, particularly in social circumstances. One faculty member said, "In this department I am afraid to be who I am. I'm not comfortable at the social events with colleagues where connections are made." Another participant, describing her very religious graduate students, said that she felt they did not understand her life and were hostile to it. She described how in communities such as theirs she would be "afraid to walk on the street" and that "somebody out there hates me." Many participants mentioned that they simply restricted their interactions with colleagues to the professional/academic and didn't discuss personal lives.

Others spoke about exclusion from career development opportunities, such as academic networks. One participant said that she was "not included in the 'boy's club'; only 'bubbly' females get in." Others spoke about not being mentored adequately and not being actively sponsored such as by nominations for awards. A number of participants indicated that they had been excluded from social events to which other faculty were invited, including dinner parties. One described an interaction with her department chair in which he described how a faculty candidate's second visit during their faculty recruitment process would be for "couples" only, and therefore it would be "inappropriate" for her to participate with her partner. The simultaneous struggle for recognition and safety in the academic workplace placed these lesbian faculty in a bind—longing to be visible and acutely aware of the risks of that visibility.

Our respondents' comments illustrate the multiple dimensions and consequences of lesbian faculty invisibility in the academic workplace, as well as the ways by which lesbian faculty navigate their intersectional invisibility. In many academic workplaces, pressures exist for lesbian faculty to remain concealed, disguised, unnoticed, and out of sight. There may not be active hostility or overt attempts to oppress or exclude lesbian faculty; instead, we see a more subtle form of systematic bias and exclusion in the academic workplace: intersectional invisibility. In multifaceted ways, lesbian faculty appear to wear a cloak of invisibility in which their sexual minority status is kept imperceptible under a mantle of heterosexuality.

Intersectional invisibility in the academic workplace occurs when lesbian faculty are not seen, noticed, or intentionally included in the context of work and social activities and connections, and when their intersectional characteristics and experiences are unconsciously distorted to conform to those of more prototypical identities. Invisibility allows the perpetuation of stereotypes about lesbian faculty because systematic contradictions of the stereotypes are not readily discernable. Lesbian invisibility encourages assimilation to the dominant heterosexuality of the workplace, promoting covering and straight-acting behavior that ultimately is costly to the individual. When lesbian faculty make individual choices to disclose their sexual identity, or when departments and their leaders create a workplace environment that is welcoming and inclusive of sexual minority identities, heterosexual norms become contested and lesbian invisibility is reduced.

We recognize that our data are drawn from only two institutions and do not generally include faculty housed in academic departments that provide quite different workplace environments, such as in humanities fields or departments that are explicitly feminist and/or gay friendly (e.g., gender studies). It is important that future research identify in detail how lesbian faculty experience the academic culture when it is one that does not render them invisible.

References

Beatty, Joy E., and Susan L. Kirby. 2006. "Beyond the Legal Environment: How Stigma Influences Invisible Identity Groups in the Workplace." *Employee Responsibilities and Rights Journal* 18(1):29–44.

Bilimoria, Diana, and Abigail J. Stewart. (2009). "'Don't Ask, Don't Tell': The Academic Climate for Lesbian, Gay, Bisexual and Transgender Faculty in Science and Engineering." *NWSA Journal* 21(2):85–103.

Boyatzis, Richard E. 1998. *Transforming Qualitative Information: Thematic Analysis and Code Development*. Thousand Oaks, CA: Sage.

Crocker, Jennifer, Brenda Major, and Claude Steele. 1998. "Social Stigma." In *The Handbook of Social Psychology, Vol. 2*, edited by D. T. Gilbert, S. T. Fiske, and G. Lindzey, 505–553. New York: Oxford University Press.

Goffman, Erving. 1963. *Stigma: Notes on the Management of Spoiled Identities*. Englewood Cliffs, NJ: Prentice-Hall.

Purdie-Vaughns, Valerie, and Richard P. Eibach. 2008. "Intersectional Invisibility: The Distinctive Advantages and Disadvantages of Multiple Subordinate-Group Identities." *Sex Roles* 59:377–391.

Ragins, Belle Rose, Romila Singh, and John M. Cornwell. 2007. "Making the Invisible Visible: Fear and Disclosure of Sexual Orientation at Work." *Journal of Applied Psychology* 92(4):1103–1118.

Smith, Charles P. 1992. *Motivation and Personality: Handbook of Thematic Content Analysis*. New York: Cambridge University Press.

Yoshino, Kenji. 2006. *Covering: The Hidden Assault on Our Civil Rights*. New York: Random House.

CASE STUDY

PROFESSOR LIU: THE MULTIPLE CHALLENGES FOR AN ASIAN WOMAN PROFESSOR IN THE SOCIAL SCIENCE FIELD

The multiple challenges for an Asian woman professor in a social science field are (a) being a woman, (b) being an Asian, (c) being a professor in social science, (d) being a feminist, and (e) being an immigrant and non-native speaker of English.

I majored in English as a foreign language in my undergraduate study. I obtained my bachelor's degree in English language and literature and taught college English for five years before I came to the U.S. for my graduate studies. My first graduate diploma was a teaching certificate: TESL (Teaching English as a Second Language). I then went on to study in a doctoral program, which led to my graduation with a PhD in [a social science]. I started teaching as an adjunct instructor when my children were young. When they went to school full-time I began working full-time as an instructor, first as a visiting assistant professor, then as a tenure-track assistant professor in [a social science field].

One day at a New Year's party, after I introduced myself to a guest of a friend, telling him of my current rank as an assistant professor, the guest commented in disbelief that after 10 years since I received my doctoral degree, I was still at the rank of assistant professor. I had to assure him it was completely true. And, it looked as if this process to obtain tenure would be even longer than 10 years. It may take a regular person with a PhD five to six years to be promoted from the rank of assistant professor to associate professor, but for someone like me, who is a woman, an Asian, an immigrant, a non-native speaker of English, a professor in a social science, and a feminist, this process could be a long, bumpy road of 12 or 15 years, if the promotion would come at all.

I have been in my current position for 3.5 years, with 7.5 years of experience teaching full-time. I am reasonably optimistic about the prospect of earning tenure in a couple of years, but the uncertainty of not getting it always hangs overhead.

I have enjoyed working with my students and colleagues in the three institutions that I worked: as a visiting assistant professor in a private college for one year, as a tenure-track assistant professor at a public two-year institution for three years, and, currently, as a tenure-track assistant professor at a public four-year institution. My colleagues have been mostly supportive.

My biggest challenge is when it's time to read student evaluations. Most student evaluations are good and constructive, but a few are not. It's extremely painful to read some of the negative student comments. In my second year at the two-year college, I was informed that (a) due to student evaluations and (b) that I had [a] record of doing research and professional presentations, there was incompatibility between me and the students in that institution. The community college's emphasis was on teaching, not on research. Therefore, I was told that my contract would not be renewed. However, in my third year my student evaluations improved from 3.0 to 4.0 out of a 5.0-point system. And, when the assistant dean who was in charge of teaching came to observe my class, I received a very good evaluation from him.

When I received the rejection of contract renewal, I felt devastated and depressed. I had to seek counseling. My self-worth and confidence suffered greatly. Four of the senior faculty in my department wrote supportive letters for me to appeal to the administration to reconsider the decision. With their encouragement and on their suggestion, I filed a complaint with the county Equal Employment Opportunity Commission (EEOC) office. Despite the evidence that there was institutional discrimination, I did not win the case. I did not have the time or resources to pursue this further. Luckily, I started a position as a tenure-track assistant professor at a four-year institution, which allowed me to conduct more research while teaching.

I believe teaching is a process of refining one's skills of delivery and becoming increasingly more artful in connecting and communicating with students, reducing student anxiety level, inspiring them to become interested and motivated in learning. It's interesting to note that for all the courses I teach, I receive an average of 4.19 for student evaluations (out of 5.0). But, for the [course that focuses on women], I receive a 3.95, [clearly] lower. This is the course where we apply feminist theories.

In my [other courses], students seldom raise the issue of my English, which is my second language (even though I have a bachelor's degree in it and spent many years practicing and working in this language; I am fluent and proficient in it). In fact, one student commented in the anonymous evaluations that I had "great vocabulary, strong accent, though." And yet, in the [course on women], one student wrote very negatively, "Can she ever speak decent English?" Another student wrote, "Fire Dr. Liu!" And another student commented, "This class is biased against everything except feminism."

Although from the same class, other students have different views. For example, the one student who sent me an e-mail stating: "Thank you for this semester. It was insightful and challenging, personally. I enjoyed it very much." One student sent me a note saying:

> Hello Dr. Liu! My name is C. M. and I was in your . . . class last summer. I was a transient student from [another school]. I know the end of the school year is near and I just wanted to see how you were doing. Unfortunately, I will not be able to take your . . . level II class. I wish I could, as I loved your class last summer. I learned so much from your class and also had fun. However, I will be taking at least one class at [your university] this summer, so hopefully I will see you! Please let me know how you are doing when you get the time.

Clearly not all students are biased against me. One student observed in the course evaluations that "the instructor was not given the respect that students generally give to American professors." Well, this is hardly surprising. Even though I have had U.S. citizenship since 2000, and in class I talk with students of my voting experiences [so they know I am a citizen], as an Asian, I am not considered an American. I am a perpetual foreigner. Such a case was evidenced with the figure skater Michelle Kwan, who wasn't treated as an American, though she was born in California. When she lost to Sarah Hughes in the 2002 Winter Olympic Games, some media outlets (e.g., MSNBC and the *Seattle Times* sports section) ran the headline, "American Beats Out Kwan!"

In short, being a university professor is a traditional male profession. Most professors are white men. They are looked up to as the respectable authority of knowledge. But if you are a woman, and an Asian, you are not perceived as an authority figure. If you speak with [an] accent, and you present a worldview that's different from some students' worldviews, such as feminism, you will be challenged, suspected, distrusted, and disrespected. When this happens, the students' learning is compromised. It is a challenge for us, too, to find out ways to meet the challenge and overcome this obstacle.

Challenges do not only come from students, however, but also from other sources too such as other departments in my institution. For example, my department chair passed the following memo to me, which came from a department chair from another unit within the same university:

> I am writing regarding the experience of some of our nursing majors who have taken [Dr. Liu's class] during the past academic year. Several have experienced what they term as communication problems with Dr. Liu. Students report that she is very nice and attempts to be helpful, but the students are not able to understand or communicate effectively with this instructor. Over the past several semesters, this problem has become severe to the level that students will not register for her classes, and either delay taking the course, or in some cases, students have registered to take the course(s) at [another university nearby]. Several of these students are "A" and "B" students. Again, I want to be clear that Dr. Liu is not rude with the students; she acts very caring toward them and for this reason they have been reluctant to "complain." They just cannot understand her.

What Can We Learn From This Case Study?

Dr. Liu takes teaching seriously, wants to excel, reflects on her teaching, and pursues ways to improve. Allies provide her with encouragement and practical forms of support. Dr. Liu ended her submission to our online survey by offering to provide us with evidence of her teaching effectiveness. This gesture suggests that Dr. Liu has internalized some of the negative messages and that even in an anonymous forum where she would have her experiences taken at face value *still* felt the need to prove her legitimacy. Despite doing everything "right" and attempting to mobilize available resources, a failure of process appears to have occurred. What resources and strategies can women academics in similar situations use to meet such challenges?

Actions Involving Individual Resources

- Listen to student feedback, but do so with some perspective. Comments can sometimes feel personal, unwarranted, or unfair. Consider the most common complaints and consider whether they have merit. Focus on constructive comments and suggestions for improvement that can inform future teaching practices. Vanderbilt University offers

constructive tips and citations for additional readings at http://cft
.vanderbilt.edu/teaching-guides/reflecting/student-evaluations/.

- Frequently self-assess what is working (and what is not working) in
  your classes and what you might do differently in the future. Use
  this information to modify teaching style, assignments, or class
  content, as appropriate. Some universities accept self-evaluations
  as supplementary evidence of one's professional development. Take
  advantage of that policy if available.

- Notice red flags along the way regarding students' perceptions. Look
  for patterns and document problems in the classroom as soon as
  they occur. Such documentation can be useful in case formal student
  complaints arise, or for subsequent reflection on course management.
  Use e-mail for dated documentation of occurrences. Keep dated
  documents/e-mails of any encounters with "problem students" that
  occur. Consider giving copies to relevant administrators to keep them
  informed and to discourage escalation.

- Connect with faculty who may face similar challenges (e.g., feminists,
  faculty of color) and meet regularly to identify and manage common
  concerns. Administrators may respond more effectively toward issues
  framed as collective rather than personal ones. Working with like-
  minded others can also reduce stress.

- Develop allies (e.g., colleagues, chairs, deans, administrators) who
  have your interests in mind. Allies may know information that
  you are unaware of such as informal rules in play on your campus
  or changing institutional values. Seek their advice and ask them to
  support marginalized faculty, in general, as well.

- Think ahead to the next phases of your career. What skills are required and how will you develop them? Build relationships with
  different mentors who can provide differing kinds of training and
  support (e.g., navigating institutional racism, developing research
  design, obtaining project funding). As always, select mentors and
  develop networks based on personal and professional goals. (For more
  on mentoring, see the next section.)

- Weigh your options. Having to leave unsupportive work environments is an unfortunate reality for some women academics. But, the
  cost of staying may be too high. Research on racism-based trauma
  affirms that situations like these may negatively impact mental and
  physical well-being (see chapter 15). Professional counseling, support
  groups, spiritual practices, and opportunities for recreation and joy
  can provide important care through difficult situations in which you
  may feel silenced or alone.

Actions Involving Institutional Resources

• Formally report incidents of sexism or racism to the appropriate sources, and take institutional structure and culture into account when doing so. This is vital to survival in hostile climates. Your chair may be the first person in the "chain of command," but deans, the office of student affairs, or others who "need to know" or who have the best ability to help resolve problems may serve as important allies. One goal in reporting is to prevent future occurrences. Without formal documentation, repeat offenders may not be noticed (see chapter 13).

• Participate in formal and informal campus networking opportunities, particularly those related to teaching and professional development. Informal groups such as faculty interest groups (FIGs) are developed and guided by faculty on topics of interest (e.g., teaching practices, issues of race or gender). Interdisciplinary FIGs allow faculty to connect across campus in ways that otherwise might not occur. FIGs work best with clearly defined structures and roles (e.g., an organizer) and assignments (e.g., readings) to produce effective discussions, but faculty can move in and out of FIGs as their interests change. Although informal, FIGs can produce powerful ideas.

• Take advantage of formal mentoring programs. Mentors offer advice and support to faculty and appear to improve job satisfaction and encourage faculty success.[1]

  ○ If your campus needs to develop its formal mentoring program, investigate effective tools being used elsewhere. The Center for Research on Learning and Teaching (CRLT) at the University of Michigan offers useful resources including, but not limited to, mentorship specific to women and faculty of color; discipline-specific mentoring (e.g., engineering, humanities, medicine); and research on mentorship, including readings targeted for administrators (see www.crlt.umich.edu/faculty/facment).

• Use alternative methods of teaching evaluations such as peer reviews to gain new perspectives. Use relevant feedback to implement changes in your teaching or as a supplement to official evaluations.

• Obtain information about departmental or campuswide evaluation scores and comments as a point of comparison. Knowing areas of improvement that your institution's students cite most frequently will contextualize your course evaluations. Share this information with supervisors if doing so is not part of the formal evaluation process.

• Reinvigorate conversations on campus about issues of inclusion and diversity. (See chapter 17 for specific tools to use.)

- Use faculty input to develop intentional and responsive policies and practices.
- Encourage formal policies and processes to require campus citizens to report uncivil or discriminatory behavior in the classroom. Collective approaches are better than thinking about each occurrence separately, which can unintentionally lead to subsequent victimization when perpetrators go unchallenged (see chapter 13).
- Develop systems of accountability.
- Decide how you want the situation resolved. Legal avenues can be time-consuming, expensive, and stressful. Before considering legal actions, evaluate whether resolution can be achieved at the university level. Many universities have mediation programs and grievance processes that might achieve desired outcomes. Similarly, consider using formal channels to place a statement in your personnel file so that your perspective is part of the official record.

Actions Involving Extrainstitutional Resources

- Use recent scholarship to get informed about how departments, schools, and campus communities effectively study and address issues of inclusion and discrimination. Good starting points for exploring basic issues and making institutional change include the following:
  - The AAUP "Statement on Teaching Evaluation," regarding the "chronic need for arriving at fair judgments of a faculty member's teaching," at www.aaup.org/aaup/pubsres/policydocs/contents/evalstatement.htm.
- Explore the literature on feminist pedagogy, which suggests that professors teaching "sensitive" topics (i.e., feminist theory, race, gender) experience unique critiques and challenges. It can provide valuable information to administrators along with validation for individual faculty who face content-related challenges.
- Seek advice from online communities such as *The Chronicle of Higher Education*'s "Diversity in the Workplace" (http://chronicle.com/forums/index.php/board,43.0.html) and "In the Classroom" (http://chronicle.com/forums/index.php/board,25.0.html) forums. See the online resources at the end of the book for information about professional organizations that might be a good fit for you. Many organizations have Listservs for members, mentoring programs, and other resources.

- Consider filing a grievance with the U.S. Equal Employment Opportunity Commission (EEOC).[2] Here are a few basics:

  o EEOC will only accept *Charges of Discrimination* involving protected categories of people (e.g., race, religion, sex, age, disability). See www.eeoc.gov/employees/charge.cfm.

  o The EEOC will not hear a complaint unless all other means of resolution are exhausted.

  o If you plan to file a lawsuit alleging discrimination on the basis of race, color, religion, sex (including pregnancy), national origin, age (40 or older), disability, genetic information, or retaliation, you first have to file a charge with one of our field offices (unless you plan to bring your lawsuit under the Equal Pay Act, which allows you to go directly to court without filing a charge). We will give you what is called a 'Notice-of-Right-to-Sue' at the time we dismiss your charge, usually, after completion of an investigation. However, we may dismiss for other reasons, including failure to cooperate in an investigation. This notice gives you permission to file a lawsuit in a court of law. Once you receive a Notice-of-Right-to-Sue, you must file your lawsuit within 90 days. We cannot extend this deadline except when the District Director gives the parties a written notice of intent to reconsider before the deadline for filing a lawsuit. If you don't file in time, you may be prevented from going forward with your lawsuit.[3]

  o If you hope to file a lawsuit, be aware of strict timelines. See www .eeoc.gov/employees/timeliness.cfm.

  o Some people may prefer the mediation process. See www.eeoc.gov/ employees/mediation.cfm.

Consult the online resources at the end of the book and the case studies in the other parts of the book for additional information that might be helpful.

Notes

1. See Kosoko-Lasaki, Omofolasade, Roberta E. Sonnino, and Mary Lou Voytko. 2006. "Mentoring for Women and Underrepresented Minority Faculty and Students: Experience at Two Institutions of Higher Education." *Journal of the National Medical Association* 98(9):1449–1459 (www.creighton.edu/fileadmin/user/hsmaca/images/News/community _newsletters/JNMA article_Aug_2006_Mentoring.pdf).

2. To avoid unwanted misinterpretations of federal guidelines, most information is quoted directly from the EEOC website. Because laws change from year to year, it would be wise to reference the website directly for the most up-to-date versions.

3. See EEOC website at www.eeoc.gov/employees/charge.cfm.

PART FOUR

HOSTILE CLIMATES
Harassment and Incivility

The "chilly climate" (Hall and Sandler 1982) for and sexual harassment of women faculty should be in the dustbin of academic history. Yet, like other systematic and systemic oppressions documented in this book, they endure. They occur in gendered organizations (Acker 1990) that have incongruous formal policies (e.g., zero tolerance for sexual harassment) and informal practices (e.g., downplaying the harmfulness of contrapower harassment [CPH]) (see Bird 2011). Part Four explores the internal strategies women faculty use to manage the personal dimensions of harassment and the external strategies to address the situation (e.g., making official reports) (Paludi 2011).

Chapter 13, "Gender Differences in Faculty Responses to Contrapower Harassment," explores harassment that occurs when the perpetrator has less formal power than his or her target. CPH manifests in many ways, typically between men students and women instructors/professors. Lampman analyzes data from 258 faculty and identifies behaviors typifying CPH—from rude, disrespectful, or disruptive behaviors to intimidation and threats. CPH can be intimidating, frightening, or dangerous. Randi, one of our respondents, provided an example:

> I recently experienced a negative event with one student who used very obscene remarks about me due to his displeasure with his class grade (after being offered numerous opportunities to make work up); these were some of the worst and most offensive comments I have ever heard from a student, which were gendered and threatening in nature. His comments were also made publicly available to others. The student met with faculty and administration, and admitted that he would not use such language against male faculty or older faculty. He apologized. The case outcome is still pending.

That the student's comments were "made publicly available" is worth discussion. Increasingly, universities (particularly public ones) record faculty course evaluations and make them available to the public through their official websites. Likewise, websites such as RateMyProfessor.com provide another public space for ratings with virtually no control over who posts comments or how many times they do so. Anonymity, combined with students' potential lack of maturity and lack of awareness about the importance of civility, may encourage harmful, vitriolic comments. This may be the case particularly for women faculty who do not fit perceptions of the "ideal professor" (i.e., "challenging" women faculty who defy expectations of being nurturing) (see chapter 11) and especially for women of color (see chapter 2). Some people may advise faculty to take such reviews with a "grain of salt," but given that course evaluations increasingly are stored digitally (thus indefinitely), they potentially impact how current and future students, colleagues, and administrators evaluate faculty. Professors have little opportunity to offer context, clarification, or rebuttal.

Increasingly, higher education is run like a business in which some view students as consumers who must be kept happy at any price. In this context, teaching evaluations play a crucial role in the tenure and promotion process. Erin, a 38-year-old Hispanic early-career academic at a comprehensive university, framed her situation as a systemic one, saying, "Students and their incessant need to demean women faculty is an issue. The department does not take this seriously enough and doesn't seem to want to understand that the evals are biased for women."

Beyond rude comments and disruptive behaviors, Lampman finds that women faculty experience harsher forms of CPH than men. Acts of intimidation potentially disrupt the classroom environment and require women faculty to use time and energy toward student management rather than more important and valued tasks of teaching and research. Additionally, women faculty suffer negative consequences to their physical health, emotional well-being, and job productivity as a result of CPH compared to men. Winona, a white 28-year-old PhD humanities student from our study, explained:

They often laugh at me in the classroom, refuse to follow rules, use profane language, and some even call me by my first name in an effort to engage in a power play. This came to a head for me in 2009, when a male student was menacing in the classroom, glaring at me, refusing to listen to directives, and then went in and out of the classroom 10 times in one session with his hands balled under his sweatshirt. (He appeared to be concealing something, possibly a weapon. I believe his behavior was meant to scare me.) I reported this to my dean of students and to the head of the department. Neither seemed worried. My department head told me that since he didn't "say anything threatening," there was not much they could do. The head did come in and observe the class. Also, the same student plagiarized a paper, so when I reported him, he was (after a battle with administration on my part) made to leave the class. I felt like collateral damage for the time that the student was allowed in my class—every day I threw up in the parking lot before/after teaching. I was scared out of my mind, but the college did not seem to care and made it seem like I was the crazy one.

Winona's narrative echoes Lampman's findings that reporting of CPH does not always lead to resolution. In this case, ineffective university processes for dealing with classroom hostilities creates a culture of silence regarding CPH. Further, it shows the emotional toll hostile student behaviors can take on women faculty in addition to the time they spend thinking about how best to manage the situation—time taken from other personal and professional pursuits. As such, CPH costs institutions as well.

In chapter 14, "Confronting Faculty Incivility and Mobbing," Gardner and Blackstone use quantitative and qualitative methods to explore how university structures create and reinforce cultures that facilitate mobbing, bullying done by groups to humiliate, isolate, silence, threaten, or damage the reputation of another person (Twale and De Luca 2008). Mobbing is about power. Using an intersectional lens, we might expect certain individuals to be its targets more than others (e.g., untenured women, women of color, LGBT women). Given their marginalized statuses, they may be more isolated, feel more stress, and possess greater uncertainty about such situations—qualities that lay fertile ground for mobbing to thrive (Twale and De Luca 2008).

Silence and fear provide the context in which bullied faculty decide how to handle it. Mary, a white 42-year-old associate professor of criminal justice at a liberal arts college, described how her chair and his administrative assistant engaged in mobbing that prevented her from being fully productive and participatory in her department. The roadblocks that she had to navigate also symbolically delegitimized her. In our online survey she wrote:

My chair and his administrative assistant had refused to allow me to have ink for my printer, forcing me to work in student computer labs. I was often kept out of departmental meetings. At times I would not receive information about a departmental meeting only to receive a call demanding to know my whereabouts and being reprimanded for not attending. . . . Once during a nasty episode of the flu I received a telephone call demanding that I keep office hours. I was forced to work without an office telephone for the entire semester after mine "died." The response after I inquired about obtaining a new telephone was, "You're dreaming." In addition, my chair refused to have my photo placed on our departmental website. I was not allowed involvement in two joint-degree programs despite the fact that at the time I was the only other ranking associate professor in my department. My department received funds with which to hire two new assistant professors last fall. I was informed of interview times and places only to show up to empty rooms. After I asked my chair about the matter he just said it was no big deal as he had opted to reschedule the interviews. Every man in the department was alerted of the changes.

Mary's intense experience was reinforced by her department's power structure. Her narrative demonstrates the angst about personal safety that often accompanies harassment, bullying, or mobbing. She continued:

There were occasions in which my e-mail account was hacked into by my chair's administrative assistant, one of my Blackboard course sites was hacked into and items removed by him, and I was intimidated on more than one occasion with the large knife carried by the administrative assistant. As a fully tenured associate professor, and the only ranking female in the department at the time, the vice provost informed me that all would be well if I filed a formal complaint. I gave the matter serious consideration as my chair has had a long and sordid history with respect to charges of discrimination and racism. I did not wish to jeopardize my employment. I finally filed the requisite complaint form; a single-page PDF web document. Within a week, my chair and his administrative assistant, a man who had, unbeknownst to me at the time, been charged with harassment of female staff and faculty on campus before, escalated their harassing behavior. One morning I arrived at my office only to discover it had been completely ransacked. It had been entered with a key. The only person apart from myself who had a key to my office was my chair's administrative assistant. Several hundred dollars in personal property including my cell phone, TV, stereo, a dictionary, class files, and textbooks were destroyed. In addition, my computer keyboard, headset, and optical mouse were torn apart. The dean then scheduled a meeting with my chair to discuss it. They decided since I had caused so much disruption with the filing of the grievance, the new associate chair was to be a junior untenured man assistant professor who had worked for less than a full year.

Like many of the women faculty who submitted accounts of mobbing to our survey, Mary was afraid of the consequences she might suffer if the mobbing continued *or* if she took formal action to stop it. Her case illustrates the inability of many colleges and universities to manage situations appropriately—not because they do not want to, but because entrenched practices and overall climate are easier to tolerate than ending them, a point made by Gardner and Blackstone.

Our respondents' narratives echo a key point from the chapters in this part of the book: Processes for dealing with incivility and harassment are often inadequate. Shonda, a 39-year-old African American associate professor at a research university, remarked:

> I find it unsettling that even at institutions categorized as "top" institutions, there are so few mechanisms to deal with attempts at bullying among faculty. Some academic institutions take an "ad hoc" or indifferent approach to protecting faculty from bullying and put up with behavior that would never be tolerated in business or corporate environments. In some cases, department chairs and leaders are appointed in the academic profession who have few skills, and who have little familiarity with the kinds of strategies that such organizations would use to identify and deal with aggressions when abuses happen from one faculty to another, though they can be good when it comes to protecting the interests of students.

To address volatile situations effectively, colleges and universities must be judicious regarding who fills leadership positions. Leaders should assume such positions because they possess the requisite skills, not because of their seniority, productivity, or "star power." Furthermore, we should not reduce these behaviors to a few "bad apples." "The legitimacy of violence is distributed hierarchically" (Acker 1998, 204); the policies and practices of academia shape members' interactions and identities. Likewise, identities and interactions shape organizational policies and practices. This is what is encouraging about seeing academia as a socially constructed, gendered organization (Acker 1990). The structure, cultures, and climates are not monolithic and static. They are subject to change and resistance. The key to effective change is strategic, targeted interventions at all levels, including climate.

The chilly climate includes everyday sexism, microaggressions, objectification, violence against women, and benevolent sexism (Vaccaro 2010). Mobbing constitutes a new aspect of the chilly climate that highlights how power imbalances manifest between coworkers, for example. In our research we were surprised by the extent of mobbing within academic workplaces. When mobbing is tolerated (or thrives), one's workplace can feel like a minefield. Such a phenomenon comes with costs to the individual and the institution; to ignore it is antithetical to the ideals of academia.

In chapter 15, "Women of Color in the Academy: From Trauma to Transformation," Davis, Vakalahi, and Scales explore how gendered institutional structures, combined with microlevel interactions with students, colleagues, and administrators, produce "racism-based trauma" for academic women of color. Building on prior research that uses an intersectional lens regarding the painful experiences of faculty women of color (e.g., Tuitt et al. 2009; Vakalahi and Starks 2010), they provide a new framework for understanding how hostile workplace experiences can result in negative long-term health concerns. They identify the consequences of race-based, unequal, and inequitable experiences as *trauma*. Their Trauma-to-Transformation model offers individual and structural-environmental strategies for dealing with harmful workplaces, healing faculty, and changing harmful institutions.

One of our respondents, Annemarie, recounted the psychological impact of mobbing when she was an assistant professor at a large state university, saying, "That stuff did affect my psyche even as I put out a stream of solid if not superior research." Unfortunately, Jean (another of our respondents) experienced severe consequences:

> [My] being exhausted and battered down is the goal of these bullies. I have spent so much time away from what I should be doing in academia and my personal life in the physical and emotional reactions as well as responding to incidents, not to mention the additional workload when students suffer from the neglect or being targeted.

In addition to the costs that targets of mobbing pay, academia pays a price as well when talented individuals are driven out of their jobs or out of academia entirely. Those who stay may feel intimidated enough to remain silent. Robbie, a 57-year-old biracial (American Indian and African American) faculty member discussed the emotional toll resulting from workplace hostility:

> I have been silenced, marginalized, and [made to disappear] to an extent that rivals the worst of international human rights crises I am aware of. I find my treatment a breach of contract, rude, disrespectful, demeaning, and traumatizing. At the time when my job was changed without my consultation I had to seek counseling for post-traumatic stress disorder; I am still in counseling. I was told that I would be fired if I complained or documented any of this abuse. I have navigated the situation by being silent. I know I have supporters, but they too are afraid.

We do not know whether Robbie's institution has a good policy on incivility, but policies alone will not prevent or curtail uncivil behavior, nor their traumatic consequences. Beyond policies that explicitly define harassment, incivility, mobbing, sexual objectification, and so on, academic institutions *must* have training, accountability, and enforcement and "procedures that *encourage*, not just allow, complaints" (Paludi 2011 375, original emphasis).

References

Acker, Joan. 1990. "Hierarchies, Jobs, Bodies: A Theory of Gendered Organizations." *Gender and Society* 4(2):139–158.

———. 1998. "The Future of 'Gender and Organizations': Connections and Boundaries." *Gender, Work & Organization* 5(4):195–206.

Hall, Roberta M., and Bernice R. Sandler. 1982. *The Classroom Climate: A Chilly One for Women?* Washington, DC: Association of American Colleges.

Paludi, Michele. 2011. "Sexual Harassment Policies and Practices." In *Gender & Higher Education*, edited by B. J. Bank, 374–381. Baltimore: Johns Hopkins University Press.

Tuitt, Frank, Michele Hanna, Lisa M. Martinez, María del Carmen Salazar, and Rachel Griffin. 2009. "Teaching in the Line of Fire: Faculty of Color in the Academy." *NEA Higher Education Journal* Fall:65–74. http://www.nea.org/assets/docs/HE/TA09LineofFire.pdf

Twale, Darla J., and Barbara M. De Luca. 2008. *Faculty Incivility: The Rise of the Academic Bully Culture and What to Do About It.* San Francisco: Jossey-Bass.

Vaccaro, Annemarie. 2010. "Still Chilly in 2010: Campus Climates for Women." *On Campus With Women* 39(2):2012–2016.

Vakalahi, Halaevalu F. O., and Saundra H. Starks. 2010. "Complexities of Becoming Visible: Reflecting on the Stories of Women of Color as Social Work Educators." *AFFILIA* 25(2):110–122.

Academic Women's Voices on Harassment, Incivility, and Trauma

The following narratives illustrate differing forms of harassment and incivility faced by women academics, ranging from subtle, interactional dynamics to overt hostility. All of them reflect the power dynamics of academic workplaces. When institutional processes for dealing with such situations are unclear or unmonitored, "superiors" can act in ways to get what they want, despite resistance by women faculty. These narratives remind us to reject individualistic explanations for people's behavior and, instead, recognize socially patterned actions that emerge from gendered university cultures and structures.

I work at a university where our female chair is extremely abusive. She was hired against the recommendation of the faculty, and has created a hostile work environment for faculty and staff. Several staff and faculty have left for other jobs in response to her abusive behavior. The chair uses faculty meetings as an opportunity to berate faculty publicly without using their names. Since the majority of the department is untenured, and most of the rest are being paid off with course release or money for administrative positions, everyone is witness to this behavior but very few speak up because if anyone says anything, the chair will just go on and on until the meeting time is over.

Several faculty and staff have complained about her abusive behavior to human resources, but their response to each person who reports is "Why hasn't anyone else complained?" when of course they have.

The chair deliberately breaks up alliances and long-standing working relationships within the faculty, and one of the saddest things about her behavior is that it is so easy to do. The environment is so hostile that our department receives few applicants for jobs despite fierce competition for positions at other schools. There have been several failed searches and the hires we have made are of extremely weak faculty who have little chance of receiving tenure.

—Jennifer, 38-year-old white assistant professor of criminology

I am a social scientist, and employed in a research unit in North America. I am subjected to tirades that are usually wild accusations based on nothing. I suffer the director's mood swings, misinterpretations of innocuous statements, vicious public sarcasm, ostracism by denying me access to project information. The list goes on. I get calls haranguing me for being a "loose cannon," "non–team player," "obsessed with my work," "unproductive." Further, I have to listen to incessant remarks about the corruption and inefficiency of people from the developing world. I am from India, and while I am aware that these problems are widespread in the developing world, they are not exclusively [sic] to it. The reiteration of this fact is not motivated by a desire to tell it how it is, but to tell me what I am. On the one hand, she threatens me with sacking and, on the other hand, railroads me into writing more grant applications—always with the threat of abuse and sacking over my head. About a talk with my director—I have tried it, but it gave her a chance to start hurling verbal missiles. She is acutely insecure, very aggressive and rude, and without a good grasp of management techniques. I am doing my project work, interviewing, analyzing, writing. However, my stress levels are incredible and I am now suffering from insomnia, crying jags, blank-outs, loss of appetite, [and so on]. I also have to deal with comments about my partner, his job, the flat I live in, the colleagues and workplaces I have been in before—all underpinned by a desire to point out that I should be grateful for being in this place, this country, this office, and someone like me does not really deserve such largesse. There is the matter of academic references. Do I have options? Can I get out and seek other (maybe even nonacademic) work? Is workplace abuse a known enough HR issue so that I could get a hearing from a future employer? How would I get around this issue of references? How would I avoid mentioning the abuse and yet explain my possible lack of good references from her? Does my situation mean that I am effectively a bonded laborer of sorts? The thing is, as time goes by, I can see the paraly-sis and inertia setting in, as I start accepting that I am an "unintelligent, incompetent, slacking no-gooder."

—Amy, 37-year-old Asian postdoc in the social sciences

I was experiencing problems with my department chair, who had hostile rela-tions with the only two other women in my department. He began to single me out for extra tasks and later extra scrutiny in ways that the two other junior male professors did not experience. I voiced my concerns to other members of the department, both male and female, and gained mixed results. Some dismissed it as just part of his character and not personal; others claimed I was simply "too sensitive"—a phrase that greatly troubled me. And others vowed to be more observant and intervene if possible. I documented every interaction and each e-mail and shared it with colleagues to make them aware of the situation. The problem eventually came to a head in a department meeting when he badgered me over comments I made in the meeting, comments that were echoed by a junior male colleague. He came to my office to argue with me about statements I made, he called me repeatedly in the office when I would not respond to his hostile attitude and eventually muscles his way into my office in a physically threatening way demanding I speak to him. Thankfully another colleague wit-nessed the action. Afterwards [my chair and I] exchanged a few e-mails and it was clear he was greatly agitated by the situation with me, but again my male colleague who agreed with my comments openly was not questioned or both-ered. As summer approached I voiced my concerns yet again to a colleague and indicated I felt unsafe coming into the office and was looking for a new job. At this point the colleague decided to take action on my behalf (I was untenured at the time and felt reluctant to move forward with complaints). He went to the provost who simply argued I should avoid the office if I felt uneasy around the chair. Eventually the senior male colleague encouraged me to seek mediation where he would also take part. I agreed and we had two senior faculty in our department sit in.

It was exceptionally stressful and it felt for most of the time I had no support from my department, or the university. If I didn't have a few friends who were willing to go to bat for me I think I would have just left the university rather than try to work through the issues. And that would be unfortunate for any other junior female faculty who came after me.

—Maya, 36-year-old Asian associate professor of political science

13

GENDER DIFFERENCES IN FACULTY RESPONSES TO CONTRAPOWER HARASSMENT

Claudia Lampman

Benson (1984) conceptualized *contrapower harassment* (CPH) to describe a situation in which an individual with less institutional power (e.g., a student) harasses someone with more power (e.g., a professor). I learned of CPH through a literature search in 2004. This search was not the basis for writing a manuscript. Instead, I hoped to find (a) evidence that other women professors, like me, had experienced intimidation, threats, and bullying from their students, and (b) guidance on how to handle it. I found validation from other academic women but most was anecdotal. I found empirical research on *sexual* harassment by students (Carroll and Ellis 1989; DeSouza and Fansler 2003; Grauerholz 1989; Matchen and DeSouza 2000; McKinney 1990). Although these studies did not consistently find gender differences in the frequency of sexual harassment from students, the two most recent found that women were more distressed by all forms of sexual attention from students, and reported more depression and anxiety from such incidents. Unfortunately, my search turned up little advice about how to handle CPH. Unknowingly, I had uncovered a hole in the professional literature regarding something practical and of personal significance. In 2005, I began research to uncover the extent to which U.S. professors (especially women) experienced CPH and what, if anything, they were doing about it.

I conducted my first study of CPH on my own campus at the University of Alaska Anchorage (UAA), a large public, open-enrollment institution. I argued that *CPH*[1] should be defined more broadly to include incivility, bullying, and aggression, and sexually harassing behaviors from students aimed at faculty (Lampman, Phelps, Bancroft, and Beneke 2009). In 2005, I surveyed all instructors on the UAA campus (including adjunct faculty) about their experiences with CPH; of these instructors 399, or approximately 62%, responded. Although men faculty reported more unwanted sexual attention and similar amounts of incivility/bullying from students as women, the women indicated that all forms of CPH were more upsetting to them, were a greater disruption to their work lives, and led to more negative consequences to their physical and emotional health.

Over the past decade, others have investigated the prevalence and predictors of CPH, including incivility, bullying, and aggression toward university faculty (Goodyear, Reynolds, and Gragg 2010; Lampman 2008, 2012; Lashley and de Meneses 2001). For example, Goodyear et al. (2010) asked 339 college faculty from nine schools to recount an incident of student incivility. Their analysis uncovered categories of incivility, including student disengagement (e.g., texting or sleeping in class), disruptive behaviors (e.g., coming to class late or surfing the Internet while in class), and instructor-focused incivility (e.g., ignoring faculty directives or expressing disdain). Additionally, they found that women professors and those who were younger and had fewer years of teaching experience reported significantly more incivility from students. Furthermore, women reported more severe experiences of incivility and more distress related to them than men.

In 2008, I surveyed a random sample of 524 faculty from 100 randomly selected U.S. colleges and universities, asking them to report on their experiences with CPH during the past year (Lampman 2012). Ninety-one percent of respondents reported at least one act of student incivility/bullying (e.g., questioning faculty credentials, challenging authority, demanding makeup exams, or making threatening remarks); 25% experienced at least one sexual form of CPH from a student (e.g., being glanced at suggestively, asked on a date, or offered sexual favors for a grade), and 1% to 2% said a student had used physical aggression or threatened them with violence. Significant predictors of student incivility-bullying included being a woman, being younger, being a member of a minority group, and having less professional experience and/or no doctoral degree. Significantly more women (63.3%) than men (50.2%) reported at least one serious incident of CPH. However, gender differences were not found regarding unwanted sexual attention or threats of violence from students.

Lampman et al. (2012) documented six major types of CPH based on a keyword/phrase analysis of respondents' descriptions of the most significant incident of CPH experienced during their careers. Each incident description was coded as containing any of the following forms of CPH from a student:[2]

- Rude, disrespectful, or disruptive behaviors or RDDB [e.g., texting in class or talking while a professor is lecturing]
- Hostility, anger, or aggression or HAA [e.g., yelling at a faculty member or throwing an object in anger]
- Challenging, arguing, or refusing behaviors or CARB [e.g., questioning a professor's credentials or refusing to follow a directive]
- Intimidation, threats, bullying, and accusations or ITBA [e.g., threatening a professor or accusing a professor of racism following an unwanted grade]
- Unwanted sexual attention or USA [e.g., flirting with or asking a professor out on a date]
- Sexual harassment or SH [e.g., offering sex in exchange for a higher grade] (Lampman, Crew, Lowery, and Mulder 2012)

A series of two-way chi-square tests of association were conducted to assess whether the presence of each type of CPH in a description was significantly associated with gender. Although women faculty were more likely than men to describe all nonsexual forms of CPH, the only statistically significant finding was that women were more likely than men to describe instances of CARB. Men faculty were more likely than women to describe incidents containing sexual behaviors (USA and SH); however, men were significantly more likely to relay an incident of sexually harassing behavior than women. These findings suggest that women academics are more vulnerable to nonsexual types of CPH than men—especially the types that involve a challenge to their authority and argumentative behaviors (similar to Goodyear et al. 2010).

Recent research has not always found clear gender differences in the frequency with which faculty report CPH. However, women are significantly more likely to suffer negative consequences to their physical health, emotional well-being, and job productivity than men, and to find all types of CPH more distressing (DeSouza and Fansler 2003; Goodyear et al. 2010; Lampman 2008, 2012; Lampman et al. 2009; Matchen and DeSouza 2000). To date, only one study has explored how faculty respond to incidents of CPH (Lampman et al. 2009). My colleagues and I found that twice as many women (10%) as men (5%) had reported a significant incident of CPH to the dean of students office at some point; the number of faculty reporting to the appropriate campus response team, however, was low (less than 1 in 10). Additionally, significantly more women than men reported taking other actions following an episode of CPH (including seeking support from colleagues and reporting incidents to department heads).

There are several possible explanations for why women may be more likely to report CPH to university administration than men. First, the kinds of CPH experienced by women are often more severe (Goodyear et al. 2010; Lampman et al. 2012). Second, women may worry more about their physical safety after a hostile encounter or one involving sexual attraction because women are more likely than men to be the victims of rape, sexual harassment, domestic violence, and child sexual abuse than men (see Crawford 2011 for a review). Third, men may feel less comfortable reporting CPH than women because doing so may threaten their masculinity. Research documents strong prescriptive gender stereotypes in American culture; we expect women to be "communal" (i.e., nurturing, caring, kind, compassionate), but men are supposed to be "agentic," (i.e., dominant, strong, competitive, achievement oriented) (Heilman and Okimoto 2007; Rudman and Glick 2008). Because men faculty may have concerns about appearing to be intimidated by students if they "violate" the prescription to be agentic, they may be less likely to seek support from colleagues following an incident of CPH. Similarly, women may be more likely than men to respond to CPH with changes to how they teach to avoid future confrontations. Although making adjustments to assignments, assessments, or teaching style may seem proactive, it suggests that women instructors feel more pressure than men to adjust their teaching practices or lower their grading standards to reduce CPH.

To date, researchers have not assessed why faculty appear reluctant to report CPH. One reason for this reluctance may be concern that reporting will take a lot of time and not lead to a successful outcome such as the student being reprimanded, put on probation, or removed from a class. Another reason is that faculty may fear becoming the target of an administrative response (e.g., being asked to give in to a student's demands by changing a grade or being blamed for the incident by a superior). Jendrek (1989) found that non-tenured professors were less likely to report students' academic misconduct than tenured faculty, possibly reflecting greater concern about job security. In follow-up interviews with respondents from the 2005 survey who indicated that they had experienced serious CPH (Lampman 2008), I found that those who had reported CPH to the dean of students office had more successful outcomes than faculty who reported it only to their chair or college dean. To decrease reluctance in reporting CPH, we must assess the effectiveness and processes experienced by faculty who report CPH. For example, how satisfied are they with how administrators managed the incident? Additionally, faculty may feel that reporting less severe forms of CPH (e.g., rude, disruptive, disrespectful, or flirtatious behavior) might not be worth the time investment or might make them look like "complainers." Thus, more severe forms of CPH, especially intimidation, threats, and bullying, might be reported more often than less serious acts.

The Present Study

The data here are from my 2008 national survey of U.S. faculty about their experiences with CPH. I explore gender differences in faculty responses to CPH and levels of satisfaction with how reports of CPH are handled by university administrators. I predicted women faculty would be more likely than men to report the most serious incident of CPH experienced during their academic careers to their department chair; the dean of their college; the dean of students; and, if serious enough, university police and local law enforcement. In addition, I expected women more than men to indicate that they had made adjustments to assignments or exams following the most serious CPH incident and sought colleagues' support to help cope. I also explored how the severity of CPH related to the likelihood that faculty would report it, making the assumption that incidents of CPH that are reported to administrators more often are more severe or extreme. I expected incidents involving ITBA to be reported more than less severe types of CPH.

The following data represent a subsample of my 2008 data:[3] 258 professors (54% women) who (a) had experienced at least one significant incident of CPH; (b) described the incident; and (c) answered a series of questions about how they responded to the "most serious incident of student bullying, aggression, incivility, or unwanted sexual attention." Questions asked whether respondents had reported the incident to their department chair, college dean, and/or the dean of students or appropriate campus entity charged with student disciplinary action; contacted the university police and/or local law enforcement; sought colleagues' support; and changed or dropped assignments or tests because of the incident. If a respondent indicated that she or he had reported the incident to a university administrator, the respondent was asked to rate his or her satisfaction with how the situation was handled.

Analyses explored how the severity of CPH related to the likelihood that faculty report it. A series of two-way chi-square tests of association explored whether reporting one's most extreme experience of CPH as a faculty member (yes or no) was associated with the presence or absence of each type of CPH.

Gender Differences in Faculty Responses to CPH

Table 13.1 shows responses regarding the most serious incident of student bullying, aggression, incivility, or unwanted sexual attention ($N = 258$). A total of 59.2% of faculty reported the incident to their department chair. Women (71.7%) were significantly more likely than men (44.4%) to report. About one in three faculty responded to the CPH by reporting it to their dean. Although women (36.0%) were more likely to report their most extreme encounter with CPH to their dean than men (25.6%), this was not statistically significant (see Table 13.1). Even fewer faculty (28.5% total) reported the student misconduct to the "appropriate person on campus for student disciplinary action" such as the dean of students. One in eight faculty members contacted the university police department regarding their most serious experience of CPH. Although not statistically significant, nearly twice as many

TABLE 13.1.

Faculty Responses to Most Serious Incident of Student Bullying, Aggression, Incivility, or Unwanted Sexual Attention Experienced During Teaching Career by Gender

Faculty Response	% of Men (n)	% of Women (n)	% of Total (n)	χ^2 (1) (p value)
You reported the incident to your department chair.	44.4 (52)	71.7 (99)	59.2 (151)	19.53** (.001)
You reported the incident to the dean of your college.	25.6 (30)	36.0 (50)	31.3 (80)	3.16 (.08)
You reported the incident to the dean of students or the appropriate person on campus for student disciplinary action.	29.1 (34)	28.1 (39)	28.5 (73)	0.03 (.86)
You contacted university police.	8.5 (10)	15.9 (22)	12.5 (32)	3.16 (.08)
You contacted local law enforcement.	0.9 (1)	2.2 (3)	1.6 (4)	0.71 (.40)
You sought the social support of colleagues.	41.9 (49)	76.3 (106)	60.5 (155)	31.43** (.001)
You changed or dropped assignments because of the incident.	1.7 (2)	7.3 (10)	4.7 (12)	4.38* (.04)

$^*p < .05; ^{**}p < .001.$

women (15.9%) as men (8.5%) called campus police. Fewer than 2% of the sample contacted local law enforcement because of their most severe experience with CPH. Although not statistically significant, 2.5 times as many women professors (2.2%) as men (0.9%) contacted local law enforcement.

As hypothesized, significantly more women faculty (76.3%) than men (41.9%) reported seeking support from colleagues concerning their most serious experience with CPH. Women faculty were more than four times as likely (7.3%) as men (1.7%) to report eliminating or changing assignments or tests because of the incident (see Table 13.1).

Satisfaction With Administrative Handling of Incidents of CPH

Respondents who reported the incident to their chair or the dean of their college (n = 151) and/or the dean of students (n = 79) indicated satisfaction with how the situation was handled. Figure 13.1 shows that roughly 60% of respondents were either "somewhat" or "completely" satisfied with how administrators handled the situation. Satisfaction rates were comparable for all types of administrators. Men had somewhat higher average satisfaction ratings regarding reports to the dean of students (M = 3.80; SD = 1.18) than women (M = 3.36; SD = 1.70), although the difference was not statistically significant: t (76) = 1.34; p = .18. Additionally, men were slightly more satisfied with how their chair or college dean handled the report of CPH (M = 3.64; SD = 1.46) than women (M = 3.56; SD = 1.49); however, the difference was not statistically significant: t (149) = 0.29; p = .77.

Figure 13.1   Faculty Satisfaction With Administrators' Handling of Report of Most Significant Incident of Student Bullying, Aggression, Incivility, or Unwanted Sexual Attention

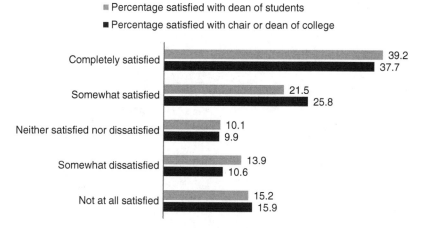

Reporting of CPH by Type of Incident

As expected, faculty were significantly more likely to report their most serious incident of CPH to their chair (χ^2 (5) = 13.1; p = .02), dean of students (χ^2 (5) = 17.9; p = .003), and college dean (χ^2 (5) = 13.1; p = .02) when it involved intimidation, threats, accusations, and/or bullying (see Figure 13.2). The likelihood of reporting different types of CPH suggests a continuum in severity of student behaviors. Faculty were most likely to report acts of ITBA, with 79% reporting such incidents to chairs, 49% reporting to college deans, and 48% reporting to deans of students (see Figure 13.2). Incidents of HAA were the second type of CPH most frequently reported, with 67% of faculty reporting it to chairs, 34% to college deans, and 32% to deans of students. Rates of reporting to chairs and college deans were consistent across the remaining categories of CPH: CARB (64% and 27%, respectively), SH (43% and 14%, respectively), USA (59% and 30%, respectively), and RDDB (56% and 26%, respectively). However, for deans of students the reporting pattern reversed: CARB (21%), SH (29%), USA (19%), and RDDB (25%). None of the types of incident was more likely to be reported to deans than to chairs—possibly reflecting a hierarchy/chain of command, familiarity, and trust.

As predicted, women faculty were more likely than men to take action following an experience of CPH. Women were more likely to consult with their department head, college dean, and colleagues and were more likely to change or drop assignments because of CPH. This greater action reflects the

Figure 13.2 Percentage of Faculty Reporting Most Serious Incident of Student Bullying, Aggression, Incivility, or Unwanted Sexual Attention During Career to Chair, Dean of College, and Dean of Students When Type of Student Behavior Was Present

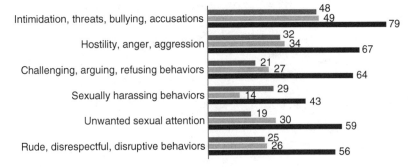

fact that women academics appear more likely to experience challenges to their authority, argumentative behaviors, intimidation, threats, and bullying than men (Goodyear et al. 2010; Lampman 2012; Lampman et al. 2012). Such behaviors may lead to greater reporting because faculty might be more concerned that students will file grade appeals or lodge complaints about their teaching methods. Although we can interpret seeking support as a positive response to CPH, the pressure to change one's teaching is a negative one. Women faculty should not feel pressured to change how they teach out of fear of CPH. Rather, we should expect students to exhibit appropriate, non-harassing behaviors. Future research should explore the types and context of CPH, and the decision-making process of adjustments that faculty, especially women, have made to prevent future incidents of CPH.

An unfortunate trend was that less than 3 in 10 faculty members reported their most serious incident of CPH to the dean of students office or other campus official with the explicit ability to discipline a student. This finding is noteworthy given that department chairs and college deans are tasked with managing faculty and courses, not students. This means that the "solutions" they suggest probably involve changes to the faculty member's behavior rather than the student's. Such responses do not address the key actors in student behavior problems or the culture in which they arise. Additionally, they imply that faculty are partly responsible for CPH. Thus, it is imperative that faculty, department chairs, and deans be well informed about the appropriate way to report CPH; although it is likely that a faculty member will first report CPH to his or her chair, the faculty member needs to be aware that the dean of students or other disciplinary body must be notified about serious CPH cases. The dean of students will keep records of a student's misconduct across all classes, not just in a single department or college. When the dean of students receives an allegation of CPH, he or she will know whether the student has been subject to prior investigations elsewhere.

The potential costs related to reporting students for CPH may explain the lower rate of reporting to the dean of students. These costs include being afraid that reporting will further aggravate an agitated aggressor; having concerns about personal safety; having concerns about negative course evaluations that could impact tenure, promotion, or pay; being blamed for the incident; or being told to meet the harassing student's demands or requests. Some faculty may fear that reporting CPH will negatively influence the student's permanent record. Potential costs likely differ by faculty gender, experience, tenure status, tenure eligibility, and type of CPH. For example, men may be less likely to report a student for unwanted sexual attention or sexual harassment than women because they perceive such incidents as less threatening compared with other types of CPH (e.g., accusations of racism, threats of harm). Similarly, some instructors, particularly new hires or non-tenure-track faculty, may not be familiar with their school's student code of conduct or know the correct process for reporting CPH.

However, potential rewards for reporting CPH exist, including decreased fear or anxiety once the CPH is being handled by administrators, closure regarding the situation, and the possibility of reducing further harassment of self and others by the offending student. The data in this chapter suggest that most faculty who reported CPH to their department chair or the dean of students were satisfied with how the situation was handled. This suggests that department chairs and college deans should encourage faculty (especially new instructors and contingent faculty) to report such events and provide guidance about how and when to do so. It is critical that faculty and administrators be familiar with the student code of conduct and the appropriate body on campus to handle student misconduct. In addition, it is important that colleges and universities create a supportive culture for reporting CPH. Appointing a faculty ombudsperson or having a campus counselor or psychologist available to help faculty experiencing CPH is a positive step that a campus can take toward creating a climate in which faculty do not fear reporting CPH and have help processing the situation.

It is critical to encourage faculty to report CPH to the dean of students. Similar to cases of student plagiarism that go unreported, when a student is not reported for incivility-bullying, aggression, or sexual harassment, it can send the message that CPH is acceptable behavior and increase the likelihood that students will engage in similar behavior in the future. Schultz (2008) suggests that students should be held accountable for even the most basic acts of incivility or disruptive conduct, arguing that noting minor disruptions or disrespectful behavior may keep it from reoccurring. Making students aware that even minor misconduct will not be tolerated sends the message that faculty are willing to take action. Faculty need to recognize the warning signs of more benign uncivil behaviors that, if left unchecked, can escalate into serious harassment (Schultz 2008).

The results of my study suggest that rates of reporting CPH should be increased; it is critical that administrators be made aware of the frequency and negative consequences of CPH and that women, minorities, and less experienced faculty are at increased risk (Lampman 2012). Furthermore, department heads need to assure their faculty that reporting will not tarnish records—especially for untenured or contingent faculty lines, more likely to be filled by women than men (West and Curtis 2006).

Finally, these results suggest that faculty are most likely to report students if the behavior involves intimidation, threats, or bullying; hostility; anger or aggression; and challenging behaviors. Previous research suggests that minor acts of incivility and more extreme acts of bullying are related constructs, and that women are more vulnerable to CPH behaviors such as these than men (Lampman 2012; Lampman et al. 2009, 2012). Although women are more likely to take action following CPH than men, they need encouragement to address all forms of CPH, report CPH to the appropriate administrator, and focus on changes in student behaviors rather than on faculty teaching.

My Experience Aiding Those Who Encounter CPH

I have taken on the post of chair of the Psychology Department at UAA and am in the position to help faculty with more than research findings. I can now guide and instruct them when they are faced with CPH. I recently counseled a faculty member in the midst of a struggle with an intimidating student. This professor fit the profile my research identified as a faculty member most likely at risk for CPH: a young minority woman who is an adjunct instructor without a PhD (Lampman 2012). I encouraged her to report the incident to the dean of students. Fortunately, this led to successful resolution; the faculty member felt supported by her department and the dean, and the student was not allowed to register for another class with this instructor. Ten years ago I did not know the right way to handle and report CPH; my inclination was to suffer in silence. Consequently, I experienced tremendous anxiety and disruption in my life. I now know that my campus has an effective protocol in place. Although I continue to experience CPH, I am no longer derailed by it. I report it, I make sure that the student and I get the help we need, and I move on. This is extremely beneficial to both me and my students. It is imperative that we disrupt the culture of silence about CPH.

Notes

1. Throughout the remainder of this chapter, *CPH* is used as an umbrella term to describe student incivility, bullying, aggression, unwanted sexual attention, and sexually harassing behaviors.
2. A complete description of the coding process and determination of inter-rater agreement is available from the chapter author upon request.
3. See Lampman (2012) for a complete description of the survey-sampling process.

References

Benson, Katherine, A. 1984. "Comments on Crocker's 'An Analysis of University Definitions of Sexual Harassment.' " *Signs* 9(3):516–519.

Carroll, Lynne, and Kathryn L. Ellis. 1989. "Faculty Attitudes Toward Sexual Harassment: Survey Results, Survey Process." *Initiatives* 52:35–41.

Crawford, Mary. 2011. *Transformations: Women, Gender, and Psychology.* New York: McGraw-Hill.

DeSouza, Eros, and A. Gigi Fansler. 2003. "Contrapower Sexual Harassment: A Survey of Students and Faculty Members." *Sex Roles* 48:529–542.

Goodyear, Rod, Pauline Reynolds, and Jannee Both Gragg. 2010. "University Faculty Experiences on Classroom Incivilities: A Critical Incident Study." Paper presented at the annual meeting of the American Educational Research Association, Denver, CO, May.

Grauerholz, Elizabeth. 1989. "Sexual Harassment of Women Professors by Students: Exploring the Dynamics of Power, Authority, and Gender in a University Setting." *Sex Roles* 21: 789–801.

Heilman, Madeline E., and Tyler G. Okimoto. 2007. "Why Are Women Penalized for Success at Male Tasks? The Implied Communality Deficit." *Journal of Applied Psychology* 92:81–92.

Jendrek, Margaret P. 1989. "Faculty Reactions to Academic Dishonesty." *Journal of College Student Development* 30:401–406.

Lampman, Claudia. 2008. "Contrapower Harassment on Campus: Incidence, Consequences, and Implications." In *Start Talking: A Handbook for Engaging Difficult Dialogues in Higher Education,* edited by K. Landis, 18–21. Anchorage: University of Alaska Anchorage and Alaska Pacific University.

———. 2012. "Women Faculty at Risk: U.S. Professors Report on Their Experiences With Student Incivility, Bullying, Aggression and Sexual Attention." *NASPA Journal About Women in Higher Education* 5(2):184–208.

Lampman, Claudia, Earl C. Crew, Shea D. Lowery, and Mikaela Mulder. 2012. "U.S. Professors Describe Their Most Serious Experience With Academic Contrapower Harassment." Paper presented at the annual meeting of the Western Psychological Association, San Francisco, April.

Lampman, Claudia, Alissa Phelps, Samantha Bancroft, and Melissa Beneke. 2009. "Contrapower Harassment in Academia: A Survey of Faculty Experience With Student Incivility, Bullying, and Sexual Attention." *Sex Roles* 60(5–6):331–346.

Lashley, Felissa R., and Mary de Meneses. 2001. "Student Civility in Nursing Programs: A National Study." *Journal of Professional Nursing* 17:81–86.

Matchen, Jim, and Eros DeSouza. 2000. "The Sexual Harassment of Faculty Members by Students." *Sex Roles* 41:295–306.

McKinney, Kathleen. 1990. "Sexual Harassment of University Faculty by Colleagues and Students." *Sex Roles* 23:421–438.

Rudman, Laurie A., and Peter Glick. 2008. *The Social Psychology of Gender: How Power and Intimacy Shape Gender Relations.* New York: Guilford Press.

Schultz, Bruce. 2008. "Recognizing and Responding to Disruptive Students." In *Start Talking: A Handbook for Engaging Difficult Dialogues in Higher Education,* edited by K. Landis, 22–25. Anchorage: University of Alaska Anchorage and Alaska Pacific University.

West, Martha S., and John W. Curtis. 2006. *AAUP Faculty Gender Equity Indicators 2006.* Washington, DC: American Association of University Professors.

14

CONFRONTING FACULTY
INCIVILITY AND MOBBING

Susan K. Gardner and Amy Blackstone

Confronting faculty incivility requires understanding how *incivility* is defined and experienced within academic workplaces. Incivility often manifests as bullying or mobbing (Koonin and Green 2004). Twale and De Luca (2008) suggest that "bullies need support from others to be successful, a bully often acts in consort with others, that is, a mob" (20). When individual bullies gain allies and networks, they become a mob. Mobbing is "ganging up on someone using rumor, innuendo, discrediting, humiliation, isolation, and intimidation in a concentrated and direct manner" (Koonin and Green 2004, 73). The ultimate goal of mobbing is to dominate, subjugate, and eliminate one's target (Twale and De Luca 2008). Mobbing affects nearly 15% of the working population in the United States (Twale and De Luca 2008).

Academia's unique cultures, typically based on isolation, ambiguity, and a high-stress work environment, may inadvertently support mobbing (Davenport, Schwartz, and Elliott 1999; Twale and De Luca 2008). Further, academic organizations are hierarchical and gendered (Acker 1990), which may contribute to creating an environment in which mobbing occurs (Allan 2011; Becher

This material is based on work supported by the National Science Foundation (NSF) under Grant No. 09-504. Any opinions, findings, and conclusions or recommendations expressed in this material are those of the authors and do not necessarily reflect the views of the NSF.

and Trowler 2001; Bergquist and Pawlak 2008; Valian 1998). This is not to say that only women experience mobbing or that men are the only perpetrators of such behavior. Both can be victims and perpetrators of mobbing (Cowan, Neighbors, DeLaMoreaux, and Behnke 1998; Ellemers et al. 2004; Twale and De Luca 2008). As Twale and De Luca (2008) note, "Anyplace where persons serve in a superordinate, managerial, or power capacity over colleagues or subordinates can set the stage for incivility and bullying" (62). But a gendered dynamic in mobbing emerges when one considers that men continue to outnumber women in positions of power in academic settings (Allan 2011), be it in administrative positions, at the rank of professor, or on important committees (Aguirre, Hernandez, and Martinez 1994; August and Waltman 2004).

Forces outside an organization may influence mobbing within it. In U.S. public higher education, dwindling economic support has driven campuses to compete for more prestige and more capital within the academic hierarchy (Brewer, Gates, and Goldman 2001; Gardner 2010). Colleges and universities seeking prestige in the academic hierarchy, known as "striving institutions" (O'Meara 2007), may be more prone than other types of institutions in supporting mobbing cultures (Twale and De Luca 2008) because they face scarce resources, changes in work expectations, and competition (Salin 2003). High workloads, time pressures, and ambiguity within striving environments may nurture mobbing (Salin 2003; Twale and De Luca 2008). Salin (2003) suggests that when job dissatisfaction is rife, bullying may occur. In striving environments, faculty job dissatisfaction may be high.

Our Study

We examine mobbing at a public institution with striving aspirations to illustrate how workers experience mobbing and to understand the relationship between mobbing and culture within a gendered organization (e.g., Acker 1990). This striving institution, Land Grant University (LGU),[1] aims to improve its *U.S. News & World Report* rankings and to increase research and grant activity. As such, LGU's culture has shifted, seeking faculty more focused on research than teaching. Given budget cuts, administrators expect more from faculty with fewer resources.

Our data come from several studies of LGU's faculty. Two surveys of overall faculty job satisfaction provide the quantitative data here, including one administered in 2009 to all full-time tenure-stream and non-tenure-stream faculty (N = 472; response rate = 49%). A follow-up, extended survey was administered in 2011 to faculty in tenure-stream and non-tenure-stream positions (N = 573; response rate = 60%).[2] In 2009, we conducted 11 interviews with women faculty who departed LGU during the years 2003 through 2008. In 2011, we interviewed 19 current women faculty from diverse ranks and disciplines. With this mixed-methods approach, we aim to provide a "more comprehensive picture" (McMillan and Schumacher 2006; see also Creswell 2003) of academic bullying, mobbing, and gendered dynamics in the LGU culture.

From the 2009 survey, *t*-test results show statistically significant differences ($p < .05$) between men's and women's experiences at LGU.[3] Table 14.1 presents differences between men's and women's responses on six mobbing items, which touch on the following four themes: intimidation, isolation, hostility, and discrediting of one's work (see Koonin and Green 2004; Rospenda and Richman 2004). The table presents gender differences in experiences of LGU's cultural context, which reflect conditions of a striving institution.

Women were more likely than men to experience all six mobbing indicators. Feeling respected by one's department chair yielded the smallest gender difference, with 86% of men and 80% of women agreeing with that item. Feeling that one does a great deal of work not formally recognized by one's department yielded the greatest gender difference, with 33% of men and 59% of women agreeing with the statement. Other gender differences include feeling isolated in one's department (9% men, 31% women), feeling excluded from the department's informal network (11% men, 36% women), feeling that one is treated with respect by colleagues (86% men, 71% women), and feeling that one's research is considered mainstream by the department (53% men, 39% women).

While 67% of men and 50% of women faculty reported a "strong fit" between their work styles and how others evaluate their work, under half (42% of men, 34% of women) reported having the resources needed to conduct research. Like other organizations with striving cultures, LGU's lack of resources coupled with faculty feelings of isolation, ambiguity, and job dissatisfaction may create an environment that allows mobbing to occur (Twale and De Luca 2008).

Although men and women reported different experiences within LGU's culture, the gender differences are far smaller than on the mobbing items (see Table 14.1). Far more women than men reported experiences of bullying or mobbing, but gender differences are less pronounced when it comes to the indicators of LGU's striving culture. This may indicate that women and men experience the negative indicators associated with a striving culture but that the consequences of that culture are more severe for women because they translate into mobbing experiences more often.

LGU's women faculty reported more hostility, greater isolation, and less support than men. But, as with other forms of gendered violence or discrimination (Quinn 2002; Reskin 2003; Uggen and Blackstone 2004), the mobbing that women faculty experience is more than an individual-level phenomenon. Although mobbing occurs at a microlevel, between individuals and small groups, its impacts are experienced more broadly. LGU's striving

TABLE 14.1.
Significant Differences in Mobbing Experiences and Organizational Culture at LGU by Gender

Survey Item	Strongly Agree to Agree [a]		Difference (%)	Significance Level (p Value)
	Men (%)	Women (%)		
Mobbing				
I am treated with respect by colleagues.	86	71	15	<.001
I am treated with respect by my department chair.	86	80	6	<.05
In my department, I feel that my research is considered mainstream.	53	39	14	<.001
I feel excluded from an informal network in my department.	11	36	25	.000
I do a great deal of work that is not formally recognized by my department.	33	59	26	.000
I feel isolated in my department.	9	31	22	.000
Organizational Culture				
I am/was satisfied with the tenure and promotion process overall.	75	60	15	<.001
I feel there is/was a strong fit between the way I do/did research, teaching, and service, and the way it is/was evaluated for tenure.	67	50	17	<.05
I have the equipment/supplies I need to adequately conduct my research.	42	34	8	<.05
I would like to receive more department travel funds than I do.	59	79	20	<.05
The department knows the options available for faculty who have a new baby.	40	37	3	<.05
The department is supportive of family leave.	57	40	17	<.05

[a] Response options for the items were presented in the form of a 5-point Likert scale (1 = strongly disagree; 5 = strongly agree). We collapsed the top two categories, agree and strongly agree, and here compare men's and women's "agree" means for each item.

culture creates a climate in which mobbing is common and often overlooked by upper administration. In such an environment, bullies remain unchecked and become empowered to continue their behavior.

Findings from the 2011 survey reveal similar patterns. Fifteen percent of faculty reported harassment, usually bullying or mobbing. More women reported being harassed than men (23% versus 9%). When prompted by an open-ended question to qualitatively describe their experiences, 80% of harassed women provided descriptions whereas only 20% of men did. There are several possible explanations for this difference. Perhaps women's experiences with harassment had a greater impact and, therefore, women felt more compelled than men to describe them. Or, perhaps men's experiences were equally impactful, but because men are not socialized to think of themselves as harassment victims, they may lack the impetus to describe their experiences. Finally, research shows that men who informally discuss their experiences with harassment are more likely than women to go on to formally report harassment to authorities (Blackstone, Uggen, and McLaughlin 2009). It is possible that men are simply less inclined to discuss their harassment, even in an anonymous survey, unless they plan to report those experiences to authorities.

Those who provided details about their harassment cited lack of institutional support for action. One woman shared, "The institution cannot or will not do much about an individual who routinely bullies her/his colleagues and has done so for years, basically destroying [the] departmental work atmosphere." Another explained:

> It took several years until one colleague addressed me and informed me of possible ways to address the situation. . . . In the hierarchical structure detailed to me there was no way to address the harassment I experienced without going through the person who was responsible for the harassing behaviors. This situation was amplified by the existing division within the department. I had no one to turn to for help.

Another woman said:

> The equal opportunity officer at the time told me, "You can't make people be nice [to] you" (after showing rude notes, and explaining a recent threatening phone message left on my home phone). The dean suggested I get counseling, to which I said, "I don't need counseling, I need a dean with a backbone."

One notable pattern in this latter case, and in others reported to us, is that administrators focused their responses on the individual *target* of the bullying rather than the perpetrators or the institutional/cultural practices that allowed or even encouraged mobbing behaviors. Specifically, the university's equal opportunity office and the respondent's dean placed responsibility on her rather than on her harasser or the institution.

Bullying by department chairs and immediate supervisors seems common. One woman said:

> My school director can be a bully. As well, he often jokingly brings up gender issues. The problem is that to survive I go along with it and joke back, which probably only encourages the behavior. I have not told him to stop. I see how he bullies other faculty and want to stay on his good side.

Many women faculty feared repercussions of working where the bully is a supervisor. One woman said, "I cried a lot. Physical pain. Nowhere to turn. Very difficult. I tried to help others and focus on my family. Ongoing and humiliating. I dreaded just to walk into the department every day."

It is not surprising that more women (21%) than men (13%) reported being slightly to strongly dissatisfied with their work. Consequently, 59% of women reported either very seriously or somewhat seriously considering leaving LGU, compared to 49% of men. When asked why they considered leaving, most women commented on aspects related to the striving environment of LGU, including a lack of resources, a lack of support, feelings of isolation, and bullying. One woman explained:

> A lack of funding, of recognition of service, of research achievements. The inability of the institution to shield a junior faculty member from departmental infighting, and bullying by faculty members. Withholding of essential information, of technical support such as printer services [and so on]. Basic attitude conveyed that I am not part of the department.

Another remarked, "Support for teaching and research at LGU has been extremely biased in that only the 'favored' boys get support here. In addition, there has been a strong culture of punishing those who disagree in any way with the administration."

The interviews with current and past LGU women faculty point to mobbing and other gender issues. One interviewee commented, "I have to say that I think if I had been a male asking, petitioning, for these salary increases there would have been a different outcome." Another shared, "There were these generational responses by men in the department. I think the older males had a very paternalistic view." Yet another said, "The worst thing was that I had a couple of colleagues, and one in particular, who were just raving misogynists. It was very difficult to work there."

Of course, bullying or support for bullying is not exclusive to men (Twale and De Luca 2008). One respondent explained:

Women can contribute to a hostile work climate equally as much as men. Like one colleague in [my department]. I know she didn't *like* the things that were going on but she accepted them and refused to stand up in any way or even admit publicly that there was a problem. She would say it to me privately but never publicly.

When asked if the environment had shaped her colleague's reaction, she replied, "I think it's definitely something that the environment fostered. If you come to a place and it's clear that women are not going to be treated equally, then very few women will actually stand up [and] say, 'This is not okay.'" Appalled, she said of her woman dean: "It was just shocking to discover that she was as much of a good old boy as [the past male dean]. I mean, hello?"

As Acker (1990) and others who analyze gendered organizational practices point out (Britton 2000; Uggen and Blackstone 2004), because women may act like bullies does *not* mean that the phenomenon is *not* gendered. Instead, the practice of workplace mobbing is one in which gender manifests itself as an organizing structure rather than an individual practice. The "good old boy" network does not necessarily exclude women. But, it is still a "boy's network" in that it promotes the existing power structure that disadvantages more women than men.

The gendered organizational culture at LGU prompted the departure of several women, including one who said: "It only got worse. I guess what you read about the cumulative effect, I think that's really true. Toward the end I would be *so* tied up in knots coming to work that I was in tears by the time I made the drive from [where I lived] to the university."

Another woman expressed her dismay about our study, given LGU's past history. She emphasized: "The university overall is hostile to women. It's like, we've had enough studies on the chilly climate for women." After receiving the e-mail asking for an interview, she said she called a former colleague from LGU. "[My colleague said,] 'What the hell is this again?' And I'm like, 'Yeah, I know, they're doing it again.' It's like, here we go again. Studying the climate for women at LGU, blah, blah, blah." The interviewee stated: "It was really about sort of people's attitudes and the climate and the bullshit and the politics and the power plays and the constant lip service to 'We value diversity, we care about women, we care about diversity,' all of this crap. I hate fake." When asked if she thought her experience would have been the same if she had been a man, this woman emphatically said, "Oh, God, no.

No. No. No. No." She laughed and again remarked, "Totally not. No. No."
She explained:

> I saw the guys sit around and sort of sneer at women's research and turn
> around and put out this stuff that's just complete fucking crap and just
> finding excuses for why this was good enough to get them tenure. You
> know, I've seen the jokes. I've seen the women who are driving ourselves
> crazy doing service, and advising, and committees, and running around
> doing all this service trying to improve the climate on campus while the
> guys do their own little thing and their one little committee and everybody
> jumps up and down about how wonderful they are.

Confronting Mobbing

At LGU, organizational and individual factors create an environment
that fosters bullying and mobbing behaviors that are most detrimental to
women faculty. Women are more likely than men to experience all six
quantitative indicators of mobbing. Additionally, the women we interviewed described cultures at multiple organizational levels—department,
college, and university—in which harassment was ignored, downplayed,
or disregarded.

Many women's experiences underscore issues of ambiguity, isolation,
and a gendered environment that fosters mobbing. These issues are exacerbated by LGU's "striving" culture, in which fewer women than men report
having the resources needed to conduct research and in which women are less
likely than men to report a fit between their own work style and the way others evaluate their work. Further, a lack of resources coupled with increased
expectations for productivity has resulted in a tense environment for faculty.
The high numbers of faculty expressing a desire to leave LGU should be of
concern to LGU's administration given that it generally costs more to recruit
new faculty than to retain current ones (California State University 2005;
University of Colorado at Boulder Task Force 2001). Administrators of similar institutions might pay heed to the repercussions for such organizational
cultures.

Unambiguous policies must be adopted to combat bullying and mobbing. These policies should clearly define such behaviors, delineating them
from sexual harassment (Twale and De Luca 2008). Policies should be for-
mulated from empirical data and require buy-in from institutional constituencies, including faculty, staff, and students. Buy-in could be obtained
through mechanisms such as information-gathering forums, surveys regarding policy revisions, and the creation of policy-writing committees including

representatives from each constituency. Equally, policies should clearly outline grievance procedures, sanctions, and actions for redress. Twale and De Luca (2008) suggest public disclosure of such incidents to demonstrate the lack of administrative tolerance for inappropriate behaviors.

Once policies are in place, university constituencies should receive routine training about these policies, their implementation, why they must be followed, and the consequences for not doing so. Policies are not useful if they are not used and people might not use them if they do not fully appreciate their purpose.

Individuals learn how to behave in an organizational culture through socialization (Tierney 1997; Van Maanen and Schein 1979). Thus, universities and their constituencies should perform regular cultural audits of the institutional environment, to understand the experiences of its members, especially those who are new. Often, those newest to an organization can most easily comment on its culture, given that an organizational culture is the proverbial water to the existing fish. By hiring external consultants and regularly gathering anonymous (or confidential) data from constituents, institutions may better understand their organizational culture. Thus, they can determine what needs to inform policies, professional development, and training. Similarly, given the socialization mechanisms at play in graduate school (Gardner 2008, 2010), graduate faculty and advisors should be cognizant of the influence they have on the next generation of faculty and university administrators. Graduate faculty and advisors who understand the impact of mobbing on individuals and institutional cultures should receive ongoing training that makes them aware of their influence and develops appropriate mentoring skills.

As seen at LGU, striving cultures that carry expectations for success on the backs of their faculty (Wolf-Wendel and Ward 2005) can create an environment ripe for mobbing. O'Meara and Bloomgarden (2011) suggest that striving environments may demonstrate less support for balancing work/family, be less likely to acknowledge and reward nonmainstream scholarship, and be more competitive and individualistic in their orientations toward faculty work/life and careers. Given the context of gendered organizations, it is not surprising that women tend to be most affected in striving settings. Institutions aspiring to attain more prestige should consider their resources, present and future, in light of these aspirations. Expecting faculty to do more with less is unrealistic and ultimately destructive when one considers the costs of faculty dissatisfaction and, consequently, attrition.

Future research should consider how different institutional environments, control (public versus private), and geographic settings influence mobbing. Further, it should explore how different groups experience mobbing and bullying behaviors based on their social locations (e.g., faculty of color versus white faculty, tenured versus non-tenured faculty, heterosexual and cisgender versus LGBT faculty, adjuncts versus full-time faculty). While this chapter examined mobbing among faculty, researchers should also consider other institutional groups such as students, administrators, and staff who create a university's culture. An understanding of workplace dynamics among all campus groups is essential in order to comprehend and eliminate mobbing and other forms of bullying. Only with a deeper understanding of these behaviors can higher education institutions work toward creating environments that reject mobbing and, instead, foster collegiality.

Notes

1. The name of the university is a pseudonym.
2. Few part-time faculty responded; overall, our results are representative of full-time faculty.
3. Although data on disciplinary affiliation, rank, race, sexual orientation, and ability status were collected, the numbers in each category were too small for effective use in analysis. Thus, we present data only on gender differences.

References

Acker, Joan. 1990. "Hierarchies, Jobs, Bodies: A Theory of Gendered Organizations." *Gender and Society* 4:139–158.

Aguirre, A., A. Hernandez, and R. Martinez. 1994. "Perceptions of the Workplace: Focus on Minority Women Faculty." *Initiatives* 56:41–50.

Allan, Elizabeth J. 2011. *Women's Status in Higher Education: Equity Matters*. San Francisco: Jossey-Bass.

August, Louise, and Jean Waltman. 2004. "Culture, Climate, and Contribution: Career Satisfaction Among Female Faculty." *Research in Higher Education* 45:177–192.

Becher, Tony, and P. R. Trowler. 2001. *Academic Tribes and Territories*. Philadelphia: Open University Press.

Bergquist, William H., and Kenneth Pawlak. 2008. *Engaging the Six Cultures of the Academy: Revised and Expanded Edition of the Four Cultures of the Academy*. San Francisco: Jossey-Bass.

Blackstone, Amy, Christopher Uggen, and Heather McLaughlin. 2009. "Legal Consciousness and Responses to Sexual Harassment." *Law & Society Review* 43:631–668.

Brewer, D. J., S. M. Gates, and C. A. Goldman. 2001. *In Pursuit of Prestige: Strategy and Competition in U.S. Higher Education*. Piscataway, NJ: Transaction.

Britton, Dana. 2000. "The Epistemology of the Gendered Organization." *Gender & Society* 14:418–434.

California State University. 2005. *Faculty Compensation and the Crisis in Recruiting and Retaining Faculty of High Quality.* Long Beach: California State University.

Cowan, Gloria, Charlene Neighbors, Jann DeLaMoreaux, and Catherine Behnke. 1998. "Women's Hostility Toward Women." *Psychology of Women Quarterly* 22:267–284.

Creswell, John W. 2003. *Research Design: Qualitative, Quantitative, and Mixed Methods Approaches.* Thousand Oaks, CA: Sage.

Davenport, Noa, Ruth D. Schwartz, and Gail P. Elliott. 1999. *Mobbing: Emotional Abuse in the American Workplace.* Ames, IA: Civil Society Publishing.

Ellemers, N., H. Van Den Heuvel, D. de Gilder, A. Maass, and A. Bonvini. 2004. "The Underrepresentation of Women in Science: Differential Commitment or the Queen Bee Syndrome?" *British Journal of Social Psychology* 43(Pt. 3):315–338.

Gardner, Susan K. 2008. "Fitting the Mold of Graduate School." *Innovative Higher Education* 33:125–138.

———. 2010. "Keeping Up With the Joneses: Socialization and Culture in Doctoral Education at One Striving Institution." *The Journal of Higher Education* 81:658–679.

Koonin, Michele, and Thomas M. Green. 2004. "The Emotionally Abusive Workplace." *Journal of Emotional Abuse* 4:71–79.

McMillan, James H., and Sally Schumacher. 2006. *Research in Education: Evidence-Based Inquiry.* Boston: Pearson.

O'Meara, K. 2007. "Striving for What? Exploring the Pursuit of Prestige." *Higher Education: Handbook of Theory and Research* 22:121–179.

O'Meara, K. A., and Alan Bloomgarden. 2011. "The Pursuit of Prestige: The Experience of Institutional Striving From a Faculty Perspective." *The Journal of the Professoriate* 4:39–73.

Quinn, Beth A. 2002. "Sexual Harassment and Masculinity: The Power and Meaning of 'Girl Watching.'" *Gender & Society* 16:386–402.

Reskin, Barbara F. 2003. "Including Mechanisms in Our Models of Ascriptive Inequality." *American Sociological Review* 68:1–21.

Rospenda, Kathleen M., and Judith A. Richman. 2004. "The Factor Structure of Generalized Workplace Harassment." *Violence and Victims* 19:221–239.

Salin, Denise. 2003. "Ways of Explaining Workplace Bullying: A Review of Enabling, Motivating and Precipitating Structures and Processes in the Work Environment." *Human Relations* 56:1213–1232.

Tierney, William G. 1997. "Organizational Socialization in Higher Education." *The Journal of Higher Education* 68:1–16.

Twale, Darla J., and Barbara M. De Luca. 2008. *Faculty Incivility: The Rise of the Academic Bully Culture and What to Do About It.* San Francisco: Jossey-Bass.

Uggen, Christopher, and Amy Blackstone. 2004. "Sexual Harassment as a Gendered Expression of Power." *American Sociological Review* 69:64–92.

University of Colorado at Boulder Task Force. 2001. *Faculty Recruitment and Retention Task Force Report.* Boulder, CO. http://www.colorado.edu/academicaffairs/fac_recruit/index.html.

Valian, Virginia. 1998. *Why So Slow? The Advancement of Women.* Cambridge, MA: MIT Press.

Van Maanen, John, and Edgar H. Schein. 1979. "Toward a Theory of Organizational Socialization." *Research in Organizational Behavior* 1:209–264.

Wolf-Wendel, L., and K. Ward. 2005. "Faculty Life at Comprehensives: Between a Rock and a Hard Place." *Journal of the Professoriate* 1:1–21.

15

WOMEN OF COLOR IN THE ACADEMY

From Trauma to Transformation

Molly Everett Davis, Halaevalu F. Ofahengaue Vakalahi, and Renay Scales

Alyssa, an African American professor at a local university, found herself experiencing heart palpitations, sweaty palms, and a feeling of being sick to her stomach after pulling into her office parking lot. Why did she have such a feeling of dread? After seeing several doctors about her high blood pressure, she recognized the feeling of dread was linked to strained relationships with faculty colleagues, a disproportionate level of work compared with colleagues, and unending challenges to prove that a woman of color can perform well in an academic setting.

Jane, an assistant professor of Puerto Rican descent, recently received a letter indicating that the promotion and tenure committee had decided that after three years her contract would not be renewed. She struggled to be a good faculty member even though some of her colleagues had been critical of her personality and called her unfriendly. Jane has diabetes, and as a result of a lot of sleepless nights and worry over her future, her blood sugar levels had become unstable. Jane was headed to class when she suddenly experienced dizziness and nausea, and that was the last thing she remembered. She awoke in a hospital to the news that she had experienced a stroke and was paralyzed on her left side. (Personal communication 2011, all names changed)

These scenarios show that women of color academics are no strangers to traumatic experiences in academia (Vakalahi and Starks 2010). Efforts to achieve access and some level of parity within academia have not always been successful. Although some inroads have been made, positions dominated by white men continue to be normative within U.S. higher education (U.S. Department of Education, National Center for Education

Statistics 2011). Women represented 41% of tenure eligible faculty in U.S. colleges and universities in 2012 (*The Chronicle of Higher Education* 2012). During the fall of 2009 statistics revealed that women faculty when viewed by racial/ethnic status consisted of American Indian (.6%), Hispanic (4%), Asian American (5.6%), African American (9%), and white (78.5%) (*The Chronicle of Higher Education* 2012). Women of color in academia are clearly underrepresented and have not always had positive or equitable experiences (Tuitt et al. 2009). The opening accounts exemplify some harmful dynamics and practices within academia. However, few researchers have analyzed these experiences through the framework of trauma. In this chapter, we use "trauma" as a conceptual framework to examine the negative workplace experiences of women of color academics. We seek to define the features of workplace-related traumatic events and explore the physical, psychological, and social costs of these events in academia (Carter 2007; Tuitt et al. 2009).

Trauma is framed broadly, as a kind of injury that harms the victim (Carter 2007; Pieterse and Carter 2010; Pieterse, Todd, Neville, and Carter 2012) physically, psychologically, and/or socially. Trauma is viewed in medicine as a serious injury or shock to the body that may become increasingly worse with reinjury (National Institute of General Medical Sciences 2012). *Psychological trauma* is a unique, individual adverse circumstance that produces psychological wounding, resulting in the person feeling emotionally overwhelmed and his or her sanity being threatened (Carter and Forsyth 2010). The common denominator of both medical and psychological trauma perspectives is harm and injury that often results in the trauma victim being unable to cope with feelings of helplessness. Racism, discrimination, oppression, and microaggressions (e.g., insults, indignities, disrespect) represent forms of trauma to women of color academics, often experienced on a routine basis and associated with a sense of chronic adversity and powerlessness (Vakalahi, Davis, and Scales 2012). This *cumulative trauma* imposes repetitive injuries that result in short- and long-term psychological, social, and/or physical consequences.

Several defining features of traumatic events can assist us in understanding how an individual experiences them. First, traumatic events are aversive and involve the nonverbal transmission of a behavior, a feeling, or an emotion that is viewed in a negative manner (Anderson, McNeilly, and Myers 1995; Guerrero and Hecht 2008). Second, traumatic events feel uncontrollable. Third, they feel unpredictable, increasing the stress and anxiety associated with them. Lastly, traumatic events threaten the person's ability to feel safe. Typically, circumstances that threaten one's safety are avoided where possible. However, workplace-based trauma is difficult or impossible to avoid, resulting in ongoing retraumatization at work.

Racism as Trauma

Carter (2007) pioneered the concept of race-based trauma: the often ambiguous, subtle, sometimes unintended experiences of racism that generate stress and result in trauma. Reactions to race-based trauma include intrusive thoughts, avoidance, emotional arousal, irritability, emotional numbness, and jumpiness (Carter and Forsyth 2010). We use *racism-based trauma* (RBT) to understand the narratives of women of color in academia regarding overt racist practices that contribute to traumatic injury (Vakalahi et al. 2012). Although recognizing microaggressions is important, the concept of RBT is broader and reflects cumulative harm to individuals who experience it (Carter 2007; Carter and Reynolds 2011; Forsyth and Carter 2012; Sue 2010; Sue, Capodilupo, and Holder 2008).

Individual and institutional racism exists in many academic settings (Miller 2009). Thus, we should expect RBT to occur in such settings and to negatively impact the physical and psychological health of women of color academics (Kersh 2012; Myers 1999). Yet, educators, physicians, health care practitioners, and the general public do not fully understand the experiences of women of color in academia from a context of trauma because of the dearth of scientific studies about their experiences (Tuitt et al. 2009; Vakalahi, Starks, and Ortiz 2007). As described by Myers (1999):

> Minority women faculty constantly battle racial and gender bias to become key players in the informal networks where real decisions are made. Some hesitate to voice their concerns for fear of being labeled by white men as domineering, or as "loose cannons." In many cases, the single African-American woman faculty member is subjected to magnified expectations and extreme evaluations. African-American women often feel pressure to outperform other white colleagues just to maintain perceived equal performance status, only to have their outstanding performance discredited due to racism or sexism. (1)

Women of color academics describe a pervasive lack of respect, challenging of their competence and credentials by students and colleagues, and work climates that manifest ongoing tensions (Clark, Anderson, Clark, and Williams 1999; Tuitt et al. 2009). Over time many women of color academics experience the cumulative effects of trauma rooted in racism. As one woman of color academic said,

> I find myself surreally bleeding from the wounds inflicted consciously and unconsciously by my students, colleagues and so-called campus community. Every day, I walk a lonely walk down the long corridor that leads to

my office, passing office after office inhabited by White colleagues who I may never really know, who cannot understand, and who would likely negate my lived experience with numerous examples of how they cannot possibly be racist. (Tuitt et al. 2009, 67)

Exposure to multiple types of trauma including RBT may impact one's ability to recover (Lepore, Miles, and Levy 1997). For example, some women of color will transition to different academic settings only to find more of the same attitudes and practices in the next job. In part, this is because the traumatic injury remains unhealed and racist practices persist in many different academic institutions. The repeated experiences in successive institutions and the commonality of the experiences of women of color in academia suggest that institutional and structural patterns within academic environments perpetuate RBT (Stanley 2006; Tuitt et al. 2009).

People experiencing trauma—including RBT—commonly feel fear, anxiety, anger, sadness, depression, low self-esteem, shame, and guilt. They may have trouble sleeping and concentrating, turn to substance abuse, or suffer physical illnesses (Carter and Forsyth 2010; Vargas 2002). Studies document the relationship among racism, high stress levels, cardiovascular disease, hypertension, and mental health issues (Brondolo, Love, Pencille, and Schoenthaler 2011; Fang and Myers 2001; Guyll, Matthews, and Bromberger 2001; Richman et al. 2007; Tull, Yah-Tyng, Butler, and Karimiah 2005). Brain scans suggest that the brain stores traumatic memories. Simmons and Matthews (2012) found that trauma can change the neural circuitry of the brain because people's experience of trauma diverts oxygen from the brain to the muscles as the body prepares for fight or flight. Additionally, Leaf (2009) identified a toxic pathway of stress that impacts bodily systems and organs:

- Heart system: hypertension, chest pain, coronary artery disease, strokes, and aneurysms
- Immune system: susceptibility to lowered immunity and autoimmune responses
- Digestive system: constipation, diarrhea, nausea and vomiting, ulcers, leaky gut syndrome, and irritable bowel syndrome

In summary, whether it occurs in the context of individuals, institutions, or cultures, exposure to RBT can lead to multidimensional, acute, and chronic negative changes in physiology, cognition, affect, and behavior.

The experience of RBT for women of color academics is linked to both institutional and interpersonal practices and policies that have historically benefited white men. Harrison's (2012) seminal report describes graphically her experience as a woman of color academic attempting to "adapt":

> The topic of racism in academia is one that can easily elicit emotionally charged "war stories" from the battles that minority academics have to fight, often on a daily basis. I could easily be brought to tears when thinking about what I have had to deal with in the classroom with students, at faculty meetings with colleagues, in the corridors, and in committee meetings in various professional contexts. Racism is pervasive, deeply implanted, painful and a violation of human dignity and rights despite the intensity with which it is denied. (18)

Her narrative, though powerful, does not fully represent the harm from being wounded psychologically, physically, and socially by such experiences. She articulates her experiences as racism, but she does not view them as a form of trauma. By recognizing the cumulative effects of racism *as trauma*, women of color academics and their allies can strategize how to survive, and academia can become more aware of the deep harm inflicted when institutions do not actively prevent racism or intervene when it occurs.

RBT appears to be pervasive among women of color academics irrespective of rank and status (Harrison 2012; Kersh 2012; Stanley 2006). Although many spend years—even entire careers—working in hostile environments, they excel professionally, a testament of their strength and resilience. Yet, why should they be expected to work harder, tolerate more racism and sexism, and bear the trauma of continual wounding and microaggressions as a way of life in academia? This should not be the status quo for women of color. Being able to circumvent the impact of trauma by proposing strategies to move "from trauma to transformation" holds the promise of bringing about change for individuals. Additionally, change within academia is needed to address inequities, power imbalances, structural racism, and policies and practices that harm women of color academics.

A Model for Change

The Trauma-to-Transformation (TT) model, shown in Figure 15.1, targets the individual and draws attention to strategies that potentially can reduce harm to individuals in the short term and produce long-term institutional and cultural change within academia. Institutional change is usually slow and uneven, but until systemic change occurs women of color must be able to function within academia at a reduced cost. Although the TT approach focuses on the individual, it is not based on the assumption that the individual woman of color who experiences RBT bears the blame for the consequences of this

Figure 15.1.   Trauma-to-Transformation Model

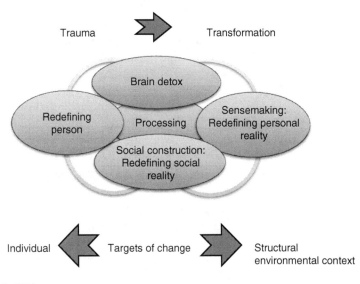

© Davis, 2014

trauma. The TT model views trauma as an injury or a wounding with its own consequences. The person-in-environment perspective, used as a conceptual framework, reflects the idea that human behavior is a function of both the person (individual) and the social environmental context (Bloom 2000; Germaine 1994). The emphasis on the development of trauma-adaptive strategies designed to promote transformation is an appropriate means to address the individual need for healing from the impact of trauma.

Goals of the TT model include harm prevention and reduction and healing for those who need it. Using an injury model approach provides a sound rationale for the active involvement of women of color in promoting their own healing. At the same time, it validates the need for advocacy and change in academia's structures and cultures. Our TT model is based on five core assumptions about the plight of women of color in academia:

1. Women of color academics routinely experience stress, wounding, and trauma (Aguirre, Hernandez, and Martinez 1994) that cause harm (Harrison 2012).

2. Trauma is a stressor that triggers a stress response characterized by physiological responses producing fight-or-flight impulses that can vary in definition from person to person (Baum 1990; Carter and Reynolds 2011; McNeilly et al. 1996). The subjective experience of a woman of color in response to ongoing trauma can vary. The individual perspective must be considered.

3. The cumulative effects of RBT include sustained harm to the individual (Carter 2007). The prospect of experiencing RBT on a regular basis with limited or no ability to prevent, reduce, or eliminate it is the source of increased harm to women of color.

4. Women of color academics need to engage actively in trauma-transforming strategies to mediate the physical, psychological, and social impact of trauma and promote self-healing.

5. Trauma transformation will occur only as change at the individual level and the institutional/organizational level occurs. Self-care for the woman of color and advocacy to promote institutional awareness and change are vital components of the transformative process.

These assumptions provide the foundation for the TT model.

The TT model views trauma as being transformed through four primary processes that involve reducing an individual's harm while promoting systemic and structural change. These transformative processes are (a) redefining the person; (b) brain detoxification; (c) sensemaking: redefining personal reality; and (d) social construction: redefining social reality. None of the processes operates exclusively or without intentionality on the part of the individual.

Redefining the Person

Redefinition involves changing how an individual views trauma and promotes environmental or cultural change to achieve transformation. Redefining one's self requires a sense of personhood. Cooley (1902) suggests that self-perception is dependent upon the perceived thoughts of others that emerge through social interaction. Thus, women of color academics whose workplace experiences are characterized by RBT will likely define themselves in relation to this kind of treatment. The idea of *internalized oppression* also provides insight into the process of defining personhood relevant to women of color in academia. When women are discriminated against, denigrated, exploited, victimized through microaggressions (e.g., daily insults), and challenged in terms of their competence, their internal view of themselves can shift. The internalized oppression results from RBT and becomes like an autoimmune disorder in which a person's body turns on itself. In the case of RBT, fears, self-doubt, embarrassment, discrimination, insults, and negative self-image become weapons for self-injury (Reiser and Mason 1990).

To move from trauma to transformation an individual has to choose *not* to be defined by RBT. Women of color academics might ask themselves, "Is my perception of who I am defined by facts or by what others have said about me?" Challenging others' perceptions and stereotypes is a first step in redefining personhood. In addition, these steps can be taken:

- Learn to recognize and confront patterns of internalized oppression by challenging the truth of perceived negative messages. Celebrate your accomplishments and strengths and take bold action to counteract negative messages.
- Connect with supportive people and those who provide affirming interpersonal exchanges. Interactions must be strength enhancing. Without support, negative messages have an exaggerated, unbalanced impact on one's sense of self.

Brain Detoxification

The second process in the TT model is brain detoxification that focuses on physiological changes occurring from trauma. When someone experiences trauma, the brain changes physiologically. First, trauma imprints the brain, storing memories of trauma. The experience of trauma can change the neural circuitry of the brain, causing it to rewire around certain brain patterns (Kolb, Gibb, and Robinson 1995; Leaf 2009). This process reflects the plasticity of the brain and its ability to change in response to trauma, thus imprinting the trauma. Second, because of brain plasticity, the brain can reorganize and create new neural connections and compensate for injury through rewiring. Third, the brain impacted by trauma can cause a disconnect between thinking and emotions, resulting in a person having extreme emotions without the ability to explain them, or the ability to explain events but with no ability to capture the emotions. The feelings of dread and anxiety experienced by Alyssa in the opening vignette, without an awareness of where these feelings came from, is an example of this pattern. For trauma to be transformed, the effects of trauma must be reversed. Leaf (2009) suggests that negative thinking is toxic to the brain and contributes to an individual's feeling powerless, hopeless, intimidated, ineffective, incompetent, weak, depressed, and/or burned out. Such thinking may result from RBT. Thinking healthy, positive thoughts releases brain chemicals that can link to negative memories and begin a transformative process. This process changes the structure of that memory, allowing a new, healthy memory to take the place of the toxic one (Leaf 2009).

The term *thought life* refers to the mental processes that continually occur and reflect how others' thinking impacts us, physically and emotionally. Leaf (2009, 46) describes the detoxification of the thought life as being accomplished through a process of "purging toxic or negative thoughts" and replacing them with a more positive thought life. A positive thought life is associated with thinking that engenders emotional stability, self-efficacy, and reduction of the physiological processes associated with the stress.

One strategy to assess the presence of toxic thoughts is to write down feelings about oneself, one's status as a woman of color in academia, one's goals, and one's prospect for the future. This list may be quite negative, especially if one has endured traumatizing experiences or internalized oppression. Negative thoughts and beliefs that are expressed on paper are moved from the brain's memories and experiences. To discharge these thoughts, positive counterthoughts should be listed on another sheet of paper (Leaf 2009). Here is an example of a negative thought (toxic) versus a positive counterthought (challenge statement):

> Toxic: "My credentials and competence are always challenged by students and colleagues; suggesting I am not good at this job."
> Challenge Statement: "Although my credentials and competence are challenged, I am confident that I have the knowledge, skills, experience, and ability to demonstrate high-level performance on this job."

After completing this exercise, the list of negative (toxic) thoughts should be discarded. This technique can be employed whenever negative thoughts return.

Sensemaking: Redefining Personal Reality

The third process in the TT model is sensemaking, which involves redefining personal reality. How do people such as Holocaust survivors, who have experienced severe trauma, manage to live a quality life despite a horrific past? Sensemaking provides one idea about how this occurs. Sensemaking is a constant process of acquiring experiences, reflecting on those experiences, and actively engaging in the integration of those experiences into one's life (Dervin and Foreman-Wernet 2003; Klein, Moon, and Hoffman 2006). This process allows one to reframe life experiences and change perceptions about situations. That is, sensemaking allows alternative ways of explaining situations that may reduce the experience of trauma, tension, or cognitive dissonance. For instance, consider this hypothetical scenario:

> Diedra cannot understand what she has ever done to her colleague Sybil to make her angry, but this colleague is always speaking badly to others about her. Sybil even encourages students to go to the department chair and complain about Diedra. Diedra is extremely depressed and agitated by Sybil's constant harassment. Diedra, as a person of faith, talks to her spiritual leader, who

explains that some people act like Sybil because they are insecure, jealous, and envious. This alternative explanation allows Diedra to feel sorry for Sybil. As a result, she is not as bothered by Sybil's actions and begins to pray for her.

By reframing Sybil's motives and behavior, Diedra reduces her personal upset and feels more comfortable in setting boundaries with Sybil and confronting Sybil's inappropriate behavior. Redefining such experiences can help transform trauma because trauma, as a stressor, can be dependent on how the individual views the situation.

Social Construction: Redefining Social Reality

The fourth process in the TT model is social construction that involves redefining the social reality. Social construction theory is based on the idea that reality is socially constructed (Berger and Luckmann 1967). In this case, trauma, as a stressor, occurs in a social context that is defined by the individual who experiences it. Narratives from academic women of color describing their lived experiences reveal a social reality characterized by RBT. The TT model is similar in focus to Bloom's injury model (2000, 2010), with an emphasis on healing first and foremost. The power of trauma to create a perception of threat, pain, and stress responses that can translate into physical symptoms and illnesses over time is formidable (Harrell, Hall, and Taliaferro 2003; Kersh 2012; Lepore et al. 1997). Redefining the social reality is a process that can reduce trauma and improve the individual's psychological, emotional, physical, and social status. Trauma is an injury that requires the injured to take an active role in promoting healing and ensuring proper treatment so that further injuries do not occur. Enhanced functioning allows for active engagement to promote change and prevent reinjury. These changes to promote healing involve being willing to use the processes identified in the TT model to engage in self-care that supports individual women's empowerment.

Overall, because both individual and structural environmental changes are necessary to deal with RBT, trauma-informed organizational changes must occur. In other words, organizations must recognize the systemic and organizational dynamics that harm women of color in academia. RBT must be recognized, understood, and eliminated. Policies and organizational processes should be created to promote climate change to reduce and eliminate RBT. Furthermore, supportive services should be available to ensure that academia produces "no harm" to women of color. The TT model is designed first to help individual women begin to transform personal trauma. Women of color must engage in self-care so that, at the end of the day, they will not become casualties of academia. As they experience healing, they will be empowered to promote organizational change, with a clear mandate to "do no further harm."

References

Aguirre, Jr., Adalberto, Anthony Hernandez, and Ruben Martinez. 1994. "Perceptions of the Workplace: Focus on Minority Women Faculty." *Initiatives* 56:41–50.

Anderson Norman B., Maya McNeilly, and Hector Myers. 1995. "A Biopsychosocial Model of Race Differences in Vascular Reactivity." In *Cardiovascular Reactivity to Psychological Stress and Disease,* edited by J. Blascovitch and E. S. Katkins, 83–108. Washington, DC: American Psychological Association.

Baum, Andrew. 1990. "Stress, Intrusive Imagery, and Chronic Distress." *Health Psychology* 6:653–675.

Berger, Peter L., and Thomas Luckmann. 1967. *The Social Construction of Reality: A Treatise in the Sociology of Knowledge.* New York: Penguin Books.

Bloom, Sandra L. 2000. "Creating Sanctuary: Healing From Systematic Abuses of Power." *Therapeutic Communities: The International Journal for Therapeutic and Supportive Organizations* 21(2):67–91.

———. 2010. "Sanctuary: An Operating System for Living Organizations." In *Managing Trauma in the Workplace: Supporting Workers and the Organisation,* edited by N. Tehrani, 235–251. London: Routledge.

Brondolo, Elizabeth, Erica Love, Melissa Pencille, and Antoinette Schoenthaler. 2011. "Racism and Hypertension: A Review of the Empirical Evidence and Implications for Clinical Practice." *American Journal of Hypertension* 24(5):518–529.

Carter, Robert T. 2007. "Racism and Psychological and Emotional Injury: Recognizing and Assessing Race-Based Traumatic Stress." *The Counseling Psychologist* 35(1):13–105.

Carter, Robert T., and John S. Forsyth. 2010. "Reactions to Racial Discrimination: Emotional Stress and Help-Seeking Behaviors." *Psychological Trauma: Theory, Research, Practice, and Policy* 2(3):183–191.

Carter, Robert T., and Amy Reynolds L. 2011. "Race-Related Stress, Racial Identity Statuses, and Emotional Reactions of Black Americans." *Cultural Diversity and Ethnic Minority Psychology* 17(2):156–162.

The Chronicle of Higher Education. 2012. *Almanac of Higher Education. Race and Ethnicity of College Administrators: Faculty and Staff in the Fall 2009.* http://chronicle.com/article/Race-and-Ethnicity-of-Faculty-Staff/128574/.

Clark, Rodney, Norman B. Anderson, Vernessa R. Clark, and David R. Williams. 1999. "Racism as a Stressor for African Americans: A Biopsychosocial Model." *American Psychology* 54(10):805–816.

Cooley, Charles. 1902. *Human Nature and the Social Order.* New York: Scribner's Sons.

Dervin, Brenda, and Lois Foreman-Wernet. 2003. "Sense-Making's Journey From Meta-theory to Methodology to Methods: An Example Using Information Seeking and Use as Research Focus." In *Sense-Making Methodology Reader,* edited by Brenda Dervin, 131–146. Cresskill, NJ: Hampton Press.

Fang, Carolyn Y., and Hector F. Myers. 2001. "The Effects of Racial Stressors and Hostility on Cardiovascular Reactivity in African American and Caucasian Men." *Health Psychology* 20:64–70.

Forsyth, John, and Robert T. Carter. 2012. "The Influence of Racial Identity Status Attitudes and Racism-Related Coping on Mental Health Among Black Americans." *Cultural Diversity and Ethnic Minority Psychology* 18(2):128–140.

Germaine, Carol. 1994. "Human Behavior and the Social Environment." In *The Foundations of Social Work Knowledge*, edited by R. Reamer, 88–121. New York: Columbia University Press.

Guerrero, Laura K., and Micheal L. Hecht. 2008. "Perspectives on Defining and Understanding Nonverbal Communication." In *The Nonverbal Communication Reader: Classic and Contemporary Readings*. 3rd ed., 6–32. Long Grove, IL: Waveland Press.

Guyll Max, Karen A. Matthews, and Joyce T. Bromberger. 2001. "Discrimination and Unfair Treatment: Relationship to Cardiovascular Reactivity Among African American and European American Women." *Health Psychology* 20:315–325.

Harrell, Jules P., Sadiki Hall, and James Taliaferro. 2003. "Physiological Responses to Racism and Discrimination: An Assessment of the Evidence." *American Journal of Public Health* 93:243–248.

Harrison, Faye. 2012. *Racism in the Academy: Toward a Multi-methodological Agenda for Anthropological Engagement*. Gainesville: University of Florida, Commission on Race and Racism in Anthropology and the American Anthropology Association.

Kersh, Renique. 2012. "In Her Own Words: Black Female Administrators: Is Stress Killing Us?" *Women in Higher Education* 20(9):8–9.

Klein, Gary, Brian Moon, and Robert Hoffman. 2006. "Making Sense of Sensemaking 1: Alternative Perspectives." *Intelligent Systems* 21(4):70–73.

Kolb, Brian, Robbin Gibb, and Terry Robinson. 1995. *Brain Plasticity and Behavior.* http://www.psychologicalscience.org/journals/cd/12_1/kolb.cfm.

Leaf, Caroline. 2009. *Who Switched Off My Brain? Controlling Toxic Thoughts and Emotions*. Nashville, TN: Thomas Nelson.

Lepore, Stephen J., Heather J. Miles, and Jodi. S. Levy. 1997. "Relation of Chronic and Episodic Stressors to Psychological Distress, Reactivity and Health Problems." *International Journal of Behavioral Medicine* 4:39–59.

Miller, Glenn. 2009. "The Trauma of Insidious Racism." *American Academy of Psychiatry Law* 37(1):41–44.

McNeilly, Maya, Norman B. Dominguez, Cheryl A. Anderson, Rodney C. Armstead, Corbett Marcella, Robinson L. Elwood, Carl F. Pieper, and Eva M. Lepisto. 1996. "Perceived Racism Scale: A Multidimensional Assessment of the Experience of White Racism Among African Americans." *Ethnicity and Disease* 6:154–166.

Myers, Lena W. 1999. "In Her Own Words: Realities of Academe for African American Women." *Women in Higher Education*. www.wihe.com/printArticle.jsp?id=18118.

National Institute of General Medical Sciences. 2012. *Trauma Fact Sheet.* http://www.nigms.nih.gov/Education/Factsheet_Trauma.htm.

Pieterse, Alex L., and Robert T. Carter. 2010. "The Role of Racial Identity in Perceived Racism and Psychological Stress Among Black American Adults: Exploring Traditional and Alternative Approaches." *Journal of Applied Social Psychology* 40(5):1028–1063.

Pieterse, Alex L., Nathan Todd, Helen A. Neville, and Robert T. Carter. 2012. "Perceived Racism and Mental Health Among Black Americans: A Meta-Analytic Review." *Journal of Counseling Psychology* 59(1):1–9.

Reiser, Richard, and Micheline Mason, eds. 1990. *Disability Equality in the Classrooms: A Human Rights Issue*. London: ILEA.

Richman, Laura S., Gary G. Bennett, Jolynn Pek, Ilene Siegler, and Redford B. Williams, Jr. 2007. "Discrimination, Dispositions, and Cardiovascular Responses to Stress." *Health Psychology* 26:675–683.

Simmons, Allen N., and Scott C. Matthews. 2012. "Neural Circuitry of PTSD With or Without Mild Traumatic Brain Injury: A Meta-Analysis." *Neuropharmacology* 62(2):598–606.

Stanley, Christine A., ed. 2006. *Faculty of Color: Teachings in Predominantly White Colleges and Universities*. Bolton, MA: Anker.

Sue, Derald Wing. 2010. *Microaggressions in Everyday Life: Race, Gender, and Sexual Orientation*. Hoboken, NJ: John Wiley & Sons.

Sue, Derald Wing, Christina M. Capodilupo, and Aisha M. Holder. 2008. "Racial Micro-Aggressions in the Life Experience of Black Americans." *Professional Psychology Research and Practice* 39(3):329–336.

Tuitt, Frank, Michele Hanna, Lisa M. Martinez, María del Carmen Salazar, and Rachel Griffin. 2009. "Teaching in the Line of Fire: Faculty of Color in the Academy." *NEA Higher Education Journal* Fall:65–74.

Tull, Eugene, S., Shea Yah-Tyng, Cleve Butler, and Cornelious Karimiah. 2005. "Relationships Between Perceived Stress, Coping Behavior and Cortisol Secretion in Women With High and Low Levels of Internalized Racism." *Journal of the National Medical Association* 97(2):206–212.

U.S. Department of Education, National Center for Education Statistics. 2011. *Digest of Education Statistics. 2010* (NCES 2011-015), Table 256. http://nces.edu.gov/pubsearch.

Vakalahi, Halaevalu F. O., Molly Davis, and Renay Scales. 2012. "Combating the Experience of Trauma in Academia Among Women of Color: A Call to Action." In Proceedings of the Hawaii International Conference on Social Sciences, Honolulu.

Vakalahi, Halaevalu F. O., Saundra H. Starks, and Carmen O. Hendricks. 2007. *Women of Color as Social Work Educators: Strengths and Survival*. Alexandria, VA: Council on Social Work Education Press.

Vakalahi, Halaevalu F. O., and Saundra H. Starks. 2010. "Complexities of Becoming Visible: Reflecting on the Stories of Women of Color as Social Work Educators." *AFFILIA* 25(2):110–122.

Vargas, Lucila, ed. 2002. *Women Faculty of Color in the White Classroom: Narratives on the Pedagogical Implications of Teacher Diversity*. New York: Peter Lang.

CASE STUDY

PROFESSOR SMITH: EARLY-CAREER MOBBING AND STUDENT HOSTILITIES

I am a 35-year-old assistant professor on my first tenure-track job at a small state university in the south—SSU. Before joining SSU, I gained two years of teaching experience in graduate school and one year in a short-term position at a liberal arts university. I've consistently earned excellent teaching evaluations and won a teaching award. I've always felt respected and welcomed. I've never doubted my ability to make a contribution to my department, university, and students. But, things are going badly.

I was assigned an official mentor, Professor Brown, who was the chair of my (new) department. Before moving, I contacted her to see about shipping my work-related materials to the office. I'd done this at my last job; it was convenient and physically easier than trying to move boxes myself. She told me there was nowhere to house the materials because I didn't have an office yet. I asked if it would be possible to store my boxes in someone's office since folks might be away for the summer. My chair said that such an arrangement wasn't really "appropriate." She sounded irritated with me for asking and I got a sick feeling in my stomach.

On one of my first campus visits before the semester's start, the office manager told me that my syllabi were too long to copy. I mentioned that they included all the assignment directions for the term. Thus, I probably wouldn't need additional copying all semester. But, I was told "no," so I cut out the assignments—saving them for later—and printed shortened syllabi.

Although I was finishing my dissertation, I became active on campus. I coadvised a student club, served as a faculty representative for Student Government, and was a coadvisor for a service organization. I created a departmental newsletter at the request of my chair (though it was never published). Although my students weren't as well prepared as others I'd had, I liked many of them. My informal and formal teaching evaluations remained good. Between teaching, service, and finishing my dissertation I worked a lot, often 65 hours a week. I felt good about how things were going, but things quickly took a turn.

In October of my first term, I received an announcement about a state-wide teaching development program that would occur in the summer. Each university in the state would select a faculty member to participate. Due to our departmental system where memos aren't copied but are routed from person to person via faculty mailboxes, I received the notice the night before applications were due. I was interested, so I stayed into the night to complete it. I left the application for my chair to review and sign and I sent her an e-mail that I'd be happy to discuss it with her when I was out of classes the next day. Since there was still a little time to apply, I left a note for the office manager asking if she could copy and distribute the memo to faculty who hadn't received it yet. (Faculty didn't have copy codes or I would have done it myself.)

The next day, my chair called me into her office to say that I had not behaved collegially by leaving the memo for the office manager to distribute. She told me that I should have *personally* gone to each faculty member to notify them of the impending deadline. I explained that I was trying to be efficient since I had only gotten the memo the previous evening. I'm not one to pass the buck, but my morning classes would have prevented me from contacting anyone until midday—thereby giving colleagues just hours to apply. Plus, I didn't really know everyone yet. Nevertheless, my chair said I should apologize to my colleagues for my behavior. I was shocked and confused. When I was ultimately chosen as one of SSU's semifinalists, the taste was bittersweet. And, I couldn't shake the feeling that something was wrong in my department.

More things began to strengthen my suspicions. My chair often reminded me of "areas for improvement" such [as] my poor handwriting on copy requests. (Granted, it is pretty bad.) I was told I didn't communicate well with the office manager although I'd never had serious communication problems in the nonprofit and corporate worlds where I'd worked previously. I began typing my copy requests and I took the office manager to lunch, asked her for feedback, and promised to "do better." But, things just didn't flow the way they normally did. I sought advice from a well-trusted academic who told me to "kill them with kindness." I tried, but it remained "chilly." I was fortunate to establish a group of friends across campus but I didn't understand the dynamics of our department. I finished my dissertation and hoped that might help (although there was never an indication that my lack of a PhD was a problem).

The following spring, during annual evaluations, my chair told me that I ranked in the bottom 1/3 when compared to my colleagues. I was told my teaching wasn't up to par and that I needed to "readjust" to SSU's ways of doing things. I was surprised since my teaching evaluations seemed good, and were comparable to my prior two teaching jobs (in the 4 range on a 5-point scale). My chair said that in light of others' excellence, I would need to improve. I feel called to teach, am reflective about my teaching, and want to be a *great* teacher. So, I was ok with trying to improve. But, the tone of the experience left me feeling belittled and disconnected.

In the fall of my second year, things went from bad to worse. One of my colleagues told me that my chair was committing "character assassination" against me across campus. He wouldn't give details but said he disagreed with what he'd heard. Students in my gender class later told me that some (men) students on campus occasionally put a swastika on my classroom door before I'd arrive—a code for "Feminazi," they thought. Increasingly, I began to dread going to work. I started playing "Accentuate the Positive" repeatedly on my commute, but it didn't help.

Then, the bomb hit. My chair said my contract was not going to be renewed because I "didn't fit in." As had been her manner, my chair told me all of this bad news in a "sweet" tone (which I read as patronizing and passive-aggressive). She also said that I had no legal grounds to fight this decision. Once I recovered from my shock, I sought feedback from others on campus, including a trusted department chair. She said that she couldn't share the details, but she "would do the same [not renew my contract] if what was being said about me was true." How could I respond to the situation when I didn't know what was being said and what was driving this situation?

Trusted colleagues suggested that I get my files from the vice president. I was unhinged at the information there—accusations I'd never been told about and almost all of it false. My chair said that I "hated male students" but also "flirted with them." She accused me of stealing office supplies and of being "disingenuous" about things such as my membership in an honor society or my participation in history club. I don't hate my men students nor do I flirt with them. I haven't stolen any office supplies. I *am* a member of that honor society and have membership papers to prove it. Likewise, I organized the club's food drive, participated in other events, and have notes and photos from meetings that show me there! To top it off, I found out from a source in the teaching center that my teaching evaluations actually ranked well, in comparison to university-wide scores.

I formally refuted the claims against me and asked that they be put in my official file. I met with my dean and the vice president for academic affairs about the situation. But, it all seemed very mechanical. Nobody really answered my questions and the evidence I offered in my defense did not seem to count. I don't understand that at all! Fortunately, I had wonderful colleagues (mostly from other departments) that supported me through this ordeal.

Ironically, in my last semester at SSU, I earned one of the campus awards for teaching excellence. This honor was inscribed on a plaque, hanging for all to see. Still, I received official notice of my contract's nonrenewal. I couldn't believe this was happening.

What Can We Learn From This Case Study?

As we consider ways to create a more equitable academy, Professor Smith's case highlights the price that individuals and institutions may pay when bullying, mobbing, and other hostile behaviors go unchecked. Like Professor Liu in the case study to Part Three,[1] Professor Smith appears to be in an unwinnable situation. She is an untenured professor in a "right-to-work" state. Thus, she has few legal protections. Further, legal battles are costly in terms of time, money, and emotional energy. What can she and women academics in similar situations do?

Before taking any action, enlist help from trusted colleagues. Identify and prioritize the short- and long-term goals that might be attainable given the culture and structure of your institution.

Actions Involving Individual Resources

- Document everything.[2] One of our heroes, Ms. Mentor, notes, "Virtually all tenure policies say that a candidate needs excellence in all three areas (research, teaching, service), although the wording varies. . . . But what often matters most is 'collegiality'—a mine field for women" (Toth 1997, 161).[3] She recommends using a tenure diary, and so do we. This effort extends beyond keeping detailed records of your teaching, service, and research to include e-mails or memos about your responsibilities, any professional agreements or promises that have been made to you, and notes from meetings with colleagues/administrators/students including who says what. Save evidence of praise and criticism regarding your performance (e.g., teaching evaluations, thank-you notes for committee work, e-mails) as well. After meetings (e.g., with your chair or dean), send an e-mail thanking those in attendance for their time. Reiterate what was said in your meeting and ask for confirmation that you are "on the same page."

o This process may sound tedious or exhausting, but rest assured, once you get a system in place, it will become second nature. Documentation allows you to preserve the details of your labor over a long period of time. If/when you go up for tenure or promotion, it will save you hours' worth of effort attempting to remember your accomplishments. Routine record keeping will allow you to compile a stronger dossier while reducing the stress of the tenure/promotion process. Documentation also provides necessary evidence to pursue formal action, if needed, including legal remedies; offers confirmation of your work to others should you need to look for a job; and affirms your worth when the going gets tough.

o Immediately document any harassment, inappropriate behavior, or situation that gets your attention and keep this information in a separate file. Record (a) the date, time, and location of the incident; (b) the parties involved (and witnesses, if applicable); (c) what happened/what was said; (d) how you felt (e.g., fearful, frustrated); (e) how you responded; and (f) to whom the incident was reported (if applicable) and how they responded (see, e.g., the University of Waterloo's "Documenting a Complaint of a Harassment" at https://uwaterloo.ca/conflict-management-human-rights/documenting-complaint-harassment). In addition to overt hostilities or inappropriateness, notice subtleties such as hostile body language or tone directed toward you. Such documentation may help identify patterns or provide a context for understanding the situation. More important, your documentation serves as evidence in formal university or police/legal actions.

• Recognize that this situation probably has less to do with you than with the culture and climate of the department and university. Even with this awareness, people in hostile work situations can experience negative effects such as depression and decreased self-esteem.[4] Professional therapy can provide a confidential forum to speak candidly and process your experience. Counselors also can suggest effective coping strategies and help with decision making.

- Expand your options. Networking, publishing, developing skills (e.g., teaching), and pursuing professional opportunities (e.g., serving as a journal reviewer, presenting at conferences) will serve you well no matter the outcome of your present situation. Should you decide to leave (or should you be forced out), time spent on these endeavors may expand your options. Consider applying confidentially for other jobs, post docs, Fulbright scholarships, research positions, and other opportunities. Although many faculty love students and have a passion for teaching, new faculty, in particular, should avoid spending too much time developing institution-specific capital (e.g., service such as committee work or advising students).

- Ask a senior colleague (or two) whom you admire, trust, and "click with" if he or she will mentor you. This can be particularly important if your university does not offer a mentoring program or if your official mentor is not meeting your needs. When considering a mentor, take into account specific goals you want to pursue (e.g., publishing an article) and whether someone outside of your department might serve you best. Meet regularly to discuss your progress, identify possible problems, and strategize ways to overcome them. Seek professional advice about workplace problems as they emerge, if that feels right for you. Your mentor may be aware of past situations that may be relevant and he or she may be able to identify resources on your campus that can help.

- Seek advice from an attorney who specializes in employment law to understand legal options. A lawsuit can be difficult to win and may only drain one's time, money, and energy. The online resources at the end of the book provide information on how to find an attorney in your area.

  - Should you go to court, your documentation of workplace hostilities can become legally admissible. If an attorney recommends that you keep such a record, that information may be protected under attorney-client privilege, which may have advantages (see www .workplacefairness.org/sexual-harassment-practical-tips).

- Engage in (or start) opportunities to meet faculty outside your department based on an academic or personal interest (e.g., a new faculty dinner/lunch club, faculty reading group). One goal of such groups is to share experiences and have fun. Additionally, these groups can help you place your experiences in a larger context and, if needed, may be mechanisms of professional support (e.g., providing letters of recommendation).

- Gather anonymous feedback from students early in the semester to inform potential adjustments to your course/teaching. Additionally, such feedback can demonstrate (a) responsiveness to students' concerns to administrators and colleagues and (b) evidence of teaching experience for potential employers.

  o Online survey managers such as SurveyMonkey.com, Zoomerang .com, and Google Forms offer free, basic versions of their software for data collection. Consider mirroring your institution's official evaluation forms but ask other questions that may be helpful (e.g., list two to three things students like and dislike about the class).

  o Review key themes with students to show that you take their feedback seriously. Point out differing experiences and explain that you aim to meet different learning styles. Briefly describe how your pedagogy is informed by course learning goals and research on teaching-learning. If possible, implement suggestions and tell them when and how you do so. For more ideas about how to make the most of student feedback see www.brown.edu/about/administration/ sheridan-center/teaching-learning/feedback-teaching/mid-semester -feedback.

Actions Involving Institutional Resources

- Exercise the legal right to copy your personnel file. Make copies of everything when permissible, and take detailed notes (e.g., date, author, contents) of every document you cannot copy. Then, formally respond to everything that you disagree with and ask the appropriate person (e.g., faculty ombudsperson, vice president for academic affairs) to place your statement in your official file. You may wish to add positive information that isn't already in the file (see "Checking Your Personnel File" at www.nolo.com/legal-encyclopedia/personnel-file-rights-33589.html). This action is primarily defensive and protective. However, should you choose legal action, possessing a list of all relevant documents may be helpful should any be lost or misplaced.
- Check relevant policies and procedures in the faculty handbook.

  o Has the appropriate process been followed?

  o When was the last time policies were updated, and by whom? For example, if faculty can be dismissed for poor institutional "fit," how is that being evaluated? Should/do faculty get written warnings about "fit"?

- ○ What is the grievance process? What assurances protect against retaliation? Consider formalizing processes whereby people are bound by institutional policy to report, for example, observed hostilities. One goal of such a system is to prevent individuals across campus from addressing such matters in a piecemeal fashion and helping prevent subsequent victimization.
- ○ Work to develop new policies, as needed, in conversation with faculty broadly.

- Discuss the situation with the head of the relevant department(s) and make an official complaint. Outline your chair's behavior and support your claims with the evidence you have documented (see "Actions Involving Individual Resources"). Because the human resources office and those in the chain of command primarily serve your employer, report incidents to those intended as faculty support (e.g., affirmative action office, ombuds office) as well. One goal in doing so is to establish a pattern of behavior that may get the attention and action of others, potentially protecting future faculty.
- Consider requesting an exit interview with key leaders (e.g., president, vice president for academic affairs, provost) if you are leaving (wait until you have a signed contract with your future employer). Because senior administrators may be unaware of the details of your situation and how institutional processes failed, you may wish to write a short, professional statement that offers constructive criticism (and praise, when due) instead of speaking from the heart. Include the formal rebuttal from your personnel file and copy the key institutional players (e.g., board of trustees, president). For more tips on how best to exit a hostile workplace, see *The Chronicle of Higher Education*'s forums such as "talking about resignation" at http://chronicle.com/forums/index.php?topic=85524.0.

Actions Involving Extrainstitutional Resources

- Use available research to explore ways your campus can best address issues of hostility. The chapters in Parts Four and Five of this volume provide a good starting point. Twale and De Luca's (2008) *Faculty Incivility: The Rise of the Academic Bully Culture and What to Do About It* identifies the importance of institutional mechanisms to prevent hostile workplace environments and suggestions for institutional mechanisms to prevent them.

- Notify the American Association of University Professors' Committee on the Employment and Status of Women (www.aaup.org; AAUP) about your experiences (after getting tenure or securing another job). Ask the committee to pay attention to your former university.
- Remember that institutions receiving federal monies are subject to federal laws about discrimination. See the online resources at the end of the book for information about who is covered and how to file an EEOC complaint.

Consult the online resources at the end of the book and the case studies to the other parts of the book for additional information that might be helpful.

Notes

1. Because there is overlap between cases and potentially useful tools and advice, we recommend reading all cases to glean the most appropriate options. Some resources and advice from Part Three (i.e., Professor Liu's case study) would be applicable here.
2. Because your employer may classify offices and their contents (e.g., computers) as university property and because offices can be breached, keep documentation only at home and on personal computers. A backup electronic copy is advisable. Note that many employers can legally read messages sent or received through work-related e-mail accounts. Some systems automatically record messages that can be used in legal proceedings. See, for example, "Email Monitoring: Can Your Employer Read Your Messages?" at www.nolo.com/legal-encyclopedia/email-monitoring-can-employer-read-30088.html.
3. See Toth, Emily. 1997. *Ms. Mentor's Impeccable Advice for Women in Academia.* Philadelphia: University of Pennsylvania Press.
4. See Lewis, Jacqueline, Diane Coursol, and Kay Herting Wahl. 2002. "Addressing Issues of Workplace Harassment: Counseling the Targets." *Journal of Employment Counseling* 39(3):109–116.

PART FIVE

TOOLS FOR CHANGING THE ACADEMY

Any one intervention is an act of resistance, not intended by itself to transform the gender relations of the organization; instead, it is through a series of interventions, each designed to subvert traditional gender arrangements, that the possibility of organizational transformation exists.

—Ely and Meyerson (2000, 133)

The research throughout this book documents challenging gender equity issues in U.S. higher education. Part Five builds on contributors' recommendations in prior chapters and focuses on the possibilities for progress. First, we provide a theoretical foundation for understanding institutional change and review broad and positive changes that have occurred in the academy regarding gender equality. Second, we discuss the importance of systemic transformation within the academy. That is, we return to the theme of the academy as a gendered organization (e.g., Acker 1990; Bird 2011; Martin 1994) and explore what it means to change the "logic" of these patterns.

In chapter 16, "Multiple Perspectives for Creating Change in the Academy," Allan argues that to address gender inequity in higher education we must consider various feminist perspectives. Otherwise, we risk overlooking potential solutions. In the final chapter, "With So Many Problems, Where Do We Begin? Building a Toolbox for Change," Ferber focuses on multicultural equity as a goal. She provides step-by-step methods to identify and overcome the structural, cultural, and interpersonal areas needing change at your college or university. Part Five ends with several case studies that exemplify recent, successful efforts for institutional transformation on several U.S. campuses.

Women's increased access to and representation in higher education is noteworthy. Since 1982, women have earned more than half of two-year, four-year, and master's degrees (Glazer-Raymo 1999). Laws ensuring equal opportunity employment, affirmative action, and localized diversity policies have contributed to women's presence at all institutional levels, including leadership. For example, national initiatives, such as the National Science Foundation's ADVANCE Institutional Transformation grants (awarded to 37 distinct universities between 2001 and 2009), identified strategies to promote the representation and advancement of women in science, technology, engineering, and mathematics fields (primarily). These strategies operated at the level of institutional structures (e.g., programs/training to overcome organizational barriers toward promotion, equity and diversity accountability structures, improved work-family policies), cultures (e.g., formal mentoring programs, work-life support programs, leadership training, network building, culture/climate audits), and climates (e.g., training on implicit bias, eliminating penalties for those who use work-family leave) (see Bilimoria and Liang 2011 for a review of ADVANCE initiatives).[1]

However, as documented throughout this book, such gains do not mean that the enduring forms of inequalities and inequities have ended. To create systemic transformation—not just piecemeal solutions—organizational change must be intentional; possess broad constituent support; and incorporate proactive, systemic interventions (Bird 2011). Inequalities must be dismantled on multiple levels: (a) *structurally*, through *policies and procedures* that privilege certain groups (often in unseen ways); (b) *institutionally*, through *institutional cultures* that shape *social interactions* between constituents; and (c) *individually*, through organizational members' *individual identities*. Thus, "change" cannot be completed in one fell swoop; progress will be uneven. For institutional transformation toward gender equity to be a responsive, emergent, creative, and ongoing organizational goal, change agents must embrace the notion that the process is "both means and ends," with "no identifiable end point" (Ely and Meyerson 2000, 113). This perspective will help organizations, and the individuals within them, to maintain vigilance against relapsing into existing patterns.

Why Multilevel Action Is Needed

We draw from Bird's (2011) theory that academia's incongruous structures, cultures, and practices create uncertainty for faculty navigating formal and informal institutional expectations. Implementing policies alone will do "little to remedy already existing incongruous, gendered bureaucratic structures"

(Bird 2011, 211) because structural constraints *and* cultural biases impede academic women's progress. Yet, throughout this book we advocate for policy-based changes because of the improvements we have witnessed from affirmative action (see this book's introduction) or responsive work-family policies (see chapter 6). However, "implementing policies that accommodate existing systems does not fundamentally challenge the sources of power, or the social interactions that reinforce and maintain the status quo" (Ely and Meyerson 2000, 112).

Another reason why strategic interventions must occur at multiple organizational levels is that this ensures deeply embedded assumptions of the academy as a gender-neutral bureaucratic organization are addressed. If, as Acker (1990) suggests, organizations possess gendered ideologies, policies and procedures, cultures, interactions, and identities, then the academy is a gendered organization (e.g., Bird 2011; Martin 1994) and change strategies must attend to these areas. Britton (2000) cautions us against assuming that bureaucratic organizations are *inherently* gendered, and doomed to perpetuate gender inequality. Although some scholars advocate eschewing bureaucratic organizations on this premise, she argues that doing so might obscure leverage points that "could improve current organizational environments to foster a less bureaucratic and thus less oppressively gendered future" (423). In short, a starting point to expose the inequitable but seemingly neutral practices, policies, interactions, and identities operating in the academy are change efforts that "address the subtle means by which systemic barriers are constructed and maintained" (Bird 2011, 211). The suggestions by Allan and Ferber in this part of the book provide a toolbox for this kind of change.

Although a complete discussion of degendering is beyond this book's scope (e.g., Deutsch 2007; Lorber 2005; Risman 2004), uncoupling gender from policies and procedures is essential to creating a more equitable academy. For example, resources "for women" (e.g., childcare at conferences) need to be reframed as legitimate resources that (any)one might need to complete his or her work, akin to the need for a cab to the airport to get to that conference[2] (see chapter 10). Change agents should address seemingly neutral but problematically gendered institutional discourses as well (Allan 2010; Ely and Meyerson 2000). For example, by implementing "family leave" policies as opposed to "maternal leave," organizations acknowledge that work-family issues are not just "women's concerns." Throughout the book, we present *institutional-level* approaches to a more equitable academy because institutional conditions shape organizational cultures and individuals' experiences in them. As such, institutional reform can improve the lives of *all* constituents.

In the case studies of each part of the book, we provide advice for individuals. Yet, *individual strategies* do not mean going it alone. Rather, individual strategies can consist of "subtle, non-threatening collective action" (Monroe, Ozyurt, Wrigley, and Alexander 2008, 223). As our case study data and the contributors' chapters illustrate, some women academics experiencing harassment, bias, or other workplace challenges are reticent to seek redress via institutional methods (e.g., ombudspersons, university counsel, formal reporting). Faculty seldom use these mechanisms, in part, because organizational cultures foster the behaviors such policies admonish (Twale and De Luca 2008). The benefits to pursuing formal remedies are unclear and can involve high costs (e.g., retaliation). Thus, marginalized faculty may rely on "incremental collective action" to navigate interpersonal situations in politically savvy ways without necessarily causing "trouble" (Monroe et al. 2008, 223). Most campuses have committed faculty, students, and administrators who challenge the status quo and reject individualistic explanations for the inequities explored throughout this book.

For progress to occur, we must apply critical feminist and race perspectives to the academy's structures, cultures, and climates because intersectional inequalities occur at all of these levels. As Chesler, Lewis, and Crowfoot (2005) suggest, institutional racism (and sexism) manifests in eight organizational dimensions that are interdependent: university/college missions; cultures; power hierarchies; the academy's membership patterns; social relations and social climate; technology; resources; and boundary management strategies. The interlocking dimensions and their contradictions (or incongruities, as per Bird 2011) can reinforce one another to perpetuate inequities and inequalities. However, they also can work at cross-purposes to provide leverage for change, effectively dismantling "historic patterns, challenging racism and sexism, and promote multicultural options" (Chesler et al. 2005, 68). For example, if a university mission espouses diversity, change agents can leverage this to demand diversification of institutional membership (e.g., students, faculty, staff, curriculum). Awareness of how inequalities and inequities operate in these key areas is critical to understanding where change is needed. Ferber's chapter suggests conducting climate/culture audits or environmental scans to clarify where problems exist.

We hope this book provides you with a sense of the breadth and depth of the gender inequities and inequalities facing women academics in the United States today. Moreover, we hope that it gives you the necessary tools and inspiration to begin disrupting the culture of silence on your campus. To dismantle such enduring patterns, practices, and policies will require the very best from us:

Courage and imagination are needed to understand [current trends in higher education] and their impacts, to counter some and facilitate others. Challenging racism [and other forms of oppression] in every aspect of our national and international life, but especially in our systems of education, is a key element for the future of a democratic, just and sustainable society. (Chesler et al. 2005, xii)

This is difficult work, but it has the potential for dramatic and positive social change, even beyond the ivory tower. We hope you will join us!

Notes

1. See also www.nsf.gov/pubs/2009/nsf0941/nsf0941.pdf.
2. This example is from Monroe et al. 2008.

References

Acker, Joan. 1990. "Hierarchies, Jobs, Bodies: A Theory of Gendered Organizations." *Gender and Society* 4(2):139–158.

Allan, Elizabeth J. 2010. "Feminist Poststructuralism Meets Policy Analysis: An Overview." In *Reconstructing Policy in Higher Education: Feminist Poststructuralist Perspectives* Edited by Elizabeth Allan, Susan Iverson, Rebecca Ropers-Huilman, 11–32. New York: Routledge.

Bilimoria, Diana, and Xiangfen Liang. 2011. *Gender Equity in Science and Engineering: Advancing Change in Higher Education.* New York: Routledge.

Bird, Sharon R. 2011. "Unsettling Universities' Incongruous, Gendered Bureaucratic Structures: A Case-Study Approach." *Gender, Work & Organization* 18(2): 202–230.

Britton, Dana M. 2000. "The Epistemology of the Gendered Organization." *Gender & Society* 14(3):418–434.

Chesler, Mark, Amanda Lewis, and James Crowfoot. 2005. *Challenging Racism in Higher Education: Promoting Justice.* Lanham, MD: Rowman & Littlefield.

Deutsch, Francine M. 2007. "Undoing Gender." *Gender & Society* 21(1):106–127.

Ely, Robin J., and Debra E. Meyerson. 2000. "Theories of Gender in Organizations: A New Approach to Organizational Analysis and Change." *Research in Organizational Behavior* 22:103–151.

Glazer-Raymo, Judith. 1999. *Shattering the Myths: Women in Academe.* Baltimore, MD: Johns Hopkins University Press.

Lorber, Judith. 2005. *Breaking the Bowls: Degendering and Feminist Change.* New York: Norton.

Martin, Joanne. 1994. "The Organization of Exclusion: Institutionalization of Sex Inequality, Gendered Faculty Jobs and Gendered Knowledge in Organizational Theory and Research." *Organization* 1(2):401–431.

Monroe, Kristen, Saba Ozyurt, Ted Wrigley, and Amy Alexander. 2008. "Gender Equality in Academia: Bad News From the Trenches, and Some Possible Solutions." *Perspectives on Politics* 6(2):215–233.

Risman, Barbara J. 2004. "Gender as a Social Structure: Theory Wrestling With Activism." *Gender & Society* 18(4):429–450.

Twale, Darla J., and Barbara M. De Luca. 2008. *Faculty Incivility: The Rise of the Academic Bully Culture and What to Do About It.* San Francisco: Jossey-Bass.

16

MULTIPLE PERSPECTIVES FOR CREATING CHANGE IN THE ACADEMY

Elizabeth J. Allan

Increased access and representation of women in U.S. higher education are indicators of progress along the path toward equity (Allan 2011; Touchton, Musil, and Campbell 2008). Yet, persistent problems remain. Women studying and working in postsecondary institutions continue to face glass ceilings and sticky floors (Iverson 2011; Reskin and Padavic 2006) and experience pay disparities. In addition, the threat and reality of sexual harassment, violence, bullying, and incivility continue to impede academic women's full participation in campus workplaces. Further, there is evidence of regression in some areas such as attempts to erode protections offered by affirmative action and antibias legislation (Gerdes 2011; Glazer-Raymo 2008a, 2008b).

Attaining and sustaining equity is vital to democratic society, yet despite decades of concerted efforts, change has been slow. What strategies are best for securing advances and increasing the pace with which we can close remaining equity gaps? Although this question is not new, we can expand the potential solutions.

This chapter presents a synopsis of research and analyses that are more fully elaborated in my report, *Women's Status in Higher Education: Equity Matters* (Allan 2011).

Approaches to equity emerge from particular perspectives about the sources of inequity. Considering the intractability of some equity problems, we must step back and examine embedded assumptions. If we overlook some perspectives in the process of identifying and *understanding* the problem(s), we may overlook strategies for *solving* the problem(s).

Even well-intentioned approaches to gender equity are framed through dominant discourses that are rarely questioned. These discourses can limit how problems are understood by failing to examine assumptions embedded in the problem frame (Allan 2008; Allan, Iverson, and Ropers-Huilman 2010; Bacchi 1999; de Castell and Bryson 1997). For example, when childcare is framed primarily as a "women's issue," it ignores that this challenge is shared by parents irrespective of gender. Likewise, if issues of sexual harassment and sexual violence are framed as "safety issues for women," strategies may focus on helping women to feel safer (e.g., through assertiveness training, better campus lighting, campus escort services). These initiatives have merit but fail to address the *sources* of harassment and violence (Allan 2003, 2011). If these equity problems were framed in terms of men's violence against women or the normalization of violent masculinity, strategies to address it would likely be different.

Given limited material and human resources, we must maximize each opportunity to advance change and promote equity. In this chapter, I suggest we will be better equipped to *solve* inequity-related problems by expanding our tools of analysis. As the previous examples illustrate, dominant lenses can eclipse other potential ways of analyzing and resolving inequity; we must identify and deconstruct the lenses. To expand the analytic toolbox, it can be helpful to review the predominant change strategies and frames for analyzing equity problems.

Since the 1970s women's movement, scholarship by and about women has grown. Scholars from a range of fields have produced knowledge about women's contributions to society, the health and development of girls and women, and the status of women in particular social arenas including higher education. The literature on women in higher education emerged from feminist scholarship across disciplines and addressed access to higher education, women students' experiences and campus climate, the advancement of women employed in higher education, research and knowledge production, curricular issues, policy, leadership, and the organization of higher education (Aisenberg and Harrington 1988; Chamberlain 1988; Rossi and Calderwood 1973).

In sum, existing research about women and gender equity in higher education is considerable. Nevertheless, persistent gender-related challenges for women in higher education demonstrate the need for continued analysis. Although the depth and sophistication of the research has evolved, it is ripe for further exploration to tease out, with more precision, complex dynamics that shape and enhance gender equity in higher education.

Analyzing Current Approaches to Promoting Equity

Multiple lenses of feminist theory have evolved in response to the central question: How do we eliminate sex/gender inequity? More recently, this question has broadened to acknowledge and incorporate fluidity of identity formations and identity-based oppression such as racism and homophobia.[1] As such, feminist theories provide valuable lenses for anyone committed to understanding equity issues. However, though exceptions exist, scholarly articles or committee reports related to gender equity seldom articulate the feminist frame(s) in which their perspectives are grounded. In fact, even research on gender equity that calls for change in the academy may shun any acknowledgment of feminist guidance as a result of general misunderstandings and hostility toward feminism and feminists. Sadly, such misunderstandings and stereotypes divide those who, in reality, share beliefs in basic feminist principles of equity and justice for all.

Within feminist theories, different approaches reflect divergent views about the sources of inequity and inequality. For example, if gender inequality in higher education is viewed from liberal feminist frameworks, the proposed remedies will differ from remedies conceived through other feminist frameworks (e.g., socialist feminist frameworks would likely see the root problem anchored in the nexus of capitalism and patriarchy; i.e., the oppression of women cannot be reduced to patriarchy alone). Similarly, while liberal and radical feminist thought value women and strive to enhance women's status, liberal feminists' focus on justice, equality, and fairness reflects the view that institutions are flawed but can be fixed through improved institutional mechanisms (e.g., improved and enforced policies). In contrast, radical feminists assert such strategies will fall short without addressing the patriarchal nature of institutions. Their central focus is on dismantling patriarchal attitudes, structures, and practices that undergird inequitable policies and practices.

Diverse feminist theoretical frames offer useful approaches to conceptualizing power, understanding complexities of inequity, and advancing strategies for change. Drawing on wide-ranging theories can broaden and deepen analyses of persistent equity problems. Thus, the likelihood of finding more effective solutions is enhanced. Further, while women, as a group, have faced shared challenges in academia, race, social class, and other aspects of identity intersect with gender and contribute to shaping one's professional status in profound ways. While women faculty share challenges unique to their role within academic organizational structures and cultures, inequities for women staff, students, and administrators in higher education exist as well.

Research on campus climate underscores complexities inherent in assessing equity (see chapter 17). It is insufficient to gauge equity progress by numbers alone (see the introduction to this book). Although women's representation is an important indicator, equity is more complex and nuanced than proportions convey. Because climate reflects the larger sociopolitical context including underlying values and norms of the broader culture, and because colleges and universities reflect society, we see common climate-related themes for women in higher education regardless of their status as students, professional staff, or senior leaders. Scholars contend that the manner in which colleges and universities are organized, the way they conduct business, and what they consider legitimate knowledge tend to privilege masculine approaches that disadvantage women and men who are committed to more collaborative and generative approaches to leadership, group process, and decision making (Asher 2010; Bensimon and Marshall 2000; Gerdes 2011). Research, including that presented in this volume, suggests that numerous factors contribute to inequitable climates, cultures, and structures of academia. However, we need more research to better understand promising approaches to transforming aspects of higher education that disadvantage women while identifying factors that help women to thrive alongside men counterparts.

Strategies to promote gender equity and elevate women's status in higher education include themes of activism, organizing, and women's networking; policy-focused strategies; mentoring; augmenting of institutional infrastructures; leadership development; altering of organizational norms and practices; and curriculum transformation including women's studies, feminist epistemology, and women-focused research centers. These predominant change strategies suggest their continued reliance on liberal feminist perspectives (Allan 2011). For example, enhanced recruitment of women, increasing availability of team sports, implementation and enforcement of antidiscrimination policies, "grooming mentoring," professional development to widen the pool of qualified job applicants, and predominant remedies for salary disparities reflect liberal feminist conceptualizations of power as a resource to be more evenly distributed between men and women in higher education.

Radical feminist influences on higher education change strategies are evident but reflect different conceptualizations of power and change including, but not limited to, developing and sustaining women's spaces, producing knowledge by and about women, valuing women's experiences through women's student centers and women's colleges, and supporting women's or feminist research and writing groups. Collective decision making and generative approaches to leadership that foreground the importance of networks, community, and empowerment are care-focused approaches informed by psychological feminist perspectives.

Strategies that acknowledge identity differences among women reflect the growing influence of multicultural, global, and postcolonial feminisms. These strategies may be similar to a range of feminist frames but acknowledge how racism and practices of colonization have shaped women's lives. For instance, Stromquist (2006) employs postcolonial and global feminist lenses. Similarly, she examines the discursive shaping of ideas about higher education conveyed in policy documents put forth by the World Bank and the Inter-American Development Bank (Stromquist 2010). Rosser (1999), who has contributed significantly to scholarship about women in science, technology, engineering, and mathematics fields, describes how postcolonial feminism and international experiences in Kenya, Saskatchewan, and Sweden provided insights for understanding biases in the production of scientific knowledge. She writes,

> The conscious de-development of southern continents under colonization by countries in northern continents in the 19th and early 20th centuries created a historical backdrop in which centuries of indigenous knowledge of the environment, health, natural resources, and appropriate technologies were erased, creating an atmosphere that allows most Western scientists to fail to challenge the notion that they have everything to give and nothing to learn from developing countries (1999, 3).

More recently, Asher (2010) draws on postcolonial feminist perspectives to examine the concept of academic leadership within higher education. She describes the "contradiction of a closed openness" in which the leadership work of women, especially women of color, is marginalized in the masculine culture of academia, even in seemingly inclusive, diverse places. She reflects on how postcolonial scholars must interrogate their own potential complicity with colonizing discourses, saying, "I also need to ask myself about the challenges and possibilities of generating scholarship that draws on the knowledge base of both East and West, both the global South and North" (Asher 2010, 72).

Examples that illustrate applications of this framework have developed from multicultural, global, and postcolonial feminist perspectives. Examples that illustrate this framework include Women of Color Summits, the Creating Global Citizens Initiative, and the At Home in the World Initiative (American Council on Education 2014) to honor contributions made by women of color and to explore and enhance internationalization at historically Black colleges and universities (HBCUs); and the University of Wisconsin's Women's Studies Consortium's named recipients for its 2010 Outstanding Women of Color in Education Awards.

Feminist socialist, poststructural, and ecofeminist perspectives for advancing women's status are less evident in the literature and in change strategies. These frames often are reflected in efforts to create space and support for new and different ways of knowing (and being) and nurturing of alternative programs and institutions that align with values and conceptualizations of power characterizing these frames (e.g., writing and research groups that draw from these perspectives and create space for dialogue and strategy development; sustainable and earth-centered approaches to conceptualizing work spaces and influencing policy development to support such practices; job sharing; and cooperative childcare arrangements). In the sense that institutions of higher education employ feminist scholars who are producing scholarship from these perspectives, academia can be understood as a vehicle for feminist scholars to challenge ways of knowing that reinforce patriarchal, racist, colonial, and other systems that can impede the attainment of equity for women.

Overreliance on liberal feminist approaches (arguably the most mainstream) may eclipse the availability and potential utility of strategies emerging from other perspectives. In light of stagnation in a number of areas, and some signs of regression related to women's status in higher education (Glazer-Raymo 2008a), the importance of alternative approaches cannot be underestimated. Perhaps the pace of change toward parity could be accelerated if we drew from more perspectives to diagnose factors that contribute to inequity and, then, to develop solutions to remedy them.

In addition to the potential benefits of applying multiple frames, there are costs for not doing so. For instance, failure to draw upon multiple perspectives for strategy development may unintentionally reinscribe *in*equity (Allan 2008; Bensimon 1995; de Castell and Bryson 1997). That is, without a multicultural lens, problems related to the status of women in higher education are likely to be conceptualized in ways that foreground perspectives of white/Western women without accounting for how race and ethnicity (among other statuses) shape experiences of women's inequity. Similarly, without an expanded lens, heterosexism and challenges for lesbian academics may not be recognized. Without an ecofeminist perspective, gender equity strategies may fail to fully dislodge ways of thinking that normalize domination of the earth and other beings; without a feminist poststructural perspective, well-intended policymaking efforts may reinscribe inequity by drawing upon dominant discourses that tend to result in the framing of gender equity as a problem of women's deficiency (e.g., lack of sufficient mentoring, lack of professional credentials, lack of confidence), rather than a problem of institutional structures and practices that privilege particular perspectives and identities.

Recommendations for Practice

Achieving equity, not simply by the numbers, is a complex undertaking. No quick fixes exist, but we can accelerate the pace of change and prevent backsliding of advances toward equity if we proceed with an expanded, rigorous analysis. This can be exceedingly difficult for many of us who simply want to "do something" to prevent injustices we see resulting from inequitable structures and practices. Enhancing problem analysis means we need to consider root causes of inequity and hidden assumptions embedded in how we think about power and change. As analytic lenses, feminist theories provide tools for understanding, assessing, and designing change strategies. Becoming more familiar with diverse feminist perspectives opens new ways of thinking with potential to catalyze more innovative and effective strategies for change.

Additionally, a strategic approach to campus equity and social change is vital and implies a well-designed and comprehensive effort that begins with a deliberate analysis of the problem and its manifestation. Deep and sustainable change must occur at multiple levels—including the intrapersonal level (e.g., individual attitudes or knowledge), the interpersonal level (e.g., communication patterns between two or more individuals), the group or department level (e.g., peer review guidelines), the entire campus (e.g., salary equity or sexual harassment policies), and the larger community (e.g., public policy). This strategic, comprehensive approach aligns with feminist values because it involves a collaborative and coalition-based approach such that multiple sectors of campus are represented and involved with analyzing the problems and formulating strategies for change.

Praxis, the integration of theory and practice, is a core principle of feminist and other change-oriented scholarship (Bracken, Allen, and Dean 2006; Lather 1991). Familiarity with a range of feminist theories can broaden perspectives on power and root causes of gender inequity. In so doing, these lenses can serve scholars and practitioners by enhancing understandings of complexities and nuances shaping women's lives and their status in higher education. Additionally, the diversity of perspectives can expand the repertoire of change strategies available to inform research and *action* based on that research. In the spirit of praxis, I offer the following recommendations:

- Promote and support opportunities to learn about diverse feminist theories for understanding women's experiences generally and in higher education. Although feminist theories are not the only way to consider enhancing women's status, they represent a rich, interdisciplinary body of scholarship related to the goal of building more egalitarian and socially just communities.

- Analyze gender equity problems and solutions through multiple feminist frames. Knowledge does not always translate to action. Putting feminist frames to use is a vital next step. Readers are urged to think broadly and within one's sphere of influence to examine particular gender equity challenges through multiple lenses. Practically, this involves developing deliberate strategies to theorize about root causes of the problem and to make inherent power dynamics explicit. For example, before pursuing strategies that appear to be "good" (e.g., professional development, mentoring), it is important to analyze how these approaches may not be transformative if they simply teach women how to adapt to perspectives and practices that privilege masculine-centered workplaces and norms.
- Invest in building campuswide coalitions that support a comprehensive approach to achieving and sustaining gender equity. For example, in faculty initiatives, ensure multiple disciplinary perspectives are represented alongside representatives from student, staff, and administrative ranks.
- Enact a collaborative approach that incorporates multiple stakeholders and perspectives (e.g., full-time faculty of all ranks, adjunct faculty, administrators, and students).
- Develop and implement change strategies (within and outside postsecondary institutions) that reflect diverse feminist perspectives. This chapter documents gains, persistent problems, and continuing complexities related to enhancing women's status in higher education. No single approach exists. However, some perspectives are more prominent than others in shaping understandings of and responses to identified problems. It may be argued that the resulting strategies have been useful, but they are insufficient. Moreover, they may eclipse the availability of other effective approaches. Thus, although we may choose to support and implement proven feminist approaches, we should work to implement strategies that reflect diverse perspectives.

Further research and activism is imperative to maintain gains made for and by women in higher education and to increase the pace of change needed to ensure all participants in higher education are afforded equitable treatment, opportunities, and climates in which to thrive and achieve their full potential. Understanding and applying multiple feminist lenses can extend what we know and open new thinking about old, seemingly intractable problems. For scholars and practitioners committed to advancing more inclusive and socially just educational environments, fostering a collaborative and strategic approach that draws on feminist theories to understand root causes and manifestations of inequity holds promise for transformative change.

Note

1. For a comprehensive review of feminist theories see "Framing Women's Status Through Multiple Lenses" in *Women's Status in Higher Education: Equity Matters* (Allan 2011).

References

Aisenberg, Nadya, and Mona Harrington. 1988. *Women of Academe: Outsiders in the Sacred Grove.* Amherst: University of Massachusetts Press.

Allan, Elizabeth J. 2003. "Constructing Women's Status: Policy Discourses of University Women's Commission Reports." *Harvard Educational Review* 73(1): 44–72.

———. 2008. *Policy Discourses, Gender, and Education: Constructing Women's Status.* New York: Routledge.

———. 2011. *Women's Status in Higher Education: Equity Matters* (ASHE Higher Education Report, vol. 37, no. 1). Hoboken, NJ: Wiley Periodicals.

Allan, Elizabeth J., Susan V. Iverson, and Rebecca Ropers-Huilman, eds. 2010. *Reconstructing Policy in Higher Education: Feminist Poststructural Perspectives.* New York: Routledge.

American Council on Education. (2014.) *Inclusive Excellence Group.* http://www.acenet.edu/leadership/Pages/Inclusive-Excellence-Group.aspx.

Asher, Nina. 2010. "How Does the Postcolonial, Feminist Academic Lead? A Perspective From the U.S. South." *International Journal of Leadership in Education* 13(1):63–76.

Bacchi, Carol Lee. 1999. *Women, Policy, and Politics: The Construction of Policy Problems.* Thousand Oaks, CA: Sage.

Bensimon, Estela, M. 1995. "Total Quality Management in the Academy: A Rebellious Reading." *Harvard Educational Review* 65(4):593–612.

Bensimon, Estela, M., and Catherine Marshall. 2000. "Policy Analysis for Postsecondary Education: Feminist and Critical Perspectives." In *Women in Higher Education: A Feminist Perspective*, 2nd ed., edited by Judy Glazer-Raymo, Barbara K. Townsend and Rebecca Ropers-Huilman, 133–147. Boston: Pearson Custom Publishing.

Bracken, Susan J., Jeanie Allen, and Diane R. Dean, eds. 2006. *The Balancing Act: Gendered Perspectives in Faculty Roles and Work Lives.* Sterling, VA: Stylus.

Chamberlain, Mariam K. 1988. *Women in Academe: Progress and Prospects.* New York: Russell Sage Foundation.

de Castell, Suzanne, and Mary Bryson. 1997. "En/gendering Equity: Paradoxical Consequences of Institutionalized Equity Policies." In *Radical In(ter)ventions:*

Identity Politics, and Difference/s in Educational Praxis, edited by Mary Bryson and Suzanne de Castell, 85–103. Albany: State University of New York Press.

Gerdes, Eugenia, P. 2011. "Trials and Triumphs of Women Leaders in Higher Education." In *Women as Leaders in Education: Succeeding Despite Inequity, Discrimination, and Other Challenges,* vol. 1, edited by Jennifer L. Martin, 1–22. Santa Barbara, CA: Praeger.

Glazer-Raymo, Judy. 2008a. "The Feminist Agenda: A Work in Progress." In *Unfinished Agendas: New and Continuing Gender Challenges in Higher Education,* edited by Judy Glazer-Raymo, 1–34. Baltimore: Johns Hopkins University Press.

———. 2008b. "Women on Governing Boards: Why Gender Matters." In *Unfinished Agendas: New and Continuing Gender Challenges in Higher Education,* edited by Judy Glazer-Raymo, 185–210. Baltimore: Johns Hopkins University Press.

Iverson, Susan V. 2011. "Glass Ceilings and Sticky Floors: Women and Advancement in Higher Education." In *Women as Leaders in Education: Succeeding Despite Inequity, Discrimination, and Other Challenges,* vol. 1, edited by Jennifer L. Martin, 79–105. Santa Barbara, CA: Praeger.

Lather, Patti. 1991. *Getting Smart: Feminist Research With/in the Postmodern.* New York: Routledge.

Reskin, Barbara F., and Irene Padavic. 2006. "Sex, Race, and Ethnic Inequality in United States Workplaces." In *Handbook of the Sociology of Gender,* edited by Janet Saltzman Chafetz, 343–374. New York: Kluwer Academic/Plenum.

Rosser, Susan V. 1999. "International Experiences Lead to Using Postcolonial Feminism to Transform Life Sciences Curriculum." *Women's Studies International Forum* 22(1):3–15.

Rossi, Alice S., and Ann Calderwood. 1973. *Academic Women on the Move.* New York: Russell Sage Foundation.

Stromquist, Nelly P. 2006. "Women's Rights to Adult Education as a Means to Citizenship." *International Journal of Educational Development* 26(2):140–152.

———. 2010. "Knowledge Capital and Excellence: Implications of a Science-Centered University for Gender Equity." In *Reconstructing Policy in Higher Education: Feminist Poststructural Perspectives,* edited by Elizabeth J. Allan, Susan V. Iverson, and Rebecca Ropers-Huilman, 215–234. New York: Routledge.

Touchton, Judy, Caryn McTighe Musil, and Kathryn Peltier Campbell. 2008. *A Measure of Equity: Women's Progress in Higher Education.* Washington, DC: Association of American Colleges and Universities.

17

WITH SO MANY PROBLEMS, WHERE DO WE BEGIN?

Building a Toolbox for Change

Abby L. Ferber

For the past two decades, the research examining the experiences and obstacles confronting women in higher education has skyrocketed. Women academics are no longer faced with a vague "chilly climate" but have ample evidence of the wide range of specific institutional, cultural, and interpersonal dynamics that contribute to what too many women experience as a hostile culture. Research documents the extent and dynamics of sexual harassment, bullying, and incivility; the problem of juggling work and family responsibilities; the ongoing salary gap; inequitable distribution of service work and mentoring; the very different expectations students often have of women faculty and of women of color faculty and how this is evidenced in teaching evaluations; insufficient family-friendly policies; and more. Additionally, we know much more about the specific challenges faced by women faculty in diverse positions, and across campus environments. Understanding how differently positioned women experience and negotiate institutional barriers is essential.

We have seen progress toward equity and equality as our understanding of issues has expanded. We are now more likely to have parental leave plans and domestic partner benefits. Numerous campuses have created gender-neutral restrooms for trans-identified campus members and lactation lounges for nursing women. Each victory is preceded by struggle. Changes rarely happen easily. It is often faculty governance structures, women's committees, and other groups of organized faculty, staff, and/or students that spend years researching issues, proposing plans and policies, and lobbying institutional leadership for change. This process can be exhausting, draining, and lead to burnout for many of those involved. Further, the time devoted to these issues takes away from research, teaching, service, family, and other commitments. Maintaining a healthy, inclusive campus climate should be the responsibility of all campus members, not just those who are most directly impacted by its problems.

More institutions are collecting detailed demographic data necessary to document and remedy a range of problems (e.g., salary inequities, problems with equitable recruitment and retention, unequal time to promotion). And, the more we grasp the depth and complexities of the problems, the more we realize simple fixes do not exist. Furthermore, the work needed at institutional, cultural, and interpersonal levels makes higher education seem impervious to change. Many equity problems are so deeply rooted and ingrained in the dominant campus culture that they are not seen as problems, especially to those in power. Thus, we need to look at academia in its entirety. We need tools that take us beyond a piecemeal approach to equity in keeping with the ideals of academia.

How do we create social justice on our own campuses? How do we strategize movement toward more inclusive cultures? Although many of us study and teach about issues of race, gender, and other inequalities, we can feel powerless when it comes to creating more equitable climates within our workplaces. Knowing what problems exist is only the first step. Creating effective change is a different issue and many of us do not have the necessary skills or training. Where do we start? My goal in this chapter is to provide readers with a toolbox for campus change that can be adapted to specific campus environments. We are not starting from scratch. The discussion that follows will introduce you to methods for identifying areas for change including environmental scans and campus climate studies to assess your campus's current conditions. I suggest six models of campus inclusion to identify where your campus is in comparison to where you want it to be. Then, I provide specific strategies and concrete steps to advance justice and equity on your campus.

How Healthy Is *Your* Campus?

The field of organization development (OD) is devoted to fostering organizational change. It draws upon theoretical insights from many disciplines, including sociology, psychology, anthropology, and history. OD incorporates diagnostic, dialogic, and intervention strategies. Marshak (2006) identified three areas of knowledge essential for OD practitioners: (a) understanding social systems, (b) understanding the hows and whys of change, and (c) understanding the role of a third-party change agent such as a private consultant. The OD literature is rich with insights to foster change.

The OD literature is based on principles of democratic change, and OD practitioners are facilitators, not consultants who propose solutions or initiate change. Under the OD umbrella are scholars who focus specifically on multicultural organization development (MCOD) intending to move organizations toward becoming inclusive and socially just.

Whereas the OD and MCOD literature addresses organizations generally, the Social Justice Training Institute (SJTI) draws on the work of MCOD research and theory regarding institutions of higher education. SJTI characterizes its model as multicultural, or intersectional; I have adapted its approach to incorporate an explicit feminist lens. I add "feminist" to be clear that racial/ethnic inclusion is not prioritized over other marginalized social identities, and to bring the intersectional focus to the forefront.

To begin, I suggest we start by identifying where we want to end up. This can be turned into a visioning activity with wide participation from constituents, or it can be predetermined by specific committees and/or campus leaders championing these efforts from the start. SJTI defines a *multicultural organization* as follows:

> [One that] values the contributions and interests of all members; members reflect diverse social and cultural groups throughout all levels of the organization; acts on a commitment to eliminate all forms of oppression within the organization, including racism, sexism, heterosexism, ageism, classism, ableism, religious oppression, etc.; includes all members as full participants in decisions that shape the organization; and follows through on broader social and environmental responsibilities. (Jackson and Hardiman 1994, cited by SJTI and adapted by Ferber, De Welde, and Stepnick 2012)

The goal of feminist MCOD is, thus, the achievement of an equitable, inclusive, and socially just environment.

MCOD scholars have developed a stage model to help you identify where your organization lies on a continuum of social justice and inclusion practice. It will help you begin planning action steps toward greater inclusion. The model consists of six stages, from organizations least accepting of difference to most accepting: (a) the exclusionary organization, (b) "the club," (c) the compliance organization, (d) the affirming organization,

(e) the Redefining organization, and (f) the multicultural organization. Based on these stages, SJTI has developed action steps to guide organizational change. Keep in mind that the MCOD model is a tool for guiding change. However, the stages are fluid; organizations may not fall neatly into one stage or another. Departments or campuses may move at different paces, some staying relatively stuck in one stage while others progress, sometimes unevenly.

Stage 1: The Exclusionary Organization

- Openly maintains dominant group's power and privilege
- Deliberately restricts membership
- Is overtly discriminatory, exclusionary, and harassing actions go unaddressed
- Is an unsafe and dangerous environment for subordinated group members

Strategic actions: The goal is to assess the current state, decrease exclusionary and discriminatory practices, and make the environment less dangerous for the physical and psychological well-being of members. To accomplish this, you will need to do the following:

- Engage in coalition building—develop relationships with other change agents across identity groups and across campus.
- Identify the interest level of top leaders regarding changes to the status quo.
- Gather data about the impact of the status quo on issues valued by campus leaders.
- Develop ways to "put a face" on the negative impact of the status quo and to make the offenses well known on campus, and possibly regionally and nationally.
- Identify internal and external demands, "levers for change" that could shift the status quo (e.g., recent bias incidents; current or potential lawsuits; decreases in enrollment and retention; priorities of state legislators, alumni, regional corporations, local/regional/national communities).
- Gather data from peer institutions, including best practices and benchmarks (see websites in the online resources at the end of the book).
- Strategize how to influence institutional leaders through existing and emerging relationships; identify those who are important to involve and assess their level of commitment to creating safe, inclusive departments and campuses.

- Identify gaps between departments and the campus in mission/ values statements, as well as policies and reporting procedures (e.g., nondiscrimination policy, hate crimes policy, sexual harassment, personnel grievances).

Stage 2: "The Club"

- Maintains privilege for those who have traditionally held power and influence
- Preserves dominant white masculine culture institutionalized in policies, procedures, and services
- Accepts a limited number of "token" women, LGBTQ faculty, and faculty of color and only *if* they have the "right" credentials, attitudes, behaviors, and so on
- Engages issues of diversity and social justice only on club members' terms and within their comfort zone

Strategic actions: The goals are to continue eliminating discrimination and harassment in the departments and on campus as well as to continue institutionalizing policies and practices to increase the safety of all members. At this point, begin assessing the current state and creating the infrastructure to implement strategies for (a) creating inclusive departments and (b) successfully recruiting, retaining, and promoting faculty and staff who demonstrate the skills and competencies to teach effectively and to provide services to an increasingly diverse student population.

- Initial assessment: Conduct a comprehensive cultural audit or campus climate survey (including the students, staff, faculty, alumni, and local community) that includes climate assessment data on recruitment, retention, promotion, tenure, performance ratings, demographics by job position and salary, grievances and hate crimes, infusion of diversity into curriculum and cocurricular activities, and other institution-specific markers of attention to diversity.
- Feedback session: Compile data and conduct feedback sessions with top leaders to diagnose the results of the cultural audit and discuss ways to address gaps.

Stage 3: The Compliance Organization

- Overtly commits to removing some of the discrimination inherent in the organization

- Provides some access to some members of previously excluded groups
- Shows no change in organizational culture, mission, or structure
- Has limited curriculum in place on gender, race, sexuality, and so on
- Has evidence of token members of marginalized groups who must be "team players"; assimilate into organizational culture; not "rock the boat," or raise issues of sexism, racism, and other forms of inequality

Strategic actions: The goals are to build and implement a data-based strategic plan for inclusivity; increase the numbers of staff, faculty, and administrators from subordinated groups; and create structures to ensure they are welcomed and embraced by the campus community.

- Develop a long-term strategic plan for inclusion, with measures of success identified and communicated widely.
- Examine and revise policies and practices to incorporate the goal of inclusion.
- Create opportunities for members of subordinated groups to meet and engage in meaningful dialogue.
- Create developmental opportunities for members of dominant groups to examine privilege, dominant culture, and explore their role in partnering to create change.

Stage 4: The Affirming Organization

- Is committed to eliminating discriminatory practices
- Actively recruits and promotes women and people of color
- Provides support and career development opportunities
- Encourages department members to be knowledgeable of inequalities
- Takes steps to transform the curriculum for increased inclusivity
- Ensures that members assimilate to the new organizational culture

Strategic actions: The goals are to continue enhancing the safety of all groups and to increase the numbers of women and faculty of color in departments/ units. At this point, increase attention to access and strategies to ensure success for all campus members. Increase skill and competencies of staff, faculty, and administrators to create curriculum, programs, services, and processes that increase engagement and the success of diverse student populations.

- Reward significant progress toward inclusion goals.
- Examine "discretionary points" in policies, practices, and unwritten rules for which bias and prejudice could result in negative differential impact and exclusion.

- Create professional development opportunities and structures that reward faculty who enhance teaching methods to meet the learning needs of all students, as well as those who integrate race and gender (and other) inequalities into their courses.
- Expand course offerings on social justice and inclusion and create requirements for students within this curriculum.
- Explicitly value publications and service work that contribute to the goals of feminism and social justice (e.g., practice-oriented publications, publications in interdisciplinary feminist journals).
- Recognize and "count" informal mentoring of other faculty and students that is disproportionately done by women and faculty of color in annual and tenure/promotion reviews.

Stage 5: The Redefining Organization

- In transition, moves beyond nondiscriminatory, nonoppressive
- Works to ensure full inclusion of women and minority faculty
- Begins to question limitations of organizational culture and structure: mission, policies, structures, operations, services, leadership, climate, practices
- Actively works toward developing a feminist, multicultural organization and curriculum
- Is committed to redesigning and implementing policies and practices to ensure full inclusion; participation; and empowerment of all members, including in leadership roles

Strategic actions: The goals are to engage the department and the entire campus community in dialogue about creating and maintaining an inclusive environment and to continually innovate, assess impact, and redesign programs, policies, and practices as needed.

- Widely communicate new norms of the inclusive organization.
- Revise performance and reward systems to be inclusive of broad methods of knowledge production and pedagogies.
- Annually analyze and revise policies, practices, and procedures to eliminate any unintended differential impact and exclusion.
- Proactively recruit women and faculty, staff, and students of color.
- Enhance community outreach efforts and partnership initiatives that can increase dialogue and responsiveness to the diverse local community and potentially support diverse recruitment and retention as well.

Stage 6: The Multicultural Organization

- Ensures that practices, policies, curriculum, leadership, faculty and staff, and other campus members represent and reflect the contributions of the wide diversity of marginalized social identity groups
- Ensures that members across all identity groups are full participants in decision making
- Actively works and values work in larger communities (e.g., campuswide, across the profession, regionally, nationally, globally) to eliminate all forms of oppression

Strategic actions: The goals are to continually reassess the current state and organizational needs of the campus community and to change, as needed, to ensure social justice on campus.

The MCOD model can be used in many ways. A specific group, such as a women's faculty committee, can use it to assess the current state of the campus or a small unit such as a department or college, then draw upon the recommended strategic actions to guide change. Another place to begin is by engaging in a dialogue about these stages with colleagues. Asking various groups of faculty, staff and/or students to identify where they see the campus can provide rich insights. This preliminary data can be used as leverage to engage campus leadership in supporting a more comprehensive and rigorous assessment of your campus's level of inclusion and social justice. This is crucial because any process that aims to create change will need the support of campus leadership.

The Cultural Proficiency Model

The cultural proficiency model (CPM) provides another framework for assessing development of individual and organizational change toward a healthy culture of equity and inclusion. Corwin Press has published a series of books, including workbooks, on the CPM that include many useful tools to facilitate individual knowledge and growth that can be added to your toolbox for institutional change. "Cultural proficiency is leading as an advocate for life-long learning with the purpose of being increasingly effective in serving the educational needs of cultural groups. Holding the vision that you and the school are instruments for creating a socially just democracy" (Terrell and Lindsey 2009, 25). Though relevant to our purposes, this model possesses limitations for higher education settings. First, it is aimed at K–12 educational settings. Second, the emphasis is on better serving a diverse student body, not other organizational constituents. Third, the notion of cultural "competence" or "proficiency" is problematic in that it seems to suggest one can achieve full understanding of all cultures and their specific needs while downplaying differences within groups and ignoring intersectionality. However, a closer reading of the CPM literature reveals a more nuanced theory and practice that addresses these concerns. Some insights in this literature are highly relevant and can be adapted for higher education settings.

The core components of the CPM include the following:

- *Guiding principles*: These provide a moral framework and set of values that emphasize eliminating the barriers posed by the dominant culture.
- *A continuum*: The continuum provides a model, much like the MCOD stages, that describes the "values, behaviors, policies, and practices existing in our schools" (Terrell and Lindsey 2009, 103). The continuum can be used as a tool to assess where a campus is in relation to desired progress toward positive social change. The stages include the following:

  1. cultural destructiveness
  2. cultural incapacity
  3. cultural blindness
  4. cultural precompetence
  5. cultural competence
  6. cultural proficiency

- *Barriers*: The model explores specific barriers including resistance to change, systems of oppression, and the dynamics of privilege and entitlement.
- *Essential elements:* These elements define a culturally proficient environment, leader, or school.

Whether one chooses to embrace the CPM or not, the texts in the CPM series provide valuable insights, activities, guidelines, and tools that faculty, administrators, and students can use toward fostering inclusive and socially just campuses and leadership. Additionally, the model emphasizes the importance of everyone involved in the process of change while simultaneously requiring work on self-transformation. A commitment to intersectional inclusion demands this of us. Frequently, social science faculty, for example, work or interact with each other in work-related silos (e.g., tasks, curricular areas, physical spaces) where they focus on one dimension of identity and inequality. They may be far less knowledgeable about the obstacles and complexities of others' experiences. Specifically, a common model on many campuses involves a structure of faculty committees such as a women's committee, a color/minority affairs committee, an LGBTQ committee, and the like. This sort of division is often mirrored in the structure of student affairs and student clubs/unions. Thus, the women's committee, for example, may have a very limited understanding of the issues facing faculty of color, and the experiences of women of color faculty may be excluded.

Diagnosis

Over the past few decades, we have witnessed a growing number of colleges and universities initiating "campus climate studies" as a means of assessing diversity and inclusion (Hart and Fellabaum 2008). Conducting a campus climate study is often the first step toward embarking upon institutional change. In some cases, these studies are initiated because of visible symptoms, such as specific incidents on a campus that signal larger problems. Other times, climate studies are conducted in the context of a campus's commitment to ensuring an inclusive and equitable environment for faculty, staff, and students. Yet, administrators and faculty often face issues with very different mind-sets. In my experience as a professor, an administrator, and a consultant, I have found that some administrators see climate studies as an admission of a problem. Thus, they refuse to support such a study, believing their campus has no significant problems regarding diversity and equity issues. This is the wrong mind-set. The decision to conduct a campus climate study should be made in the context of recognizing that we live in a society characterized by vast inequality, in which racism, sexism, heterosexism, and other systems of oppression and privilege shape everyone's lives, as illustrated throughout this volume. As the editors of this book suggest in the book's introduction, addressing structural and cultural inequalities requires a proactive, not reactive, approach. No one escapes this system. Despite our best efforts, creating a healthy campus climate in this environment requires ongoing commitment and vigilance. Just as doctors recommend an annual exam to monitor health and detect problems early, every campus that is committed to inclusion should undertake a climate study and continue to monitor issues of equity regularly. I recommend two useful diagnostic methods for campuses, departments, or other campus units: an environmental scan and a campus climate study.

The Environmental Scan

While a climate study (explained in the next section) is an essential tool, if the resources and support are not available for it, another option is an environmental scan. The following environmental scan, adapted from SJTI (2010) is diagnostic:

Reflect and note what is currently in place in each of the areas that either values or creates obstacles to the creation of an inclusive, gender-progressive, socially just department and campus. The list begins with items that are somewhat easier to identify than those near the end. This is not an exhaustive list, and not all items may be relevant. However, it provides a starting point for consideration. Individuals, groups, and other campus units should review the list and create their own based on their specific context.

1. Department and/or campus mission statement, vision statement on diversity, values and goals about inclusion
2. Administrative support for a broad campus commitment to inclusion and social justice (e.g., standing committees on inclusivity and diversity, women's faculty committee)
3. Behavioral expectations and policies regarding nondiscrimination, inclusion, and social justice
4. Demographic data for administrators, faculty, staff, and students (e.g., degree of diversity present, recruitment and retention demographics, promotion rates, time to tenure)
5. Demographic data regarding rape, assault, hate crimes, sexual harassment, and other transgressions based on minority status
6. Support systems for women, people of color, LGBTQ constituents, and differently abled populations (e.g., committees, clubs, support centers, mentoring programs)
7. Recruitment and search practices (e.g., dual hiring opportunities, diversity champions)
8. Equitable distribution of resources such as office or lab space
9. Availability of gender-neutral restrooms
10. Performance reviews that take into account inclusive behavior and values or contributions to diversity
11. Salary equity
12. Grievance policies and procedures

13. Response systems and processes for harassment and bias
14. Assessment structures to measure campus climate regularly (e.g., surveys, focus groups, exit interviews)
15. Structures to address issues of discrimination (e.g., human resources department, equal employment opportunity/affirmative action offices, ombudspersons, diversity offices)
16. Curriculum (e.g., Are there gender/women's studies and race/ethnic studies departments? To what extent are issues of race, gender, sexuality, and so on integrated across the curriculum? Does general education curriculum include diversity requirements?)
17. Faculty teaching development opportunities (e.g., curriculum transformation, teaching methods, skills to manage difficult dialogues)
18. Family-friendly policies and practices (e.g., partner benefits, part-time [tenure-track] appointments, job sharing, stopping the tenure clock, paid family leave, eldercare supports, on-campus daycare, lactation spaces)
19. Formal recognition that students' evaluations of faculty are often shaped by gender, race, and other social identity stereotypes and bias
20. Department and campuswide communication about the goals of inclusion
21. Feminist/social justice knowledge and competency among administrators, faculty, and staff
22. Professional development, training, and educational opportunities for administrators, faculty, staff, and students around issues of diversity and inclusion
23. Degree of safety on campus for students, staff, and faculty from subordinated groups
24. Scholarship on diversity issues (e.g., gender, race, sexual orientation) valued for tenure and promotion
25. Explicit and implicit norms about what it takes to succeed and to be viewed as a valued campus contributor
26. Decision-making processes throughout the university and departments or units including an emphasis on inclusiveness
27. History of efforts toward inclusion and social justice
28. [Add others that you identify]

The Campus Climate Study

Campus climate studies are often treated as internal documents. Hart and Fellabaum (2008) identify The National Academy of Sciences' Committee

on Women in Science, Engineering, and Medicine website (http://sites.
nationalacademies.org/PGA/cwsem/PGA_045079) as the only public compilation and clearinghouse of campus climate studies. In their meta-analysis
of 115 studies, they found no clear consensus on what "campus climate"
refers to, and a range of methodologies used. Further, the studies varied in
focus on one or more of the roles of students, staff, and/or faculty, and on
social identities (race, gender, and/or sexual orientation/identity). In 112 of
the studies, gender was the most common focus; 58 analyzed race/ethnicity,
and 21 analyzed sexual orientation. Other studies addressed disability (8),
religion (6), age (4), and socioeconomic status/class (3). Hart and Fellabaum
conclude:

> Because our data source is a web page designed to focus on gender issues,
> it is not surprising that we found that the climate studies included gender
> as a salient characteristic in nearly every case. However, what was surpris-
> ing is that nearly half of the studies concentrated on only one identity
> characteristic, either gender or race/ethnicity. These studies failed to take
> into account the interlocking nature of identity and how these mutually
> shaping identities may contribute to differing experiences and perceptions
> of campus climate (Hill Collins 2000). (Hart and Fellabaum 2008, 230)

Furthermore, they identified a key issue for anyone preparing to undertake
a campus climate study to consider in advance. They highlighted the question of who should conduct the research, arguing that there are advantages
and disadvantages to relying upon internal or external researchers, including
issues "of cost, bias, perceptions of researcher(s) by those participating and
those implementing recommendations based upon the study, and methodological expertise" (Hart and Fellabaum 2008, 231). Based on their analysis, they recommend a mixed-methods approach that provides quantitative
and qualitative data; an intersectional approach that includes all historically
underrepresented identity classifications; and a transparent, accessible process that communicates all findings to all campus constituents. They argue
that the research should be embraced as an ongoing process that will be
monitored and repeated regularly to increase accountability. Therefore, the
research findings should be used to guide change on campus and inform
future practices (e.g., hiring, promotion, salary increases).

Locating campus climates studies, or "multicultural audits" within the
context of "participatory-action-research," Chesler (1998, 174) argues that
simply increasing knowledge about the campus should not be the primary or
only goal. Instead, "organizational improvement and empowering organization members for change has at least an equal priority" (1998, 174). Therefore, he emphasizes turning to internal leadership, empowering those involved

in the process, and simultaneously working to increase internal capacity for ongoing assessment. He outlines recommended steps to guide this process including an effort to educate and build dialogue across the campus community regarding equity in higher education. Chesler's approach is noteworthy in that the process of conducting the climate study is not merely a tool for identifying the problems, but a key part of the change process. That is, the work leading up to the study and the process of conducting the study are designed to directly impact the campus culture and its various constituencies.

Additionally, campus climate studies vary widely in how much data they collect, and the kinds of issues and questions they examine. Hart and Fellabaum (2008, 231) suggest that campuses draw upon "frameworks, like Peterson and Spencer (1990) and Hurtado et al. (1998:231), to inform the types of data to be collected and to provide a mechanism to compare between campuses." Combining a campus climate study with the MCOD stage model may be particularly useful. The MCOD model can inform decisions regarding what kinds of data to collect and provide a tool for evaluating the data results. The campus climate results can be used to assess where the campus climate falls within the stage model, which then provides recommended next steps and strategic actions to guide the process of change.

Chesler (1998, 172) argues that the vast literature on the specific problems and experiences of diverse faculty teach us about the need for change. However, to begin any specific change agenda on a campus, it is essential to "particularize and specify the conditions of discrimination, and the hopes for diversity and multiculturalism, in each distinct organizational setting." The tools provided in this chapter and in the online resources at the end of the book can assist you with those efforts on your campus. Indeed, it is our responsibility, once we recognize the disturbing breadth and depth of inequity in higher education so well documented throughout this volume, that we begin looking at our own specific campuses, assessing where we are, and charting a course for change.

References and Recommended Resources

Battle, Conchita Y., and Chontrese M. Doswell, eds. 2004. *Building Bridges for Women of Color in Higher Education: A Practical Guide for Success*. Lanham, MD: University Press of America.

Berry, Theodorea Regina, and Nathalie D. Mizelle, eds. 2006. *From Oppression to Grace: Women of Color and Their Dilemmas in the Academy*. Sterling, VA: Stylus.

CampbellJones, Franklin, Brenda CampbellJones, and Randall B. Lindsey. 2010. *The Cultural Proficiency Journey: Moving Beyond Ethical Barriers Toward Profound School Change*. Thousand Oaks, CA: Corwin Press.

Chesler, Mark A. 1998. "Planning Multicultural Audits in Higher Education." *To Improve the Academy*, Paper 400. http://digitalcommons.unl.edu/podimprove-acad/400.

Clayton-Pederson, Alma R., Sharon Parker, Daryl G. Smith, José Moreno, and Daniel Hiroyuki Teraguchi. 2007. *Making a Real Difference With Diversity: A Guide to Institutional Change.* Washington, DC: Association of American Colleges and Universities.

Cress, Christine M. 2002. "Campus Climate." In *Women in Higher Education: An Encyclopedia,* edited by A. M. Martinez and K. A. Renn, 390–397. Santa Barbara, CA: ABC-CLIO.

Ferber, Abby L., Kristine De Welde, and Andi Stepnick. 2012. "Creating a Gender Progressive Department." Workshop presented at a conference of Sociologists for Women in Society, St. Petersburg, FL, February.

Garcia, Mildred, Cynthia Hudgins, Caryn McTighe Musil, Michael Nettles, William Sedlacek, and Daryl Smith. 2001. *Assessing Campus Diversity Initiatives: A Guide for Campus Practitioners.* Washington, DC: Association of American Colleges and Universities.

Goodman, Diane J. 2001. *Promoting Diversity and Social Justice: Educating People From Privileged Groups.* Thousand Oaks, CA: Sage.

Guerrero, Lisa, ed. 2008. *Teaching Race in the 21st Century: College Teachers Talk About Their Fears, Risks and Rewards.* New York: Palgrave McMillan.

Harper, Shaun R., ed. 2008. *Creating Inclusive Campus Environments for Cross-Cultural Learning and Student Engagement.* Washington, DC: NASPA.

Hart, Jenie, and Jennifer Fellabaum. 2008. "Analyzing Campus Climate Studies: Seeking to Define and Understand." *Journal of Diversity in Higher Education* 1(4):222–234.

Hill Collins, Patricia. 2000. *Black Feminist Thought.* New York, NY: Routledge.

Hurtado, Sylvia, Jeffrey F. Milem, Alma R. Clayton-Pederson, and Walter R. Allen. 1998. "Enhancing Campus Climates for Racial/Ethnic Diversity: Educational Policy and Practice." *The Review of Higher Education* 21:279–302.

Jackson, Bailey W. 2006. "Theory and Practice of Multicultural Organization Development." In *The NTL Handbook of Organization Development and Change,* edited by B. B. Jones and M. Brazzel, 139–154. San Francisco: Pfeiffer.

Jackson, Bailey W., and Rita Hardiman. 1994. "Multicultural Organization Development." In *The Promise of Diversity: Over 40 Voices Discuss Strategies for Eliminating Discrimination in Organizations,* edited by E. Y. Cross, J. H. Katz, F. A. Miller, and E. W. Seashore, 231–239. Arlington, VA: NTL Institute.

Jackson, Bailey W., and Evangelina Holvino. 1988. "Developing Multicultural Organizations." *Journal of Religion and Applied Behavioral Science* 9(2):14–19.

Lesage, Julia, Abby L. Ferber, Debbie Storrs, and Donna Wong. 2002. *Making a Difference: University Students of Color Speak Out.* Lanham, MD: Rowman & Littlefield.

Lindsey, Randall B., Stephanie M. Graham, R. Chris Westphal, Jr., and Cynthia L. Jew. 2008. *Culturally Proficient Inquiry: A Lens for Identifying and Examining Educational Gaps.* Thousand Oaks, CA: Corwin Press.

Mabokela, Reitumetse, and Anna L. Green, eds. 2001. *Sisters of the Academy: Emergent Black Women Scholars in Higher Education.* Sterling, VA: Stylus.

Marshak, Robert J. 2006. *The NTL Handbook of Organization Development and Change: Principles, Practices, and Perspectives.* John Wiley and Sons.

http://www.worldcat.org/wcpa/servlet/DCARead?standardNo=078797773X&st andardnoType=1&excerpt=true.

Messer-Davidow, Ellen. 2002. *Disciplining Feminism: From Social Activism to Academic Discourse*. Durham, NC: Duke University Press.

Musil, Caryn McTighe, Mildred García, Cynthia A. Hudgins, Michael T. Nettles, William E. Sedlacek, and Daryl G. Smith. 1999. *To Form a More Perfect Union*. Washington, DC: Association of American Colleges and Universities. www.aacu.org.

Musil, Caryn McTighe with Mildred García, Yolanda T. Moses, and Daryl G. Smith. 1995. *Diversity in Higher Education: A Work in Progress*. Washington, DC: Association of American Colleges and Universities.

Peterson, Marvin W., and Melinda G. Spencer. 1990. "Understanding Academic Culture and Climate." *New Directions for Institutional Research* 1990 (68):3–18.

Rodriguez, Nelson, M., and William F. Pinar, eds. 2007. *Queering Straight Teachers: Discourse and Identity in Education*. New York: Peter Lang.

The Social Justice Training Institute. 2010. "Creating Social Justice on Campus: Sharing Best Practices and Lessons Learned." Workshop presented at White Privilege Conference, La Crosse, WI.

Terrell, Raymond D., and Randall B. Lindsey. 2009. *Culturally Proficient Leadership: The Personal Journey Begins Within*. Thousand Oaks, CA: Corwin Press.

Wolf-Wendel, Lisa, and Kelly Ward. 2003. "Future Prospects for Women Faculty: Negotiating Work and Family." In *Gendered Futures in Higher Education: Critical Perspectives for Change*, edited by B. Ropers-Huilman, 111–134. Albany, NY: SUNY Press.

Woodard, Virginia Spiegel, and Johnnie M. Sims. 2000. "Programmatic Approaches to Improving Campus Climate." *NASPA Journal* 37:539–552.

Suggested Websites

Diversity Web (http://www.diversityweb.org/)

Association of American Colleges and Universities' (AAC&U) On Campus with Women (http://www.aacu.org/ocww/)

POD Network (http://www.podnetwork.org/)

Sociologists for Women in Society (SWS) (http://www.socwomen.org/web/)

American Association of University Professors (AAUP) (http://www.aaup.org/aaup)

College and University Work-Life-Family Association (CUWFA) (http://www.cuwfa.org/)

CASE STUDIES OF RESISTANCE
AND FEMINIST CHANGE

We conclude our book with four real-world case studies that illustrate successful, feminist institutional transformation. These cases reflect "small victories," while illustrating the difficulty of academic landscapes to change swiftly and significantly. These successes occurred, in part, because the change agents targeted institutional structures and cultures (i.e., the policies and procedures, interactions, identities, informal norms, and values). Further, they illustrate potential overlap between the strategies for gender equity reforms (e.g., networking, policy initiatives, changing organizational norms, and activism) (see chapter 16). Finally, the changes documented in these cases resulted in improvements to academic work settings that benefited those who work and study there. The changes include:

- Development of a women's resource center for all members of a campus community
- Creation of nursing rooms and lactation spaces accessible to any member of a campus community
- Development of family-friendly work-life policies via a faculty union
- Establishment of a permanent campuswide work-life committee charged with policy oversight, policy recommendations, and educating administrators on work-life issues

The Sociologists for Women in Society's (SWS) Committee on Academic Justice facilitated a workshop titled "Feminist Change in the Academy" (2010) that featured a panel of four SWS members who explained their experiences participating in feminist change at their institutions. We offer their experiences to illustrate which lessons that readers can apply on their campuses.

Undergraduate Student and Faculty Organizing: Lobbying for a Women's Center

Laura Logan, Hastings College

In [the] 2005–2006 academic year, after several women students at my undergraduate university (the University of Nebraska at Kearney) reported being victims of sexual assault, it became clear to a group of feminist students—who also happened to be members of the Women's Studies honor society—that services and resources for women on campus were too limited. We did not have a women's center on campus, though other feminists on campus, particularly Women's Studies (WS) faculty, had lobbied for a women's center in the past. The time seemed right for another concerted effort to get a women's center, so our group of WS students decided to conduct a petition drive to lobby for a women's center.

With strong support from WS professors, we sat in the student union and other heavily trafficked campus locations and asked students to support our efforts with their signatures. We employed a variety of strategies to obtain signatures such as reaching out to students in other departments and in organizations (including sororities) that we thought might be particularly supportive. Ultimately, we gathered hundreds of signatures. Additionally, we and others wrote letters to the local paper, the university paper, and to the university chancellor.

Ultimately, our efforts resulted in a formal meeting with the chancellor in the spring of 2006. During that meeting, we presented the petition and letters of support, which led to a thoughtful discussion. Before the meeting was finished, the chancellor agreed to support the development of a Women's Center, to be in place by the fall—which is exactly what he did.

Feminist faculty were essential to this activist effort. They explained some of the previous efforts to get a women's center on campus, which helped us strategize our actions. They steered us away from unnecessary conflict and helped us learn a bit about university politics. Finally, I think faculty's guidance prevented us from taking an ineffective approach. As one student noted, we were quite inclined to "go all Norma Rae." However, a lighter touch and the effective strategies provided by feminist leaders on our campus were more effective.

Feminists ADVANCE-IT at URI

Jessica Holden Sherwood, Johnson & Wales University

When I arrived at the University of Rhode Island in 2006, it was in the midst of a second-round NSF ADVANCE-Institutional Transformation grant. These grants are designed to improve the proportion of women faculty in STEM disciplines (see http://uri.edu/advance). Early in the project, the leadership team planned micro- and macro-level changes, presuming that targeting individuals and the institution would yield positive results. Previous experience had taught the leaders to expand their targets. For example, imagine a department where faculty respond positively when asked about gender equity (the individual level) and where work-family policies are on the books at the institutional level. One might imagine how things would be different if only one level of support were in place. The ADVANCE team embraced Barbara Risman's theory (see *Gender and Society* 2004, 429) that gender must be analyzed on the individual, institutional, and interactional levels. The ADVANCE interventions expanded to include the interactional level, with workshops on departmental climate, training on the mentor-mentee relationship, gatherings to build campus social capital, and more.

I had been serving on the URI Work-Life Committee, which was formed as part of the ADVANCE grant. But, as the NSF suggested, it remained permanent after the grant's conclusion.

Feminist victories due to this work at URI include: paid parental leave policy, guidelines for dual career assistance, and an award-winning new lactation program. Also, the Work-Life Committee educates administrators about the necessity of work-life programs. We show that improvements for women can also be improvements for men employees and for the institution overall. It's been gratifying to apply feminist theory to create real-world change.

Nursing Social Change in the Academy Through Lactation Spaces

Julia McQuillan, University of Nebraska, Lincoln

I gave birth almost nine years ago. I was committed to breastfeeding my child, but it was a challenge for me. The two months' maternity leave from my university was essential to establishing a good nursing relationship with my infant. My department was supportive; I brought my infant to my office often. Through challenges with nursing I became involved with a support group at a local nonprofit organization, Milkworks. Once my daughter and I mastered nursing, I sought to help other women by joining the Mayor's

Commission on Breastfeeding—which became the Healthy Kids 2010 Breastfeeding Coalition and, eventually, the Nebraska Breastfeeding Coalition. Milkworks also held "You Can Do It! Return to Work and Breastfeed" workshops. Through these activities I gained a reputation on campus as a breastfeeding advocate.

A few years ago an undergraduate student contacted me after she ran out of ideas to find a place to pump while going to school. She was having trouble finding places to pump, and a staff member told her that she should not be in school if she had a lactating child or that she should no longer nurse if she wanted to go to school. I was quite distraught by this and told her that I'd do what I could. I called the staff person in charge of the room and found the same negative attitude. I kept asking, "There is nothing that can be done? In the three-story building that houses your department, there is not one little space that a woman can have privacy to pump?" I got similar comments: Does she really need to breastfeed? Does she really need to be in school? I tried bringing in some authority by using my status on the Chancellor's Commission on the Status of Women. (I thought of them as my "posse" in this situation.) Still I met resistance. At this point I did not realize that my approach was a problem—I was looking for an ad hoc solution, but clearly depending upon individual goodwill was a bad idea—we needed structural change.

I tried a new approach. I looked around campus for possible lactation spaces, but continued to face resistance. In the short run, I had the undergraduate student—who had a night class and no other options—use my office at night. We had a system that allowed her in and then she locked my door. I never met her—we never crossed paths—but I was pleased she had persevered and stuck with nursing.

I brought the issue to the Chancellor's Commission on the Status of Women. The chancellor and his advisor wrote a lactation policy and designated several spots on campus as lactation/nursing spaces (e.g., in the Student Union). The Americans With Disabilities compliance officer also took on this cause. The formal "Lactation Policy" is now on the web: www.unl.edu/chancellor/policymemoranda/20090901-Lactation-Policy. And, the university provides refrigerators for storing milk, too. The university's lactation policy is much more helpful than attempting to cajole individual staff or department chairs to support lactating students. Additionally, the work to institutionally accommodate lactation—similar to any other necessary accommodation because the university was originally designed for able-bodied men—was essential to helping lactating students.

Our sociology department has been a leader for change, creating a dedicated lactation room out of a storage closet. This room is beautifully painted, has a rug, a table, lamp, plug, rocking chair, and changing table. The department obtained matching funds from the college and the chancellor to complete the renovation.

This experience demonstrates the value of institutional change over ad hoc solutions, the power of having a Chancellor's Commission on the Status of Women committee with direct access to the chancellor and the ability to challenge "business as usual," and the benefit of flexible administrators. All of this happened at the same time that the university was formalizing many work-life flexibility options and disseminating information to guide faculty. Relevant lactation information was added to the list of many other policies and programs on campus.

Feminist Change in Work-Life Policies: The Case at U-Mass Amherst

Joya Misra, University of Massachusetts Amherst

My example of feminist change in academia comes from my experience with the Massachusetts Society of Professors (MSP), the faculty union at the University of Massachusetts Amherst. In the early 2000s, the union took on the issue of work-life policies, which resulted in the university adopting policies to support work-life balance. In part, this change has occurred due to the work of the Joint Administration-MSP Work-Life Committee. This committee was bargained for by the union and meets regularly every semester. It possesses the power to bargain for work-life policies without waiting until contract bargaining (usually every three years). The committee includes feminists (and others) in the administration and on the faculty. Generally, we have the same goals in mind—to increase support for, lessen turnover of, and increase the diversity of our faculty.

Our work-life/care policies provide for many of the "usual suspects" such as health and dental insurance and life and long-term disability insurance. Also, faculty have access to a sick leave bank that allows them paid leave when they are ill. A range of bereavement leaves, unpaid leaves, tuition remissions, and other supports are available, as well as health care and dependent care spending accounts. The most recent work-life policies developed by MSP and the Joint Work-Life Committee include policies meant to support parental caregiving and care for partners, parents, or other household members:

Family Sick Leave: Paid leave for 5 days, 30 days, or one semester to care for seriously ill family or household members.
Care Postponement of Tenure Decision Year: One-year delay on tenure decision year related to the care of a seriously ill family or household member.

Paid Parental Leave: One semester paid leave during the semester of or the semester following the birth or adoption of a young child for tenure-line faculty. Full-time contract faculty employed for six years are eligible for this benefit, too.

Parental Postponement of Tenure Decision Year: One-year delay on tenure decision year related to the birth or adoption of a child under 5.

Partner Employment Program: Consideration of partner hire without a national search to recruit or retain tenure-line faculty; initial contract funded equally by the provost, initiating unit, and host unit.

Child Care Assistance: A fund dispersed to newly hired faculty to help subsidize childcare costs.

The change in the university is remarkable. Many, many faculty have young children, including pre-tenure faculty. Both departments and colleges are adjusting to the idea that we now have clear and effective policies to support caregiving for parents, partners, children, and others. Additionally, the Work-Life Committee has developed a tool kit (adapted from one developed by the University of California) to train chairs and deans in the implementation of these policies and to help address changing the *culture* as well. Cultural change is the next step—as we move from policy development to ensuring that policies are implemented well and equally to all faculty.

All in all, our Work-Life Committee has had a tremendous impact on policies at the university, and we believe it is beginning to help shift the culture around caregiving on campus. These outcomes are in keeping with feminist ideals because they offer necessary supports that benefit faculty and the university as a whole.

ONLINE RESOURCES

General Issues in Higher Education

American Association of University Professors (AAUP) (www.aaup.org)
Provides career resources, research, and recommendations on diversity, research and statistics, information on family leave, stopping the tenure clock, institutional support for childcare/eldercare, balancing work and family, and resources for contingent faculty.

- The Committee on Women in the Academic Profession DIRECT (Committee W): "formulates policy statements, provides resources, and reports on matters of interest to women faculty and the academic community" (www.aaup.org/about/committees/standing-committees#womencom).
- The *Annual Report on the Economic Status of the Profession* provides salary data (www.aaup.org/AAUP/pubsres/research).
- *Academe*, AAUP's magazine (http://www.aaup.org/reports-and-publications/academe).
- Issues in Higher Education (www.aaup.org/AAUP/issues/).
- Resources on Balancing Family & Academic Work (www.aaup.org/issues/family-work%C2%A0/resources-balancing-family-academic-work).

American College Personnel Association (ACPA) (www.acpa.nche.edu)
A national student affairs association for undergraduate and graduate students, student affairs faculty, educators, officers, organizations, and companies engaged in the campus marketplace.

- The Standing Committee for Women (www.myacpa.org/search/site/%E2%80%A2%09The%20Standing%20Committee%20for%20Women).

For the purposes of this document, generally we quote organizational descriptions verbatim from official websites. We acknowledge and thank Abby Ferber for providing us with information about many of these resources, including their descriptions.

American Council on Education (ACE) (www.acenet.edu)
A coordinating organization of all institutions of higher education in the United Staes focused on providing leadership for institutions and influencing public policy.

- The Inclusive Excellence Group (www.acenet.edu/leadership/Pages/Inclusive-Excellence-Group.aspx)
- The ACE Women's Network (www.acenet.edu/news-room/Pages/ACE-Womens-Network.aspx)

American Federation of Teachers (AFT) (www.aft.org)
Best known for efforts on behalf of pre-K to 12th-grade teachers, AFT also offers resources for higher education faculty, including contingent faculty. See its data center and statements about "tenure, shared governance, contingent labor, teacher education and technology" (www.aft.org/about/) for use in campus organizing efforts. AFT also has resolutions on the following:

- Promoting faculty diversity in higher education
- Academic freedom in the twenty-first-century college and university
- Shared governance in colleges and universities
- The truth about tenure in higher education

Association of American Colleges and Universities (AAC&U) (www.aacu.org)
Focuses on liberal education. However, it provides a variety of women-focused resources:

- AAC&U's Program on the Status and Education of Women (PSEW) offers *On Campus with Women*, an online publication about issues relevant to women academics (www.aacu-edu.org/ocww).
- Campus Women Lead (CWL) (www.aacu.org/campuswomenlead/).
- Campus Women Lead Listserv for administrators, faculty, staff, and students to share information about professional development opportunities for women in higher education (http://list.aacu.org/mailman/listinfo/aacucampuswomenlead).

International Professors Project (IPP) (www.internationalprofs.org)
"A non-profit global network of professors who have begun working as 'Academic Citizens of the World' on university campuses in developing countries around the world."

Resources Specifically for Women in the Academy

American Association of University Women (AAUW) (www.aauw.org)
Works toward the advancement of equity for women and girls through advocacy, education, and research. Provides a wealth of research conducted and position papers on topics such as family and medical leave, pay equity, and civil rights.

Association for Women in Science (AWIS) (www.awis.org)
A national advocacy organization championing "the interests of women in science, technology, engineering, and mathematics across all disciplines and employment sectors."

Center for the Education of Women at the University of Michigan (CEW) (www.cew.umich.edu)
"Dedicated to encouraging and enhancing the education and careers of adult women through programs and services, advocacy and research. . . . CEW's research and advocacy inform and encourage institutions and government to adopt policies that support work-life integration" (www.cew.umich.edu/about/ and www.cew.umich.edu/action/statenatladvo/worklife).

- See Women of Color in the Academy Project (WOCAP) at www.cew .umich.edu/leadership/wocap.

National Association for Student Personnel Administrators (NASPA) Women in Student Affairs (WISA) (www.naspa.org/constituent-groups/ kcs/women-in-student-affairs)
Intends to "give voice to the needs of women in student affairs and to provide professional development opportunities through both regional and national activities designed to address gender equity and prompt personal growth."

University of Venus (uvenus.org/about/)
"A collaborative venture bringing together the voices of GenX women in higher education from around the globe."

Women in Academia Report (http://WIAReport.com)
Weekly online newsletter featuring stories related to women's administrative positions, awards or honors, and research related to women and girls. The website includes information about recent books and statistics related to women in higher education.

Women in Higher Education (www.wihe.com)
Monthly newsletter that includes reports on recent research, lawsuits, conferences, leadership issues, and so on. Also lists jobs for women in higher education administration.

Resources on Racial/Ethnic Diversity in the Academy

Diverse: Issues in Higher Education (http://diverseeducation.com)
A publication containing news and information on a variety of issues concerning diversity in the academy.

The Hispanic Outlook in Higher Education Magazine (www.hispanicout look.com/home/)
The only "Hispanic educational magazine for the higher education community."

Mujeres Activas en Letras y Cambio Social (MALCS) (www.malcs.org)
A "national organization of Chicanas/Latinas and Native American women working in academia and in community settings with a common goal: to work toward the support, education and dissemination of Chicana/Latina and Native American women's issues."

National Center for Faculty Development and Diversity (NCFDD) (www.facultydiversity.org/)
"An independent professional development, training, and mentoring community of over 40,000 graduate students, post-docs, and faculty members." The center is "100% dedicated to supporting academics in making successful transitions throughout their careers." It offers on-campus workshops, professional development training, and intensive mentoring programs (www. facultydiversity.org/?page=About_Us).

Sisters of the Academy (SOTA) (www.sistersoftheacademy.org/membership/)
SOTA aims to "create a network of Black women in higher education to foster success in the areas of teaching, scholarly inquiry, and service to communities[;] to facilitate collaborative scholarship among Black women in higher education[; and] to facilitate the development of relationships to enhance members' professional development."

Women of Color Research Network (WoCRn) (www.wocrn.nih.gov)
Through the National Institutes of Health (NIH), this organization was created "to pursue, in a new way, the innovative capacity and enhanced inclusion of women of color in the research enterprise, both at NIH, and

throughout the scientific community" (http://sigs.nih.gov/wsa/Pages/Bulletin Board.aspx). The website highlights conferences for women of color in STEM fields and provides an online discussion forum.

Resources on Family-Work Issues

College and University Work-Life-Family Association (CUWFA) (www.cuwfa.org)
Aims to "provide leadership in facilitating the integration of work and study with family/personal life at institutions of higher learning" by offering professional support, gathering information on relevant issues, and contributing to "the understanding and development of the work-family field."

Families and Work Institute (www.familiesandwork.org)
A nonprofit research center that provides statistics and resources related to workforce and work-family policies (e.g., 2014 National Study of Employers; www.familiesandwork.org/2014-national-study-of-employers/).

MIT Work-Life Center (http://hrweb.mit.edu/worklife/welcome)
Provides numerous resources for MIT employees (e.g., policies, contacts, reports) and also serves as a model for other campuses.

Work and Family Researchers Network (WFRN) (https://workfamily.sas .upenn.edu/content/about)
Formerly the Sloan Work and Family Research Network, WFRN is an international organization of interdisciplinary work-family researchers, policy makers, and practitioners. See, in particular, "University Based Work-Family" links at https://workfamily.sas.upenn.edu/content/work-and-family-links# university.

Resources for Adjunct/Contingent Faculty

AdjunctNation.com (www.adjunctnation.com)
A clearinghouse of information for non-tenured faculty, including reading materials, job search information and tips, interviews, and discussion forums (e.g., teaching online, job hunting, using technology in the classroom).

The Adjunct Project (www.adjunctproject.com/about-the-project/)
The website includes a member-driven spreadsheet regarding adjunct pay, benefits, and other working conditions created by more than 1,500 contingent

faculty workers across the United States. Also, it includes an active blog about adjunct-related matters (http://adjunct.chronicle.com/category/blog/).

- The Contingent Academics Mailing List (http://adj-l.org/mailman/listinfo/adj-l_adj-l.org) is affiliated with The Adjunct Project.

Adjunct Voice (http://theadjunctvoice.blogspot.com)
"A virtual meeting place for part-time/adjunct university faculty members from across the U.S. to have a voice: share your ideas, experiences and concerns!"

The Chronicle of Higher Education's **Forum "The Nontenure Track"** (http://chronicle.com/forums/index.php/board,52.0.html)
A place to "talk online about your experiences as an adjunct, visiting assistant professor, or other contract faculty member." Requires subscription to access.

Coalition of Contingent Academic Labor (COCAL) (http://cocalinter national.org/)
An informal grassroots coalition of activists working for contingent faculty. Seeks to bring greater awareness to the situation of contingent faculty in higher education, organize for action, and build solidarity.

Coalition on the Academic Workforce (CAW) (www.academicworkforce. org)
A "group of higher education associations, disciplinary associations, and faculty organizations committed to addressing issues associated with deteriorating faculty working conditions and their effect on college and university students in the United States."

The Delphi Project on the Changing Faculty and Student Success (www. thechangingfaculty.org)
Offers a variety of resources to assess and improve contingent faculty working conditions within specific institutional contexts. In particular, see its tool kits for creating institutional change.

H-Adjunct (www.h-net.org/%7Eadjunct/)
An "open, inter-disciplinary forum for issues involving adjunct, part-time and temporary faculty at universities, colleges and community colleges." Sponsored by H-Net (Humanities and Social Sciences online).

Modern Language Association (MLA) (www.mla.org)
A disciplinary association for fields in languages and literature. Features a searchable database of contingent faculty statistics and interactive data collection function at www.mla.org/acad_work_search.

New Faculty Majority (NFM) (www.newfacultymajority.info/equity/)
"Dedicated to improving the quality of higher education by advancing professional equity and securing academic freedom for all adjunct and contingent faculty" in a variety of ways. The website features resources including a listing of relevant legal references about state and federal policies and news updates on legislation relevant to contingent faculty.

- NFM's blog "Precarious Faculty Rising" promotes an open exchange of ideas and information about higher education and professional issues, especially concerning adjunct and contingent faculty (see http://thenewfacultymajority.blogspot.com/2012/07/message-from-nea-contingent-faculty.html).

Resources for Legal Action[1]

Equal Employment Opportunity Commission (EEOC) (www.eeoc.gov)
Provides resources for individuals seeking to "file a lawsuit alleging discrimination on the basis of race, color, religion, sex (including pregnancy), national origin, age (40 or older), disability, genetic information, or retaliation" (www.eeoc.gov/employees/lawsuit.cfm).

- EEOC will only accept Charges of Discrimination involving protected categories of people (e.g., race, religion, sex, age, disability). See www.eeoc.gov/employees/charge.cfm.
- If you hope to file a lawsuit, be aware of strict timelines. See www.eeoc.gov/employees/timeliness.cfm.
- "Federal Laws Prohibiting Job Discrimination Questions and Answers" gives information about who can file lawsuits, deadlines, and what kinds of information you will need. See www.eeoc.gov/facts/qanda.html.
- To locate the EEOC office nearest to you, see www.eeoc.gov/field/index.cfm.
- Regarding the mediation process, see www.eeoc.gov/employees/mediation.cfm.

National Employment Lawyers Association (NELA) (www.nela.org/ NELA)
"NELA is the country's largest professional organization that is exclusively comprised of lawyers who represent individual employees in cases involving employment discrimination and other employment-related matters." Provides a "Find a Lawyer" directory at www.nela.org/NELA/index.cfm?event= showapppage&pg=members&configid=105.

U.S. Department of Justice (www.justice.gov/crt/complaint)
For employment discrimination involving a group or class of individuals, "the Attorney General has authority to bring suit against a state or local government employer where there is reason to believe that a 'pattern or practice' of discrimination exists. Generally, these are factually and legally complex cases that seek to alter an employment practice, such as recruitment, hiring, assignment and promotions, which have the purpose or effect of denying employment or promotional opportunities to a class of individuals."

Workplace Fairness (www.workplacefairness.org)
"Believes that fair treatment of workers is sound public policy and good business practice, and that free access to comprehensive, unbiased information about workers' rights—without legal jargon—is an essential ingredient in any fair workplace." The website provides information from a variety of Internet sources (e.g., the "Job Survival " section includes links to information on topics such as "Sexual Harassment—Practical Tips," "Proving Discrimination," "Blowing the Whistle," and "Getting Help From Government Agencies").

- Question/answer links are a starting point for someone seeking to identify whether his or her experience fits within the legal confines of "harassment" or "discrimination." See www.workplacefairness.org/ raceharassment and www.workplacefairness.org/discrimination.
- To access information about the closest EEOC office *and* the agency that handles workplace discrimination in your state as well as information about cross-filing paperwork and relevant deadlines, see www.workplacefairness.org/complaintdisc.
- To find a lawyer or law firm in your area that handles cases relevant to your situation, see the "Attorneys" link at www.workplacefairness. org/find-attorney. (Selecting the state you live in may produce better results than entering your zip code.)

Feminist and Women's Academic Organizations by Discipline[2]

Social Sciences

Anthropology

Association for Feminist Anthropology (AFA) (www.aaanet.org/sections/ afa/)
A section of the American Anthropological Association (AAA), AFA intends to foster feminist perspectives within anthropology, facilitating communication among feminist anthropologists and feminists working in other fields, offering information on gender issues within AAA and in society, and supporting the integration of feminist research from the subfields of the discipline.

Committee on the Status of Women in Anthropology (COSWA) (www.aaanet.org/committees/coswa/index.htm)
A committee of the American Anthropological Association that monitors gender discrimination within the field of anthropology.

Women in Archaeology Interest Group (www.saa.org/ForMembers/ InterestGroups/WomeninArchaeologyInterestGroup/tabid/158/Default .aspx)
A branch of the Society for American Archaeology (SAA) with objectives to foster the involvement of women in all activities promoted by the society, improve contacts among women archaeologists, provide a broader forum for the discussion of and action on issues of interest to COSWA (women in anthropology) and archaeologists interested in gender studies, and promote improvement in work-life issues. The Archaeological Institute of America (AIA) also has a group called Women in Archaeology Interest Group (www .archaeological.org/interestgroups/156). Its purpose is to understand and promote the position of women within AIA through various programs and publications.

Economics

Committee on the Status of Women in the Economics Profession (CSWEP) (www.cswep.org)
A committee of the American Economic Association (AEA), founded "to eliminate discrimination against women, and to redress the low representation of women, in the economics profession. . . . CSWEP is comprised of women and men in the diverse areas of the profession—academia,

government, and business. . . . Makes an annual report to the AEA on the status of women in the economics profession, and engages in other efforts to promote the advancement of women" (www.aeaweb.org/committees/cswep/mission.php).

International Association for Feminist Economics (IAFFE) (www.iaffe .org)
An "expanding group of scholars, policy professionals, students, advocates and activists interested in empowering and improving the well-being of women—and other under-represented groups around the world" (www .iaffe.org/pages/about-iaffe/).

History

Committee on Women Historians (CWH) (www.historians.org/govern-ance/cwh/index.cfm)
A standing committee of the American Historical Association, with goals "to advocate for the interests of women in the historical profession and within the American Historical Association; to advocate for women's and gender history; to foster an inclusive scholarship that challenges and transforms the practice of history, both substantively and methodologically."

Coordinating Council for Women in History (CCWH) (http://theccwh .org)
An organization for women in the historical profession "committed to exploring the diverse experiences and histories of all women." Affiliated with the American Historical Association.

Political Science

Association for the Study of Black Women in Politics (ASBWP) (www.apsanet.org/content_8537.cfm)
ASBWP is a section of the American Political Science Association that advances "research on Black women in politics in the United States and across the globe . . . [and] recognizes the specific issues and concerns that are unique to African American women in the academy in general and within the political science profession in particular. As such, the ASBWP is also committed to recruiting and mentoring women of African descent in academia."

Committee on the Status of Women in the Profession (www.apsanet.org/content_3693.cfm)
A committee of the American Political Science Association that monitors the status of women in the profession at all levels, reporting periodically to the

membership at large on its findings. It advances research on women as well as on issues of concern to women and works closely with other groups to share information and to ensure fair and equal treatment of women throughout the profession.

Women and Politics Research (www.apsanet.org/sections/sectionDetail .cfm?section=Sec16)
A section of the American Political Science Association to "foster the study of women and politics within the discipline of political science."

Women in International Security (WIIS) (http://wiisglobal.org/wordpress1/)
"The only global network actively advancing women's leadership, at all stages of their careers, in the international peace and security field."

Women's Caucus for International Studies (WCIS) (www.isanet.org/ISA/ Caucuses/WomensCaucus.aspx)
"WCIS is devoted to upgrading the status of women in the profession of international studies. WCIS seeks to promote equal opportunities for women in their professional lives, from graduate school admissions through all stages of employment. WCIS also seeks to promote women's professional development, both in academic and non-academic professional careers in international studies. As a section of the International Studies Association, the WCIS serves as an advocate and liaison to the ISA for these purposes. WCIS also works to encourage mentoring networks for women in the profession and organizes workshops and roundtables at ISA conferences focusing on topics of concern to women in the profession" (www.isanet.org/ISA/ Caucuses/WomensCaucus/AboutWCIS.aspx).

Women's Caucus for Political Science (WCPS) (www.apsanet.org/~wcps)
"Seeks to improve the status of women in the profession of political science by promoting equal opportunity for women political scientists in employment, promotion [and] tenure decisions, as well as graduate school admissions [and] financial aid decisions. . . . WCPS meets during the annual meeting of the American Political Science Association."

Psychology

The Association for Women in Psychology (AWP) (www.awpsych.org)
A "scientific and educational feminist organization devoted to reevaluating and reformulating the role that psychology and the mental health field generally play within women's lives. It seeks to act responsibly and sensitively with regard to women by challenging the unquestioned assumptions,

research traditions, theoretical commitments, clinical and professional practices, and institutional and societal structures that limit the understanding, treatment, professional attainment, and responsible self-determination of women and men, or that contribute to unwelcome divisions between women based on race, ethnicity, age, social class, sexual orientation or religious affiliation."

Society for the Psychology of Women (www.apa.org/divisions/div35/) Provides "an organizational base for all feminists, women and men of all national origins who are interested in teaching, research or practice in the psychology of women." The society's purpose is "to promote feminist scholarship and practice, and to advocate action toward public policies that advance equality and social justice."

Sociology

American Sociological Association (ASA) (www.asanet.org) Within the ASA there are the "Sex and Gender Section" (http://www2.asanet. org/sectionsexgend/) and the "Section on Sexualities" (http://www2.asanet. org/sectionsex/). Both promote professional activities related to these topical areas as well as the scholars who teach and conduct research on women and LGBT issues and provide advocacy for those populations.

Sociologists for Women in Society (SWS) (www.socwomen.org) Provides resources and research on a range of issues impacting women in academia and inequality in society. Sponsors local and regional chapters and publishes *Gender & Society*, a leading peer-reviewed journal on the scholarship of gender. Features a multitude of "Fact Sheets" that serve to summarize recent research on issues ranging from violence against women, to LGBT parenting, to women in science. SWS meets twice per year (summer meetings are concurrent with the ASA meetings, and winter meeting locations vary).

Humanities

Art

Committee on Women in the Arts (CWA) (www.collegeart.org/committees/women.html) A committee of the College Art Association (CAA) that "promotes the scholarly study and recognition of women's contributions to the visual arts and to critical and art-historical studies; advocates for feminist scholarship and activism in art; develops partnerships with organizations with compatible missions; monitors the status of women in the visual-arts professions; provides historical and current resources on feminist issues; and supports emerging artists and scholars in their careers."

Women's Caucus for Art (WCA) (www.nationalwca.org)
"Founded in 1972 in connection with the College Art Association (CAA). WCA is a national member organization unique in its multidisciplinary, multicultural membership of artists, art historians, students, educators, and museum professionals."

Classics

Women's Classical Caucus (WCC) (www.wccaucus.org)
An affiliate of the American Philological Association that fosters "feminist and gender-informed perspectives in the study and teaching of all aspects of ancient Mediterranean cultures and classical antiquity. [WCC] strive[s] to advance the goals of equality and diversity within the profession of Classics, to foster supportive professional relationships among classicists concerned with questions of gender, and to forge links with feminist scholars in other disciplines" (http://wccaucus.org/the-womens-classical-caucus-home/why/).

Communications

National Communication Association (NCA) (www.iupui.edu/~ncafws/about.htm)
In the NCA, there are the Feminist and Women's Studies Division and the Women's Caucus. The mission of the Women's Caucus is "to advocate for women's improved status, voice, and opportunities in the discipline." The Feminist and Women Studies Division "is interested in themes related to feminist studies in communication."

Organization for Research on Women and Communication (ORWAC) (www.orwac.org)
"Promotes dialogue, discussion, research, and scholarship concerned with women, feminism, gender, oppression, and social change." ORWAC is affiliated with the Western States Communication Association and publishes the journal *Women's Studies in Communication.*

English, Foreign Languages, and Comparative Literature

Committee on the Status of Women in the Profession (www.mla.org/comm_women) Part of the Modern Language Association (MLA), the committee investigates and reports on the situation of women within the profession and promotes the study and teaching of women's literature. The MLA also has an interdisciplinary division known as the Division on Women's Studies in Language and Literature.

Music

Committee on Women and Gender (www.ams-net.org/committees/csw/) Formerly called the Committee on the Status of Women, the Committee on Women and Gender is part of the American Musicological Society. It "promotes gender equity and feminist scholarship in musicology and related fields" and provides informal mentoring and links to other organizations concerned with the status of women in the academy.

Section on the Status of Women (www.ethnomusicology.org/?Groups_ SectionsSSW)
As part of the Society for Ethnomusicology, the section supports ethnographic, historical, and theoretical scholarship on women and musical performance. Also supports the exploration of academic women's professional needs in the field of ethnomusicology.

Philosophy

Association for Feminist Ethics and Social Theory (FEAST)
(www.afeast.org)
"Dedicated to promoting feminist ethical perspectives on philosophy, moral and political life, and public policy. Through meetings, publications and projects, [FEAST hopes] to increase the visibility and influence of feminist ethics, as well as feminist social and political theory, and to provide support to emerging scholars from diverse and underrepresented populations."

Committee on the Status of Women (CSW) (www.apaonlinecsw.org)
Documents gender-related issues within the field of philosophy and proposes solutions to them. Produces the Newsletter on Feminism and Philosophy.

Society for Women in Philosophy (SWIP) (www.uh.edu/~cfreelan/SWIP/)
SWIPA holds a small conference for each regional division and a session at the national American Philosophical Association's meetings. It also hosts a members-only Listserv for its three divisions (Eastern, Central, and Pacific).

Society for Women's Advancement in Philosophy (SWAP) (http://student groups.fsu.edu/organization/societyforwomensadvancementinphiloso phythe)
A graduate student group modeled after SWIP. (See previous entry.)

Religious Studies

Status of Women in the Profession Committee (www.aarweb.org/about/ status-women-profession-committee)
Part of the American Academy of Religion, it "recommends policies and good practices to assure the full access and academic freedom of women within the Academy and develops programs to enhance the status of women in the profession."

Natural Sciences

Biology

Committee on the Status of Women in Microbiology (CSWM) (http://forms.asm.org/Policy/index.asp?bid=22282)
Within the American Society for Microbiology (ASM), this standing committee "periodically collects data on the training and employment of women microbiologists; studies legislation affecting women microbiologists; interacts and cooperates with similar committees in other scientific organizations; encourages women microbiologists to participate in ASM activities; and advises ASM on matters concerning the status of women microbiologists."

Women in Cell Biology Committee (WICB) (www.ascb.org/index.php?option=com_content&view=article&id=86&Itemid=12)
Part of the American Society for Cell Biology, WICB provides career support and advice for its members. The committee members "respond to reports of discriminatory practices, offer a speaker referral service to help program organizers identify women speakers, and produce monthly columns for the ASCB Newsletter."

Women in Plant Biology Committee (WIPBC) (www.aspb.org/committees /women/index.cfm)
A standing committee within the American Society of Plant Biologists (ASPB) with a mission to promote the inclusion of women plant biologists in all aspects of ASPB and the profession.

Chemistry

American Chemical Society (ACS) (www.acs.org/content/acs/en.html)
Provides a rich collection of resources on women and women of color in
STEM fields that "empower women chemists of color to maximize their
opportunities in the chemical profession while cultivating an environment that fully engages these members" (www.acs.org/content/acs/en/
membership-and-networks/acs/welcoming/diversity/wcoc-about.html).

Women Chemists Committee (WCC) (http://membership.acs.org/W/WCC/)
Serves the members of the American Chemical Society to attract, develop,
promote, and advocate for women in the chemical sciences.

Computer Science

Association for Women in Computing (AWC) (www.awc-hq.org)
Dedicated to the advancement of women in technology, including computing, business, industry, science, education, government, and the military,
through networking and programs.

Committee on the Status of Women in Computing Research (CRA-W)
(http://cra-w.org)
Part of the Computer Research Association. An action-oriented organization
dedicated to increasing the number of women participating in computer science and engineering research and education at all levels.

National Center for Women & Information Technology (NCWIT)
(www.ncwit.org)
"A non-profit community of more than 500 prominent corporations, academic institutions, government agencies, and non-profits working to increase
women's participation in technology and computing. It believes that inspiring more women to choose careers in information technology is not about
parity, but about innovation, competitiveness, and workforce sustainability."

Women in Technology International (WITI) (www.witi.com)
"WITI's mission is to empower women worldwide to achieve unimagined
possibilities and transformations through technology, leadership and economic prosperity."

Engineering

Society of Women Engineers (SWE) (http://societyofwomenengineers.swe
.org/index.php)
An educational and service organization that empowers women to succeed
and advance in the field of engineering, and to be recognized for their life-
changing contributions as engineers and leaders.

Women in Engineering ProActive Network (WEPAN) (www.wepan.org)
A national organization that "works to transform culture in engineering education to attract, retain, and graduate women" (www.wepan.org/displaycommon.cfm?an=4).

Women in Optics (http://spie.org/x1845.xml)
Part of the Society of Photo-Optical Instrumentation Engineers (SPIE); "promotes personal and professional growth for women through community building, networking opportunities and encouraging young women to choose optics as a career."

Women in OR/MS (WORMS) (www.informs.org/Community/WORMS)
A forum within the Institute for Operations Research and the Management Sciences (INFORMS) for women in operations research and management science "to encourage interest in the field of operations research and the management sciences[;] to encourage discussion and interaction among individuals having interest in the issues facing women and their relationship to the profession of operations research and the management sciences[; and] to advise the INFORMS Board on aspects of issues facing women in the profession of operations research and the management sciences and to keep the INFORMS Board apprised of developments in this area."

Geology/Earth Science

Association for Women Geoscientists (AWG) (www.awg.org)
"An international organization devoted to enhancing the quality and level of participation of women in geosciences and to introduce girls and young women to geoscience careers" (www.awg.org/about/index.htm).

Association for Women Soil Scientists (AWSS) (www.womeninsoils.org)
An organization that supports the establishment and maintenance of high standards for professional women soil scientists, and provides assistance and encouragement for women, particularly those seeking employment in the field of soil science.

Learning Sciences

Women in Learning (WIL) (www.womeninlearning.com)
An organization founded by a graduate student and run solely by graduate students and postdoctoral fellows. WIL "offer[s] a forum in which students or post-docs doing scientific research in the broader field of Learning Theory,

Behavior, Memory and Neuroscience can seek advice, support, and guidance on the advancement of [women] researchers."

Mathematics

Association for Women in Mathematics (AWM) (www.awm-math.org)
Its purpose is "to encourage women to study and have active careers in the mathematical sciences."

Neuroscience

Women in Neuroscience (www.sfn.org/careers-and-training/women-in-neuroscience)
Part of the Society for Neuroscience (SfN); highlights achievements of women neuroscientists, educates members around issues of gender bias, addresses challenges that women neuroscientists may face in their careers, and provides training and professional development for women neuroscientists.

Physics

Committee on the Status of Women in Physics (CSWP)
(www.aps.org/about/governance/committees/cswp/index.cfm)
Established as part of the American Physical Society (APS) in 1972 "to address the encouragement and career development of women physicists."

Umbrella Organizations

Association for Women in Science (AWIS) (www.awis.org/index.html)
A national advocacy organization championing "the interests of women in science, technology, engineering, and mathematics across all disciplines and employment sectors."

Committee on Women in Science, Engineering, and Medicine (CWSEM)
(http://sites.nationalacademies.org/PGA/cwsem/PGA_045036)
"A standing committee of the National Research Council (NRC). Its mandate is to coordinate, monitor, and advocate action to increase the participation of women in science, engineering, and medicine."

Institute for Women in Trades, Technology and Science (IWITTS)
(www.iwitts.com/index.html)
Provides tools to successfully integrate women into men-dominated careers such as technology and law enforcement through training, publications, products, e-strategies, and research projects. Their audience includes educational institutions, police departments, employers, and women and girls themselves.

National Alliance for Partnerships in Equity (NAPE) (www.napequity .org)
"A national organization committed to the advancement of equity and diversity in classrooms and workplaces" (www.napequity.org/about-us/mission/). Be sure to check out its resource page, including the list of related organizations at www.stemequitypipeline.org/Resources/OnlineResources/Organizations.aspx.

Sigma Delta Epsilon/Graduate Women in Science (SDE-GWIS) (www.gwis.org)
Formed by women graduate students at Cornell University in 1921, their mission is to "advance the participation and recognition of women in science and to foster research through grants, awards, and fellowships."

Professional Fields

Business

American Accounting Association (AAA) (http://aaahq.org/about/ directory2008/sectionregion2008/gia.htm)

The Gender Issues and Worklife Balance Section of the AAA has the "overall objective of facilitating interaction among Association members regarding gender issues as they relate to accounting practice, research, and education." It sponsors sessions(s) and programs at the annual and regional meetings of the association; publishes a newsletter; and provides assistance to members regarding research, education, and employment.

Gender & Diversity in Organizations (GDO) (http://division.aomonline .org/gdo/)
A division of the Academy of Management; its mission is to "generate and disseminate knowledge about gender and diversity within and outside of organizations, to embrace diverse perspectives in organizational research and education, and to support social justice through the inclusion of marginalized voices in members' research and practice."

Education

American Council on Education (ACE) (www.acenet.edu/AM/Template. cfm?Section=Home)
Provides links to the office of women in higher education with the goal of supporting the advancement and retention of women in higher education.

American Educational Research Association (AERA) (www.aera.net)
AERA "strives to advance knowledge about education, to encourage schol-arly inquiry related to education, and to promote the use of research to improve education and serve the public good" (www.aera.net/AboutAERA/ tabid/10062/Default.aspx). It has several standing committees to address concerns related to gender, class, and race/ethnicity (www.aera.net/Abou-tAERA/KeyPrograms/SocialJustice/tabid/10188/Default.aspx):

- Critical Examination of Race, Ethnicity, Class, and Gender in Educa-tion. Its purpose is to "promote the integrated study of race, ethnic-ity, social class, and gender as lenses for performing critical analyses and evaluations of prevailing theory and practice on education" (www .aera.net/SIG027/CriticalExaminationofRace,Ethnicity,Class/ tabid/11754/Default.aspx).
- Committee on Scholars and Advocates for Gender Equity. It emphasizes "research and action for gender equity and invites members who engage in gender equity research and advocacy to look to the committee as a resource and voice for their interests" (www.aera.net/AboutAERA/KeyPrograms/ SocialJustice/CommitteeonScholarsAdvocateforGenderEquity/ tabid/10942/Default.aspx).

Law

Commission on Women in the Profession (www.americanbar.org/groups/ women/about_us.html)
Part of the American Bar Association (ABA), "the Commission assesses the status of women in the legal profession, identify barriers to advancement, and recommend to the ABA actions to address problems identified."

Medicine

American Medical Women's Association (AMWA) (www.amwa-doc.org)
Works to "advance women in medicine and improve women's health . . . by providing and developing leadership, advocacy, education, expertise, men-toring, and strategic alliances" for physicians and medical school students.

Group on Women in Medicine and Science (GWIMS) (www.aamc.org/ members/49354/gwims/)
Part of the Association of American Medical Colleges (AAMC), GWIMS provides support to address gender-related inequities and improve pathways for women to contribute fully to academic medicine. GWIMS offers profes-sional development seminars and other sessions at AAMC annual meetings.

Social Work

Council on the Role and Status of Women in Social Work Education

(Women's Council) (www.cswe.org/About/governance/CommissionsCouncils/15550/15556/32301.aspx)
A council of the Commission for Diversity and Social and Economic Justice, a body within the Council on Social Work Education (CSWE). The Women's Council is "responsible for the development of educational resources relevant to women's issues within social work education. The council works to eliminate all procedures within academia that hinder the full participation of women, makes recommendations to the Board on all matters of policy, and initiates and coordinates programs and activities related to women in social work education."

National Committee on Women's Issues (NCOWI)
(www.socialworkers.org/governance/cmtes/ncowi.asp)
Reports on a regular basis to the National Association of Social Workers' (NASW) board of directors on policy matters; works with the NASW Program Coordinating Committee; and develops, reviews, and monitors NASW programs that affect women.

Women's and Gender Studies

National Women's Studies Association (NWSA) (www.nwsa.org)
Seeks to "illuminate the ways in which women's studies are vital to education; to demonstrate the contributions of feminist scholarship that is comparative, global, intersectional and interdisciplinary to understandings of the arts, humanities, social sciences and sciences; and to promote synergistic relationships between scholarship, teaching and civic engagement in understandings of culture and society" (www.nwsa.org/content.asp?contentid=19).

Notes

1. Pursuing legal remedies to bias and discrimination can be time-consuming, expensive, and stressful. If successful, one *may* recoup costs related to attorneys' fees, court costs, and other expenses associated with legal action in addition to other compensation. Before weighing legal action, consider your goals and ways to achieve them (e.g., at the university level, through mediation). In fact, the EEOC echoes what we have argued throughout this book: that "*preventing* employment discrimination from occurring in the workplace in the first place is preferable to remedying the *consequences* of discrimination" (www.eeoc.gov/eeoc/outreach/index.cfm; emphasis added).

2. Created by the Committee for Academic Justice (a subcommittee of Sociologists for Women in Society), Laura M. Carpenter and Gail Murphy-Geiss, August 2008. Expanded and updated by Andi Stepnick and Kristine De Welde, February 2011, "Disrupting the Culture of Silence" Workshop. Edited for this book, November 2014.

ABOUT THE CONTRIBUTORS

Elizabeth J. Allan is professor of higher education, University of Maine, Orono.

Candice P. Baldwin is director of the Multicultural Center of Academic Success at Rochester Institute of Technology in Rochester, New York.

Diana Bilimoria is KeyBank Professor, and professor and chair of organizational behavior, at Case Western Reserve University in Cleveland, Ohio.

Amy Blackstone is associate professor and chair of the sociology department at the University of Maine, Orono.

Corinne Castro is assistant professor of sociology in the Department of Sociology, Political Science & Geography at Texas Lutheran University, Seguin.

Molly Everett Davis is associate professor and codirector of field education at George Mason University in Fairfax, Virginia.

Doreen A. Dedjoe is a senior research analyst at Siena College in Loudonville, New York.

Kristine De Welde is associate dean of University-wide Programs and Faculty Engagement in Undergraduate Studies and associate professor of sociology at Florida Gulf Coast University, Fort Myers.

Abby L. Ferber is professor of sociology, director of women's and ethnic studies, and director of the Matrix Center for the Advancement of Social Equity and Inclusion at University of Colorado, Colorado Springs.

Shanyuan Foo earned her master's degree in sociology from Boston College.

Susan K. Gardner is associate professor of higher education at the University of Maine, Orono.

Monica D. Griffin is director of Community Studies and Engaged Scholarship and the Sharpe Community Scholars Program, and executive associate professor of education at the College of William and Mary in Williamsburg, Virginia.

Robert J. Hironimus-Wendt is professor of sociology at Western Illinois University, Macomb.

Laura Hirshfield is assistant professor of medical education and sociology at the University of Illinois at Chicago.

Jessica Holden Sherwood is assistant professor of social sciences at Johnson & Wales University in Providence, Rhode Island.

Barret Katuna is visiting assistant professor at the University of Connecticut, Storrs.

Adrianna Kezar is professor of higher education at the University of Southern California, Los Angeles.

Julie A. Kmec is professor of sociology at Washington State University, Pullman.

Claudia Lampman is professor and chair of the psychology department at the University of Alaska Anchorage.

Gretal Leibnitz is coprincipal investigator on the NSF ADVANCE project at Washington State University, founder of the national ADVANCE Implementation Mentors (AIM) Network, and executive director of ProActualize Consulting.

Laura Logan is assistant professor of sociology at Hastings College in Hastings, Nebraska.

Kristin Marsh is associate professor of sociology and is a faculty member in women's and gender studies at the University of Mary Washington in Fredericksburg, Virginia.

Julia McQuillan is professor and chair of the sociology department at the University of Nebraska–Lincoln.

Joya Misra is professor of sociology and public policy at the University of Massachusetts, Amherst.

Briana Keafer Morrison is an assessment specialist for sciences at Washington State University, Pullman.

Penny A. Pasque is associate professor of educational leadership and policy studies and women's and gender studies at the Center for Social Justice, University of Oklahoma.

Karen Pyke is associate professor of sociology at the University of California, Riverside.

Cecile H. Sam is a research specialist in the Consortium for Policy Research in Education at the University of Pennsylvania, Philadelphia.

Renay Scales is director of faculty development and associate professor of family medicine at Kentucky College of Osteopathic Medicine, Pikeville.

Catherine Richards Solomon is professor and department chair of sociology at Quinnipiac University in Hamden, Connecticut.

Andi Stepnick is a professor in the sociology department at Belmont University in Nashville, Tennessee.

Abigail J. Stewart is Sandra Schwartz Tangri Distinguished University Professor of Psychology and Women's Studies at the University of Michigan, Ann Arbor.

Halaevalu F. Ofahengaue Vakalahi is associate dean and professor in the School of Social Work at Morgan State University in Baltimore, Maryland.

Amy S. Wharton is professor of sociology and director of the College of Arts and Sciences at Washington State University, Vancouver.

volume makes a significant contribution to the literature on the role of race and gender in American universities. Summing Up: Highly recommended."

—*Choice*

"Compelling narratives that illuminate experiences of women in the academy. The essays highlight the diversity that exists among 'women of color,' not only in terms of their racial and ethnic identity, but also in the multiple facets that are integral to their identities, including family, relationships, and commitments to their community and faith. The concerns addressed in these pages underscore the relentless (institutional) cultures and practices that continue to relegate the professional contributions of women of color to the margins. This book makes a significant contribution. Readers will emerge with a keen understanding of the concerns that continue to impact women scholars of color. This book provides hope that such understanding will inform and influence institutional policies and practices."

—*The Review of Higher Education*

22883 Quicksilver Drive

Sterling, VA 20166-2102   Subscribe to our e-mail alerts: www.Styluspub.com

Related books from Stylus

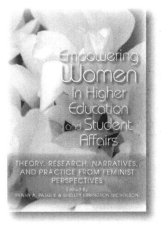

Empowering Women in Higher Education and Student Affairs
Theory, Research, Narratives, and Practice From Feminist Perspectives
Edited by Penny A. Pasque and Shelley Errington Nicholson
Foreword by Linda J. Sax

"Anyone interested in the experiences of women in the world of academia will learn from consulting this collection."

—Teaching Theology & Religion

"The authors and editors have done a remarkable job conveying the multivocal, multilayered, and complex nature of feminist inquiry. . . . Overall, the theory, practice, and research contributions were most impressive. . . . The narratives, in turn, were extraordinary."

—Journal of College Student Development

"It offers practical wisdom for those experiencing barriers in their own career progression and those who may wish to serve as a mentor. . . . This book would be an excellent recommendation for young professionals seeking insight for professional development or perhaps even women graduate students. It would serve as an excellent common book for a women's studies or higher education leadership course, or even for a circle of colleagues on your campus."

—NACADA Journal
National Academic Advising Association

From Oppression to Grace
Women of Color and Their Dilemmas within the Academy
Edited by Theodorea Regina Berry and Nathalie Mizelle

"Berry and Mizelle have assembled an impressive array of 19 scholarly essays focusing on the dilemmas, challenges, and opportunities of women of color in the US academy. The contributing authors—women of African, Native American, Latina, East Indian, Korean, and Japanese origin—narrate their positive and negative experiences at predominantly White universities. . . . These real-life stories of discrimination, resistance, and survival provide the minority viewpoint, and illustrate the profound consequences of race and gender in the academy. This